Madeline Patte-on,

Frontispiece Horace Alexander, 1927

GANDHI'S INTERPRETER

GANDHI'S INTERPRETER

A Life of Horace Alexander

by
Geoffrey Carnall

Foreword by Philippa Gregory

EDINBURGH UNIVERSITY PRESS

Edinburgh University Press Ltd
22 George Square, Edinburgh

www.euppublishing.com

Typeset in Sabon and Gill Sans
by Servis Filmsetting Ltd, Stockport, Cheshire, and
printed and bound in Great Britain by
CPI Antony Rowe, Chippenham and Eastbourne

A CIP record for this book is available from the British Library

ISBN 978 0 7486 4045 4 (hardback)

CONTENTS

DEDICATION

This book is dedicated to Woodbrooke Quaker Study Centre, Birmingham, still committed to making the world a more just and peaceful place.

'I have come here as a matter of pilgrimage, because it is this Settlement [Woodbrooke] it was that spared and sent Mr Horace Alexander to us at a time when we were in need of a friend.'

M. K. Gandhi, 18 October, 1931

'What then is the Spirit of Woodbrooke? – it is the spirit which forces men and women to realize their mutual responsibility in life; it teaches them to think of others, and not to take thought alone for their own comfort, pleasure or salvation. This Spirit I hold must grow to pervade all classes of the community, irrespective of rank or station, class or race. It is a spirit that will raise men by its unselfishness; will broaden their views, so that where now they see but creed and dogma they will see Truth. It will indeed teach that we, the children of humanity, being brothers and sisters, must serve one another in the love of all mankind, to the benefit of all life and the advancement and ultimate perfection of those who are yet to come.

'Surely the Spirit of Woodbrooke teaches us patience in trial, resignation in affliction, humbleness in success, and virtue in whatever position in life it has pleased God to place us. Above all, the Spirit of Woodbrooke is the Spirit of True Fellowship.'

Jomo Kenyatta, Easter 1932

FOREWORD

I first met Geoffrey Carnall, who was to be my supervisor for the four years of study for my PhD, in his small office at Edinburgh University in 1980. I was an energetic Marxist-feminist student, a former journalist, with cropped hair in staunchly corduroy dungarees, and he was a quiet thoughtful man with studious horn rimmed glasses and an endearing habit of saying 'aha' in reply to most comments, which – as I learned – gave him time to pause for thought.

Of all the things I learned from him, that pausing for thought was perhaps the most valuable. Not that I have ever achieved it in my own life! I am by temperament impulsive; but his passions: for scholarship, for peace, for social justice, run deep and slow. The 'aha' was more than the acknowledgement of someone truly listening: it was also a chance to think about the reply.

He taught me so many other things too. A rigorous and fierce regard for the detail of writing history: from punctuation (this is the man who taught me the use of the semi-colon which has enriched my writing and clarified my thinking) to the correct form of a footnote. My first version of my painfully wrought thesis was rewritten word for word after his insistence on accuracy in the text. For a mild-mannered man committed to peace he has a fierce adherence to precise thinking and precise expression. How I wish that had satisfied him! When I arrived with much heartache at the penultimate draft, he commanded a total retype of everything: for there were too many typing errors. He was a hard task-master, and he taught me a standard of work which sits before me always, even now, nearly thirty years on.

His demands were high but his teaching was gentle. Silent students were encouraged to sit and think, if they could not scrape up one word to say. I grew accustomed to his quiet and formal tutorials. For the first two years he called me Miss Gregory and I – knowing he was a committed Quaker and would not welcome any honorific title – merely called him, inelegantly: 'You'. As the years went on any my studies continued we developed an understanding. With his wife Elisabeth, he attended my wedding, and they were among the first visitors when I had my baby, Geoffrey merely observing that the arrival of Victoria might delay the current chapter of the thesis. Years later, when Victoria was grown and attended Edinburgh University herself, she stayed with them for her first term. I could not have written my first historical novel without reading the eighteenth century novels that I undertook under his supervision. But equally, I could not bear to start my first fictional biography, based on a real person, without writing to him to demand that he lift the embargo he had unwittingly placed on my imagination.

It was a casual aside in a seminar on John Stuart Mill (which owing to the vagaries of my old typewriter I always wrote as John Stuart Nill, which Geoffrey delightedly took as a coded revelation of my true opinion of the philosopher). Geoffrey remarked that he could not tolerate novels that deployed real historical characters, his imaginary instance was: 'What do you think of giving the suffrage to women and would you pass the marmalade Mr Mill?' With my new proposed novel, *The Other Boleyn Girl*, shaping itself in my mind, very much based on a real character: Mary Boleyn – I had to write to Geoffrey and ask him if it was 'all right' to go ahead. Of course, he had no recollection, either of that seminar, or of the aside, but he took a mischievous delight that his casual remark was haunting me. He gave me exorcism from the remark and read my subsequent books with, I think, some pleasure.

Early on in our relationship I discovered his wry and self-deprecating humour, his love of word-play, his intense sense of the ridiculous, and his joy at the smaller follies of the world. But some follies he could not condone. I was amazed to learn that he had been arrested for demonstrating against the glamorising of war at the world-famous Edinburgh Military Tattoo. In his trial his defence was embellished with a reference to Aristophanes' comedy *The Peace*, which he delivered to the court in the style of Aristophanes, to the considerable entertainment of those present. He was triumphantly acquitted, the court accepting that it was perfectly proper to make such a protest. I learned from this incident of the grit that exists, beneath his quietly spoken pacifism. The subject of Horace Alexander is thus particularly appropriate for such an author and this biography has been a labour of love for ten years, and is Geoffrey's tribute to his mentor, with whom he travelled in India in 1949–50. Britain continued military conscription for some years after the Second World War, and Geoffrey registered as a conscientious objector. The tribunal allowed him to work in India and Pakistan with the Friends' Service Unit from early October 1948 until late July 1950.

Horace Alexander was the senior Friend in the subcontinent, based in Delhi, and was very much part of efforts made to prevent the outbreak of war in February 1950, when there was a massive exodus of Hindus from East Bengal (Pakistan) and Muslims from West Bengal (India). Geoffrey himself took part in fact-finding missions crucial to reducing the tension created by inflammatory rumours.

As a young man, Geoffrey observed Alexander's quiet detachment as he worked as a mediator and fact-finder at a time of great political tension, with

India and Pakistan on the brink of war. He learned that Alexander had been one of the few people trusted by the independence movement in India, and played a significant role in the peaceful transfer of power from a suspicious imperial power to an even more suspicious emerging independent state.

That Geoffrey has dedicated so many years to this biography, which he described cheerfully to me as a work about a relatively unknown pacifist by a relatively unknown academic, alerted me that this book was a story of genuine significance, telling the story of an ordinary man who, inspired by the great idea of peace, was able to play an extraordinary part in one of the major events of the twentieth century. In a private email to me, in his most engaging and idiosyncratic style Geoffrey wrote:

> I have lately been intrigued by the thought that my first book, 'Robert Southey and his Age: the Development of a Conservative Mind', narrates the sad story of someone who went Wrong – while my last book narrates the inspiring story of someone who went Right. Who says that age makes one melancholy! (Robert Burton, actually, but the question is rhetorical.)

I am left only to hope that Burton is wrong and that age never makes Geoffrey melancholy, and also that this is not his last book.

Philippa Gregory
Philippa Gregory is alummna of the year 2009, Edinburgh University. Her first novel *Wideacre* was published in 1987, her most recent novel is *The White Queen*.

PREFACE

While Horace Alexander's activities took place in a world different in so many respects from that of the early twenty-first century, they have a clear bearing on current issues. His characteristic technique of listening attentively to participants in a conflict, and thus discerning ways of resolving it, deserves much more examination than in practice it has received. One reason for this, apart from the huge investment in military methods which makes other methods seem of marginal relevance in the real world, is that such an approach depends so much on the personality and previous record of each individual mediator. Alexander was immensely strengthened in his role by his familiarity with Gandhi and Gandhi's combination of intractability and friendliness, mixed with a certain deviousness which some (like Alexander's father-in-law John William Graham) believed put his integrity in question. Richard Symonds told me that British officials found Alexander 'slippery'. They had, he said, a better opinion of his co-worker Agatha Harrison, who was 'straight', though misguided. This, too, was an effect of personality. No one who knew her could ever forget the irresistible assurance with which she accepted the integrity of those she encountered, and their ability to resolve the conflicts in which they were engaged.

Alexander himself had a curiously detached, almost judicial manner, which suggested a personality that was never flustered or thrown off-balance. His Cambridge friend Nick Bagenal regarded him as the embodiment of 'pure reason'. This was an acquired manner, for his impatience with people close to him like his fellow Quakers could be explosive. But when professionally engaged, as it were, and he had to deal with political partisans ranting away about their evil adversaries, he would sit sadly with downcast eyes, until something less confrontational was said, when he pounced (it is the only appropriate word) and insisted on developing its implications. It was his ability to identify potential areas of agreement that made him an accomplished interpreter, in the literal sense of translator of an unfamiliar language, where Gandhi's intentions were concerned, both to the British Government and to his fellow Quakers.

I saw a good deal of Alexander in India in the latter half of 1949 and early 1950, and his personality left a strong impression which I have tried to convey in my account of his life. It is an impression that makes it impossible for me to dismiss out of hand initiatives that on the face of it seem naive or over-ambitious. In particular, his hope that the former Woodbrooke fellow Fritz Berber might have some ability to affect the foreign policy of Nazi Germany was clearly mistaken, and yet this and other contacts with the German foreign ministry might usefully have been much more fully exploited by the British Government at the time. And when, after 1947, he found himself championing Jawaharlal Nehru's policy of non-alignment, he could feel that his approach to conflict resolution had at last become something to which the world had to pay some attention.

Alexander himself has up till now attracted almost no attention, and I know of only two specific assessments of his role in relations between Britain and India, that of Hugh Tinker in 'The India Conciiation Group: Dilemmas of a Mediator' (1976), and Suhash Chakravarty in *The Raj Syndrome* (1989). Dr Chakravarty sees him and Agatha Harrison as examples of an 'imperial sensibility', unable to reconcile themselves to the prospect of a completely independent India.[1] This assessment would have come to them as something of a surprise, but it is not essentially different from Dr Tinker's judgement that C. F. Andrews, Agatha Harrison and Horace Alexander provided an acceptable face of imperialism.[2] Congress leaders could always feel that they had friends in Britain, and this eroded their radicalism.

Did this mean acquiescence in an unjust social order? Maybe it did, but one should also remember the extreme injustice inseparable from violent conflict. Enterprises like the second Iraq war have done something to discredit what has long been a prevailing militarist orthodoxy: it is now commonplace to say that 'there is no purely military solution'. In exploring what follows from this realisation, the experience of people like Horace Alexander will come to be more fully appreciated. His work required him to operate inconspicuously, behind the scenes. He should now spend a little time centre-stage.

ACKNOWLEDGEMENTS

Many people have helped me in the making of this biography, but to three friends I am particularly indebted. The first is the late Richard Symonds, Alexander's deputy in the Friends Ambulance Unit in Calcutta in 1942–3, who later worked with him in the terrible hostilities that followed the partition of the Indian subcontinent in 1947. Throughout the writing of the book he was a constant source of encouragement and information. He read the entire text, but I am disappointed that he did not live to see it published.

That it has been published at all is due to Philippa Gregory, who, appreciating that a biography of an unknown Quaker by an unknown author is not a recipe for commercial success, agreed to sponsor the book for publication by the Edinburgh University Press. I am grateful for her good opinion of the book, and rather stunned by her generosity. She will have her reward in heaven if not elsewhere.

Finally, I owe a great deal to Cecilia Sibinga, Horace Alexander's stepdaughter. She has been ready to help me at every turn, and I am touched by her confidence in my portrayal of a much-loved stepfather, even when the portrayal was not altogether flattering. She gave me the run of the large collection of books and papers still in her care, and I realise that the materials she has looked after so faithfully could provide the basis for two or three more books on Horace's life and times.

Members of Horace's wider family have helped me in several ways. Lucy Brown was preparing an edition of the letters of Horace and Olive before her untimely death, and her memories of Olive Graham Alexander gave me a greater sense of her personality than I could possibly have gained from the printed records alone. Jenny and John Graham had vivid memories of Alexander in his later years in Pennsylvania. I am grateful to Roger Sturge and other family members for helping me financially to travel to Pennsylvania to spend time in the archives of the American Friends Service Committee, and to meet people who had known Horace. I had particularly useful conversations with Margaret Hope Bacon, Tessa Cadbury and Mary Hoxie Jones.

I learnt much about Horace's time as leader of the Friends' Ambulance Unit in Calcutta in 1942–3 from Pamela Bankart, Leslie Cross and Sujata Davies, usefully supplemented by some acute observations in a letter from Clement Alexandre. Duncan Wood gave invaluable assistance in writing the narrative of Horace's excursion to China in the spring of 1943, and another member of the FAU's China Convoy, Parry Jones, sent me a splendidly entertaining account of Horace's journey through western China with a lorry-load of medical supplies. To Gray Peile, also a member of the China Convoy, I am indebted for a description of the extraordinary substitutes for petrol that these lorries necessarily had to use.

Hallam and Margot Tennyson knew Horace in his time in India immediately after the war, and I greatly enjoyed Hallam's account of Horace's visits to the FAU village project at Pifa, when he was received like royalty. Margot was a refugee from Nazi Germany, and had affectionate memories of Woodbrooke, where Horace oversaw her studies. Brenda Bailey had had the same experience, and described how she had told him that she wanted to resign her membership of the Society of Friends. 'Well, that's all right', he said. 'Write me an essay on why you want to.' She wrote the essay and decided she didn't want to resign after all.

Several people around Woodbrooke had interesting memories, particularly of Olive. Winifred Hyde remembered Horace's tenderness in his care of her; Monica Sturge recalled stimulating tutorials with her, providing materials for intense discussion afterwards. Joan Barlow recalled how her husband Ralph and Horace used to take boys who had been in trouble with the law on bird-watching expeditions. Much else was told me about Horace the bird-watcher, but Duncan Wood's ornithological biography, *Birds and Binoculars*, allows me to neglect this important side of his life. I should mention, though, that it was bird-watching that drew him to his young neighbours in Swanage, Trev Haysom and Ilay Cooper. Trev lent me his collection of letters from Alexander – a correspondence which continued almost to the end of his life.

S. K. De helped me at an early stage of my work on this book, and gave me invaluable guidance on the people whom it would be useful to meet. Marjorie Sykes, too, was exceptionally well informed about who might give me an insight into Horace's way of working. Roger Carter shared with me a sympathetic appreciation of Fritz Berber's difficult predicament. Other helpful interviews were with Alison Bush, Cecil Evans, John Linton and Sir Geoffrey Wilson. Raj Kothari told me about his father's determination to see that a worthwhile film about Gandhi was made, and kindly lent me his unpublished book about the evolution of Richard Attenborough's production.

David Gray and Chris Lawson were on the staff of Woodbrooke in 1992 when they encouraged me to undertake this biography, and I have appreciated their continuing interest. This is the place to express my gratitude to the Joseph

Rowntree Charitable Trust for giving me a grant for travel at the outset of my work, and a second grant to pay for residence for five weeks in Woodbrooke to get the writing finished.

Several people have read parts of the text, and I have learnt a good deal from their observations: I should particularly mention Sharon MacDonald and Edward Milligan. Professor Judith Brown gave me valuable advice about the structure of the book.

For me it has always been a pleasure to work in the libraries and archives containing the publications and documents related to Horace. My greatest debt is to the library in Friends House in London, and to Josef Keith, whose knowledge of the manuscript collections there has been invaluable. I have been a reader in the National Library of Scotland for over fifty years, and can testify that the courtesy and efficiency of its staff are exemplary. I am grateful too to the staff of the Edinburgh University Library, the British Library in London (including the India Office Library), the National Archives in Kew, and in Cambridge the libraries of King's College, Trinity College and Churchill College. Across the Atlantic I was given generous assistance in the archives of the American Friends Service Committee (AFSC) in Philadelphia, and the Peace Collection in Swarthmore College.

I must thank the following institutions for their kind permission to quote from copyright material: Friends House Library in London, the Woodbrooke Library in Birmingham, and the AFSC archive in Philadelphia; the National Archives and the India Office Library; the Provost and Scholars of King's College, Cambridge, the Master and Fellows of Trinity College, Cambridge, and the Bootham School archive in York. I am also grateful to Ann Spokes Symonds for permission to quote from the published and unpublished writings of Richard Symonds; similar permission has been given by Annette Wallis for the use of the writings of her father, Corder Catchpool. Peter Hogg was happy to allow me to make extensive use of the letters of his mother, Dorothy Hogg. Sir Crispin Agnew of Lochnaw permitted me to quote from the letters of his father, Sir Fulque Agnew, which have been published by Edinburgh University's Centre for South Asian Studies (2001). I am also grateful to the present Earl of Halifax for permission to quote from a letter of his grandfather's.

A quotation from Bernard Shaw's *Fabian Essays* is included by kind permission of the Society of Authors on behalf of the Bernard Shaw Estate. Two quotations from the work of G. Lowes Dickinson are included by kind permission of the Provost and Scholars of King's College, Cambridge 2010. Material from J. Maynard Keynes's *Essays in Biography*, 1972, Macmillan Press Ltd is reproduced with permission of the Royal Economic Society and Palgrave Macmillan. Judy Kirby has allowed me to quote freely from *The Friend*.

I should add a special word of thanks to Stuart Morton for his efforts to trace a particularly elusive copyright holder. Unsuccessful efforts have been made to trace a copyright holder for the letters of Agatha Harrison, but any breach of copyright is unintentional and could be corrected in a future edition.

Finally I must thank the staff of the Edinburgh University Press for seeing this book through the press in a friendly and considerate way.

It is customary on these occasions to thank one's spouse and family, and I am certainly glad to testify to the devoted interest my Elisabeth has always shown in the book as it was being written, and the support she has always given me. But more than that, over many years we have been colleagues in the task of helping Edinburgh's Peace and Justice Centre to continue its precarious existence. It is a commitment of which Horace Alexander would have warmly approved.

Geoffrey Carnall
Edinburgh, September 2009

ILLUSTRATIONS

ARCHIVE SOURCES

American Friends Service Committee, Philadelphia Archives
Bootham Archive, Bootham School, York
Churchill College, Cambridge: Philip Noel-Baker collection
Cotteridge (Birmingham) Preparative Meeting minutes
LSF (Friends House, London) MSS: FSC/IN; FSC/R/SP; Temp. MSS 42; 577; 971
India Office Library MSS: L/P&J: Irwin, Viceregal correspondence; MSS L/PO/6
King's College, Cambridge, Modern Archive (KCMA): Oscar Browning MSS
National Archives, Kew: Cab. 65.11; Foreign Office papers, 371, 800
Sibinga, Cecilia: Private collection, to be transferred to the Library of the Society of Friends, London
Sturge, Roger and Hilda: Private collection
Trinity College, Cambridge: R. A. Butler papers
Woodbrooke Quaker Study Centre, Birmingham: HGA MSS; Logbooks

ABBREVIATIONS

AFSC	American Friends' Service Committee
FAU	Friends' Ambulance Unit
FSC	Friends' Service Council
FSU	Friends' Service Unit
HGA	Horace Gundry Alexander
KCMA	King's College Modern Archive Cambridge
LSF	Library of the Society of Friends, London

1

THE MAKING OF AN INTERNATIONALIST

Early years

The Society of Friends – the Quakers – originated in the great upsurge of radical religious and political movements that subverted the established order in England in the middle of the seventeenth century. It affirmed the intrinsic equality of all human beings: no distinction between men and women, no need for any kind of clerical elite. Everyone could pay attention to the promptings of the spirit, though the potential anarchy that this might have fostered was tempered by the strong sense of community that found expression in its meetings for worship. This sense of community has enabled it to adapt to new conditions and survive into the twenty-first century.

One of its most characteristic features has been its peace testimony, utterly denying 'all outward wars and strife and fightings with outward weapons, for any end or under any pretence whatsoever'.[1] In a world where fighting with outward weapons is taken for granted, this conviction has prompted the Friends to find alternatives, and since the latter part of the nineteenth century to do so in an energetic and ingenious way. No one illustrates this preoccupation better than Horace Alexander. I worked with him, admired him immensely, and held him in great affection. Hence this book.

He was born in Croydon, a few miles south of London, on 18 April 1889. He was the youngest of four brothers. When drafting some autobiographical notes almost ninety years later, he remarked that the same month of 1889 also saw the birth of Arnold Toynbee, Stafford Cripps, Charles Chaplin and Adolf Hitler. The historian, the politician, the film actor and the dictator could all be described, in their various ways, as energetic, enterprising and original; and although Alexander denied any belief in astrology, he evidently felt some satisfaction in this odd link with such tireless achievers. Certainly he showed a strikingly tenacious determination to work in a practical way for a more humane and peaceful world.

He came of Quaker stock on both sides of his family, and found inspiration in the example of his paternal great-grandfather William Alexander. In the late eighteenth century he had been a foreman in Chatham naval dockyard, but became convinced of the truth of Quaker principles, and resigned. He took up school-teaching, and had at least one famous pupil, the chemist and philanthropist William Allen: 'a man', says Alexander feelingly, 'who influenced Governments and Emperors'. Strictly speaking he influenced one emperor only, the Russian Czar Alexander I, but as he may have thus had a hand in drafting the first practical blueprint for general agreed disarmament – part of the original plan for the Holy Alliance after the Napoleonic Wars – the exaggeration is pardonable. Horace Alexander's major role-model, though, was quite clearly his own father, Joseph Gundry Alexander, who died in 1918. In 1921 he published a biography of his father which can be seen in retrospect to foreshadow several aspects of his own career. It is no uncritical exercise in filial piety. While the loving labour of going through his father's letters and papers had evidently given him a fresh sense of his achievement, the author is in many ways remarkably detached. He evokes his father's strong evangelical faith: 'the life and words of Christ were to him real, life-giving and invincible.' But, he goes on,

> most men have not this faith today. . . . Orthodox religion is discarded because it has lost touch with life; but we are still at a loss for a new way of salvation. We are in need of some deep faith that will remain unshaken by life's calamities. It may not be quite the same faith that my father had; it will not express itself in the same words, but if it is expressed in unconquerable effort towards human welfare the spirit is always the same.[2]

Nearly thirty years later he was to body forth this faith in helping to start the Fellowship of Friends of Truth.

Joseph Gundry Alexander was a barrister with a special interest in international law, which led him (in 1872) to go to Paris to study the subject at the Sorbonne. He combined study with evangelistic mission work which involved much collaboration with non-Quakers. 'In later life', his son remarks with evident approval, 'he found among his fellow-workers in good causes men with little or no profession of religion at all.'[3]

These good causes included support for the annual peace congresses that met in various major cities in the years before the First World War, and the strengthening of international law against slavery. But his great concern was the ending of the opium trade, so profitable to the finances of the Government of India and so deplorable in its effects in China. This was a campaign that enjoyed wide support in evangelical circles in the latter part of the nineteenth century, and in its antagonism to British rule in the subcontinent it anticipated the anti-imperialist rhetoric of a later era. The campaign's monthly magazine, *The Friend of China,* was harsh in its judgements. British rule was upheld by bayonets.

> If you want to watch the maximum of arbitrary power and the minimum of popular interference with affairs of state, you must go to India. If you desire to study the temper of a people who are taxed at the pleasure of foreign masters without any voice either as to the raising or disposal of the funds, you can do so in India.[4]

Alexander was tireless in harrying supporters of the status quo, and when the Government accepted the need for a full inquiry into the issue, and set up the Royal Commission Opium (1893–5), he followed it around India, encouraging and criticising – his attentions probably as welcome to the Commission, John Palmer Gavit suggested, 'as a wet and waggy dog'.[5] After an often frustrating struggle, a measure of success was finally achieved in 1906 with the great Liberal victory in the British elections, when 250 of the new MPs were pledged to support abolition. In the wake of this triumph, J. G. Alexander revisited China and other countries in southern Asia to underline how strongly British public opinion supported the proposed new measures. In Kuala Lumpur he was greeted with an address of welcome printed in gold on silk. It lamented the dreadful calamity of opium –

> When shall we have an end of it?
> Fortunately we have now a true-hearted virtuous person
> to save us
> In the person of Mr. Alexander, who is a pioneer in the
> gallant work.
> He comes with all speed from the head office of the
> Society,
> Despite all difficulties he uses all efforts to
> suppress the opium trade.[6]

His efforts in this campaign brought him friendship with a number of Chinese, some of whom visited him in England. One of these was Dr Wu Lien Teh, whose special concern was the eradication of bubonic plague in Manchuria. In March 1918 he wrote a warmly appreciative obituary of J. G. Alexander in the *Peking Daily News*, part of which is quoted in Horace Alexander's biography of his Father. He praised him for keeping the opium issue alive in Britain, in spite of discouragements, so that when the political opportunity eventually came there was an educated public opinion ready to apply the necessary pressure. He had the gift of infinite patience, tenacious, uncompromising, sustained by 'faith in the complete invincibility of his cause'.[7]

The presence of such Chinese visitors, along with many more French colleagues in philanthropic work, helped to reinforce a sense of cooperation in good causes that transcended national boundaries. J. G. Alexander spoke French fluently, so that his sons early became used to the idea that cultural barriers did not have to be barriers at all. Horace says in his own autobiographical notes that his father was palpably a world citizen long before the idea of world citizenship became current. But although in this respect the Alexander household was accustomed to wide horizons, the four sons were brought up in what was in many ways a rather restricted environment. There was little appreciation of the arts, and of course the theatre was morally unacceptable. Only Gilbert, the eldest brother, made friends outside the family circle. The other three found bird life more congenial.

He was introduced to the discipline of Quaker silent worship at the midweek morning meeting in Croydon, some time in 1893. He sat quietly as he had been instructed, until he heard outside in the road the pattering of many feet. He could not help remarking on this occurrence: 'Sheep; and I think . . . ' – at which point his mother said 'Hush!' and his observation remained incomplete.

The 'hush' was probably spoken very gently. Josephine Alexander's letters show her to have been a kindly and considerate woman, deeply religious, but not inclined to burden her family with needless scruples. When she died, in 1940, one of the letters of condolence came from Christine Deacon of West Hartlepool. She said that her own mother had been greatly comforted by the knowledge that Josephine did not think it wrong to knit on Sundays.

> Mother always had trouble with her conscience about doing it until she knew that someone else of her own generation, and a good woman and a Friend, also found knitting a help in the 'employment of those hours on the first day of the week not occupied in Meetings for Worship'.

Most of what is known about Horace's childhood relates to birdwatching. The beginnings of his ornithological passion are vividly described in *Seventy Years of Birdwatching*. It was inspired by his uncle, Herbert Crosfield, who was a devoted birdwatcher in spite of having to work long hours in his London office, and devoting his Sundays to strictly religious activity. On Horace's eighth birthday, by which time the family had moved from Croydon out to Tunbridge Wells on the Kent–Sussex border, he was given *The Naturalist's Diary: A Day Book of Meteorology, Phenology and Rural Biology*, compiled by a local meteorologist, Charles Roberts.

> One page was devoted to each day. The left half of the page was divided into sections covering Weather, Plants flowering, Birds nesting, singing or migrating, Insects appearing and so forth. The second half of each page was left blank for the owner-recorder of the book to enter his own observations.

As it happened, a few weeks earlier, on 25 March 1897, his uncle Herbert had nearly missed his train to work in order to tell young Horace that there was a chiffchaff singing in the garden.

> For the next hour or so I wandered round the front garden, listening in high rapture to that Chiffchaff, watching the slender brown warbler flitting from tree to tree. Once at least it came very close to me in a low bush. Still in memory I can see it dashing out after insects, its tail gently wagging, the song coming fitfully as it flitted hither and thither.[8]

That early chiffchaff became the first entry in the *Naturalist's Diary*. By the time of his birthday he had also seen his first swallow for the year, and on the 18th itself a nightingale obliged by singing in a copse near his home. 'I was well away with regular recording.'

Expeditions with Uncle Herbert on his occasional free Saturdays were the chief recreation of the younger Alexander boys. The more sociable Gilbert, says Horace, was 'driven almost to distraction' by his brothers' obsession. Certainly the surviving natural history diaries occasionally suggest a tactless cockiness that might well have been hard to endure. Thus, on the train that was taking father and sons to the Paris Exhibition of 1900 (there was much mission work to be done on such occasions) a fellow-traveller had stated that there were no small birds left in France, and that you could travel for hours without seeing any birds at all. The eleven-year-old Horace proceeded to list birds seen between Tunbridge Wells and Newhaven, and between Dieppe and Paris. What he saw, the diary records, 'proves that the gentleman must have been reading his newspaper instead of looking out of the window.'[9]

These diaries are preserved at Bootham, the Quaker boarding school in York where the three younger brothers were sent. Horace went there in 1903, having previously spent two years at a newly-established preparatory school near Malvern, the Downs School at Colwall. This was conducted by a Quaker couple, Herbert and Ethel Jones, and in these early days there were only four or five pupils. In 1980 Alexander wrote to the school about his experiences there, and his testimony suggests that his ornithological knowledge was genuinely valued. One late evening in the early summer of 1902, Herbert Jones came to the dormitory, saw that Horace was still awake, and told him to come downstairs. He obeyed, wondering what awful crime he had committed. He found Jones at the door, listening intently to a far-away buzzing sound. '"Is that a nightjar?" . . . "Yes, I believe it is," said I, though I am sure that at the age of thirteen I had never heard a nightjar before, and slunk back to bed.'

Evidently young Horace found Jones rather formidable, but Ethel Jones was more approachable and warmly encouraging. One day she was reading an enthusiastic account of the dawn chorus, and unwisely said that if one of the boys ever woke early she and they could go out and listen to it.

> Three or four days later, I knocked on their door about 5 o'clock, and Mr Jones came to see if one of us had been taken ill. 'No,' said I, 'we want to go out and hear the dawn chorus.' The incredulous Mrs Jones nobly got up and took us out. We were much too late for the dawn chorus, but we had a rapturous time walking through the dew-soaked grass.[10]

The boys' offer to try again another day an hour earlier was declined, but Alexander's keenness was acknowledged in a prize he was awarded: a book by R. A. Proctor, *Half-Hours with the Telescope*, published in 1902, the year that it was presented. He was commended for his 'Public Spirit', as shown in his work for the school's Natural History and Magazine Clubs.

Prep-school life seems to have been pleasant enough, but Bootham was a good deal more stressful. He says he was not particularly happy there, offering as an explanation that he was no sportsman. The explanation carries conviction when one reads an essay contributed by F. E. Pollard to the Bootham Centenary book. Games, he remarks, are 'vital elements in the spiritual life of a school'.[11] What Horace thought of that spiritual life comes out clearly in an oddly bitter remark he made many years later about his paperback book, *India since Cripps*. The Government people may think he knows more about conditions in India than is good for him – or them. 'But they need not worry. I too have been through the British educational system. It is contrary to my nature to be indiscreet, except of course in our Quaker way.'[12] He evidently found the public-school ethos oppressive, and this view was not substantially changed, as we shall see, when he experienced such schools as a teacher. One compensation, admittedly, was that it helped him to cope with British officialdom. He knew their world from the inside. And fortunately for him at Bootham he genuinely liked cricket, sufficiently at least to qualify as scorer for the school team. On his first visit to India he amused himself with speculations about the popularity of cricket in the sub-continent, suggesting that it embodied a kind of mystical discipline congenial to the Indian mind.[13]

He made some good friends at school, notably Philip Baker (later Philip Noel-Baker) and George Clark (the historian), but, as he noted in a letter to Rachel Sturge some years later, these two were very close friends with each other, and in his last few terms he felt he saw little of them, and was stranded among people he didn't really know. He was not a 'reeve' (the Bootham word for a prefect), 'and any authority or respect that I had in the school seemed to disappear'. Unlike his brothers he wasn't even awarded the Natural History Exhibition, though he knew that he was a much better naturalist than some who had held it in the past. Baker and Clark got leaving scholarships, but he left with nothing. 'Life seemed a solitary, miserable thing, and I retired into my shell, and became proud, aloof, jealous and bitter against fate.'[14]

He related one curious incident from this period in a letter to Olive Graham (Rachel's sister and his future wife). Members of the school debating society were required to deliver a one-minute impromptu speech on a given topic, and, says Horace, 'the villainous committee' told him to talk about whisky. He assumed that the intention was to mock his morose and puritanical disposition, and he was furious. Fury made him cool, 'and I expatiated without any difficulty, and in a voice of scorn, on the great virtues of whisky as a drowner of sorrows, and a soother of grief'. He sat down with a sense of triumph, relishing the silent amazement with which his tour de force was received (15 October 1917).

Evidence directly from his schooldays suggests that things were not always as stressful as this. He took obvious pleasure in his solitary birdwatching, and was for a time President of the school's Natural History Club. He appreciated visiting lecturers like Oliver Pike who pioneered the photography of birds: a talk by this ornithologist was illustrated by numerous coloured slides, some of which, Horace remarks temperately, showed their colours 'quite well' (15 February 1905). A diary entry for 4 February 1905 acquires interest from Horace's later concern with cooperative and gregarious behaviour in birds. A coconut was hung up somewhere in the school to feed garden birds. A robin was feeding there, and was approached by a great tit.

> Knowing that both were pugnacious birds I wondered very much what would happen. The Great Tit flew onto the string suspending the cocoanut, and then flew down. The Robin did not attempt to drive it away, but departed at once, though whether because it had finished, or was afraid of the Great Tit I do not know, but should think probably the latter.[15]

Horace contributed occasionally to the periodical produced by the school's Essay Society, *The Observer*. He championed Sir Edwin Landseer against Ruskin's strictures, on the ground that he evidently knew more about animals and showed his knowledge in his painting. There is also a characteristic discussion of parliamentary reform. Good government, he insists, is not a matter of imposing the will of the majority. In Queen Elizabeth's time, the country was divided into large confessional groups – moderate Protestant, Puritan and Catholic. If one could suppose any one of these groups to have won a parliamentary majority, it would have trampled its opponents underfoot. But this would not have been an expression of the general will.

> Elizabeth's own choice of a via media, however, which would have been an impossible choice for the parliament to have passed, very well represented the country as a whole, as almost all, though not actually satisfied with the arrangement, at least found it tolerable.[16]

The liking for moderate-minded managers was to persist and develop: he came to admire the political skills of Sir Robert Walpole, for example, finding 'something delightful in the clever way in which he used the arts of secret diplomacy to end wars, instead of making them.'[17] John Morley's short biography of Walpole illustrates the unusual 'union of tact and patience with immovable determination' that characterised so much of Walpole's conduct of foreign policy. Morley is particularly impressed by Walpole's restraining influence in the crisis following the Treaty of Vienna in 1725, when the Spanish seemed set to reconquer Gibraltar and their Austrian and Russian allies were believed to be promising support to the Stuart claimant to the British throne. Walpole refused to sanction active military intervention, and in due course the various threats evaporated.

> We may almost wonder even in our own enlightened day [Morley's biography was first published in 1889], how a minister could dare to be as sensible as Walpole. Though this resolute tardiness in recourse to arms exposed him to taunts of pusillanimity then and since, he was speedily justified by the event.[18]

Morley makes abundantly clear that Walpole's career had much that was distinctly unedifying, but he is convinced that his underlying intentions were good, and that he achieved much of the good he intended. And certainly the young Horace Alexander was not exactly predictable in his application of Quaker principles. The same Bootham essay on parliamentary reform insists that the franchise should be confined to those who are reasonably well informed about the issues. Those not willing to inform themselves and who yet persist in voting, ought, 'to use Mr Brayshaw's phrase, . . . to be gently but firmly shot'.[19]

'Mr Brayshaw' was A. Neave Brayshaw, fondly remembered by Bootham Old Scholars for his archaeological excursions and the 'hot toast and potted meat in his room, and the books there, and his kind chatty way'.[20] His engagingly lilting voice may still be appreciated in a tape of humorous verse readings preserved at Woodbrooke. One of them, which begins with the eohippus who knew he was going to be a horse, is an improving parable about the fallacy of supposing that things have to remain the way they are, and Neave Brayshaw's smooth delivery is a splendid vehicle for subverting the certainties that sustain the Establishment in every time and place. Something of his possible influence on Horace Alexander can be gleaned from the address given to the Friends'

Guild of Teachers at Woodbrooke in January 1914, on 'Spiritual Ideals of Education'.

> The man of action, that is of faith, always stands to be shot at more than does the man who lies low. It is not necessarily the latter who makes the fewer mistakes, but those which he makes are less easily recognized, and, on that account, they are the more insidious. . . . Of those who launch out into the deep it is true that some are foolhardy and some are drowned, and it is easy to show that from this fate those who stay on shore are always safe; it is not so easy to say how many faithless ones have starved for want of that which only can be gained by launching out.[21]

In later years, as we shall see, Horace Alexander was apt to alarm colleagues by impulsive actions and gestures. He may well have felt egged on by the spirit of Neave Brayshaw.

The Bootham teacher with whom Alexander remained in closest touch in after life was Hugh Richardson, the science master. He had been at King's College Cambridge, and may have influenced Alexander's own decision to seek admission there. Horace recalls his 'fertile and original mind', and his prophetic awareness of the functional approach to world government. He welcomed the undermining of national sovereignty by international bodies organised, like the Universal Postal Union, for specific and limited purposes. He visited the Alexanders' family home in Tunbridge Wells in 1912 for a meeting of the Friends' Guild of Teachers. At that time there was press speculation about tensions between Germany and Russia in connection with the German ambition to develop a Berlin–Baghdad railway. This was at odds with the Russian ambition to have unrestricted access to the Mediterranean Sea. Hugh Richardson suggested that where the German railway crossed the relevant Russian railway, one line should go under the other by a tunnel, thus eliminating the need for giving either party a superior right of way. The idea remained nothing more than a mealtime topic of conversation, but Horace was impressed by its sheer ingenuity: always a desirable talent when there are conflicts to be resolved.[22]

Hugh Richardson was the eldest son of David Richardson, director of a tanning firm in Newcastle-upon-Tyne. It was an exceptionally talented family. David's pamphlets on economics were 'original and full of thought'. One son, Arthur, was a painter of some distinction, and father of the actor Ralph Richardson. Another son, Lawrence, was an amateur astronomer whose work earned him an honorary degree from Durham University. Yet another, Gilbert Hancock Richardson, was a linguist who was a champion of the idea of an international language, preferring Ido to its better-known rival Esperanto. One daughter, Edith, was a poet and painter; the other, Catherine, was a physician and an accomplished musician. The youngest child, Lewis Fry Richardson, was the meteorologist who became a pioneer of scientific peace research.[23]

Cambridge before 1914

Alexander left Bootham in 1906 and did not go to Cambridge until the autumn of 1909. He speaks vaguely of being held back by ill-health, and it seems he was afflicted with a persistent bronchial condition. He did, however, spend the autumn term of 1906 at the Woodbrooke Settlement in Birmingham. Woodbrooke had been founded in 1903 as a Quaker study centre, presided over by the notable Biblical scholar Rendel Harris, and assisted among others by the ebullient Neave Brayshaw from Bootham. Horace's one term as a student at Woodbrooke was also Neave Brayshaw's last, and a farewell song, entered in the first Woodbrooke logbook, testifies to his power of instructing and expanding the minds of his hearers. As usual, Horace testified to his own enthusiasm for ornithology, contributing to the logbook a three-page essay on the birds of Woodbrooke.[24] He appears in the term's group photograph, looking remarkably mature for his seventeen years. He was evidently not a docile student, to judge from a letter, half a century later, from a contemporary, Edith Wood. He had written to her for some reason (the letter does not survive), and she responded warmly, greatly cheered by hearing from 'the very "Horace Abiram" I knew in 1906'.[25] Why Abiram? Well, he was a subversive Israelite who, with others, complained to Moses and Aaron that they had exalted themselves above the assembly of the Lord [Numbers 16,3]. In what sense Horace expected the earth to open and swallow him up is not clear, but he was evidently felt to be an audacious fellow.

After the term at Woodbrooke, there are for more than a year few details about Alexander's activities on record. He spent the winter of 1906–7 in Switzerland with his mother, and was presumably one of the two sons who met their father at Southampton, on 25 July 1907, after J. G. Alexander's final and triumphant visit to China and Japan.[26] It is clear that in these formative years of his late teens he spent much time bird-watching on his own. In 1908 he came to know Miss E. L. Turner, a dedicated ornithologist and photographer, and in May 1909 she invited him to spend a week in her houseboat on Hickling Broad in Norfolk. It was, he says in his autobiographical notes, 'a week of pure ecstasy for me'. He particularly recalled paddling round in a canoe, observing the wealth of bird life in the Broads.

Because of the long delay before he entered King's College Cambridge to read for the History Tripos, he was evidently advised to consult one of the tutors at King's about what he should be reading. The tutor consulted was Oscar Browning, then reluctantly on the point of retirement. He had done much to make King's a centre of historical scholarship, and although he was felt, with reason, to be a difficult colleague, he was immensely sociable, and tireless in his patronage of promising young men. He was for many years Treasurer of the Cambridge Union, and President of the Footlights Club.

His Sunday evening 'at homes' were the noisiest and most uninhibited social events in the Cambridge calendar. He was notorious for cultivating the acquaintance of the great, a trait that is neatly commemorated in a cartoon by Max Beerbohm, drawn in 1908, entitled 'Mid-Term Tea at Mr Oscar Browning's'. Horace saw it in April 1913, and told Browning that it represented him 'as introducing several pale, nervous-looking undergraduates, all exactly alike, with evident joy, to a large assembly of courtiers in various startling costumes'.[27] Horace was mistaken about the 'courtiers': Browning's guests are all recognisably contemporary kings, emperors, and the like. But the 'evident joy' of an enthusiastic patron is exactly right, and it is clear from Horace's own letters to Browning how stimulating a relationship it was for him.[28]

Alexander's first letters, dated 6 and 19 April 1908, show that Browning had told him to read Gibbon's *Decline and Fall of the Roman Empire* and Macaulay's *History of England*. The tone of the letters is remarkably self-assured, in marked contrast to that of similar letters from one of Alexander's contemporaries, Noel Compton-Burnett, brother of the novelist. Compton-Burnett is stilted and deferential; Alexander is cheerfully outspoken. Of Gibbon's history he remarks that 'the size of the thing alone appals me'; and of Macaulay's, 'I am afraid he is rather too brilliant for my liking.' Later in the year, Browning had suggested buying a book in a Harmsworth edition, which would be inexpensive. Alexander refused to buy anything published by Harmsworth, not because the man was conservative, but because anyone 'who can go to such lengths as Harmsworth does in the Daily Mail to get money does not deserve a farthing of my money'. As Browning had contributed to the Harmsworth *History of the World*, this was scarcely tactful. Alexander does indeed offer an apology of a sort: 'I am afraid you will think it not much good giving advice to such a hopelessly scrupulous person'.[29]

In the autumn of 1908 he attended extension lectures on England under the Stuarts, given in Tunbridge Wells by A. E. N. Simms, finding them stimulating and wonderfully fair-minded. He entered on a rapid study of the religions of the world, starting from Gibbon's attitude to Islam, and moving on to the great prophets of India. He decided that Buddha was a 'pessimist', which he didn't care for, as the human race had 'advanced enormously in the last 2000 years, or even in the last 500'.[30] For some reason Browning seems to have doubted whether Alexander's optimistic affirmations were genuine, as in his next letter (3 December 1908) he insists that he was indeed no pessimist but an optimist – 'at least generally'. He concludes, 'I remain yours very optimistically, Horace G. Alexander.'

Alexander spent another winter holiday, evidently for his health, in the south of France, travelling by sea to Marseilles, and then staying for some time at Hyères, not far from Toulon. Then in May, as already noted, he had the blissful holiday in the Norfolk Broads, and thus strengthened he was able to embark on his studies in Cambridge with some confidence.

Looking back on his initiation into Cambridge life, he remembers himself being acutely self-conscious, never sure that he wasn't saying or doing the wrong thing. On one occasion he wanted to buy a ticket for a Greek play, but from sheer inexperience of theatre-attendance failed to recognise the box-office, and found himself in the dressing-rooms. He was rescued by a distinguished gentleman who 'with amused politeness directed the bashful fresher to the box-office'.[31] While this diffidence may have been an element in his feelings, it is not at all the impression created by the letters written at the time to Oscar Browning, now living in Bexhill and doubtless relishing all the Cambridge news that young protegés like Alexander could transmit to him. On the contrary, they conjure up a young man delighted by the bustle and animated companionship of a society which assumed that its members would play a distinguished part in a world that was ripe for improvement. Many years later he recalled how he was apt 'to join everything that seemed new and exciting and progressive', and so enrolled in the newly formed Cambridge University Fabian Society, thus coming to know Rupert Brooke (President) and Clifford Allen (Secretary).[32] The atmosphere is felicitously suggested in J. M. Keynes's memoir, 'My Early Beliefs':

> It was exciting, exhilarating, the beginning of a renaissance, the opening of a new heaven on a new earth, we were the forerunners of a new dispensation, we were not afraid of anything . . . . Even at our gloomiest and worst we have never lost a certain resilience which the younger generation seem never to have had.[33]

The resilience was certainly to remain an enduring element in Alexander's character.

It was a society that was notoriously tolerant of homosexuality, but there is no indication that this touched Alexander except as a reinforcement of the tendency nurtured in schools for boys at the time to disregard the female sex generally. What emerges from the letters is an immeasurable satisfaction in the ordinary routine of college life. After he had been at King's for a few weeks, he gave Browning an account of a typical day: 8.30 breakfast, then reading the paper or writing letters, followed by a light diet of morning lectures - 10 to 12 noon, or merely 11 to 12 noon. The afternoon was spent on the river: he was the cox in the Senior trials. Doubtless, he explains modestly, they wouldn't have used him if they could have found anyone lighter. After tea he would settle into some real work, and go to bed any time between 10pm and midnight. He enjoyed writing the weekly essay, partly perhaps because he always found himself 'discussing some present day problem by mistake'.[34]

Browning had evidently expressed anxiety about Alexander's being 'by nature too much of a hermit', but the young man rejected the suggestion with spirit: 'I have', he said, 'had three years of enforced solitude, . . . and though I should live to be 100 I don't believe I could ever want it again'.[35] Well, he did live to be 100, and no doubt didn't want it again, though part of his appetite for bird-watching grew out of the respite it afforded him from human affairs. But as he put it in the same letter, he liked to have visitors even when he was busy. 'I get quite intoxicated with the delight of having friends at hand to talk to on the subjects one naturally thinks about at this time of life'.

He seems in fact to have spent too much time socialising for his academic health, and was only awarded a third class in his first-year examination. But Browning himself, and Alexander's tutor J. H. Clapham, wrote to him very encouragingly, and he resolved not to let this setback disturb him overmuch. On reflection, too, he wondered whether he may not have wantonly antagonised his examiners by his habit of relating historical events to some principle: 'I can't study history as if it were an end in itself, even for a moment; I can't bury myself in the past, and don't want to, either.' He was readily dissatisfied with his instructors, and complained fiercely to Browning about a Dr Tanner, whose lectures on the English civil war proved much less congenial than those given in Tunbridge Wells by A. E. N. Simms. He had difficulty, he wrote, in listening to him calmly and in silence, 'and so the best policy to adopt will be to cut his lectures until he gets into a more temperate frame of mind – or until I do!' As he remarked, 'I am hopelessly argumentative'.[36]

He certainly had no inhibitions about arguing with Browning. He was delighted to find that Browning advocated an 'international point of view', but questioned his support for universal military training.

> Personally I go as far as to believe in the Tolstoy scheme, even if it did mean a martyr nation; I think if England were to end as a martyr nation it would be the greatest service she could possibly render to the world, but I believe the conscience of nations has got far beyond the point at which such a thing would occur. I know these schemes are called wildly impractical. They are, to my mind, extremely practical, except in the sense that everything is impractical for which the majority of people are not prepared yet.[37]

Not that as fellow-Liberals they had radical differences to cope with. They could rejoice together at the Parliament Act of 1911, which substantially reduced the powers of the House of Lords. There was, Alexander told Browning, 'a scene of great animation' in the King's reading room on the morning when news of one of the crucial votes came through, 'and the conservatives shrank into the background to nurse their wrongs'.[38] There was talk of creating a large number of Liberal peers to secure the passage of the Bill, and Alexander speculated on the possibilities. Browning himself, generally known as he was as O.B., could become 'Lord Rippleswell of Obi, which I believe to be the name of a river in Siberia'. He then listed possible titles for such distinguished Kingsmen as Keynes, Pigou, Clapham, John Sheppard and Lowes Dickinson, and added that he feared the House of Lords would then usurp the powers of King and Commons alike, 'for its prestige would be overwhelming'.[39]

At the end of his second year he took the first part of the History Tripos and obtained a decent second class: Clapham told him that his Political Science paper was awarded a first-class mark, and his immediate reaction was to take International Law in his third year, partly because it might help him in a future career as a barrister. partly because of its 'vast importance in promoting the peace of nations'.[40] Clapham, however, advised him to continue with the Political Science, and he did so. The advice was good: in June 1912 he took Part II of the Tripos, and was awarded a First. This qualified him for a College Foundation Scholarship, and his tutor, J. H. Clapham, asked him to serve as Secretary to the King's College Political Society – a great compliment because, as he told Olive Graham, 'all the Secretaries have distinguished themselves in afterlife'. In his third year he had been Secretary of the Walpole Society, and now he moved on to being its President. As if that wasn't enough, he also served on the Cambridge Union's Kitchen Committee.[41]

Gaining a First was an appropriate climax to a year that had been successful in other ways. He had become something of a public figure. He was secretary of the College's Walpole Society, which organised debates, and also of its Social Work Committee, which was a King's variation on the more traditional missions to the working classes.[42] He helped in the editing of the King's magazine, *Basileon H*, and thus oversaw the first publication of Rupert Brooke's 'The Old Viczrage. Grantchester'. He managed to create a good deal of controversy, agreeing, for example, to a suggestion that the Walpole Society should discuss 'the licensing of harlots'. The College authorities prohibited the topic, and the Walpole Society protested. Alexander told Browning that they could not compromise in such a matter. Free speech must win the day: 'I feel very strongly, myself, that until sexual and other matters, usually regarded as delicate, are publicly discussed by responsible people in a thorough manner, progress towards the moral perfection of society must necessarily be slow.'

Browning obliged with a supportive postcard, but it wasn't needed as the College withdrew its objection, to the disquiet of the wider University community, where, said Alexander, the position was 'misunderstood'. But this would do more good than harm in the end: 'At any rate the Walpole has gained in vigour enormously; every debate since has been good, and the attendance large.'[43]

His concern for free speech was matched by a concern for free movement. He led an agitation for the abolition of 'signing in' to College, and had the satisfaction of achieving this. Browning was not over-pleased, but Alexander insisted that the practice was incongruous with the general condition of freedom in King's.[44]

Alexander even found himself the subject of a scandalous paragraph in the *Cambridge Review*, which alluded coyly to an incident in the Backs when he and another undergraduate, Sidney Russell Cooke, had a misunderstanding with a Proctor, who charged them with indecent behaviour, doing so in strong language. They were actually engaged in the innocent and scientific task of marking the location of night-birds, and they lodged a vigorous protest that embarrassed the Proctor considerably. The *Review* got hold of this story by way of the vastly amused Philip Baker, and affected to compare Horace's interest in night-birds to Caterina da Valbona's interest in nightingales in the *Decameron* (5.4). But why, Alexander and Cooke inquired in the following issue, 'seek analogies from Boccaccio when Keats expresses all the truth? Your correspondent is no less fallible than the proctor: it is to be hoped that he will have less cause to repent his folly.'[45] Telling the story to Browning, Alexander was evidently pleased with their reply, remarking smugly, 'I rather think we have scored'.[46]

At the time, his greatest triumph must have seemed the Walpole Dinner, which it fell to him to organise in February 1912. In spite of much anxiety beforehand, it proved to be an uproarious success. The dons undertook a reading of Act 3 of *The Importance of Being Earnest*, and the vivaciously erudite John Sheppard demonstrated his theatrical powers in a parody of the *Oedipus* as then acted in Covent Garden: 'He did the whole thing, audience and all, and kept everyone in a hopeless state of laughter all the time.'[47] This was the famous Max Reinhardt production, with John Martin-Harvey in the title role. No one who saw it, said the reviewer in *Punch*: 'is likely to forget the repulsive hideousness of the scene where the King rushes out with bloody eye-sockets, flings himself against a pillar of the palace and howls at the top of his voice.'

As he groped his way through the audience to the exit, people were seen hiding their eyes in horror.[48]

There was a huge cast, drawn from the drama students and boy scouts of London, whose moans and cries and shouts set the air throbbing (*Daily Telegraph*), and who raised their white arms – 'a sea of white arms it was' – in agonised supplication (*The Times*). Gilbert Murray, whose translation was the one used, exclaimed that 'the half-naked torch-bearers with loin-cloths and long black hair made my heart leap with joy'. Their free and natural movements as they raced up and down the steps of the palace were for the *Punch* reviewer 'the most engaging feature of the evening's novelty'. They invaded the auditorium: a small cartoon in *Punch* shows a late-arriving member of the audience being pursued to his seat by a crowd of yelling citizens of Thebes.[49] John Sheppard evidently conjured all this up in his one-man performance.

Even in his old age he could delight extra-mural classes with the versatility of his dramatic evocations of Greek drama: a talent surely anticipated by Walt Whitman in his celebrated claim, 'I am large, I contain multitudes'.[50] Alexander's ecstatic appreciation of this performance demonstrates the keen conviviality that was to be an enduring element in his character.

Looking back at his Cambridge career years later, Alexander attached a good deal of importance to his friendship with Philip Baker. Baker was a popular and successful undergraduate who became, among other things, President of the Cambridge Union. They used to walk to Jesus Lane Meeting on Sunday mornings, generally arriving about ten minutes late, possibly because they were engaged in absorbing conversation. Baker and Alexander, together with John Rickman (who later became a distinguished psychiatrist), enjoyed being a subversive fraternity in the Meeting, directing 'a powerful onslaught on all species of Young Friendism' - meaning Young Friends whose enthusiastic devotion inspired but sometimes alarmed their elders.[51] They 'vanquished H. T. Hodgkin on a memorable occasion, proving that missionaries were pernicious, and that every influence of western civilisation in the East was bad. I believe', Alexander added with relish, 'we made him quite miserable.'[52] T. R. Glover fared no better, but John William Graham was more congenial, being a Kingsman himself. He remembered the Political Society of his own day fondly, and his adoration of the place, on almost his first visit for twenty-five years, helped to convince Alexander even more of 'what a really glorious place King's is and has been'.[53]

Philip Baker used to rehearse his Union speeches to Horace: 'he said I was a good trial audience', Horace remarks in his autobiographical notes. Horace himself made only two speeches in Union debates, the first on 3 May 1910, addressing a motion on Irish Home Rule. The report in the undergraduate magazine *Granta* noted that he made some interesting remarks, but gave no hint of what they were. 'His delivery is unusual; but there is no reason why he should not speak again. We hope he will.'[54] The hope was not realised for a long time, but one ingredient in the speech was indeed served up again, and with acclaim. He had concluded with a crisp peroration about 'England standing between the Irish people and their destiny'. Philip liked this, and next time the issue was debated (24th January 1911) made use of it at the end of his speech. 'It provoked loud applause', says Horace, adding wryly, 'When I had said it, a year earlier, it had produced scarcely a ripple!'[55]

When he did make another speech, some two-and-a-half years later, it was on behalf of another oppressed nation, Persia, victim of the imperial rivalries of Russia, Britain and Germany. But by that time, as we have seen, a great deal had happened to enhance his self-confidence and sense of direction. In retrospect he gave much of the credit to a chance remark of Philip Baker's. Philip said that he envied Horace:

> 'You always seem to be able to take an unconventional view of things, whereas I am only able to do just what everyone else does.' . . . Here was I trying desperately but unsuccessfully it seemed to be a conformist, to be acceptable among the brighter stars of Cambridge; the very last thing I was trying to do was to be unconventional. And yet here was my best friend apparently telling me that my tendency to do the wrong thing rather than the conventional thing was a virtue.[56]

No doubt the remark precipitated changes for which he was already well prepared. And clearly many of his friendships at King's were very significant.

His relationship with Arthur Happell is particularly interesting in view of their later very different association with India. They knew each other well, as they both came from Tunbridge Wells. During the summer of 1913, Alexander succumbed to a vicious attack of typhoid fever after a holiday in Italy, and during his convalescence Happell took him out in a bath-chair, energetically pushing him up- and downhill. After the war, Happell joined the Indian Civil Service, and Alexander met him twice on his first visit to India in 1927–8. He was decidedly unsympathetic to Indian nationalist aspirations. Even so, Alexander remarks, Happell still made him welcome 'as an old friend from King's.[57]' And that of course was the point: the freemasonry of King's was stronger than any disagreement, however profound.

The strongest influence on Alexander at this time was probably that of his third-year tutor Goldsworthy Lowes Dickinson. Dickinson, more than anyone, embodied the King's ethos which he was always to value so highly. In Dickinson's own words, it produced people who were

> unworldly without being saintly, unambitious without being inactive, warmhearted without being sentimental. Through good report and ill such men work on, following the light of truth as they see it; able to be sceptical without being paralysed; content to know what is knowable and to reserve judgment on what is not. The world could never be driven by such men, for the springs of action lie deep in ignorance and madness. But it is they who are the beacon in the tempest.[58]

He had published some much-admired *Letters from John Chinaman* in 1901, celebrating the virtues of Chinese civilisation in contrast to that of Europe, and his predilections were congenial to someone from a family with such close links with China. Horace helped to start an Anglo-Chinese Society in the university, and was its first Secretary (Lowes Dickinson agreed to be President). His Chinese interests prompted him to attend a meeting of the economics society run by J. M. Keynes. A friend, Archibald Rose, was reading a paper on the Chinese economy, and Alexander rashly joined in the discussion, lamenting, as Lowes Dickinson might have done, that China seemed set to follow the path of industrialisation, undermining her ancient culture. He was flattered when Keynes treated his rather amateurish contribution with respect, agreeing that as there was a prospect of a world surplus of industrial production, it was all the more crucial to sustain existing food producers. This was not at all the point Alexander was trying to make, though doubtless it was flattering to be taken seriously, even on the basis of a misunderstanding. But he was already developing and extending Dickinson's questioning of European values.[59]

He did this in an environment which was increasingly cosmopolitan. A striking illustration of this was a pair of conferences held in the summer of 1910, one in June, at the Caxton Hall, Westminster, on 'nationalities and subject races', and the other, even more ambitious, a month later at the University of London – a 'Universal Races Congress'.[60] Gilbert Murray's opening address at the earlier conference was a cogent and witty attack on attitudes of racial superiority.

> If ever it were my fate to administer a Press Law, and put men in prison for the books they write and the opinions they stir up among their countrymen, I should not like it, but I should know where to begin. I should first of all lock up my old friend Rudyard Kipling, because in several stories he has used his great powers to stir up in the minds of hundreds of thousands of Englishmen a blind and savage contempt for the Bengali . . . And in case Mr Kipling should feel lonely in his cell, I would send him a delightful companion, Mr Anstey of *Punch* –

in which periodical Indians are caricatured as cowardly, vain, untruthful and bombastic, he continues. When, Murray concludes, rulers show jealousy of their subjects, wishing 'to keep them out of power not because they are unfit for power, but because they are too obviously fit', then they have 'forfeited their claim to stand among the great leaders and governors of the world'.[61]

As already noticed, when Alexander spoke in the Union for the second and last time, he did so in a debate about Persia, on 26 November 1912. He was supporting a motion condemning Sir Edward Grey's policy there, which was widely held to be an appeasement of Russian ambitions in Persia in the interests of European power politics. There is no record of what Alexander said, but according to the report in the *Cambridge Review* (28 November 1912) the motion was opposed in terms that would have irritated him, with references to 'backward peoples' and 'picturesque bandits'. At this time Alexander was associating himself with the circle around the Professor of Arabic in the University, Edward Granville Browne, who was an ardent champion of the Persian national reformers, and a fierce critic of the ideology of imperialism. As he put it in the preface to his book *The Persian Revolution of 1905–1909*, many people saw Persia as a backward country which could only be 'developed' by some European power, whether the Persians liked it or not. But for

Browne, Persia had its own 'generic perfection' which would be lost if its people were compelled to imitate an alien culture.

> No material prosperity, no amount of railways, mines, gaols, gas, or drainage can compensate the world, spiritually and intellectually, for the loss of Persia. . . . Many European journalists and other writers have made merry over the idea of a Persian Parliament, repeating like so many parrots the expression 'comic opera' on almost every page. Yet I venture to think that there was more reality and more grim determination in this Persian struggle than in our own European politics, with their lack of guiding principles, their conferences, and their sham conflicts.[62]

He was resigned to the fact that many of his friends did not share his admiration for the Persians, 'a great and talented people' with much to contribute to the 'intellectual health of the world'. He put this down to their ignorance of the people involved, or – in the case of his good friend and orientalist Edward Denison Ross – exposure to the demoralising influence of the European establishment in India.[63] Denison Ross remarks on his enthusiasm for many causes that were at odds with imperialist orthodoxy, including Irish Home Rule, and this may explain why it was Browne whom Alexander first approached to be President of the Anglo-Chinese Society, even though Lowes Dickinson must have appeared in retrospect to be the obvious choice. Browne declined the invitation, but maintained an interest because of parallels between the predicament of China and of Persia. He invited Alexander, a few weeks before the Union debate, to dine with him to meet a Captain Stokes who had up-to-date information about the state of things in Persia.[64] Evidently Alexander continued to concern himself with the Persian question, because as late as 28 April 1914 there is a letter from Browne to him lamenting the evaporation since 1912 of public anger about Grey's treatment of Persia. Retribution 'for this wicked crime' will surely follow, Browne insisted, perhaps in India or in Ulster, 'but I doubt if the dead can be restored to life again'.

Browne's influence at this time is apparent in a paper that Alexander read to the Political Society in 1913. His subject was foreign policy, which he remarked was conducted in a much more secretive way than were domestic affairs. This secrecy made it easier for ministers to fail in their duty to support oppressed nations. Far more could have been done to support constitutional government in Persia and China, and there has been a shameful acquiescence in the condemnation of the leader of the opposition in Egypt. The choice is not one between mere words and war. Support can be strong without being aggressive.[65]

It must be admitted that Alexander gives little indication of how precisely support is to be offered. He mentions the zeal on behalf of the oppressed shown by Palmerston and Gladstone, but that, after all, implies the deployment of the occasional gunboat. And when he says, in conclusion, that 'whenever the integrity of a nation is in danger . . . we must be willing to sacrifice a good deal', he anticipates the circumstances that seemed so decisive to most of his contemporaries when Germany invaded Belgium in August 1914. They did not, in the event, seem decisive to Alexander, and it is important to understand why.

The few years before the outbreak of war saw not only an increase in cosmopolitan sentiment, but also an awareness of the importance of international institutions. The Brussels periodical *La Vie Internationale* regularly published impressive lists of international conferences, from those of spiritualists and freethinkers to the Young Women's Christian Association, from campaigners for women's suffrage to campaigners against alcoholism. A particularly innovative institution of international cooperation was founded in Rome in 1905: the International Institute of Agriculture. This was the result of many years' campaigning by an American businessman, David Lubin, who saw the importance of reliable and detailed information about harvests worldwide as a way of defeating speculators. The Institute had a large staff receiving and processing data from official sources, and its publications became an indispensable resource for everyone concerned with the distribution of agricultural products.[66] Horace Alexander had particular reason to be aware of this organisation, as his brother Christopher joined its staff at an early stage.

The efflorescence of such organisations reinforced the impression that the world was becoming more cooperative, less willing to tolerate a resort to brute force. Nowhere is this more evident than in the writings of Norman Angell, whose book *The Great Illusion* (first published in 1909 as *Europe's Optical Illusion*) was immensely influential. Briefly his thesis was that in a modern commercial society war simply made no sense. There was no rational motive to justify it. While nations were still perfectly capable of going to war – and indeed were arming themselves for this purpose with immense enthusiasm – they did so because journalists and politicians were deluded. They acted on assumptions that were all very well for Congo savages, cattle-lifters or South American adventurers, but were unworthy of sophisticated people who understood their own self-interest. 'Are we to assume', Angell inquired, 'that the Governments of the world, which presumably are directed by men as far-sighted as bankers, are permanently to fall below the banker in their conception of enlightened self-interest?'[67] It is in everyone's interest to maintain economic stability. In financial matters, internationalism is total. The Labour movement, too, finds itself under pressure to internationalise itself. Enlightened liberals in Britain and Germany have far more in common than they have with their militaristic fellow countrymen. J. G. Alexander was concerned to make the same point in support of his own belief in world federalism. Horace Alexander suggests that in promoting this belief his father was giving salience to actually operative forces of which it is all too easy to lose sight. He was drawing attention to the 'signs of a growing international spirit; to show the people of each nation that those of other nations were, not merely in ideal, but increasingly in fact, their friends and fellow-workers'.[68]

Quakers generally were predisposed to welcome the Angell doctrine. J. W. Graham devotes a whole chapter to it in his *Evolution and Empire*, published in 1912. He relates it to the great Christian insight that we are all members one of another, and adds the more mercantile consideration that armies and navies entail more expense than they are worth: 'the insurance premium is too high for the risk.' Unfortunately, like Alexander in his foreign policy paper, he invokes an argument that in August 1914 could be turned against him. The happiest countries in Europe, he claims, are small states whose independence is guaranteed by treaties, not by arms. He is thinking of Switzerland, the Scandinavian countries, Holland and, alas, Belgium. 'How the mere names call up dignity and cleanliness and public well-being', he exclaims. 'How free and democratic these states are. How pleasant their populations; how well-educated and intelligent.'[69] Much good their education and intelligence did them when they stood in the way of the German armies, objectors might, and did, readily remark.

The fact remains, as the Alexanders and Graham insisted, that we are indeed all members one of another, and Angell did seem to have found a way of translating this into practical politics. His ideas were particularly influential in Cambridge, where on 13 February 1912 there had been a notable debate in the Union on naval rearmament. Robert Yerburgh, President of the Navy League, spoke in favour of maintaining an unquestionable superiority in Britain's naval establishment; Norman Angell was the leading speaker on the other side, and persuaded a sufficient majority of those present to support him, 203 to 187. Philip Baker was Vice-President that term, but it seems to have been the Secretary, Harold Wright, who actually secured Angell's attendance. He became a leading champion of Angell's approach to international relations, and worked closely with people of similar sympathies, like Lowes Dickinson and Lord Bryce. His personal convictions on peace and war were, according to Norman Angell himself, very much of the Quaker kind.

> There should be certain things in the intercourse of civilized nations, as in that of civilized men, which simply 'are not done'. To maim, torture, starve, disembowel, poison, kill, often the weak and powerless, because you – or the many you's that make your nation – wanted something the other refused to surrender, could never seem to Harold good or necessary.[70]

His overriding concern, though, was to promote rational discussion, to create an atmosphere, a public opinion, which would encourage politicians to act reasonably. He was willing to consider what might be of value in any ideas about war prevention, and welcomed any development that seemed to point in the right direction.

Norman Angell and Harold Wright interested conservative politicians such as Lord Esher and A. J. Balfour in their practical approach to such issues, and this led to the establishment of the so-called Garton Foundation for promoting the study of 'international polity'. Associated societies were started in most British universities, the Cambridge one being described by Harold Wright as a sort of Kinder-Garton Foundation. There was also a journal called *War and Peace*, along with conferences at Le Touquet and Old Jordans – the latter being held just before the outbreak of war in 1914.

Such an inclusive, unsectarian mode of campaigning against the institution of war might well generate the kind of hopes that led Philip Baker to say (according to Horace) 'I doubt if there will ever be another war'. The Hague conferences of 1899 and 1907 were, as Alexander remarked in his autobiographical notes, 'developing a broadly based international law, which would enable the Sovereign States of Europe to live in peace through law. The next conference might well produce an agreement for the reduction of armaments.'

In retrospect it is easy enough to see how excessive this optimism was, how insufficiently grounded in the facts of human behaviour. The arms race continued unchecked – irrationally, no doubt, but irresistibly; and as readers of the short stories of Saki (H. H. Munro) will appreciate, there was plenty of sophisticated rejection of rational pacifism in the years just before the war. But it was not absurd either to feel that Angell's was the voice of the future. In the event the wave of enthusiasm for his ideas only made the catastrophe of 1914 more shattering for his disciples. On his reasoning, the war should have been prevented by the enlightened self-interest of financiers and business people. It could be argued that the outbreak of war simply showed the sheer potency of old illusions, but the overwhelming mood was one of bewilderment and incomprehension. Angell put it crisply: 'Everybody wanted not to go to war. Everybody has gone to war. The action we did intend, we have not taken.'[71] He went on to speak of 'this essential helplessness of men', a conviction that was widespread. Lowes Dickinson noted 'the dumb impotent feeling of the gulf between nature, the past, all beautiful true and gracious things and beliefs, and this black horror of inconceivability that nevertheless was true'.[72] W. B. Yeats's comment on the Irish troubles is apposite:

> The night can sweat with terror as before
> We pieced our thoughts into philosophy,
> And planned to bring the world under a rule,
> Who are but weasels fighting in a hole.[73]

Alexander may have felt that much should be sacrificed if the integrity of a nation was threatened, but the sacrifice could not be allowed to include the metamorphosis of man into weasel. And his distress was perhaps the greater because of the way he saw himself as a modest contemporary of greater men, who would know how to run the world for its own good. In an enthusiastic letter to Browning in February 1913 he celebrates the greatness of some of the people in his year, such as Philip Baker, Noel Compton-Burnett and Freddie Hardman, and hopes they will reflect their glory on to him. He had no clear vision of his own future: he turned down an opportunity to be a private secretary to the Liberal politician Herbert Samuel, feeling too independent (and not knowing enough German); he had some thoughts of following his father's vocation as a barrister, and took relevant Law examinations (Roman Law – 'detestable stuff', he said – and International Law); he wondered whether he might take tutorial classes for the Workers' Educational Association.[74] Meanwhile he lingered in Cambridge, till the way should become clearer.

While he was very much at ease in this Zion, and always remained deeply attached to its libertarian ethos, seeing little point in the relative austerity of his upbringing, he was conscious of some insufficiencies. He did not take to the idea that art could be a substitute for religion, and felt that the prevalent Cambridge aestheticism left life rather empty. He strongly endorsed Keynes's admission in 'My Early Beliefs' that the exhilarating rationalistic optimism of pre-1914 Cambridge ultimately impoverished life, ignoring as it did powerful and valuable springs of feeling, 'the spontaneous, irrational outbursts of human nature', and the emotions inspired by 'the order and pattern of life amongst communities'.[75] In his late autobiographical notes, Alexander contrasts 'My Early Beliefs' with the memoir published in the same posthumous volume about the German financier, Dr Melchior, with whom Keynes negotiated in the period between the Armistice and the Versailles Treaty.[76] He did so with an intrepid disregard for the Allied prohibition of personal contact with the defeated enemy, and Alexander saw this as the effect of a moral passion which one could hardly detect in 'My Early Beliefs'. But Cambridge generated people who could redeem the world, even if they could not explain why.

The First World War

The war of 1914 changed Keynes, of course, as it changed everyone else, not least Horace Alexander. As it happens, we have a record of his state of mind on the eve of war in a paper entitled simply 'Peace'. Internal evidence indicates that it was written in mid-July, when he was reading at the British Museum, and lunching regularly with two members of its staff, his fellow Kingsman and orientalist Arthur Waley, and Denison Ross, newly returned from India. Alexander begins by referring to Philip Baker's too hopeful prophecy that there would never be another major war, and dates this a year previously.

> Since then Europe seems to have been fast slipping back to anarchy and barbarism. . . . But it is just at such times as these, when we might so

> easily be struck dumb by the frustration of all our hopes – it is now, if ever, that there is most need for us to make our voices heard.

He repeats his conviction that international law will continue to work for greater justice, thus reducing the demand for war, and that friendship between individuals will reduce the bitterness of conflicts. But he realises that if war comes, peace advocates will be mocked. Very well, then. When our puritan ancestors were defeated, they 'humbled themselves before their Maker, and with great humility and self-abasement prayed that they might see in what way they had been unfaithful'. With fierce emphasis, Alexander insists that there is a great work to be done:

> If we would only do what comes to our hands to do, and do it as well as we are able, I am convinced that we should find ourselves beginning to move the world, not only to a higher destiny in the remoteness of the future, but to something tangible, something better and nobler – even though not just what we expected – and that immediately, tomorrow or even today.[77]

The note struck in this paper was not one to which his friends were accustomed. As Nicholas Bagenal, one of his King's contemporaries, put it, he had always thought of Alexander as the embodiment of a type, 'the intellectualist *pure* and *simple*'. There was an 'unfathomable gulf' between this type and 'the artistic type' represented by Duncan Grant.[78] The gulf could be accounted for 'by the inability of the one to feel and the other to think'. Alexander had upset this analysis by giving 'visible and outward signs of definite feelings! How dare you? I suppose the next thing will be that Duncan will write a book.'[79]

The letter to Bagenal that betrayed 'definite feelings' will have been one announcing his engagement to Olive Graham in the summer of 1917, but Alexander's capacity for passionate feeling is sufficiently evident in an essay he contributed to *The Friend* in September 1914. 'The Glamour of War', was inspired by the agonised discussions he and his friends had after war had broken out. He found that although many of his circle knew Rupert Brooke well, the poet's patriotic response to the crisis was not much shared: they emphatically did not thank God for matching them to this hour: 'It was a grim business, that would undermine, perhaps destroy, the things we most cared for: but what did we do about it?'

Noel Compton-Burnett, brother of the novelist, and a Fellow of King's, 'the most unmilitary man imaginable', Alexander wrote, 'the gentlest, most open, most understanding of my Cambridge friends', was deeply exercised by the pressures to enlist. 'It is all very well for you', he told Alexander, 'you are a Quaker, so you have a conscience about it.' Alexander thought he must have assured his friend that 'his objections to fighting were at least as fundamental and "conscientious" as mine', but it didn't convince him. Noel Compton-Burnett enlisted, and was killed in 1915.

Many others suffered the same fate. The greatest grief was caused by the death of one of his closest friends, Tommy Stone. Little is known about him, except that in the autumn of 1911 he went on a holiday in the Pyrenees with Alexander, when they quarrelled a lot. The quarrelling features in one of Alexander's strangest writings, 'A Friend's Friend'. It was never published. He imagines himself as a German soldier who killed an Englishman, and was curiously haunted by the experience, as though the Englishman were his real self, and he had committed suicide – but was still alive. Years afterwards he visited England and came to know a man who seemed to be both attracted to him and yet often incomprehensibly angry with him too. It turned out that he was a friend of the man whom the narrator had shot, and to whom the narrator bore an uncanny similarity.

> What you said just now about not liking people who talked about beautiful things was too awful. Because once before the war he and I went to the Pyrenees together, and the evening we got there we were going by train up the valley, and presently the Moon appeared over the mountains. We hadn't been talking much; I think he had been reading. . . . Anyhow, I couldn't resist any longer, and so I said, indistinctly and rather afraid I might annoy him by saying anything, 'Have you noticed the Moon?' – no more than that. He was very annoyed. 'Yes', he said, 'I saw it half an hour ago, and now you've spoilt it all.' And that was just what you said half-an-hour ago. Good God, I do hate you![80]

It isn't easy to disentangle the complexities of this relationship, but the anguish is unmistakeable. And it was the cumulative effect of these deaths that was really devastating. They were all people, said Alexander in his autobiographical notes, 'who might have helped to turn the world away from the suicidal courses its leaders seem to have led us into.'

'The Glamour of War' is a less tormented piece than its later counterpart 'A Friend's Friend', but it is still powerful evidence of the writer's misery at the onset of war. Alexander writes as a birthright Friend, strongly convinced of the peace testimony, and believing war to be 'the most stupid and ridiculous barbarism ever invented'. Then war came: 'neutral territory had been violated; it was evidently useless to suggest "submitting the matter to arbitration".' What could be done but fight for Belgium? His friends enlisted, though with heartburning and doubt.

> They saw still the stupidity of it, and they must have felt secretly that their life was worth more to the world than their death. . . . As they went they said to me, enviously I think, 'It is all right for you; you are

> a Quaker and have a conscience about it.' If ever I cursed Quakerism I cursed it then. Had I a conscience? What was a conscience? I could not say; another of these religious shibboleths, probably. My hatred of war was the same hatred my friends had. They had gone to fight, to die. I must do the same.

So he imagines himself training for war, and then going to the front. He takes part in an attack, and realises that the gun he has fired has felled a German soldier. He could think of nothing but his conviction that he had killed this man: 'I thought I had killed my dearest friend.' In fact he was only injured; the author, too, was injured though he hadn't realised it. He helped him back to safety, and they were in hospital together, where they discovered they both had the same horror of war. 'It seemed strange that two men with such a horror of killing should meet on a battlefield.' An old soldier comments that most people feel like that at first, but they swallow it down pretty quick and get over it. If not, they get killed.

It is curious to find Alexander anticipating the theme of Wilfred Owen's 'Strange Meeting' so early in the war, but to some extent the idea of the soldier as victim, feeling solidarity with fellow victims, was an established one: it is effectively used in H. W. Nevinson's *The Plea of Pan* (1901), for example. Anyway, it helped Alexander to think his way through to his anguished conclusion: 'Perhaps, after all, it is better even to submit heroically to an alien Government than to kill men of other nations in order to keep liberty. It is a hard alternative.'[81]

The alternative was the harder because of the intense public pressure on young men to join the army. Some relief was provided by Philip Baker's initiative in forming the Friends' Ambulance Unit, which demonstrated that objectors to war were still willing to undergo its perils. Alexander himself was influenced by this feeling, and in the early weeks of the war he thought of volunteering for the Friends' War Victims Relief organisation. His doctor objected, no doubt because of the bronchial condition. As time went on he saw his real duty elsewhere, encouraged perhaps by the vigorously iconoclastic attitude of his fellow Kingsman and Quaker, John Rickman. Rickman was scornful of the excessively improvised nature of the FAU ('Some of the dressers have been studying medicine for 6 weeks, isn't Phil amazing? Poor wounded!'). He also deplored the motives of many of the recruits:

> It is pathetic to see the way many of those going are just cowtowing to public opinion, many of them think that this is good work instead of enlisting, as though the military can impose a standard for men to live up to: I deny them the right![82]

The vigour of Rickman's assertion of his right to go his own way was exceptional. Most of Alexander's associates were utterly disorientated by the outbreak of a war that ought not to have happened. The one thing that could be done, on Angellite principles, was to make sure that it didn't happen again, and from the very outset Lowes Dickinson, in particular, began thinking on lines that were eventually to be embodied in the League of Nations.

E. M. Forster, in his biography of Lowes Dickinson, remarks that he may well have invented the phrase 'League of Nations'.[83] His further claim, that Dickinson was also the first to formulate the idea, is not literally true. Andrew Carnegie had outlined the idea in his second Rectorial Address to the students of St Andrews University (17 October 1905), and followed it up in an address to the Peace Society in London in May 1910. In the latter, he said that he had put the proposal to the late Liberal Prime Minister, Henry Campbell-Bannerman, on the eve of the 1907 Hague Conference. Would Britain welcome an invitation to join such a league?' Campbell-Bannerman replied, 'No party in Britain dare refuse.'[84] It was in 1910 that Carnegie established his Endowment for International Peace, and that Theodore Roosevelt, in accepting the Nobel Peace Prize, looked to the formation of 'a League of Peace' which would guarantee the security of all nations ('by force if necessary').[85]

Then, too, Philip Noel-Baker's father, the MP J. Allen Baker, had been campaigning for a 'League of Peace' in the years before the war, and in 1909 had put the idea to the German Kaiser, who was not unsympathetic. On the eve of war, the British Foreign Secretary Sir Edward Grey wrote to the German Chancellor that if the current crisis could be safely passed, he would promote a scheme to ensure peace among the European Powers. 'The idea', he went on, 'has hitherto been too Utopian to be the subject of definite proposals'.[86] It was precisely the 'definite proposals' that Lowes Dickinson was concerned to supply, and his first public presentation of them was in a pamphlet published early in 1915, *After the War*. Here he uses Allen Baker's term, a 'League of Peace', which would require states to submit disputes to arbitration or conciliation, and would introduce measures of disarmament. The pamphlet was given earnest endorsement in an editorial in *The Friend* (26 March 1915). The warmth of the endorsement reflected the concern of many Friends to take up the work laid upon them a month earlier by Norman Angell. He appealed to the Society of Friends to take a fuller part in propagating its peace principles, 'explaining intellectually a truth which you hold intuitively by the Inner Light'. It was Friends' role to show that 'greater than all instruments of despotism is the spirit of man, man's unconquerable mind'.

> You are going to be one of the few Cities of Refuge left. This war is not going to end war, and . . . it is not going to end militarism. If war and militarism are ended it will not be by an army, it will be by the humble teacher trying to understand life, about how things work, and trying to help others to understand.

Angell was appalled by the temper, the moral atmosphere that had grown since the outbreak of war – bitter, cruel, vengeful. Yet even so 'the curious thing is that everyone knows that finally we have got to come to abolishing war, or war will abolish us'.[87]

The Society of Friends was initially as stunned by the outbreak of war as were many other groups dedicated to bettering the world. But at the end of September 1914, a conference was organised at Llandudno in North Wales to help Friends sort out a response to the challenge, and the Society settled down, uneasily, to the position presented week by week in the pages of *The Friend*, that of a threefold service: to bear witness to the Peace Testimony, prepare for post-war reconstruction, and help relieve suffering. There was an Emergency Committee for Helping Aliens, a War Victims' Relief Committee, and Philip Baker's Friends' Ambulance Unit. This general position was by no means unanimously acceptable. In the early months of the war there was a vigorous correspondence in *The Friend* about the rights and wrongs of enlistment. But the Society as a whole maintained a strong witness against all war, including this one. As a 1915 Yearly Meeting minute put it, the peace testimony was 'one which comes welling up from within. It springs from the very heart of our faith.'[88]

It is in this context that one can appreciate the urgency with which many Friends sought help to think through the problems thrust upon them by the war. Joseph Alexander made an initial attempt in November 1914 to persuade Friends to publish an appeal for peace, invoking a speech by Herbert Asquith, the Prime Minister, that looked towards a future world order based upon 'public right' and not force. He supported this with a draft of a pamphlet that Horace had written, entitled *Peace! Peace!!*, arguing that an immediate peace would be better than one reached six months later. The title was not derived from Jeremiah's denunciation of those who have healed the people's wounds lightly, saying 'Peace, peace,' when there is no peace Jeremiah, 6.14, but came from one of Alexander's seventeenth-century heroes, the gentle and cultivated Lord Falkland. A footnote explains that he met his death in one of the first battles of the Civil War, crying 'Peace, peace!'

Joseph Alexander consulted several of his friends about the practicability of making such an appeal, but the responses were generally negative. Isaac Sharp thought it would engender nothing but lengthy argument, Arnold Rowntree believed that Prussian militarism needed 'a severe check' (though emphatically not 'a fight to a finish'), Rendel Harris, while sympathetic, did not think the time ripe, and Henry Hodgkin was troubled by the thought that a Quaker peace initiative might be interpreted in Germany as a semi-official admission of defeat. Hodgkin went on to say, though, that an initiative from American Quakers would not be open to such an interpretation, but might not carry much weight.[89] Still, though he did not see his way clear in November, his involvement with the formation of the Fellowship of Reconciliation in Cambridge in the last four days of 1914 evidently opened up fresh possibilities. This organisation developed out of pre-war work by Allen Baker and others to organise a world alliance to promote friendship through the churches. In a conference in Constance, held just as war was breaking out at the beginning of August 1914, it was resolved that in every country the churches should be enlisted in 'a joint endeavour to achieve the promotion of international friendship and the avoidance of war'. Thanks to the Kaiser's interest in the conference, the delegates got away in the last through train to the Netherlands, and there was a memorable parting at Cologne station where the German pastor Siegmund-Schultze had to leave his fellow delegates, embarking on a dedicated wartime witness to the ideals of a truly universal church.[90] At the Cambridge conference Hodgkin was one of the principal speakers, and Alexander attended, along with about 130 others. Hodgkin himself lost no time in organising a Quaker 'War Sub-Committee', comprising fifteen Friends. Alexander suggests that most of the names were selected by Hodgkin, but it was a sub-committee of Meeting for Sufferings rather than of the long-established Peace Committee, and if normal nominating procedures were observed preparations for the committee must have been going on alongside those for the Cambridge conference. John W. Graham, Alexander's future father-in-law, chaired the sub-committee, and Alexander became secretary.

The new sub-committee first met a couple of days after the founding conference of the Fellowship of Reconciliation, on 2nd January 1915, and over several months a pamphlet, *Looking towards Peace*, was prepared, which was subsequently distributed to Quaker meetings throughout Britain – Alexander himself sending out those for meetings in the southern half of the country from his rooms in King's College. It was agreed to assign consideration of a number of specific problems to particular members, and some articles arising out of this exercise – all by Graham – were published in *The Friend* in April 1915 ('Limits to the Use of Force', 2 April, 'The State and the Individual', 9 April, 'War as a Moral Tonic' and 'Offensive and Defensive Warfare', 16 April, 'A Divided Loyalty', 23 April). At Yearly Meeting in May it was agreed that a committee should be formed to deal with war and peace issues. Again Alexander was appointed secretary, and one of its main tasks was to call a conference of sympathetic organisations outside the Society to coordinate work for peace. This ought not to have been necessary, as it was precisely the function of the National Peace Council to facilitate such coordination, but the Council was at that time paralysed by divisions over the rightness of the war, and the Quaker initiative was timely. It brought in organisations like the FOR and E. D. Morel's Union of Democratic Control. The UDC was inspired by the conviction that wars were the fruit of secret diplomacy. As George Lansbury, who also attended the founding meetings of the FOR, put it, 'Good, clean-living, honest-dealing men in private life, become double-faced, downright liars when dealing with international affairs.'[91]

The conference proposed by Yearly Meeting met on 24 and 25 June 1915, and considered the principles needed to create a just peace, and once again a committee was formed to carry the work forward, and once again Alexander was asked to serve as secretary. Charles Roden Buxton chaired the committee, and the principles sketched in the conference were widely discussed through the winter of 1915–16. The final document was endorsed by a number of distinguished people in what might be called the Liberal establishment and in the Labour movement: Leonard Woolf and Lord Courtney, for example, and Margaret Bondfield (later to be the first woman to become a Cabinet Minister), along with Robert Smillie of the National Union of Mineworkers.

At this point, though, conscription was introduced, and Alexander's efforts to continue his administrative work for the developing peace movement did not appeal to the tribunals that looked at his conscientious objection. His talent evidently impressed them, as a Military Representative suggested he might do useful work at the War Office. In the end he was exempted from military service on condition that he worked as a schoolteacher. At the time he felt reasonably happy about this, as he saw history teaching as an opportunity to develop more peaceable attitudes in the young. Looking back on the experience in his old age, he wasn't sure that he ought not to have insisted on absolute exemption. It's all very well shaping the mind: the trouble is that the mind is all too apt to be undermined by emotion.

Before settling into his first appointment, at a school in Warwick, he had a striking experience of the immediate aftermath of violent conflict. Not content with being secretary of various peace committees, Alexander was also secretary of the Yearly Meeting Young Friends Committee. In this capacity he was appointed a representative to the 1916 Dublin Yearly Meeting. It should have taken place early in May, but this was just after the Easter Rising, and it had perforce to be deferred to the beginning of June, and met even then under restrictions. When peace issues were discussed, the Clerk felt compelled to rule out of order any consideration of the impact of conscription, and even of post-war reconstruction. This can hardly have been congenial to a campaigner like Alexander, and one hardly likes to imagine what he thought of the opening contribution from William Thompson, who insisted that nowhere in the Gospel is it suggested that it's wrong to 'uphold the social fabric by force'. Familiarity with his own father's evangelical faith enabled Alexander to understand the appropriate way to intervene in this atmosphere, and intervene he did, tactfully recalling that at the recent Yearly Meeting in London Friends had shown themselves very conscious of the possibility of speaking about ideals without sufficiently living up to them. 'Our duty', *The Friend* reports him as saying, 'must be the consecration of our whole life to the service of Christ'.[92]

He did not restrict himself to attendance at Yearly Meeting sessions. He made friends with Cecil Neill-Watson, elder brother of two of his Bootham schoolfellows, and clearly a man sympathetic to Irish nationalism, as of course was Alexander. He told him about De Valera's escape from execution – attributed by Neill-Watson to the power of prayer, though Alexander thought Dev's Spanish nationality was more relevant. Anyway, he was being kept in solitary confinement, and Alexander took back to England details of the case for C. Delisle Burns, who was involved in getting it reviewed. Alexander also looked into the possibility of having visits organised to interned Irishmen held in English prisons, and the Quaker MP Arnold Rowntree took this idea up. But the political climate was unfavourable, and nothing came of it.

Alexander's most adventurous initiative while he was in Dublin was to visit a supporter of the Rising who lived in the Wicklow Mountains. Again it was Cecil Neill-Watson who took him, and Alexander evidently proved a good listener as the Sinn Feiner thought he must be an American: 'he could not believe that an Englishman could be so sympathetic to the Sinn Fein point of view.'[93]

2

THE HUMANISING OF AN INTELLECTUAL

Olive Graham

A Young Friend who could make himself acceptable both in the oppressively evangelical atmosphere of the 1916 Yearly Meeting in Dublin, and in the home of an ardent Irish republican; someone who was evidently much in demand as a secretary to organisations working under pressure, and on whom a military officer could cast covetous eyes as a valuable recruit to the War Office – someone, moreover, who impressed at least one Cambridge colleague as a kind of archetypal embodiment of pure reason – what could he have been like? In some ways he was distinctly insecure and lacking in confidence. In the letter to Rachel Graham, already referred to in the first chapter in connection with his schooldays, he suggests that although he often felt solitary and unregarded, and suspects that Rachel may too, this feeling can be 'a proof of unusual, rather exceptional gifts, which are not properly understood by the normal, average being'. He hasn't yet found his vocation:

> I am such a queer shape that no hole seems made for me to fit into. But so far I have refused to fit myself permanently into a hole that I could see wasn't really mine. I have wriggled about in a good many that happened to be vacant, and in doing so I hope I have made myself more able to fill the hole that will turn up some day. Not that I ever expect to fit

Figure 1 Olive Graham Alexander, *c.*1925

> beautifully into any imperfect structure as the structure of the world is and for ages will be.[1]

The same letter says that his time at Cambridge had saved him from the worst of his unhappiness, 'and perhaps Olive will complete my salvation!'

'Olive' was Olive Graham, Rachel's elder sister, to whom he was now engaged to be married. They were daughters of John W. Graham, whom we have already encountered as an enthusiastic exponent of Norman Angell's ideas and a mainstay of Quaker peace witness in the First World War. Olive herself was a lively and independent-minded young woman. She went to the Quaker school at Sidcot in Somerset, where she had a problem with hymns, refusing to sing lines which expressed beliefs she couldn't accept. But as she had a penetrating voice, this made her more conspicuous than quite suited her, so she stopped singing altogether.[2] This theological scrupulosity seems to have grown on her. When she spent a couple of terms at Woodbrooke, in the autumn and spring of 1911–12, the log-book records that the Mission Study Circle based its discussions on a book by W. H. T. Gairdner, *The Reproach of Islam* (1909). Gairdner presents Islam as 'the foe which the Church of Christ has to attack', and he has harsh things to say about the moral tone of Muslim countries.[3] According to the log-book, this was not allowed to pass unchallenged. 'Some', it says, 'were brave enough to question the absolutely unprejudiced veracity of the author.' It is tempting to suppose that Olive may have been one of the bold questioning spirits.

She went on to read History at Somerville College, Oxford, and gained second-class Honours. She then spent a year at the London County Council teacher training college in Clapham. Her assertive character did not fit easily into the rather rigid regime there, and she earned a reputation as a trouble-maker, with a face and manner too 'aristocratic' for her station in life.[4] She had the satisfaction, though, of learning that her complaints about both the curriculum and the boarding arrangements had been responded to, though only after she had left to join the staff of the Quaker school for girls in York, the Mount.[5]

It was at this time that she first encountered Alexander when they were both members of the Young Friends Committee. She was at once struck by his appearance, 'a cross between Voltaire and a large toad', she told her mother. She had tried to draw him, 'because I thought it was quite the most amazing and fascinating thing I'd ever seen produced in the male line'.[6] This might not seem the most promising start, but the correspondence carried on between them in the months that followed shows vividly how their relationship developed.

A characteristic early letter from Alexander (23 December 1916) responds to an attempt by Olive to interest him in a certain John S. M. Thomson, who was perplexed about what his next move should be in finding suitable work. Alexander is puzzled:

> I can't think what sort of a being he is, nor what I can possibly do for him. Personally I think a man who prefers social work to any other kind of work in the world must be a fool. In spite of the fact that I once helped to run the King's College Social Work Committee and thoroughly enjoyed it, the mere sound of the name 'social work' always makes me groan – chiefly, I think, because I associate it with the names of Percy Alden and Lucy Gardner . . . the two most insufferable bores on earth.

He conjectures that John Thomson thought Olive might be helpful because of a natural mistake:

> He imagines that your large-mindedness is typical of Young Friends, and does not realise that the typical Young Friends are of the type that were antagonised by him at Woodbrooke, and that you are merely a young friend, who happens to be a member of the Y.F. Committee chiefly because that Committee (or rather the Y.F. originators of that Committee) have been trying to broaden its basis. This nearly leads me into a disquisition on the wiles and subtleties (unintentional and therefore the more successful) of the typical Y.F.

Evidently a young man with a good conceit of himself, not suffering fools, or even weighty Friends, gladly, and, though significantly impressed by Olive's 'large-mindedness', unconscious of how crushing his dismissal of John

Thomson must have seemed. Olive had described him (13 November 1916) as 'an able man' with 'a very living concern', whose difficulty in finding appropriate work made her wonder whether Friends were as ready to cope with the post-war world as they ought to be. Anyway, in her next letter (28 December 1916) she gamely picks herself up, apologises for being a thorough nuisance, says she 'laughed much over your description of John' and encourages him to forget about the poor man as 'the wit expended in the two pages of your letter is bound to give John Thomson a strong presentative activity in your mind', if an opportunity offered to help him in future. The letter goes on to mention that she had met Bernard Shaw recently at the home of Charles Trevelyan. 'I don't like him,' she said, 'though I can't help admiring his cleverness.' One wonders if Alexander took the hint.

Half a year later, on 3 May 1917, his tone is much more serious. Yearly Meeting in 1917 had adopted the findings of the Committee on 'War and the Social Order', and this was vigorously taken up in the Young Friends' meeting. Alexander obviously felt that things were on the move, and said that Olive had given quite an impetus to his year of secretaryship. He admits to fright because he feels even less competent to face the situation than before. The spirit of Quakerism needed to be brought into the lives of 'every socialist and labourite under fifty. And I feel less suited to do that than to do almost anything.' He felt better able to preach to the rich than the poor – 'I have always felt their need was greater'. But he wasn't sure.

Evidently that summer they became increasingly attracted to each other. In retrospect he perceived that the main motive he had for attending Young Friend Committee meetings was that Olive would be at them. He returned from one in February with a face so radiant that a fellow schoolteacher immediately perceived what was happening. An intimation of this phase of their relationship appears in some affectionate teasing by Alexander. He was responding to a letter she had written from a Student Christian conference at Swanwick in Derbyshire (22 July 1917). She had found the proceedings profoundly misguided: what is usually called Christianity, she said, with its emphasis on belief as such, is on the wrong track. People now are 'awake to the spiritual force in the world and realising the spiritual power they each can have and surely that is the essential thing – and to clog it all up with a system to be believed seems disastrous.'

Alexander described this (29 July 1917) as a 'fit of paganism', and claims that she shouldn't have been writing all this to him but edifying her pious colleagues with it. It would have done them good. Perhaps she was just getting into practice. Anyhow, Horace reflected, 'it's a good thing I have never profaned that sacred temple.'

In the latter part of August, presumably – though this is not clear – as a member of the Young Friends Committee, Alexander embarked on a 'travelling in the ministry' in South Wales. Olive gave him the name of one of her Somerville friends who lived there, and he also stayed with a Warwick colleague whose home was near Swansea. Before he set out, he felt impelled to write a kind of proposal of marriage to Olive. He had, he said, over the past year wondered increasingly 'whether our friendship either had, or might some time have, something in it more intimate than normal friendship.' But there was a difficulty. He had never met a woman of his own age 'to whom I could talk for five minutes without becoming unspeakably bored.' (One wonders whether, in the heat of composition, he may not have left out a 'her' before the 'becoming'.) He had concluded that marriage was not therefore for him, although he regarded every new woman with curiosity to see if she might conceivably do. So what about Olive? 'You (I remember now) specially engaged my attention' – he crossed out 'attention' and substituted 'anticipation' – 'by reason of the intelligence of your father and brother.' And the anticipation was justified, for when he first met her at a Young Friends committee she disagreed with him, formidably, about something to do with America. He found himself becoming more and more attracted to her, but had never made the opportunity 'to have it out with you, and try to discover some working agreement'. He had feared spoiling the atmosphere, was anxious that he might be rebuffed, and did not quite trust his own constancy. He was somewhat reassured by the fact that his enduring friendships with men had grown stronger after sometimes unpropitious beginnings, and perhaps this was true in this instance also.

> If you think our friendship can suitably become, sooner or later, more intimate, we should both give the matter our most serious attention, with a view to arriving at a more definite [deleted] complete accommodation when we meet at York next month.[7]

This must be one of the coolest proposals of marriage on record, and might almost have come from the pen of Jane Austen in her most satirical vein. His own self-criticism in the letter is pertinent: 'Probably you will wonder what on earth I am driving at: but then that is just my own difficulty. I don't know what I am driving at – at least not quite.'

Fortunately Olive knew perfectly well what he was driving at, and responding by return of post (23rd August 1917) she reassured him that he must not worry about the affair's not going further if it seemed the wrong thing. She once lost her heart to a missionary, but realised she couldn't be a proper companion for him, and withdrew, heartbroken (but not for long).[8] She did find some parts of the letter rather appalling, though. He found women boring? 'I have a thoroughly female mind . . . and moreover I don't want to have a male one – so if the woman you marry must have a male one, clearly I am not she.'

She was sure that a good marriage was the best thing, but all other marriages are hell. So they were right to be cautious. And she also felt it right to add a remark of her parents' kitchen-maid: 'the man who marries me has got to marry me with my temper.' Her chief anxiety was that she had wilfully deceived her parents into thinking there never could be anything but ordinary friendship between them, and now her father might be writing 'demanding pounds of flesh and such'.

Olive's response was just what he wanted. He wrote immediately (24 August) that the previous letter had been an elaborate exercise in concealing his own meaning from himself. He apologised for his remarks about the female mind, which came from an affectation of being a confirmed bachelor: she was having a devastating effect on his most cherished prejudices. He went on to say that he had talked to his parents about the engagement, and they were most understanding. He had also written to his brother Christopher, now stationed on the western front. They had always been very close to each other, though their conversation was almost exclusively about birds: 'when there does happen to be something rather important happening to us we incline to tell each other as a sort of parenthesis to ornithology!'

It is not clear what Olive thought about being viewed in a parenthesis, but her father was not amused, though certainly amazed, 'utterly amazed', she told Alexander, 'could say nothing but "my dear girl, he didn't behave like a man in love", with which I heartily agreed' (27 August 1917). This did not please Alexander at all. Indeed, it made him 'furiously angry'.

> How could he tell whether I was in love? And what does he mean by being in love anyway? And do any two people fall in love in the same way? And if he says I haven't fallen in love, I confess it, frankly: I have not fallen, I have gradually slipped. (29 August)

Olive agreed (31 August) that her father had very limited views on the subject, and that it was precisely the nonsense talked about the love of men and women that caused all the unhappy and mediocre marriages that there were. Her earlier prediction about pounds of flesh was all too justified, and her father was determined to talk to Alexander about money matters. She begged him to remember that John William was actually the dearest father in the world, 'and if his ideas are mediaeval on one or two points, well let us smile.' There was also to be a conference with Joseph Alexander: 'The prospect of our two Papas discussing affairs is really most entertaining. I hope they will enjoy themselves and it really doesn't much matter what they say, does it?' (5 September).

Perhaps it didn't, but the meeting on 6 September does seem to have been rather gruelling for Alexander. He told Olive (7 September) that they had taken the money business 'horribly seriously'. John William considered that Alexander couldn't marry on less than £300 a year, and that someone contemplating earning a living by lecturing on Quaker and international subjects could hardly hope to earn so much. 'I merely grunted', Alexander told Olive, adding that he was tempted to say that if he could earn £297.10.6 , perhaps Olive could earn the balance of £2.9.6 – 'but I was afraid that would fill them with horror'. Quite right, Olive told him later; 'Father would have jumped right down your throat if you had made the suggestion.' It would have savoured of feminism, 'his pet abomination' (10 September).

But although the fathers agreed that Alexander and Olive would have to reconcile themselves to a long engagement, Alexander did not allow their prudence to affect his great happiness. In his letter of 7 September, he regretted that 'these older people do not know how many generations or decades we have lived through in having all life cut away from round about us just when we were entering into the full joy of its meaning.' But, he went on, 'there is still joy in life after all. . . . The hunger for it', he admits, 'is so great that I dare not seize it suddenly, for fear it should taste bitter after all.' And he recalled the deaths of his Cambridge friends, Freddy Hardman in October 1914, and worst of all Tommy Stone's a few months later: 'After that the death of other friends of mine left me quite cold. But the wound of March 1915 never really healed at all. . . . When I enter into it again like this it still bleeds a little.'

If he seems aloof and cold and incapable of being ruffled or stirred, that is why.

*

At the end of August Olive had developed chickenpox, which was an infuriating frustration for her. Her brother Michael, who was in the Navy and engaged in the relatively humanitarian business of minesweeping, had just got some leave: she wanted to rejoice with him over her engagement, but had to be kept in isolation. Contemplating the situation made her angrier and angrier: one thing the Graham family was genuinely good at was 'family jubilations and killing the fatted calf', and now it couldn't. But having exploded to Alexander, she went on to the more congenial task of relating some of the difficulties created by keeping the engagement undisclosed for the time being. Alexander had been the subject of a conversation between Olive and one of her friends, Margaret Lloyd, who said that he rated high in intellectual ability among Young Friends, and wondered who would make him a suitable wife: 'We discussed her in theory. I said she should be plump, placid, pudding-perfect and of the harmless mildly-adoring type – which at least took the limelight off me!!' (?2 September).

Alexander somewhat obtusely took this to mean that Olive did consider herself 'plump, placid, pudding-perfect, brainless and wildly-adoring' (evidently quoting from memory), and looked forward to 'tyrannising' to his heart's content (4 September). Olive may have taken this in the facetious spirit in which it was offered, but she was more concerned about his reaction to some of the photographs of herself which she sent him at about the same time:

'The photographs of you in that swanky velvet affair make me shudder', he said; 'they shall be destroyed!' (5 September). She explained: 'The "swanky velvet affair" was a case of daughterly acquiescence, and if I had sorted them you would not have seen any such' (10 September). Olive did not find in her mother a congenial spirit, and was apt to express impatience with her well-meant efforts to improve her daughter's character.

This appears vividly in her mother's reaction to an unconventional idea that occurred to Olive in this same letter. She suggested to Alexander that she should come as soon as possible to Tunbridge Wells to meet his parents, although she knew she'd be embarrassed and put butter in the tea. Alexander (11 September) welcomed the suggestion ardently: his mother would be 'tremendously pleased'. Olive could send a telegram about the time of her train, and if she were starving on arrival he could take her to a café, and then they could have a walk on the common. 'Even if it's raining', he remarked with enthusiasm, 'we might sit in a shelter and shiver, or else find a quiet corner in one of the cafés.'

Doubtless this letter might have alarmed the most tolerant of parents in that generation, and the Grahams forbade any such departure from the proprieties. Her mother warned her that she was 'making herself cheap', and so on: 'I can't write it down', Olive told Alexander in her next letter (12 September). 'I think it ended with a quotation from Longfellow' – evidently the ultimate nauseating detail. 'I suppose', she went on, 'decent "feminine modesty" or something is left out of my composition.'

The Longfellow quotation was, I suspect, the then familiar admonition from 'Maidenhood': 'O, thou child of many prayers! Life hath quicksands, – life hath snares.'

Alexander had no wish to be seen as either a quicksand or a snare, and tactfully accepted (14 September) that she might not have been sufficiently recovered from chickenpox to travel. But he did very much want her to meet his parents, as Olive felt was only sensible (12 September): his mother 'had really better see the real me. . . . The real me does not want to have an idealised me to compete with.'

In the letters that passed between Olive and Alexander through the autumn and the following spring, one can see the process of discovering 'the real me' on both sides. She confessed (5 September) to a phobia about birds which she, not unreasonably, supposed might be an obstacle to their good relationship: she didn't mind snakes, spiders or worms, but dead birds, or birds flying close to her, gave her the horrors. Alexander reassured her (7 September) that his interest was not in stuffing birds but in observing 'their habits and emotions when unaffected by the proximity of the human species, in particular their migrations and their song'. He had persuaded Miss Turner to organise 'wait and see' photographs, taken by a camera placed near regular feeding grounds:

'a wholly new and attractive brand of bird photography.' A letter some six weeks later expressed the hope that Olive would be able to appreciate the individuality of birds: a dull-looking one might be rare, might be graceful. Not, he added sternly, that it would do her any good with him to feign excitement (19 October).

Birds may not have turned out to be a serious problem, but Olive's mother was a perennial trouble to her: 'I can feel affection for Mother when she is not there', Olive explained, 'or I have not just got a letter from her' (8 March 1918). Alexander was on affectionate terms with his mother, but felt the contrast between the warmth of the younger part of the Graham family and the undemonstrative coolness of the Alexander brothers. He had a good relationship with Christopher, but little attachment to Gilbert and Wilfrid. An account of their religious attitudes (5 November 1917) is revealing. Gilbert, the eldest, 'incredibly social', scoutmaster, landworker, thought of himself as a Friend, but seemed to Horace 'an ordinary nonconformist'. Wilfrid, too, the scientist, was a fairly nominal Friend.

> He shares my philosophy of being all things to all men, but whereas my interpretation of it is that one should enter into all the peculiarities of the people one meets, he has a horror of peculiarities, and prefers to be so conventional in everything that no one can possibly get annoyed with him. And I'm afraid that's just what does annoy me, which is shockingly unfraternal.

Alexander's concern to enter into people's peculiarities, and his essentially convivial disposition, certainly led him into some odd situations. In King's he was on friendly terms with a scapegrace called Barringer, who insisted on calling Alexander 'Jesus', and was once found drunk on the steps of the college chapel, explaining that he was 'looking for Jesus', though whether he meant Alexander or the Son of God was not clear. At Warwick School, too, he was far from puritanical in the company he kept, and was ready enough to join in a party of pleasure. He told Olive that he once accompanied a colleague to Birmingham for an evening out. They had a champagne supper at a hotel near Snow Hill.

> After that we went to some absurd performance or revue, which I found extremely dull, and then I found he had made an appointment with two 'classy' females in the revue; and I had an immense struggle (of argument) outside before convincing him that we must catch the 11.0 train to Warwick, and not go home with the milk, ending in a wild rush for the train and victory for me; and I daresay you helped a good deal!

While he always tried to make a merit of being a 'friend of publicans and sinners', he admitted to Olive that 'but for my Quaker training and comparative impecuniosity I should have been one myself'.[9]

No doubt the sense that Alexander was far from being a model Quaker as then understood was part of his attraction for Olive. In the spring of 1917 she read Ethel M. Dell's stirring novel *The Way of an Eagle*, and – she informed Alexander a year later – enjoyed it very much 'because something about the man reminded me of you. I can't remember what it was exactly.' (31 March 1918). The day following she happened on the novel again:

> I lay on a sofa there the whole evening and read it again and the only real likeness I can now find between Nick and you is that you are both strange to look upon and have light eyelashes and brows!! (1 April)

In fact Ethel M. Dell's hero Nick Ratcliffe could be taken as a kind of romantic metamorphosis of certain aspects of Alexander. Nick Ratcliffe's ugliness (he has a yellow complexion and pinched, wrinkled features) is suffused with a 'perpetual suggestion of simmering activity'. Although seeming recklessly light-hearted, he has indomitable determination – 'the pluck to go on fighting when you know perfectly well you're beaten' – and with a hint of molten passion that could make him demonic. And if anyone wonders what could have been construed as demonic about Horace Alexander, Reginald Reynolds' cautionary tale, considered in a later chapter, should be kept in mind: 'Horace could imitate with ease The laugh of Mephistopheles.'[10]

More pertinent, maybe, is the moment of real fury when he learned that John William Graham had doubted his love for Olive. Like the Grahams' kitchen-maid, he certainly had a temper, and did not always control it.

But with Olive he seems always to have been steadily affectionate. Indeed, some of his contemporaries seem to have found his affection somewhat too vehement. Gwen Marriage (née Pickard), an active Young Friend at the time, used to complain that his enthusiasm for his fiancée was excessive. It was all very well for him to feel that way, no doubt, but he showed a scant regard for the customary reticences of Quakerism.[11] The lovers' correspondence does admittedly have its moments of strain and stress, including one episode which might be described as a tiff. Olive's brother Dick and Alexander had exchanged drafts of a paper that was eventually to be completed as their joint work, *An Essay on Human Association*. On 5 November 1917 Alexander sent Olive a copy of his own paper for comment, and added a few observations on other people who might be able to help. He classified them according to his estimate of their intellectual competence, as A or B or C. Among the As were Lowes Dickinson, Norman Angell, John Sheppard, Gerald Shove (pre-eminently), G. D. H. Cole, G. N. Clark, and Dick Graham himself. Modestly he rated himself on the border between A and B. He remarked that he couldn't think of any woman who rated an A, apart from George Eliot, who was dead. He could think of three who might be considered B. Olive was not among them, but he awarded her a special position as one who would have 'a female intuition of my intellectual shortcomings (that is not intended to be disparaging)'. It may not have been, but Olive was somewhat provoked. She responded instantly:

> Good heavens! man! if I were one or two degrees nearer sanity you should have your paper back by return of post. – You know really and truly you are rather the limit. You seem to be continually trotting me out like a prize horse to judge my points and to see how nearly they approach to the standards you set up. I didn't ask you for this to show off my intellectual attainments. Of course if you sent it me in order to judge them I suppose it is candid of you to say so.

She objected to the way he made her self-conscious, and thought she might dry up altogether if he went on like this. As for disparagements of her sex in general, these left her cool. She was quite able to resist the desire to become an extreme feminist, 'which would be the natural result of your attitude' (6 November).

Before the letter ended, she allowed herself the half-forgiving remark that she felt Alexander wouldn't have spoken quite as candidly as he had written in this matter. She supposed that when they were married he would have to go away every three weeks or so in order that she might have the benefit of his inmost thoughts.

Alexander response (8 November) was initially defensive, conceding that his mother always said he was too analytical, 'but I find the more I analyse people (like horses if you like to put it that way) the more good things I discover in them'. His critical faculty was always at work, even when other things were uppermost in his mind, as in his spoken ministry in Meeting for Worship. But then he abandoned his defences:

> Oh, Olive, Olive, there are times when I feel very acutely that you will find it intolerable to live with me; but I think it only is that it would be intolerable to spend our whole lives writing to each other. To live together, yes, that is what I want; and the only reason why I sometimes write dreadful things to you that I would never say is that your presence banishes the evil motive that prompts them.

Olive had no difficulty in relenting. She responded (9 November) that she had nearly written once again about the 'intellectual categories' because she feared she might have made him feel that he had hurt her, but then she left it: 'We'll have a great talk about it.' She remarked that she herself had a reputation for being critical and analytical.

Alexander was in fact distraught at this time by the news that Christopher had been very seriously wounded, though definite confirmation of his death was not received until early December. There was a period of many weeks when it was unclear exactly what had happened to him. Olive understood the torture of having to imagine all the possibilities:

> God help us to help him [Christopher] by using the great spiritual forces which rule the world. I've never believed in them so completely as in these days when we have been struggling apart and yet together, and it gives me new hope of what we can do for him (9 November)

Alexander's reaction to the uncertainty was to hope that Christopher died of his wounds rather than live a hopeless cripple (12 November), but when death was confirmed it was still hard to bear. Olive had given him the newly published autobiography of John Morley, with whose rationalism he felt so strong an affinity, and a letter of 30 November makes clear what pleasure the gift had afforded him. John William Graham reviewed it in *The Friend*, and when Alexander went to his parents after the news had come, Joseph asked him to read the opening paragraph.

> How can we avoid [wrote Graham] giving greater honour to those who, without the profound emotion and the joy of heart which the fellowship of Christ brings to her conscious followers, maintain their austere way by the light which glows within them, and build of hard-won materials a religious consciousness which wears well, though their words speak not much of praise and adoration.[12]

It was all true of Christopher, Alexander told Olive: father and son found it too much for them, and broke down. In his bereavement, Horace reflected earnestly on the qualities where his brother did better than himself, in being more patient and more willing to avoid 'high argument'. And a patience foreign to his temperament, and an avoidance of intellectual pretension, did indeed become characteristics of Alexander in his maturity.

*

In an essay which Alexander had published in the *Friends' Fellowship Papers* for 1916, he expressed the fellow-feeling he shared with Christopher, as with other friends who had enlisted. It was entitled 'Revolution', and began by defending conscientious objectors against G. K. Chesterton's charge that they made revolution impossible. Alexander pointed out that on the contrary it was violence that had actually subverted many revolutions, while mild, obscure characters like Francis of Assisi and John Woolman had inspired enduring revolutionary developments. The present war was a major disaster because it was inhibiting the goodwill and intelligence needed to create a peaceful international order. But it was still possible for people to be caught up in the business of warmaking and to 'regard war and the passions of war with utter loathing and contempt'. Such people were comrades in the great task of peacemaking, and would 'have the opportunity so to develop international life that all men will be interested in its support and none will contemplate its rupture with any feeling but horror – if they ever contemplate such an absurdity at all'. Alexander evidently felt that it was the special responsibility of the out-and-out pacifist to proclaim the message, 'Peace now, and complete abolition of armaments.' Such a pacifist won't advocate half-measures, 'though he will welcome anything tending in the right direction – if he is sure it is tending that way – and will urge those who cannot go further to go as far as they can.'[13]

The essay is tentative and not altogether coherent, but an opportunity soon arose to develop Alexander's response to the war in a more effective form. From 1916 onwards, plans were made to hold a world conference of Friends to reconsider the peace testimony as soon as the war was over. In preparation for this conference, seven commissions were set up to look at different aspects of peace witness: the fundamental basis of the peace testimony, national life and international relations, personal life, education, the life of the Society of Friends itself, propaganda, and international service. Both Joseph and Horace Alexander were invited to join Commission 2, on national life and international relations, as were John William Graham and Horace's old science master, Hugh Richardson. The Commission 2 report, when eventually published in 1920, consisted of essays by individual contributors, Hugh Richardson, for example, writing on international cooperation, and John William Graham on the police and the army. Alexander contributed an essay entitled 'Peace, the Perfection of Liberty'. In it he expounds what he claims is the principal contribution of Quaker experience to the problem of government: identifying the 'general will' or 'sense of the meeting' by means of conference.

> The good man will always find points of contact with the self-revelation of the most hardened sinner. Always our first impulse should be, not to destroy those whose actions or opinions we disapprove, but to understand their motives and their justification.[14]

Richard Graham was also invited to contribute a paper on 'partnership', in which he looked at the worldwide scope of industrial and intellectual interests, and the possible role of the League of Nations in this context. The existence of a world economy meant that economic sanctions would exert considerable pressure on a refractory nation.

It looks as though, in preparing these papers for the conference, Alexander and Graham were moved to attempt a more radical analysis of the basis of a peaceful international order, and in due course they produced the short book, a draft of which Alexander tactlessly offered to Olive as an intelligence test for his friends and acquaintance. 'An Essay on Human Association' is an investigation into 'the various ties that actually bind men and women together' a firmer basis for the study of institutions than any abstract theory of rights.

The firmer basis is needed because the huge social changes in the industrialised West 'have not been accompanied by corresponding changes in the established forms of association'.[15] There is still a fixation on the territorial sovereign state, with an uncritical acceptance of its unique claim to loyalty. On the contrary, voluntary and creative association is a higher form of organisation, and should be recognised as such. The authors' emphasis is consistently on the people who enter into associations, and whose humanity has within it the potential for development and, hence, reconciliation. Conciliation is the only way to reach permanent settlements, for it is an educative process which leads to genuine consent or at least acquiescence from all parties.[16] The idea of military domination of the world is a petty ambition, and futile: 'great achievements, like the reconciliation of two able, vigorous, suspicious and hostile peoples, are beyond its powers.'[17] Conciliation, the authors allow, can appear to be unavailing, and if so there is nothing more to be done, or rather –

> nothing but the application of tireless patience and the use of every opportunity of bringing reason to bear on the unreasonable community. If there is in all men a final response to reason, patience will be ultimately rewarded. If there is not, greater heroism can be shown by unyielding endurance than by blind revolt against the inevitable. But the truth is that human beings are not nearly as unreasonable as we often pretend they are.[18]

While 'An Essay on Human Association' has a decidedly Quaker flavour, it is clearly part of a widespread interest at the time in theories of social pluralism, an interest heightened by the inordinate claims of the state under war conditions. This is explicit in Leonard Woolf's pioneering study, *International Government* (1916; see Woolf 1923), which exposes the fallacy of seeing the world as neatly divided into compartments called states, relating to each other only in terms of their statehood. On the contrary, modern states are in perpetual and intimate and intricate relationship with each other. Complete independence is a legal fiction.[19] Pluralist theories had originally been developed by historians such as F. W. Maitland and J. N. Figgis, and are explored in various ways in the early writings of G. D. H. Cole and Harold Laski. One of the most impressive expressions of this view of society is L. T. Hobhouse's *Metaphysical Theory of the State* (1918), a critique of ideas developed in Bernard Bosanquet's *Philosophical Theory of the State* (1899). Bosanquet, following Hegel, sees the state as 'the supreme community' in which moral relations are organised. Hobhouse denies this, remarking that many well-established relations cross national boundaries – relations commercial, religious, intellectual, artistic. These are forerunners of a world community, for which the conditions have now matured.[20] The state came into being for certain specific purposes, and in the future it might well be adapted, expanded, changed and even abolished.[21]

Hobhouse's downgrading of the state is elaborated by G. D. H. Cole in publications from this period. In *Social Theory* (1920) he considers

> the position of voluntary and functional associations in Society, in their relation to national States, and their position as being often international associations in the multiplicity and possible conflict of loyalties and obligations for the individuals in simultaneous membership of several such associations.[22]

Too optimistically, he detected signs of a worldwide movement towards industrial freedom and self-government. Even the increasingly authoritarian character of the Soviet Union was to be understood as a temporary phase enforced by war. The pressure removed, 'the bureaucracy and "State-like" Soviets' will together atrophy so far as economic functions are concerned.[23]

When Alexander and Graham had completed their own book, Alexander sent it to Lowes Dickinson for his opinion, and his old tutor gave it qualified approval, a B+ rather than an A. He was evidently not altogether happy with pluralist theories, feeling that 'the current reaction against "sovereignty" rather extreme from a lack of experience of the evils of anarchy, of which you speak rather lightly.'[24] Lightly or not, the book clearly illuminates the approach to conflict and mediation that Alexander was to adopt throughout his life. There is, for example, a paragraph in a discussion of religious association which anticipates his view of the universalism that was the basis of the Fellowship of Friends of Truth: the Church Universal that will come by 'the extension of the humble spirit which does not claim or hope for all knowledge for itself, and allows that others who differ may yet possess much of the truth'.[25] The book is at its strongest when it conveys something of this temper. It is most dated in its concluding attempt to envisage the organisation of a world society, based upon a bewildering complex of associations to which as many decisions as possible will be devolved.

The book was offered to Allen and Unwin for publication, but it was rejected. It survives only as a typescript in Alexander's papers.

*

While collaborating with Richard Graham on their book and developing his relationship with Olive, Alexander had changed schools, moving from Warwick to Cranbrook School in Kent. While at Warwick he seems to have found a congenial enough role for himself. He edited the school magazine, *The Portcullis*, and encouraged J. D. Franklin, Captain of the School and of its rugby team, to compose a 'hitherto unknown' passage from Thucydides with a distinctly pacifist message. He involved himself in debates, including one on military reprisals, and played the part of Mr Spuds, the Agricultural Representative on a mock-tribunal for conscientious objectors (evidently a very light-hearted affair). Predictably he enlivened the programme of the Natural History Society, astonishing its members with his photographs of birds on Holy Island – photographs that had needed great patience and perseverance to obtain. Although cricket was not one of his enthusiasms, he played his part in the staff-school match on 16 June 1917: he was out for a duck, but made two catches.[26]

Even so, all was not quite well, because when he ventured, early in the autumn term of 1917, to make a complaint about the school food, the headmaster had replied that the food was all right but that Alexander's discipline and examination results were all wrong, and that he had better leave at Christmas, or sooner. The situation was saved by his ornithological friend Miss Turner. She was head cook at the Cranbrook military hospital, and had heard that the boarding school in the town was in need of a history master. One may infer that she had put in a strong word for Alexander, as he told Olive that the headmaster, a sensible and radical parson called Charles Frederick Pierce,[27] had been unworried by disparaging reports about discipline and examination results. On the contrary, he would 'help me in my weak places no end'. Alexander was unusually exhilarated at the prospect: 'I always did believe I was a man of destiny!' (17 September 1917).

And on the whole he found Cranbrook as congenial as he anticipated. He decided that he was perhaps too sober to be a great success as a teacher, telling Olive that he hadn't the inventiveness in presentation that she had, or her brother Dick. Even so, he was pleased that in general he got on very well with the boys (2 November 1917). He gave an amusing account of a school debate on whether bachelors should be taxed. One boy who spoke in favour of the idea 'made the most comical remarks about me, and appeared to be suggesting that I was a rakish philanderer.' Alexander summed up for the opposition, and asked the House to vindicate his character. Afterwards the boy came to see him, quite upset, and said that he'd only 'intended to suggest that all ladies naturally would fall in love with me: so I forgave him' (4 November).

Three days later the news that Christopher had been seriously wounded upset him so much that he lost his temper with a silly youth and gave him a vast imposition. The class, he told Olive, was fearfully subdued. Afterwards he explained to the boy what was the matter, and told him to forget about the imposition. 'He went away looking scared.' He asked Olive to be strong for him, for he was so weak. He was greatly moved by the kindness the boys showed him, leaving him in peace when he was 'taking prep'. He sat there reading Keats's *Endymion*, and copied out the opening of Book 2, which struck him poignantly with its evocation of the 'sovereign power of love', manifest even through 'the mist of passed years': 'One kiss brings honey-dew from buried days'. He had certainly come a long way from the 'intellectualist pure and simple' seen by Nick Bagenal.

This is if anything even more apparent in his reaction to an attempted suicide by a 13-year-old, the younger of two brothers. As it happens, Alexander had come to know the elder brother in the sixth form quite well, and no doubt this brought the trauma home to him the more forcibly. He told Olive that the boy had been overcome by a sense of friendlessness, 'revealing the nakedness of "the public school system" in its full horror.' Alexander was grieved that the boy had felt unable to take any of the masters into his confidence, and he was quite angry with the attitude adopted by Pierce. The headmaster said simply that the boy was 'deranged'. Alexander, uncharacteristically, swore:

> Damn him! Of course that may not represent the spirit in which he will deal with him, but I'm horribly afraid it is. Oh, damn, and it's just the sort of occasion when I do believe I could help, and I'm such a fool I don't know how to intrude myself into the business. (15 March 1918)

The following day, by way of comment on Pierce, he exclaimed 'Oh – these strong men who can't sympathise with weakness!' (16 March 1918).

So far as he could, Alexander certainly did his best to neutralise the 'horror' of the public school system. He adopted a deliberately egalitarian mode in his dealings with the boys. He told Olive that he had no liking for dignified severity: 'when I try it I always break down into a grin' (28 June 1918). In the years immediately before the war, some ardent educational reformers had been developing methods which rejected the formal modes of the traditional classroom. Maria Montessori was a major inspiration, but her ideas were taken up by pioneers already predisposed to welcome them. Edmond Holmes, a former school inspector, wrote a book that was particularly influential in its critique of mechanical obedience: *What Is and What Might Be* (1911). Even as moderate a reformer as Guy Kendall wanted his readers to take seriously the ideal which Montessori set before herself, 'the regeneration of humanity through education'.[28] The reforming impulse is memorably satirised by the reliably reactionary and anarchic Saki in 'The Schartz-Metterklume Method', but readers who wish to appreciate what was really involved should immerse themselves in H. Caldwell Cook's splendid treatise *The Play Way* (1917), with its celebration of the school as a place of joyful activity.

Alexander himself was acquainted with the work of Norman MacMunn, a teacher in Stratford-upon-Avon, whose *Path to Freedom in School* (1914) saw 'the teacher's mission as something glorious and beautiful and inspiring' working a revolution that would create a new type of human being. He evolved what he called the 'differential partnership' method, in which each member of the class prepared a different aspect of the topic covered in each lesson. Alexander seems to have followed the method rigorously on only a few occasions, but he in any case encouraged animated participation by his classes, and it was quite exceptional for him to take centre-stage. On one memorable occasion he did indeed do just that. At Easter each class was required to have a session on the crucifixion, and Alexander told his lot that he was going to talk to them for the whole period – which he had never done before. 'Someone demanded if I meant I was going to preach a sermon, and I said that was exactly it. Suppressed cheer!' The 'sermon' made a pacifist case in terms adapted to the boy mind: he pointed out that the crucifixion was opposite to the disciples' expectations, but that it made good sense all the same. Gentle people have a greater authority than people whose assertiveness irritates and alienates us. He worked around to the conclusion that the best service to others consisted in 'trying to keep them good-humoured and amused, and to get the maximum amount of fun out of life', keeping cheerful in the most depressing times.[29] He felt that this last bit went down particularly well, and if the reader is disposed to disparage it as optimism of a somewhat crass banality, it is worth remarking that many years later these were the terms in which he commended the exemplary leadership exercised by Gandhi at the height of the post-independence communal riots.

On one occasion Alexander felt that he had allowed his libertarian approach to get out of hand. Accompanying the school's cricket team back from an 'away' match, he chose to ignore the fact that they were smoking cigarettes, the prefects being the worst offenders – 'obviously quite old hands'. In this 'den of uproarious smokers' he was full of schoolboy spirits himself, utterly forgetful that he was a schoolmaster, catching the holiday mood and the joy of those looking forward to going to Oxford. He noticed that the coachman and some of the passers-by were scandalised by such an unedifying spectacle, but this only put him on his mettle. It was afterwards, when Pierce asked him about how the match had gone, that the enormity of his lapse from the schoolmaster role dawned on him, and he confessed all. Pierce took it very well, but was rather shocked to find how established the smoking habit was among the senior boys.[30] Alexander went to bed 'perfectly wretched', and read the crucifixion story for consolation. He asked Skipper, one of the boys involved, to bring the team to his room after chapel. Pierce spoke to them beforehand, 'so they had a dose of him'. Then they lined up in Alexander's room in awful silence. He said he wanted to apologise, and felt horribly mean, 'not in going to Mr Pierce, but in letting them smoke and misbehave'. He suffered because he felt that he had lost any claim he might have had to their respect, and their confidence, which he valued no less. He couldn't say more, he told Olive, and thought they would go,

> but then Skipper came across the room and held out his hand and said they thought just as well of me as ever, or something like that, and we shook hands, and all the others followed in turn silently, and everyone with the kindest, frankest look, which I met through swelling tears, that fairly broke me when the last had gone.

If this sounds too much like an episode in a school story from the Religious Tract Society, the final detail at least is deliciously profane. The team had far too high a regard for Alexander to believe that he had betrayed their confidence, and put it about that 'some old parson saw them and told Pierce!' (23 June 1918).

Pierce evidently had a considerable regard for Alexander, who refers to conversations where they disagreed strongly, but remained friendly. In November 1917 he mentions to Olive that he had been expounding pacifist principles to Pierce over tea, and that the headmaster had conceded that an international conference of Christians would be a sound idea (5 November). The following May, when three leading Friends were prosecuted for refusing to submit Quaker publications to censorship. he had 'an immense further talk with Mr Pierce': 'We left off as far from agreement as ever. I respect him for caring to encourage me to say such things as I did last night, but I think he is hopelessly bigoted in some respects!' (21 May 1918). Bigoted in matters of peace and war, probably, but not in ecumenical initiatives. Shortly before he left Cranbrook, Pierce and Alexander had a discussion which led to the thought that there was scope for occasions of united worship in Cranbrook, of a kind that might appeal even to those who seemed indifferent to religion. 'We might set an example to the towns and villages of England. We might save the national life, by giving a fresh religious inspiration to it, by bringing a sense of unity and comradeship and trust amongst "neighbours"' (9 July 1918).

But the deepest satisfaction for Alexander during his time at Cranbrook seems to have come in his discussions with sixth-formers working for university entrance examinations. One of these candidates, who had written a good essay on the Oxford reformers, had also attempted one on 'the future of the world' which was disappointing. Alexander had a long session with him in which he explained how the present war had affected the generation that had come of age just before 1914:

> seeming like an overwhelming avalanche that cut off every bright prospect and robbed us of our companions in life, and left us desolate, broken and embittered. Then something of the passionate hopes of that lost generation, and of how the 'future of the world' depended on our responsibilities and on our efforts. . . . Man seemed to have had both all that is meanest and all that is most generous brought to the surface, and all the future depends on which we build.

The young man was cynical about 'fine emotions', and Alexander felt challenged to express the passionate convictions of his own generation 'in a way that meant something real and rational to him'. There was a great satisfaction in exerting his best powers in the expression of his deepest nature, 'and that, to my mind, is man's greatest work. At King's you could do it every day' (30 May 1918).

*

If at this time Alexander felt the passionate hopes of a lost generation with peculiar force, it was because he was still coming to terms with the death of his father. Joseph Alexander had been deeply depressed by the outbreak of war, feeling 'altogether out of date and helpless in the cause of peace',[31] but had none the less devoted himself to the efforts being made by Lowes Dickinson and others to develop the idea of a League of Nations. He was tireless in supporting conscientious objectors, and taking his share of Quaker administration. He celebrated the New Year of 1918 by announcing to his family that he was going to fit in an Adult School committee, attendance at Maidstone Quarter Sessions, and a visit to a CO in prison, all in one day, and then go back to London for his regular monthly committees.[32] And then there were the more purely sociable engagements, as on Monday 14 January when he planned to take some Basuto chiefs to the London Zoo, and meet Alexander afterwards for tea.[33]

But the strain was too great, more especially under the burden of grief for the death of Christopher. Early in February he was taken ill, and on the 26th he died.

Getting married

Horace and Olive saw their intended marriage as a modern Quaker partnership, carrying forward the concerns to which they were both so passionately committed. They felt in a quite different world from that of their parents, and their correspondence is apt to treat parents with a certain air of patronage. A few days after he had learned of the engagement John William Graham asked his daughter whether she and Horace had ever discussed any questions relating to married life. 'I told him we had discussed Family Reading. I thought that would give the "heavenward journey" touch.' He had also asked whether Horace's second letter had contained a proper proposal of marriage (evidently Olive had shown him the excruciatingly embarrassed first letter). 'I said it did! It sounds like a lie but it was nearest to the truth I could get for the previous generation.'[34]

As time went on they did indeed have some strenuous discussions of 'questions relating to married life'. One that showed Olive in a distinctly feminist mode was when Horace unguardedly referred to his future wife as a 'helpmeet'. He had expressed anxiety about people asking his advice, and wrote that it would be a relief to turn to his 'helpmeet', 'if you don't object to that very Old Testamentish idea of a wife' (4th April 1918). She did object, strongly. It was an 'absurd concoction of a word . . . founded in some illiterate creature's use of Genesis.' For good measure she added that there was nothing in the Bible about marriage with which she could agree (April 1918).

The interpretation of the Bible could cause little trouble between them, but Horace's somewhat casual reference, in one of his letters, to the possibility of their having children disturbed Olive considerably. He had remarked that it was strange

> that in writing about my affection for you and Mother I didn't mention what was in the back of my mind, that for years I have longed to see Mother a grandmother, and that I feel that more than your motherhood just now. (24 May 1918)

This sentence reduced her to tears. She had feared that Horace's mother would be disappointed if she knew of their intention to have no children for the time being, 'and then when you say things like that it tangles me all up again' (25 May 1918). She explained her feelings more fully three days later. She had quite thought that Horace felt they shouldn't start a family at Cranbrook, and then his letter sounded as though he wanted children as soon as might be.

> I felt absolutely at sea as to what you thought about anything. – That puzzledness and an overwhelming sense of my own unfitness to cope with all these things were, I rather think, the chief things which reduced me to tears – it seemed as if you had suddenly brought the distant future tumbling about my ears and I knew not where I was.

She was also somewhat upset that his 'sudden veering round' should have been prompted by his mother's wishes in a matter which affected her so profoundly. She admitted this to him rather reluctantly, but felt that she should because, she insisted, 'I feel I must try to explain all I can' (28 May 1918).

Horace had to reassure her that his temperament, his puritanical upbringing, and the 'rather obnoxious frankness, including plenty of incidental indecency, in University atmospheres', had made him 'slow to be stirred to any sexual desires at all. Of course', he added, 'they are there all right, but they do not form an important or permanent part of my life' (30 May 1918). In any case, he felt that all married couples should live together for a few months 'before launching out on the family business'. But, realising that he was still not quite striking the right note, he conceded that 'the whole attitude of a man and a woman to the physical side of marriage is quite different, and always will be, and probably ought to be; and it's fairly hopeless to understand each other' (27 May 1918).

In principle Olive held views about sexuality which were enlightened and 'modern'. In the previous October she had written to Horace that prostitution was a consequence of the belief that sex was unclean, which it couldn't be, since it 'blossomed in little children'. She had once overheard prostitutes in the women's washroom at Charing Cross station discussing their plans for the evening, and was sickened by them. She was equally angered by her mother (as so often) who was in the habit of saying at weddings that 'she was so sorry for the girl'. But although she rejected her mother's attitude, some maternal inhibitions evidently remained as Olive seemed as embarrassed by the subject as Horace was. There was something else too. Olive did have grounds for anxiety about her health. In the letter of 28 May when she was trying to explain her distress at the reference to children, she said that in purely practical terms she would want to have her house running easily before embarking on a family, and 'I must get well and strong'. She did not yet have this confidence, and already there were signs of the condition that was to disable her so soon after her marriage. In the autumn of 1917 she developed 'neuritis' in one of her arms. In November Horace expressed concern that she hadn't seen the doctor earlier about her condition, and warned her that she should never disregard 'brother ass' when he needs a little gentle coaxing (5 November l917). Her mother, too, was free with advice which, she complained, her daughter never took: 'She was sorry I had neuritis but was not in the least surprised' (13 November l917).

The letters contain a number of references to Olive's painful arm, but no obviously sinister developments seem to have occurred before the marriage. The main burden of preparation lay on Horace in finding a suitable house in Cranbrook. The first possibility, a house called Springfield, had too much ground to look after. and with a rent of £35 a year was rather expensive. He said that he looked forward 'with horror to a sort of endless burden of property, the thought of which makes me sick' (6 April 1918). But by the end of May he had found a house with the modest rent of £16 a year. The accommodation was modest too: water from a pump outside the back door ('so bringing in water should be fairly easy', he wrote bravely), and of course an outside toilet, draining into a cesspool: they could spend £50 on connecting this with the main drains. There were two rooms and a kitchen downstairs, and two rooms upstairs, one of which 'the selfish MAN annexes as his dressing room study' (3 June 1918).

While domestic arrangements for the couple seemed to be sorting themselves well enough, the correspondence is subtly burdened with a sense of anxiety which found expression in a number of specific problems. The least of these was the little matter of who was to be Horace's Best Man. The proper and conventional choice would have been Horace's eldest brother Gilbert, but Horace found the idea unpalatable as he was sure Gilbert would harass him all the time. Olive's mother might not approve, but he wanted Michael Graham to perform, partly, he admitted, because he reminded him of Tommy Stone, 'about my most intimate friend really, though quite different from all other King's people' (16 February 1918). Horace obviously needed to feel that his marriage was going to affirm things that were important to him in his past life, as is rather painfully apparent in the disagreement he had with Olive over where the wedding was to take place. Olive would have liked it to be at the Grahams' holiday home in Allonby in Cumberland, but Horace was distressed at the idea that his recently widowed mother might not be able to attend: she would hardly have been able to travel so far (4th June 1918).

> I suppose men are just as incomprehensible as women [he wrote on 6 June]. I felt very much on the point of shedding tears. I seemed to feel that if we were married at Allonby without Mother or anyone I should feel as if our marriage were a symbol of the end of my family life.[35]

Eventually they agreed to have the wedding on classic Quaker ground at Jordans in Buckinghamshire. But there was still a further difficulty, though one in which Horace and Olive were in warm agreement. They objected to the traditional wording of the marriage vow used in Quaker marriages. The offending phrase was the one about the couple's being loving and faithful partners 'until it shall please God by death to separate us'. Horace had suggested that the promise should apply 'throughout our mortal life, and resting in the hope of a deeper union hereafter'. But they were advised that this was unacceptable if the marriage were to be legally valid. They felt so strongly about the matter that they were prepared to consider marriage in a registry office, but in the end it did not come to that. Josephine Alexander thought they might make an initial explanation of their objections, and then – as it were under protest – go through with the old formula.[36] But Olive felt that this would make those attending think about the formula rather than the wedding itself, and it would be no better if a kind of footnote were to be added at the end.

> I think it may be pleasanter for everybody if we are just hypocrites and make no fuss. The real thing about weddings certainly does seem to be how best to suit everybody else! I am longing for it all to be over, but at the moment I can't see beyond the jubilating crowd and my internal misery – but I really think it will be better to endure the internal misery and let the crowd jubilate.[37]

It should be added that John William Graham did not let the matter drop, and that, largely at his instigation, the form of words to be used was referred to a weighty Committee on the Marriage Declaration (set up in July 1922), and considered at length at the 1923 Yearly Meeting. After a good deal of agonising and further reference to a committee, the wording now current, 'as long as we both on earth shall live', was adopted.[38]

The wedding took place on Tuesday 30 July. A few days before, Horace had spent a few days bird-watching in Dungeness, arriving there full of mental fever and bodily exhaustion. 'Magically', he wrote on the 28th, 'by yesterday morning I found that all the small wranglings of our poor nature mattered nothing in the light of nature, and in presence of its peace and power.' This was emphatically not Olive's state of mind: she wrote on the 28th that she had had 'three horrible days'. Horace had not done enough to get the wedding arrangements sorted earlier, 'and then went to Dungeness in the midst of the chaos.' She relented sufficiently to concede that she had written 'a horrid letter', but it is alarming to think what effect Horace's all too tranquil letter will have had when she received it the day before the wedding. One hopes that the peace and power of nature inspired Horace to say the right thing to his overwrought bride.

Whatever the state of mind of the principals, Olive's father was in excellent spirits. Two weekends before the wedding he had been involved in a prayer meeting in Manchester for peace. It was somewhat provocatively held in the open air, and was riotously broken up by a crowd singing 'Rule Britannia' to drown out the pious strains of 'O God Our Help in Ages Past'. A report in *The Friend* (2 August 1918) suggests that a good time was had by all. John William Graham's cheerful mood is vividly expressed in the leading article he wrote for *The Friend* of 16 August, with the title 'Where God Dwelleth'. It expresses a chastened but buoyant optimism about the prospects for a peaceful world, in spite of the fact that 'the Government, the press, the multitude, the educated class, all deny our testimony'. There are, he insists, many signs that a readiness for peace and cooperation does exist.

It was with a concern to reinforce this movement of the spirit that Horace and Olive planned, in the first months of their marriage, to 'travel in the ministry' to young Friends all over the country. As they were together, the surviving correspondence throws no light on their first visits, or indeed on Horace's final terms at Cranbrook. The obituary Horace wrote for the *Woodbrooke Journal* in 1942 records that Olive's disabling illness (probably multiple sclerosis) first showed itself in 1918 as she was hurrying to catch a train in Nottingham, when her legs gave way under her. Thereafter Horace had to continue the travelling alone, and the letters resume. In July 1919 he was in Bristol and Somerset, and then in Saffron Walden in Essex. A visit to Northampton was followed by one to Bournemouth: both were difficult, though in different ways. In Northampton the group was 'distinctly uneducated and "Arryish"', though the discussion went well enough (8 July). In Bournemouth he stayed at the home of the Misses Brown, 'two large, loud-voiced, energetic, frigid, semi-evangelical, middle-aged ladies', and his meeting was at their aunt's house. She was even more formidable, a stately lady of 78 who had known Horace's grandfather. She insisted that he should have a Bible by him, though he told her that he didn't think he'd need it.

Evidently at this time Olive was still hoping that her condition would improve. She and Horace planned to attend the first major post-war Quaker conference together: it was at Oriel College Oxford in mid-September, and Dr Henry Gillett was to make arrangements for them. In the event she wasn't able to go, and Horace's letters to her are a striking record of his sense of alienation from the Society at this time. He told her that he felt no real affinity with those attending the conference:

> I have no Quaker friends unless you count J[ohn] R[ickman],[39] who really doesn't count – and, in their several ways, your two brothers. And I never shall have. Quakerism means a good deal to me, but in some ways not the deepest things. I am a human being first, and a religious propagandist or emotional worshipper with others of the divine long after. And it is as a human being that I have made all my intimate friendships, and have married you.[40]

The conference, which was concerned with 'ministry and visitation', did not allow for the sense of doubt and darkness that oppressed Horace, and was indeed seized with an 'intensity of conviction of "a message" to be given' that left him rather desperate. He was relieved somewhat by the genial company of Herbert Corder and Barratt Brown ('Barry'), who enlivened breakfast and the late evening with stories described in one place as 'low' and in another as 'lewd', and enjoyed a brief visit to Barratt Brown's home a few days later, describing himself as 'very content today in this household of happy paganism'.[41] But although Barry may not have been one of the excessively pious type so deplored by Horace at this time, his reflections on the conference in *The Friend* of 17th October emphatically proclaim a message, a message of the rebirth of Quakerism under the stresses of war, in which Friends have renewed their connection with 'the frequenters of guardrooms and lock-ups and gaols'[42] There is a buoyancy and exuberance here which is in striking contrast to Horace's depression.

The depression was not only caused by anxiety for Olive, but uncertainty about his own future career. Olive herself refers to his 'endless applying' for academic posts.[43] For some time, though, he had been in touch with a Rugby businessman and Quaker, Frederick Merttens, who was concerned to establish the teaching of international relations at Woodbrooke, and saw in Horace an eminently suitable person to do this.[44] But H. G. Wood for one was by no means convinced that a new appointment needed to be made, and Horace wondered whether he would have to go back to Cranbrook and implore Pierce to reinstate him as a history teacher. He saw one of the trustees, J. H. Barlow, at the Oxford Conference, who told him that nothing had as yet been settled. And when, shortly afterwards, he learned that he had been appointed for one probationary year, he was still not exactly enthusiastic about it. He told Olive that he had been a good Quaker earlier in the year, but had rather overdone it, and now felt that he never wanted to go to meeting again: 'But I suppose I must keep up appearances till my Woodbrooke appointment is confirmed a year hence! There now, there's an unquakerly sentiment for you' (24 September 1919). Olive matched this unquakerly sentiment with one of her own, describing a certain Anna Matilda as 'a cat' for making a disagreeable remark about her brother Michael. She suggested that she and Horace were like herself and Dick when they had measles: 'each trying to make out we were worse than the other' (28 September 1919).

The day following his 'unquakerly' letter, Horace arrived in Woodbrooke, and surveyed the situation without enthusiasm. The library was poorly equipped so far as his future work was concerned: no international law at all, and only a conventional set of books on European history and politics. The following Sunday, 28 September, he attended Selly Oak meeting, and felt colder about it than he had even in his most 'pagan' days at Cambridge. There was ministry from several 'raw-minded Evangelical-socialist people', and he found himself 'observing the working of their minds' with a certain detached interest. The house they were to live in did not help, either. It was 61 Linden Road: far too big, generally uncomfortable, and with a larder that stank of stale fish – penetrating his nostrils even when smoking a cigarette. He felt utterly miserable and lonely.[45]

This was a passing mood, however. He evidently enjoyed working on his lectures on the development of constitutional democracy in Europe. He ranged widely in his preparation, reading, for example, J. A. Froude on Erasmus. This probably means Froude's *Life and Letters of Erasmus* (1894a), but he may well have known also the earlier *Short Studies on Great Subjects*, where there are three lectures on Erasmus and Luther as complementary figures in the history of the Reformation. Alexander sees Erasmus as 'the most excellent person who ever lived': 'I do approve of every bit of his character. He is such a magnificent instance of the man who saw all sides of things and yet was "great" even in the vulgar sense'.[46]

Froude's biography shows Erasmus indefatigably trying to work for peace between the Catholic and Protestant parties as the struggles of the Reformation unfold, warning his Catholic friends that the only cure for the troubles is for the Church to mend its ways. This seems unlikely to happen, with the result that the country will be laid waste, and Germany and the Church be ruined. If only someone could have the sense to approach the Lutherans in a friendly spirit![47] For Froude, particularly in the 'short study', Erasmus is an ultimately tragic figure who became progressively more alienated from the society of his time. He sees, moreover, some justice in this: Erasmus's latitudinarian attitudes might have led to infidelity among the educated, while leaving the uneducated to their superstitions. For Luther, nothing but the truth would do; as for Erasmus, he preferred truth, if he could have it, but if not, 'he could get on moderately well upon falsehood'.[48] Erasmus was too closely associated with the existing order; Luther came from, and appealed to, the humble folk who had less to lose from revolutionary change. As we have seen, Alexander felt unable to cope with uneducated people, and reluctantly decided that his mission had to be to the elite. In this context Erasmus was an attractive if worrying role-model. How splendid if he could work with some Luther of the twentieth century. And of course in Gandhi he found him.

In the autumn of 1919, though, Gandhi could hardly have been even a name to him. He pursued his Erasmian path, greatly cheered by a useful visit to Birmingham's second-hand bookshops, finding what must have been a reviewer's copy of W. H. Dawson's recently-published book *The German Empire*.[49] Dawson was a historian who had dedicated himself to interpreting Germany to a British audience, and his scrupulously fair assessments of German policy under Bismarck and his successors had no trace of wartime distortions. They were indeed a good example of the kind of approach that Alexander hoped to bring to his international course at Woodbrooke. A couple of weeks later he took possession of a fine set of the *Cambridge Modern History*, thus seriously beginning to repair the deficiencies of Woodbrooke's library.[50]

He was further cheered by a visit to Cambridge around 18 October, primarily to attend a Council meeting of the Royal Society for the Protection of Birds, but also to resume his connection with a much-loved place. He had dinner at King's as a guest of Lowes Dickinson, who greeted him in a way that held up the queue of dons proceeding to the high table. They all shook hands with Alexander as they passed, and, he told Olive, 'I stood there feeling as if I were George Windsor or somebody'. Flattering though this attention was, it was the RSPB that gave him most pleasure. He saw W. H. Hudson for the first time, and admired his extraordinarily mobile face. Shown a picture of a ringed plover, 'he looked as if he suddenly saw all the Ringed Plovers of his experience, in every kind of circumstance on every sandy shore of England'.[51] Alexander also found a connection between his bird-watching and his interest in the newly founded League of Nations. The meeting agreed to see in what ways the League might provide international action for the protection of birds.

On 21 October 1919 Olive came to live in Birmingham, staying at first with a Mrs Wilson. The correspondence therefore ceases for a time, and other sources have to be consulted to find out something about Alexander's teaching. That he did not feel altogether comfortable in Woodbrooke at first is apparent from a letter that John Rickman wrote to him in January 1920. 'You sicken at Woodbrooke's surface-contact revolutionism', Rickman observed; and, speaking with the authority of one who had witnessed the Russian Revolution at first hand, added:

> I should sicken at it too. They are rebels, sickly gut-less rebels in love with Jesus because he was gentle. You want to bring another idea into

> Woodbrooke, that of hard work, historical, close thinking, sympathetic; a love for Jesus because of his passion for unity with the struggles of men (which made him gentle).
>
> Woodbrooke wants to be rebellious, advanced. You want it to be statesmanlike, practical. Their minds are fevered. You want to cool their fever with a dose of history.[52]

In time, Alexander came to find in Woodbrooke a model of the good international society, and this probably was due in part to the tone and temper of his courses, as we shall see in the next chapter. Before going on to that, though, there remains one piece of family business to record.

With the end of the war, it had become possible once again for unofficial travellers to go abroad, and Alexander was anxious to go to Rome as soon as possible to wind up his brother Christopher's affairs. He didn't want to go alone, and in November he persuaded Dick Graham to accompany him. He hoped to get in touch with pacifist people in Italy, and looked for help in doing this from Philip Baker and from the Japanese Quaker Inazo Nitobe, who was passing through London to take up a senior position in the secretariat of the League of Nations. And of course his old mentor Oscar Browning, who had been living in Rome for some years, would be a great support.

Alexander and Graham arrived in Rome just before Christmas, enthusiastically greeted by Browning, who found them accommodation and evidently rather overwhelmed them with his conversation. He wanted to discuss Victorianism and Georgianism, which Alexander felt was wasting their precious time: 'In some respects', he told Olive ungratefully, 'he is an intolerable old man, but we must be kind and patient with him, I suppose'.[53] But they evidently enjoyed their Christmas Day dinner in the pension. They were encouraged to wear funny hats, and Alexander actually won second prize, 'chiefly on account of two immense newspaper whiskers'. The climax of the visit was, however, a family lunch with Aldo Cerri, one of the employees at the Institute where Christopher worked. His father had fought with Garibaldi in 1870, and Christopher was evidently honoured as a gallant soldier. In spite of the awkward feelings that this admiration must have engendered, Alexander and Graham experienced a feeling of welcome that moved them very deeply. The meal was lavish, and they were plied with red and white wine. When they were served with coffee they thought they were safe, but no: a round of toasts followed. 'It was a most happy and delightful party.' There was a freshness and friendliness about it, 'all totally unlike anything one could ever possibly experience in England'.[54]

Alexander met Christopher's chief, Professor Provenzal, on several occasions, and found that he was the editor of *Il Nuovo Patto*, a journal devoted to the creation of a tolerant world view, and therefore prepared to print the 'message to all men and women' adopted by Meeting for Sufferings on 5 December. This message expressed Friends' desire to stretch out their hands in fellowship across frontiers:

> 'We call upon all men everywhere to unite in the service of healing the broken world, to bear one another's burdens, and so fulfil the law of Christ.'[55]

Alexander also found another journal that would print the message, and take an article on the religious and ethical basis of an effective League of Nations. Alas, at this point he was struck down by flu, and could do nothing further than conserve his strength to travel home in time for the new term.

3

THE DISCOVERY OF GANDHI

International studies

The lectureship at Woodbrooke was part of a widespread concern, extending well beyond the Society of Friends, to promote the study of international relations. In *The International Anarchy* (1926) Lowes Dickinson was to record his dismay at the failure of policy-makers to learn the lessons of the world war, but he was none the less encouraged by an awareness of 'currents below the surface which do not find expression in policy'.[1] Dickinson himself saw this 'new world fermenting underneath' as manifesting itself in a great work of education. 'Internationalists', he insisted in *Causes of International War*, 'must contend with imperialists for the mind and soul of the peoples'.[2] Against a background of the chaos and confusion in central and eastern Europe that erupted after 1918, the need for a better understanding of human conflict was a matter of urgency. At the same time as Alexander was starting his courses, a chair of international politics was being established in Aberystwyth by David Davies, formerly a secretary to Lloyd George. The post there was first held by Alfred Zimmern, who later worked for the League Secretariat in Geneva, and then moved to a similar chair in Oxford. Davies and Zimmern agreed with Theodore Roosevelt and the American 'League to Enforce Peace' that military power was essential to a successful international order.[3] Such an order would owe more to 'the living experience of Versailles' than it would to the academic dreams coming out of The Hague.[4]

It is true that the 'living experience of Versailles' turned out to be a bitter disappointment for Zimmern. He wrote later that an exhausted continent looked to President Wilson, Lloyd George and Clemenceau to bring lasting justice and 'appeasement'. They failed: they fumbled with the tiller, and the devil seized it.[5] Versailles was a monument to greed and rancour. This view was widely shared in the liberal establishment, including many of the 'academic dreamers' Alexander had known at Cambridge. In his *Economic Consequences of the Peace*, first published in December 1919, J. M. Keynes had exposed the inevitable disaster that would follow the treaty's deliberate attempt to impoverish Central Europe. Earlier in the year, on 24 May, the *Manchester Guardian* published a protest from forty influential writers and academics, including Julian Huxley, J. K. Jerome, A. D. Lindsay, John Masefield, Gilbert Murray, R. H. Tawney, H. G. Wells and Leonard Woolf, condemning the draft treaty, inspired as it was by vindictiveness and fear, on which it was 'impossible to establish any true League of Nations'. It would, they said, lead only to mutual aggression, increased armaments, a perpetual danger of war. No nation could be expected to accept the terms imposed on Germany 'otherwise than under duress, or with any intention of keeping them a day longer than such duress can be maintained'.[6]

None the less, the League had within it the possibility of development, and Alexander accepted it for what it might become. He started a branch of the League of Nations Union in Bournville, accepting the support of those who felt able to endorse the idea of a League of Nations rather than the League that they'd actually got.[7] The ideas informing his early years at Woodbrooke may be studied in a book he published in 1924, *The Revival of Europe. Can the League of Nations Help?* He bases his analysis on the Woodbrooke experience itself. Working there has enabled him to make contact with intelligent people from many countries, exchanging opinions and knowledge 'in an atmosphere of rare candour and mutual regard'. The immediacy of this experience makes political issues 'burn with human passion, as no newspaper paragraphs or hasty journeys can do'.[8] Awareness of the passion is crucial for Alexander, because unless conflicts are probed to the depths, it isn't possible to learn and apply the lessons that need to be learnt. But if the probing is genuinely undertaken, conflicts can be resolved. In his concluding chapter, he insists that a 'sense of right' is more powerful than fear. Indeed, if the League of Nations bases itself on military force, it will fail.

> The League must act by persuasion, by reason, by the publication of truth, by agreement – at the worst perhaps by refusal of intercourse. And the astonishing discovery is made, that the representatives of a State are much more likely to be reasonable and conciliatory if they know that their neighbours have only reason and truth and common sense as weapons behind their arguments.[9]

E. H. Carr could well have taken this as an extreme example of the utopian illusions he criticised in *The Twenty Years' Crisis* (1939), but in making this claim Alexander was evidently thinking of his own experience at Geneva, when he visited the Third Assembly in September 1922. There was already a small Quaker group in the city, started just after the war by Ethel and Herbert Jones, the couple who had founded the Downs School in 1900, and thus had care of Horace when first he left home. Herbert was the secretary of the International Bureau for the Protection of Native Races. They held regular discussion meetings, and were in touch with many organisations based in Geneva. The Joneses themselves had left Geneva for a time in the latter part of 1921, and seem not to have been there when Alexander made his visit. The Clerk of Geneva Meeting, Madeleine Savary, kept the work going, and eventually, in the autumn of 1923, premises were found for a permanent Quaker Centre.[10]

Alexander went to Geneva with the support of Friends' Peace Committee, who encouraged him to take this service (6 July 1922), and then contributed £5 towards his expenses (3 August). He reported back to their meeting of 5 October. Earlier in the year he had written a booklet, *The Moral Basis for a Treaty of Peace*, in which he called for a revision of the Treaty of Versailles on the lines of President Wilson's 'Fourteen Points', which had been the basis of the armistice of November 1918. Alexander emphasised the importance of cooperation, justice, humanity, penitence and humility if an enduring settlement were to be achieved. 'Nations that try to dominate ultimately perish; but the meek shall inherit the earth.' Evidently he had taken copies with him to Geneva, but felt they had not had much effect. Peace Committee minutes record that 'the opportunities for direct propaganda were not great'. But he was deeply impressed by the atmosphere of the League sessions themselves. In *The Revival of Europe* he recalls the Haiti representative's exposure of oppressive measures against tribespeople in the newly mandated territory of South-West Africa. The speech ensured that something was done about it, for openness and fairness tend to prevail in the Assembly.[11] He was equally struck by the skill shown by diplomats like Robert Cecil in handling vehement disagreements. 'Patience, restraint, goodwill, candour, courage – these qualities are often found at Geneva, and found in combination.'[12] Geneva also undermines traditional loyalties in the interest of a higher loyalty to international well-being. At the Third Assembly, Alexander had the pleasure of hearing a New Zealand representative criticising Britain and India for their unsatisfactory policy on opium exports.[13] And Alexander was particularly encouraged by the way the League was beginning to take an interest in what would formerly have been regarded as issues purely internal to a particular state. 'There is no more sanctity about the State', he said, 'than about many of the other organisations man has formed for controlling and assisting his social relationships.'[14]

In Geneva, in fact, Alexander felt that he detected intimations of the international order sketched in the 'Essay on Human Association'. He stood deliberately opposed to the assumptions made by David Davies and Alfred Zimmern in the Aberystwyth school of international studies. For Zimmern, the nation-state was

> the only principle on which an effective international organisation in the public interest can be built up in the modern world. The day is past and over when churches or guilds or other non-territorial forms of association could claim to be equal to the task of providing justice and liberty for mankind.

Those, he insisted, who 'deny this duty of civic dedication are, consciously or unconsciously, trying to bring anarchy into human society.[15] Lowes Dickinson would have agreed, and clearly Alexander had a formidable task ahead of him to validate an approach to international relations so much at variance with received opinion.

The Woodbrooke timetable gives some idea of how he organised his own inquiries into the subject. In his first term, the autumn of 1919, he gave one lecture a week on the history of internationalism, and another on governments and parties in Europe. In the following summer term he added a series on 'international problems', and in the autumn another on 'Europe since the Peace'. In the spring term of 1921 he gave his first series on the League of Nations, and in the summer extended his view to 'the Empire' and to constitutions and parties outside Europe. He was evidently trying to build up a comprehensive picture of the international system, and to relate this to the personal experience of internationalism in Woodbrooke itself.

His experience as a schoolteacher willing to try his hand at experimental methods served him well in the informal atmosphere of the college. His lectures were notably clear and objective, and his willingness to take other people's opinions seriously was good training for his later interventions in daunting conflict situations. It was good training too for an effective style of leadership. Richard Symonds, his deputy in the Friends' Ambulance Unit in Calcutta many years later, was much impressed by the excellence of the briefing he received from Alexander on Indian and Quaker history while they were on their way to India. (The wartime journey took five weeks, so there were no time constraints.) He added that while Alexander was Unit leader 'he was remarkably modest and receptive to ideas which we newcomers threw out, always willing to have his own ideas criticised.'[16] The effectiveness of the FAU's work clearly owed something to this.

After Alexander's first visit to Geneva, he had occasion to write to H. G. Wood, who was away travelling in the eastern Mediterranean. He told him something of the current batch of students at Woodbrooke, and in particular mentioned three of them: Fritz Berber, a Bavarian Methodist from Munich,

Willi Schubert; from Vienna; and Reginald Reynolds, from his own birthplace, Croydon.[17] Berber, who had arrived in poor physical shape from severe malnutrition, was now restored, and impressed Alexander with his gentle modesty, his many interesting ideas, his rejection of superficiality. Schubert, by contrast, was 'full of humour, and almost childish enjoyment of things'. (Years later, Alexander recalled the 'immense gusto' with which Schubert had conducted an impromptu jazz band at a Woodbrooke entertainment.[18]) Reynolds was 'a youth of complete assurance, who began by treading on everyone's corns, and still bubbles over frequently, though he is certainly becoming acclimatised.'[19]

All three were to play a significant part in Alexander's life, Schubert in his understanding of the League of Nations, Berber in his contacts with Nazi Germany, and Reynolds in working for Indian independence. Reynolds is the most conspicuous figure of the three in the Woodbrooke log-books of the time, taking, for example, the Quaker *Advices and Queries* as the model for some queries of his own, including 'Are you careful not to take more than your share of cake at tea?'[20] Alexander thought to make fun of this over-confident young man in a mock-review of a trashy novel entitled *Records of Reggie*, writing on the assumption that this must be Reynolds himself. The Reggie of the novel is said to utter 'lightning sallies' that are witty and amusing. 'You will want to hear', says the reviewer, 'some of his witty and amusing lightning sallies', but he has to disappoint his readers. 'Probably', he continues, 'if you engage him in conversation afterwards he will give you some illustrations.'[21] There is much else of this jocularity which evidently nettled Reynolds considerably. In the following term he responded with a telling 'cautionary tale' in the manner of Hilaire Belloc. It was entitled 'Horace, who walked in the Paths of Sin and was finally compelled to dwindle out a Miserable Existence in Purgatory'. The opening lines set the tone:

> For Libel gross, and brazen Slander,
> None equalled Horace Alexander,
> Whose History I here disclose . . .

Reynolds passes rapidly on to Horace's death, when, through some kind of confusion, he was mistaken for a saint and admitted to heaven. Here he continued his ornithological pursuits ('Helped by the wings he now possessed'). At this point Reynolds shows a complete misunderstanding of Alexandrian bird-watching by making Horace stuff a bird of paradise, thus providing the celestial authorities with a reason for despatching him to hell. Here he found many old friends from many parts of the world.

> They met, and talked, in clubs and stations:
> 'Why not', said they, 'a League of Nations?'
> – Which Horace thought a splendid plan;
> And there the trouble first began.

The Autocrat of Hell surveyed
Aghast, the League that Horace made;
And recognised in H.G.A.
A Rival Power – anyway,
Horace could imitate, with ease,
The laugh of Mephistopheles;
At Politics and Knavish Tricks
Odds were on Horace – twelve to six;
At leading sheep in paths of evil,
No precedence had Mr Devil – [22]
While as to libel, as to slander,
No peer had Horace Alexander!!!

He is eventually banished to a 'sad and sorry / Suburban villa in Purgatory'.[23]

However much the two men sparred with each other, their subsequent relationship suggests that there was little bruising on either side. But one wonders what the deferential Germans made of Reynolds' 'lightning sallies'. A number of Schubert's letters to Alexander survive, and their tone is certainly very different. On the point of leaving England to return to Vienna he expresses gratitude for the way Alexander had made Woodbrooke 'a spiritual starting point or perhaps turning point, which will direct my whole life and will help me to overcome the difficulties I shall have to face [in] the next years.'[24]

The correspondence shows how carefully Alexander kept in touch with his old students and gave them support. Schubert found life in the impoverished Vienna of the immediate post-war years too disheartening to bear, and in December 1924 he travelled to Geneva in search of work, possibly with some encouragement from Alexander. He had certainly written to a Miss Blomfield asking her to help Schubert, which she did by lending him books for an examination for applicants for an indexing post. At first his only employment was typing library cards at the YMCA, and he was pessimistic about his chances of finding a vacancy in the League Secretariat, since so much depended on the satisfaction of national interests. But in the following April he was appointed to a post in the Disarmament section under the direction of Salvador de Madariaga.[25]

The correspondence that follows is of great interest in showing the strains to which the international ideals of the League were subject. Schubert himself complained about the preponderance of English nationals in the Secretariat – 133 out of 350, a figure that would not have included the humbler clerical positions. He remarked that there were only four other Austrians employed there, three of whom were typists. The fourth was a former cavalry officer who believed in a strong army, union with Germany, and smashing the French. Fortunately he was in the Economics section, where his deplorable views could do little harm. Schubert himself was strongly Austrian in his outlook. He wrote an article for *The Friend* on the injustice of Italy's annexation of the South Tyrol, and objected strongly to another article there by John S. Stephens on Czechoslovakia which included a favourable account of the nationalist Sokol movement in that country.[26] He was also distinctly anti-Semitic, disapproving of the acceptance by Woodbrooke of a Jew from Berlin, 'one of the tolerable kind', but not the right person to understand and interpret the religious message of Friends.[27] He dismisses the objections that Alexander evidently made to this kind of remark as mere ignorance: 'You are not 'against' Jews because you don't know them. I was not 'against' Americans because I did not know them. It does not seem to be true that intercourse guarantees mutual understanding!'[28]

He worries that the Japanese Friend, Inazo Nitobe, an Assistant Secretary-General of the League, is somewhat anti-German, though fair-minded enough not to let it affect his impartiality. 'Very often such dislikes are physical ones just as with me regarding Jews'.[29]

It is unfortunate that Alexander's side of the correspondence has not been preserved, particularly when the two friends disagreed – sometimes strongly. In one letter Schubert refers to a 'thunderstorm' that had burst over him in response to a criticism (also not found) of British opium policy in China. 'You must never take my emotional letters serious!' pleaded Schubert.[30] And yet in a sense it was important for Alexander to take them 'serious', because of the corrective they provided to what might be called the officially optimistic view of the League. Schubert felt that Alexander was in any case too apt to adopt this optimism, as in his pamphlet on the League and national minorities.[31] Early on in his time in Geneva he had formed an estimate of League participants which was to remain constant:

> In the League of Nations there are two kinds of people: the idealists who are very keen but do not understand anything, and the experts who are not at all keen but understand everything. The latter win the battle in most of the cases. Not only in the field of drugs.[32]

Schubert was writing in the middle of a League conference on measures to control opium trafficking. If only for reasons of filial piety, Alexander would in any case have felt a deep concern in this matter, but Schubert's glib formula challenged him to show that the idealist could become an expert without losing his keenness. As we shall see in the next section, it was a challenge that Alexander was more than ready to take up.

Schubert's life was cut tragically short in 1930 when he was poisoned by some pollution in the Lake of Geneva while he was bathing there. The previous year he had published a revaluation of the 'dogma' of state sovereignty in the era of the League, and he would have been an invaluably unpredictable observer of the rise of the Nazi movement in the 1930s. He might also have been an understanding confidant of his fellow Woodbrooker Fritz Berber, who was to become something more than an observer.

Berber had returned to Munich after the autumn term of 1922, and was studying law with a view to becoming a judge. He was involved in much of the radical political discussion generated in a turbulent city – the scene of Hitler's abortive putsch in 1923. One contribution that he made to the Munich Youth Circle (Jugendring München) in 1924 was published, and will be considered in a moment. In the autumn of 1926 he returned to Woodbrooke as a college fellow, and remained there till the following summer. He was closely associated with Alexander's teaching of international affairs, and in the summer term ran a short course of his own on German political life. Alexander wrote a short account of Berber in April 1979 and remarked that it was he who first interested him in Gandhi.

> India had always seemed strange to me, and the reports of Gandhi if anything only made it stranger. Fritz insisted that Gandhi was demonstrating that a man even in political leadership, could follow his conscience in all that he did. 'Conscience' was for him the key word for Gandhi. I believe it has always been the key word for Fritz, who has had some of the hardest decisions to make that a man can ever face.[33]

Berber's paper for the Jugendring München explains clearly what he meant by 'conscience'. The paper's subject was 'justice', and in it he set up a kind of Pauline antithesis between the old politics and the new. The old politics is that of an unredeemed, instinctual humanity, concerned with utility, with honour, with power. The new politics is defined by conscience, the capacity of a human being to attend to the voice of God. In every individual there is a capacity for this politics of conscience, but it has to work itself out in the context of things as they are. This puts a peculiar strain on those who try to be obedient to conscience. They have to endure tension, take on burdens, be prepared to be homeless. Berber goes on to say that Germany has a special vocation at the present time because of what it has learned in the trauma of defeat. The greatest praise that Germans give to public figures is that of genuineness, Echtheit.[34]

Everything relating to Berber reinforces the impression of an exceptionally solemn person, with no sense of humour. Woodbrooke did not allow him to continue thus unchallenged. The log-books, indeed, suggest that he was found irresistibly entertaining. He is revealed as a hypochondriac, always taking pills, unable to sleep because of various kinds of noise, and because he was cold – above all because he was cold. His suffering was relieved by the purchase of a heavy eiderdown, which encouraged him to cancel the arrangements for his own funeral.'[35]

His classes were held to be strenuous: one student's poem in the log-book describes how 'He lets us go to wild conclusions leaping, 'clusions leaping, Then he tells us what things really truly are.'[36] The only actual specimen we have of his seminar manner is noted in a log-book entry for 18 May 1927: 'Fritz, giving us a concrete example to illustrate a point, asks us to imagine him going into a room 10 inches by 3 inches by 1 inch. Our imaginations, however, fail us.' The log-book fails to make clear whether or not this was an illustration of some aspect of German political life.

*

In the cheerful atmosphere of Woodbrooke – where 'God Save the King' might be heard sung to a jazz accompaniment, and a rendering of 'Christians Awake!' in the bass part only 'quite brought the house down'[37] – Alexander continued to develop his analysis of international institutions. Olive, in spite of her disabling physical condition, devoted the vigour and high spirits so evident in the courtship letters to sustaining the Woodbrooke community. She edited the *Woodbrooke Journal*, which kept past students in touch with each other and did much of the administrative work needed to organise the reunions of Woodbrookers in various parts of Europe.

These reunions were often the occasion for wider travel so far as Alexander was concerned. After a reunion in Elsinore in Denmark in August 1923 he went to Berlin with H. G. Wood, then down to Prague and on to Vienna to see Willi Schubert, and thereafter to Budapest, then Munich, and finally the Rhineland, at that time under French occupation. In an assessment of this tour, evidently written immediately on his return, he emphasised the acuteness of the conflicts that divided central Europe, and above all the dire hardship suffered by many Austrians and Germans. Vienna and the Rhineland were in a particularly distressing state: he wondered whether one solution for Vienna's problems might not be to move the headquarters of the League of Nations there from Geneva. He noted the pervasive anti-Semitism, at its most intense in Munich, where Jewish people dared not show themselves. He saw many swastikas in the city – this was just before Hitler's 'putsch' – an emblem worn by 'weedy idealists rather than strong barbarians'. Fritz Berber was his host in Munich, and he took him to the opera, where one could almost imagine oneself back in imperial Germany. But, as Berber pointed out, many of the beautifully dressed women there were also obviously half-starved, but Alexander was struck by the resilience, the 'undying fire' which somehow coped with conditions well-calculated to engender bitter hatreds.[38]

The next reunion, in 1924, was in Barchem, east of Arnhem in the Netherlands. At the same time and until mid-September Olive attended the clinic of Emile Coué at Nancy in eastern France.[39] On her journey there she was accompanied by Alexander and her youngest sister Agnes, and Agnes remained with her throughout. Coué's advocacy of auto-suggestion in the treatment of many conditions attracted much attention in the 1920s, and an exposition of his method like Harry Brooks's *The Practice of Autosuggestion* (1922) helps one to understand why Olive felt that some benefit might be obtained from it. She certainly illustrated Coué's conviction that we should not allow disease to destroy us by allowing our minds to dwell on it – but on the contrary we should 'oppose it and destroy it by a stream of healthful and dynamic thought'.[40] They stayed in a pension conducted by a flamboyant lady whose conversation was 'as good as a play', but whose anti-Protestant and anti-German prejudices caused the sisters some discomfort. Olive appreciated the wonderful atmosphere created by Coué in his clinics, and diligently carried out the exercises he suggested. But no improvement resulted and besides she grew weary of 'Madame'. In the end, admittedly, she wondered if she had misjudged her, as when they were about to leave 'Madame' expressed great kindness, hoped she would come back, and 'longed to see me well when I was "si jeune".' Olive was deeply affected by this sympathy, and (she told Alexander) had a good cry: 'I suppose one must be allowed to be sorry for oneself sometimes.'[41]

Opium

While the most obvious concern of the League of Nations was with the resolution of international conflicts and with related policy areas such as disarmament, it was also associated with a variety of initiatives in social policy, notably the International Labour Office. One area of concern proved to be of special interest to Alexander, that of the various attempts to control the traffic in narcotics, more especially opium. As we have seen, his father had made it the main business of his life to expose the connivance of governments, more especially the British-controlled government of India, in the export of opium for non-medical purposes. Alexander was not quite so zealous in the matter: indeed, he confessed that although he had the greatest admiration for Joseph's anti-opium work, 'I had always found opium a very dull subject'.[42] Dull it may have been, but it was a major issue on the international scene. Two major conferences on the opium traffic were planned in Geneva for the winter of 1924–5 – one on the suppression of opium use in Asia, the other on limiting the production of opium and coca derivatives to medical and scientific purposes. These conferences became the focus for a great deal of renewed campaigning by religious and welfare organisations, and in the United States they were seen as a test of the League's effectiveness in changing the world for the better.[43]

In India the Congress Party and the National Christian Council had made common cause in attacking the Government of India's connivance in sustaining opium consumption, and in particular the dependence of the Assam government on revenues derived from opium sales. Gandhi's friend Charles Freer Andrews had been investigating the situation in that province. It so happened that shortly afterwards, in December 1923, he had to travel to England for medical treatment, and stayed with Jack Hoyland, who had been a colleague of his at St Stephen's College in Delhi. Hoyland was on leave from his work in India and living in Birmingham. He had known Alexander in Cambridge, so it was natural enough to think of him as possibly helpful in anti-opium work. It was not so natural for Alexander to be persuaded. He regarded Hoyland as 'one of those big-hearted, impulsive child-like people who go about the world breaking into china shops and frozen hearts and other fragile places'. The Indian connection did not help. 'I distrusted the Indian outlook, or what little I knew of it, and people who got Indo-mania.' He felt there was too much religiosity about it all, and preferred the matter-of-fact Chinese. He did agree to meet Andrews, however, and was persuaded to undertake a limited task over the period leading up to the League conferences.[44] He was to act as joint secretary for a British Committee on India and Opium along with an Indian colleague, Tarini P. Sinha. Sinha had been an active supporter of the Indian National Congress in Allahabad, and had been particularly concerned with anti-alcohol and anti-opium work, spending some time in the USA for the World League against Alcoholism. The committee would educate public opinion, and make some kind of submission to the conference itself.

The kind of work performed by the committee may be studied in its main and fairly widely circulated publication, a booklet entitled *The Opium Evil in India: Britain's Responsibility*. This was a reprint of articles by Andrews in the *Manchester Guardian*, with an introduction by Alexander and Sinha. It did not appear until January 1926, nearly a year after the League conferences, and was presumably an attempt to maintain the momentum of the League's work. Andrews emphasised that the revenue problem was not insoluble, but it was essential that a firm decision should be taken by the government to accept that opium consumption must be discouraged. This the authorities in India were not willing to do.

Unsurprisingly, the main success of the committee before the Geneva meetings was to enlist the support of Friends' executive body, the Meeting for Sufferings. At its April meeting it welcomed the work of the All-India Society for the Suppression of the Opium Traffic, and set up its own opium sub-committee. It prepared a statement for the first conference, and sent Alexander to represent the Society and deliver the statement, which he did on 22 November. But on that day he also had a more interesting message to pass on. Two days earlier, Gandhi himself had sent him a telegram: 'Please tell convention all India wants complete stoppage opium traffic save for medical purposes.' As the official Government of India representative had been arguing that it was politically impossible for the 'alien government' to adopt prohibitionist tactics in the sub-continent, this intervention was acutely embarrassing.[45] Alexander was not, however, totally unsympathetic to the

British position. He wrote later that at Geneva he formed the opinion that they were 'getting a overdose of blame for honestly defending a policy that other Governments . . . silently intended to maintain'.[46] And there were real difficulties in the way of restricting opium use.

Any hopes that Alexander may have had that his intervention in Geneva would mark the end of his commitment to the anti-opium work were soon disappointed. Of course the campaign had to be carried forward, not only through the booklet already mentioned, but in articles in the press and in the organisation of appeals. One theme that emerges from the publications issued in this period is that joint action against opium use is the kind of initiative that will draw together people of goodwill in India and Britain. C. F. Andrews wrote that his 'one hope for a union of East and West is along these moral and humanitarian lines',[47] and in an article published in the *Times of Assam*, Alexander made the same point adding ('with all respect and diffidence') that he believed that: 'the people of India may find that such a campaign of purification is a greater help towards Self-Government than any purely political agitation.'[48]

Andrews was anxious that Alexander should come and assess the situation in the East for himself. Alexander could see the sense of this, as he felt that viewing the problem from a distance left many relevant questions unanswered. What attitudes did ordinary people in India and countries further east actually adopt towards opium use? What did the educated elites think? What really was the record of the various governments involved in administering legislation? Much was asserted on all sides, but the assertions seldom carried conviction. There was another reason for going: what was to be made of M. K. Gandhi? As we have seen, in the session of 1926–7 Fritz Berber had awakened Alexander's interest in the way Gandhi was illustrating a new kind of politics in his obedience to 'conscience'. Moreover, his colleague on the India and Opium Committee, Tarini Sinha, was closely involved with the swaraj campaign, so much so that in the aftermath of the 1926 General Strike, he travelled across to Alfreton in Derbyshire to encourage the striking miners there to use the technique of non-violent non-cooperation. He was arrested for his pains, and charged with sedition, but he was defended in court by none other than Jawaharlal Nehru, and the charge was withdrawn.[49] All this will have heightened Alexander's interest in the Indian situation, and he decided to apply for leave from his duties at Woodbrooke during the 1927–8 session. With the assistance of a Selly Oak Colleges Travelling Fellowship he was able to go to India, Malaya and the Dutch East Indies.[50]

As it happened, his visit coincided with a vigorous renewal of Nationalist campaigning. The appointment of the Statutory Commission chaired by Sir John Simon to consider Indian constitutional development caused outrage in India because of its exclusion of any Indian members. It was boycotted by a wide range of political organisations, including even the moderate Liberal

Federation, and from the time of its arrival on 3 Feburary 1928 it was harried by demonstrations carried out on a large scale. The upsurge of political energy may have contributed to the slightly nervous conclusion of a report from a two-man delegation from the British Trades Union Congress, visiting the sub-continent at the same time as Alexander: 'We felt growing upon us very strongly an apprehension that we were in the presence of tremendous forces which sooner or later would be applied to a great expansion of manufacturing activity.'[51] Alexander, too, was to become aware of these 'tremendous forces'.

At the end of July 1927 he began his tour with a journey through central and southern Europe, bringing himself up to date with developments in Geneva and the Balkans. From Greece he passed over to Egypt and travelled in one ship to Aden and in another on to Bombay. In this last stage of his journey one of his fellow travellers was his old friend from King's and from Tunbridge Wells, Arthur Happell. Happell was now well established in the Indian Civil Service, and no friend to nationalist agitation. In a letter of his written in February 1922, shortly after his arrival in India, he said it was 'quite certain' that it would be a very long time before Indians could govern their own country – say 200 years. Now he told Alexander that what ordinary Indian villagers wanted was a good, just 'father', and that there was little chance of their finding such fathers among the educated classes in India.[52]

Although Alexander was predisposed to be far more sympathetic to Indian aspirations than any British official was likely to be, he began his time in the sub-continent with distinctly less sympathy with the nationalist cause than he came to have. This is more apparent in the journal letters to Olive on which he based the book which describes his journey, *The Indian Ferment* (1929), than it is in the book itself. Thus, in his account in the book of his first encounter with a vehemently nationalist Indian, in Sohagpur in mid-India, he does not include his own response: 'I pointed to the dangers and difficulties of self-government and how hard a task it was to turn self-government into good government, requiring self-discipline, widespread political education, devotion to duty and so on. I quoted Bernard'[53] – and there, tantalisingly, the narrative breaks off: a page is missing. The most probable Bernard for Alexander to quote in this context would be Bernard Shaw, and it is tempting to suppose that he was invoking the authority of one of Shaw's contributions to *Fabian Essays* (1889), the lecture entitled 'Transition', in which he insists on the necessity of 'cautious and gradual change':

> The young Socialist is apt to be catastrophic in his views – to plan the revolutionary programme as an affair of twenty-four lively hours, with Individualism in full swing on Monday morning, a tidal wave of the insurgent proletariat on Monday afternoon, and Socialism in complete working order on Tuesday.[54]

This would have been a pertinent text to throw at a nationalist who was denouncing all the works of the British Raj as evil: how, after all, was the transition from British Raj to *Swaraj* to be managed? Alexander was not persuaded by this man, a lawyer: 'I found him charming, friendly, misguided, illogical, irresponsible'. He was reminded of Korean wrath against the Japanese, or German wrath against the French for their occupation of the Ruhr: the passion was understandable, but not a basis for policy.[55] He was reassured by the attitude of the Servants of India Society, whom he encountered in Poona. They 'frankly accept the British connection as ordained, in the inscrutable dispensation of Providence, for India's good.' Self-government is the aim, but it 'cannot be attained without years of earnest and patient effort and sacrifices worthy of the cause.' The members he met were much interested in the Birmingham Social Diploma and in the work of Woodbrooke itself. All very congenial.[56]

But, disconcertingly, Alexander found that the League of Nations, the chief focus so far as he was concerned of hopeful development in the world, was generally regarded as a 'gilded pill': 'at the heart of it is the Imperialism of the Western Powers'. Soon after his time in Sohagpur he was in Nagpur, where Jack Hoyland had arranged a series of meetings on the League. The occasion that made most impact on Alexander was a debate at Amraoti, 100 miles west of Nagpur. One of the most powerful speeches was made by a local lawyer, who launched a ferocious and well-argued case against the League and its many failures. After that, Alexander was relieved that the League was supported by as many as 70 votes to 250, and cheered himself with the thought that some people had been disgusted by the lawyer's speech, and 'had seen through it'. Afterwards he spoke to the lawyer, and found that 'his cynicism quite crumpled up before a few "idealistic" suggestions'.

> Cynicism of that kind is only skin-deep in most Indians. This man seemed to me thoroughly unattractive; and yet his worldly 'realism' fell away when I suggested that for us who were still young (everyone within earshot was young except himself) it was a fine thing to have a chance of influencing the world . . . and that it was better to spend one's life straining – perhaps in vain – for the ideal, rather than to add to the excessive amount of cynicism from which the world already suffered.[57]

The somewhat priggish tone of all this was doubtless a natural reaction to the thoroughgoing rejection of anything associated with the British, and one wonders how much longer he might have continued in this mode if he had not, while in Nagpur, encountered a sympathetic Irish ICS man. He was 'the terror of many of his brother officials because of his unorthodox views', including the idea that the Indians would manage self-government quite as well as half the states of Europe. Alexander had to agree, thinking of the Balkans, and perhaps

Spain and even France.[58] The full significance of this appears if one recalls a remark made in his European tour in 1923, when on his way to Budapest the boat in which he was travelling down the Danube was stuck in some shallow water. The tugs that came to the rescue were extremely inefficient, and the captain of the stranded vessel itself was manifestly incompetent. Alexander 'began to understand why the British Empire continues to grow while some others diminish'.[59] Clearly, though, no one was suggesting that the Hungarians should lose their independence, and if the Hungarians could cope, why not the people of India, no matter how scornful the efficient British might be of their capacity for self-government?

And in fact, how inefficient were the Indians? When, later, Alexander was visiting Santiniketan, Rabindranath Tagore's ashram in rural Bengal, a fire broke out in one of the outbuildings. Tagore and Alexander had been visiting a neighbouring village at the time, and saw the fire from a considerable distance. They rushed back, and on their return half an hour later found that the fire had been admirably dealt with. Students and school pupils had immediately formed double rows between the three wells and the burning shed, and passed buckets of water along so effectively that the fire was brought under control, and damage to other buildings prevented.[60]

This incident may have done more to convince Alexander of India's capacity for self-government than the denunciation of British attitudes which he listened to from Tagore, 'great impression' though that made on him. Tagore might lament the alien nature of the British system, its lack of imagination and insight, the intolerable arrogance of British people in India, creating a slave mentality, but if the Indians themselves had been as hopeless in an emergency as the arrogant Britishers claimed, it might not have been sensible to accelerate progress towards independence.

Anyway, it is clear that one way and another his visit to Santiniketan was decisive in converting Alexander to the nationalist cause. His conversion was reinforced by the attitude of some of the British officials to his main concern, the opium traffic. Before travelling to Bengal he had spent a few days in Delhi, and had had a session with the excise official chiefly concerned with opium matters, one Richard Tottenham. In *The Indian Ferment* he is perfunctorily mentioned as 'T' and no more is said about him, but the relevant journal letter makes clear that Alexander was exasperated by the interview. Tottenham himself was 'well-fed, amiable, condescending, omniscient', and made clear that the Government of India could never contemplate reducing the production of opium to a level sufficient only for medical and scientific purposes. Rajputs eat opium, he said, just as Scots drink whisky. So far as exports went, the Government would eventually meet its international obligations. 'Curiously enough', Alexander remarks, 'he said nothing of its obligations to the people of India.'[61] Significantly, Tottenham's departmental head, Sir B. N.

Mitra, was much more satisfactory, anxious to listen and manifestly concerned for the welfare of his fellow countrymen.

Early in December, while based in Calcutta, Alexander went on a short visit to Orissa. This province contained areas of high opium consumption, and in addition had been suffering serious flooding. Alexander found that far fewer resources had been made available to relieve distress in Orissa than had been the case in similar crises in western India, and that there was much evidence of government neglect.

> I returned to Calcutta feeling more ashamed, more disgusted and sick with the present government of India, more angry and rebellious than I had ever been in my life. I think what I felt most was the callousness of those who should know better.[62]

Later in December he spent two weeks in Assam, this being the province with by far the highest level of opium use. While Richard Tottenham had merely irritated him, the District Commissioner of Dibrugarh (unnamed) managed to make him seriously angry. It is true that on this occasion Alexander was accompanying the delegation from the British Trades Union Congress already mentioned. It consisted of Albert Arthur Purcell (a Labour MP) and Joseph Hallsworth.[63] Purcell's ebullient personality may well have antagonised the Commissioner, and besides he had read a 'very misleading paragraph' about Alexander in the *Times of Assam*, which did not help. Even so, when all allowances had been made, the District Commissioner was intolerable.

> He spent much of his time reviling the Assamese people, and especially the politicians; and an unfortunate Indian official, his junior, had to sit and hear it all, and occasionally say 'Yes' when appealed to to confirm some foolish allegation.[64]

Fortunately, Alexander had an introduction to the Governor of Assam, Sir Laurie Hammond, who was much more satisfactory, though the book gives no details. The journal letters are more illuminating. Hammond is described as a sympathetic and liberal-minded man who was well aware of the evils of opium, and concerned to cooperate with the nationalists to suppress it. Alexander also talked to the Excise Minister, the Rev. Nichols Roy, and got him to admit that the Government couldn't give up so much revenue all at once.

> In the Provincial Council they will never admit that revenue matters at all. On the other hand I was able to tell him and the Governor that my Swarajist friends had all assured me that they were prepared for heavier taxation, to make up for the loss of revenue: this they won't admit in the Council. So I had the pleasure of betraying both sides to the other. In fact there is real goodwill on both sides between the Governor and the Swarajist leaders, so I think my double betrayal may have done some good.

He left Assam with a more hopeful feeling about the Government, and he continued to accept that it was acting in good faith. The trouble was that the lack of trust between officials and politicians was too great to be overcome by such kindly deviousness as Alexander employed. In the printed text he bleakly concludes that 'Government and popular leaders cannot work together today; there is too much mutual suspicion.'[65] And in *Narcotics in India and South Asia* he expresses the wish that the Government could come to terms with the Congress Party and obtain its active support. Until that happened, social reform was scarcely possible, or at least seriously hampered.[66]

After Assam, Alexander spent a day or two before Christmas in Darjeeling with John William Graham, who was also visiting the sub-continent and reaching conclusions much at variance with his son-in-law's. They must have compared notes, perhaps with some heat. Alexander told Edward Milligan years later that 'there was no meeting of minds at all – his father-in-law was solely preoccupied with all the material things (roads, etc.) the British had done.'[67] But in any case the approach of the two men to their visits could hardly have been more different. Graham was exhilarated by the sheer number of the lectures he had given to large audiences. He estimated that he must have addressed about 30,000 people altogether. Alexander took C. F. Andrews' advice not to accept invitations to lecture if he could possibly avoid it, but to stay long enough in a few places to make real friendships.

> Wherever possible, in whatever company I found myself, I tried to find out what was in the minds of others without at first giving expression to my own convictions, showing only that I was anxious to learn and to understand.

It isn't surprising that Alexander's convictions were changed by this experience, whereas Graham remained in full possession of his preconceptions. For him the Indian character was disfigured by moral weakness, lying, bribery, stealing, cheating were endemic. Hinduism had no strength or charm to withstand Christianity. 'It lives in the past. There is a vast mass of helpless inertia: that is all.'[68]

At the end of the month, Alexander went south to Madras to witness the closing sessions of the Indian National Congress being held at that time. His account of this in *The Indian Ferment* emphasises the huge scale of the meeting, but also the very considerable skills manifested in debate. J. M. Sen Gupta, the Mayor of Calcutta and a Cambridge graduate, secured a hearing for a resolution that many Hindus found unpalatable. 'I am sure', Alexander remarks, 'if he is ever a responsible Minister, he will be capable of persuading his followers to accept measures they really detest.'[69]

His old friend Happell was working in Madras, and Alexander saw a good deal of him. *The Indian Ferment* refers briefly to their discussions, Happell insisting on the incapacity of Indians for self-government, Alexander feeling that a spirit was working in India which people like Happell did not perceive. His one concession to 'imperialism' was that he still felt ordinary Indian villagers might be looking to the British rather than to their own leaders for any escape from their misery. If such expectations could be answered, there would be a strong case for maintaining the existing regime.

> But I am afraid we have largely failed. Or rather, perhaps, we have done all that we can do. We have sown the seed, but our Western methods of tending the crop will not do. If it is to ripen, those who know the nature of the soil must tend the crop, even though they seem to us incompetent.[70]

From Madras Alexander went south to Ceylon and from there to the Dutch East Indies. He found less racialism there than in India, and the people more prosperous and better fed. But basically the situation of an alien government was similar. Some of his experiences with Christian missionaries helped to confirm him in his ideas about the nature of true Christian witness. At Solo in mid-Java he found that the Calvinist missionaries were very successful in making converts, but the converts weren't necessarily improved in character. He left the place with a heavy heart: 'success turns the Christian missionary from humble service to proud domination.'[71] The journal letters reveal a more specific source of depression. Alexander was disturbed by the capacity Calvinist missionaries had to make a non-Calvinist like himself feel 'a worm'. They knew about Woodbrooke, and hated what they knew. Anyone with a Woodbrooke connection was immediately suspect.[72]

While Alexander felt no repugnance to Christian orthodoxy as such, provided there were fruits of the spirit to validate it, his encounters with missionaries were often stressful – too stressful to find full expression in the printed text. Thus in Benares he had stayed with the Hudson family, who seemed to him 'to have a most appalling Wesleyan theology, but they were extraordinarily kind to me, and are obviously beloved by many people in Benares.' He adds that he went to a harvest thanksgiving on a wet Sunday night, and then had to lead family evening prayers. 'That nearly finished me off.'[73] None of this is in *The Indian Ferment.*

From Java he returned to India by way of Malaya and Burma picking up information about opium as he went. He was accompanied in Calcutta by an Indian Quaker, Nalin Ganguly, who introduced him to a number of academics who could brief him on India's economic disabilities. He also met Professor Radhakrishnan, the philosopher who was later to become President of the Republic of India. He had only recently returned from a visit to the West, where his lectures had been a great success, and he had had discussions with Cambridge people well known to Alexander, like J. M. Keynes and Lowes Dickinson. It should have been a comfortable occasion for Alexander, but clearly it was nothing of the sort. Radhakrishnan felt that no one in Britain had much understanding of the Indian perspective, and indeed the only person who did have an inkling seemed to be Lord Haldane. As for British Labour people, they had little sympathy with the independence movement, because besides being hopelessly unimaginative, they felt that if India controlled her own tariff policy it would ruin the cotton industry of Lancashire.[74]

After this somewhat sobering beginning to his return to India, he found all the more encouragement in the next stage of his journey. C. F. Andrews joined him in Calcutta, and together they went to Santiniketan for the spring festival, where Alexander was deeply impressed by the performance of a play for the season, with Tagore himself playing the part of the Blind Minstrel who shows the way to renewal of life.[75] It was the Easter message in an Indian idiom, validating the possibility of hope, a promise that would sustain him in his quest.

After this interlude, Alexander travelled to Delhi, where he stayed from 9 to 21 March as the guest of the Principal of St Stephen's College, S. N. Mukarjee, who - he discovered - had been a contemporary of his at Cambridge. There was some opium work to be done: he visited an opium shop with a Miss Campbell who was President of the Women's Christian Temperance Union, and his presence alarmed an elderly man who thought he might be starting to take the drug: 'He kept calling to me in Urdu . . . pleading with me not on any account to begin taking opium. . . . It was poisonous stuff and I should be ruined.'[76] By now, though, Alexander's interest was mainly in the political situation, and he was anxious to meet the leading politicians and to attend a meeting of the Legislative Assembly. The debate that he heard there (on the Finance Bill) reminded him of 'the Puritan leaders of the Long Parliament making their "Grand Remonstrance" against Charles I.' Perhaps recalling the extension lectures in Tunbridge Wells twenty years earlier, he pointed out that Charles was convinced that his rule was for England's good, and that some of the parliamentary leaders were narrow-minded men with an eye to their own class interests. None the less, 'the call to liberty is a noble call'. Motilal Nehru and Lajpat Rai will be honoured as Pym and Hampden are.[77]

From Delhi Alexander travelled to Ahmedabad and to the ashram of that great puritan M. K. Gandhi. It was strikingly ascetic in contrast to the joyous aestheticism of Tagore's educational centre at Santiniketan, but he found it no less a happy place, particularly in its children, who were in the habit of accompanying Gandhi on his daily walk. 'He marches briskly along with half a dozen children dancing along beside him, and the favoured one of the day (each in turn, I fancy) holds his hand.' Alexander had several talks with Gandhi in the early morning, cutting up vegetables in preparation for the main meals of the day, but it was at his first, formal, interview, at 4 o'clock one afternoon, that a good understanding was reached. During his travels he had been increasingly distressed by the unwillingness of Indians to believe that the British could ever understand their needs or sympathise with their aspirations. He had pleaded for patience, but without success, even with a friendly citizen of the world like Radhakrishnan. Gandhi, at least, might be more persuadable.

And he was, though not immediately. 'Well', he said, 'first we want you to get off our backs.' Alexander made clear that he was well aware of that, but the problem was 'how the mind of Britain could be so changed as to perceive that we have become a burden on the back of India, and that we need not be and must not be so.' As they talked, Gandhi showed that he appreciated that the British would want to feel that they were doing the right thing because it was the right thing, and not just because of the pressure of events. He was quite willing to go along with this.[78]

The full significance of the meetings with Gandhi is perhaps somewhat muted in *The Indian Ferment*, though Alexander does conclude that, together, Gandhi, Tagore and the Servants of India Society are working for the growth of a strong, enlightened people. He is less reticent in an article he wrote for the *Woodbrooke Journal* on his return. Gandhi, he wrote, is essentially a Quaker, or rather:

> the kind of man my ideal Quaker would be: a man full of practical sense, intensely alive to present evils, to injustice and cruelty, spending himself in the effort to overthrow them; wise and tolerant, sympathetic and affectionate, wonderfully modest; but above all deeply religious, sure of himself insofar as he is sure of divine guidance, seeking not his own will but the will of God, to whose voice he is ever attentive.[79]

Clearly Alexander had found a leadership more dependable and inspiring than anything he had known before. And like the two TUC men, he was impressed by the potential of the people – the 'big-hearted, full-souled mass of workers' as Purcell and Hallsworth described them.[80] This sense of a power with which it would be right to cooperate was above all what he brought back from his travels. As he put it, in 'Silence: An Indian Adventure',

> wherever I went – most of all among the Servants of India, at Santiniketan and at Sabarmati – I was dimly conscious of some new element, difficult to define, but real – as if some deep impulse of spring-time were stirring – that made my war-sick European heart and mind throb with fresh hope. It was like the sight of the first summer migrant to the bird-lover after months of frost and snow and biting east-winds.[81]

In this mood the rest of his time in India passed quickly. He revisited the Friends' mission in Central India, where he was impressed by the way Geoffrey Maw had earned the confidence of local people - a model of the kind of service that the British could still offer. Then back to Bombay, and to Britain.

4

QUAKER INTERVENTIONS

Tagore at Yearly Meeting, and some consequences

As we have seen, Alexander lost no time on his return in affirming his support for Gandhi's leadership of the Indian national movement. It was a view associated at the time with the radical left wing in British politics, and did not instantly appeal to many Quakers. This was all the more apparent because of the accelerating tempo of nationalist campaigning in India itself. In 1928 a series of All-Party Conferences in India responded to the Simon Commission by drafting a scheme for Dominion status, usually called the Nehru Report after its principal author Motilal Nehru. Alexander thought highly of the document, considering that its approach to the communal problem was exceptionally enlightened. In essentials, communal conflicts resembled the 'minority problem' in the states created by the Treaty of Versailles. 'It would be well', said Alexander in an unpublished paper evidently written at this time, 'if the States of Europe had the prospect of being governed by men of such enlightenment' as the authors of the Report. In any case, its proposals,

> formulated after long discussion, and taking advantage of several earlier proposals, indicate pretty clearly the mind of educated India today; and it is unlikely that any more modest proposals will be accepted by those Indians whose co-operation we are bound to seek.

They provided an opportunity to meet the acknowledged leaders of India on a basis of equality, with respect and with confidence. 'Such an approach', he concluded, 'will get an immediate response from India, and may be for the lasting benefit of two continents.'[1]

In fact, the Nehru Report was being contemptuously dismissed in the British press ('half-baked, superficial, impracticable, unrepresentative, alien to the spirit of the East, clever devices for bargaining'): alienation and misunderstanding were thus further intensified. And of course there were many in India who regarded Motilal's moderation with impatience. At the Congress session in Calcutta in December 1928, Motilal's son Jawaharlal, and other younger leaders like Subhas Bose, argued in favour of *purna swaraj*, complete independence. A compromise was reached, agreeing to give the Government of India a year to accept the recommendations of the Nehru Report, failing which there would be a demand for complete independence, backed by a campaign of civil disobedience.

There was no great expectation that the 'year of grace' would elicit a positive British response, and throughout 1929 Gandhi was touring different parts of India preparing his hearers for the 'fiery ordeal' of civil disobedience, and incidentally himself igniting a bonfire of foreign cloth in Calcutta, the signal for a campaign to boycott such imports. But at the end of May a Labour government was elected in Britain which was rather more disposed than its predecessor to pay attention to Indian aspirations. The Viceroy, Lord Irwin, was himself anxious to win the support of moderate nationalists for measured progress towards self-government, and after consultation with the new Secretary of State for India, Wedgwood Benn, he issued a declaration (31 October 1929) that 'the natural issue of India's constitutional progress . . . is the attainment of Dominion status'. The steps to be taken to this end would be the subject of a Round Table Conference in London.

A joint statement by senior Congressmen and Liberals gave a conditional welcome to this initiative, but among younger activists there was too vehement a determination to press for complete independence to allow any agreement on the basis of Irwin's declaration. At the session of Congress held in Lahore at the year's end, while there was much lobbying and bargaining, the upshot was a stirring call to independence by the Congress President, Jawaharlal Nehru. At midnight on the 31st the tricolour flag of an independent India was raised amid general acclaim.

Back in Britain there began to be an increasing readiness to accept the validity of the Congress claims. Suhash Chakravarty, in his useful account of Krishna Menon and the India League, has shown how groups throughout the country were being formed to support Indian aspirations. Menon himself was tireless in organising such groups, and among other initiatives secured cooperation from the Adult School movement, a network closely associated with the Society of Friends.[2] In August 1929 Alexander himself made contact with Menon to develop the campaign in Birmingham,[3] and the Birmingham Council for Indian Freedom organised a well-attended meeting in Birmingham Town Hall some time in January 1930, with Alexander in the chair. Most significant of all, perhaps, was the conversion of the editor of *The Spectator*, Evelyn Wrench, to the view that the case for Indian self-government deserved respectful consideration. Wrench was committed to the idea of the Commonwealth as an association of free peoples, and Menon played some part in persuading him to apply this principle to India. *The Spectator* was very much of an establishment weekly, but it deliberately opened its columns to a balanced discussion of the issues. This did not please some of its readers, who complained that it might be lending its influence to 'deep-laid schemes for breaking up the connexion of England with India'. But the editor replied that 'telling the politically-minded in India that they are naughty children and must be kept permanently in the schoolroom will, in our view, lead inevitably to the breaking-off of India from the British Commonwealth'.[4]

As it happened, Alexander also had access to a first-hand account of developments in India from his former Woodbrooke charge, Reginald Reynolds. In 1929, Reynolds, being in a state of uncertainty about what he should do with his life, had taken up a suggestion of Alexander's that he should spend some time with Gandhi in India. Alexander recalled that in the vivid journal-letters that Reynolds was sending back to the Friends' Service Council, he was clearly uneasy about the militant course of action adopted by Congress, feeling as he did that the Labour Government genuinely wanted to meet India's just demands.[5] On the other hand, he admired Gandhi as much as Alexander did, and agreed to carry the message that Gandhi addressed to the Viceroy formally announcing the campaign of civil disobedience. The salt tax – uniquely oppressive to the poor – was the first manifestation of imperial rule to be targeted, and the attack was initiated by a march from the Sabarmati ashram to Dandi, on the coast north of Bombay, with meetings organised at every stop. It was at Dandi on 6 April that Gandhi committed a technical breach of the law by picking up a handful of salt from the beach. A month later he announced he would lead a raid on the Dharasana salt works, and at this point, on 4 May, he was arrested. Protests and demonstrations erupted all over India.

It was at this time of high tension in India, and corresponding alarm and estrangement in Britain, that Rabindranath Tagore arrived in Britain to deliver the Hibbert Lectures in Oxford. These lectures, subsequently published as *The Religion of Man*, were a definitive exposition of his synthesis of opposing philosophical systems, coming to him 'through the same unseen and trackless channel' as did the inspiration of his songs. If he referred to Indo-British relations, he did so obliquely through the Indian colonists who figure in the *Ramayana*, representing 'the change of the people's aspiration from the path of conquest to that of reconciliation'.[6] But reconciliation was a long way off in May 1930, though Tagore was very much committed to it. He was ready to brave nationalist indignation at his acceptance of a visit from the Governor of Bengal just as Gandhi was preparing his campaign, thus gaining a useful grant for his educational work from the British authorities. Through his contact with Alexander it had been possible to appoint one of his young Bengali scholars, Amiya Chakravarty, as a fellow of Woodbrooke, and while in Britain Tagore himself made his base there, thus opening up the possibility of forging further links between the Quaker settlement and Santiniketan.

The Woodbrooke log-book vividly communicates the excitement which Tagore's arrival created. As early as 29 April he was thought to be coming soon. On the 30th it seemed that he was not coming soon. Next day he was coming in a week, the day after in a fortnight, the day after that – some time! On the 12th he was expected hourly, and on the 13th he actually arrived. A few hours after his arrival, Amiya Chakravarty's wife Haimanti gave birth to a daughter, who of course had to be named by Tagore, and was: Shaimonti, or little red flower.

Tagore lost no time in writing to the *Manchester Guardian*, deploring recent measures in India, which showed Britain to be an exploiter and upholder of race supremacy (16 May), and in Woodbrooke itself he gave a talk warning his hearers against the mechanical forms of modern civilisation, to which people too readily adapt themselves, so becoming part of a deadening process.[7]

As a prophet of undogmatic religion who was moreover a Nobel prize-winner and the founder of an educational institution with which Friends were in sympathy, it was natural for Friends in an adventurous mood to invite Tagore to address a special session of Yearly Meeting. In his 'Indian Adventure' manuscript, Alexander claims that he had wanted him to talk about Santiniketan and his educational ideals, and how Friends could cooperate with him. With his distinguished figure, fine face and beautiful voice – a magical combination of the aesthete and the prophet – the effect would have been irresistible. But it was 24 May, Empire Day as it was then celebrated, and the papers were full of reports of further attacks in India on salt works, with accompanying arrests, together with claims that Moscow was exploiting Indian troubles for the benefit of world revolution. While *The Spectator* called for greater imagination and sympathy on the British side, the Labour-supporting *New Statesman* had been assuring its readers that Gandhi's day was over, that revolution and violence were inseparable, and that the Government must now be prepared to deal with a revolutionary India, 'stimulated in an incalculable degree by a prophet whom it could not follow'.[8] Tagore had his differences with Gandhi, but this kind of dismissal was intolerable. The truth must be told, a gathering of Quakers was one where he might make some impression, and, if we may believe a rather indignant Alexander, C. F. Andrews and Jack Hoyland positively encouraged him to speak out, against Alexander's judgement and behind his back.[9]

It may not have been the most prudent thing to do, but it was great theatre. There is in any case an inherent drama in sessions of Friends' Yearly Meeting in London. The thousand or so people present are accustomed to sustained periods of silence which heighten expectancy and enhance attentiveness. Tagore's exotic presence would intensify this sense of drama, the more so because of his coming from a troubled land with an uncertain future, inextricably linked with Britain's. In the gallery there were many young people, eleven years old and upwards. The somewhat older 'Young Friends' were in the body of the hall, though they were to meet separately – and to some effect – on the following day. And of course there was a full attendance of older Friends, from all over the country.

Alexander himself introduced the session, hoping that those present would search their hearts in penitence for whatever was preventing their two peoples from coming into a union of hearts. Perhaps a call could be made for 'repentance at the foot of the Cross of Christ': a sense of national humiliation might disperse the clouds of bitterness. Then Tagore spoke. He condemned British rule in India as a life-destroying machine, disfigured by a 'dark chasm of aloofness instead of the living touch of sympathy'. He pleaded for 'a generous co-operation from both sides' and a willingness to make allowances for the weaknesses in human nature in order to keep a faith in human nature. He urged his hearers to affirm their trust

> in the life that creates and not in the machine that constructs, in the power that hides its force and blossoms in beauty, and not in the power that bares its arms and chuckles at its capacity to make itself obnoxious.[10]

Jack Hoyland was quick to underline Tagore's message by comparing the struggle for Indian freedom to the campaigns against slavery, and urging Yearly Meeting to pass Tagore's message on to the Labour Party. But this was far from the feeling of some of those present, and their convictions were forcibly expressed by John William Graham, who was evidently not best pleased at this moment with his son-in-law. He was sorry that Yearly Meeting had entered on a political discussion, but felt it necessary to deny that Britain ruled India in order to aggrandise itself. Rabindranath Tagore and Mahatma Gandhi created much too favourable an impression of their fellow countrymen, who in the mass were difficult and childish. To leave India now would be to enslave it the more, because of its many hostile divisions. What Tagore and Andrews should be doing ('Horace too', one imagines him thinking) is getting Gandhi to stop his rebellion.

Although succeeding speakers were generally more sympathetic to Tagore, Graham had made a wholehearted endorsement impossible. The text of Tagore's address had been published as a Friends' Service Council pamphlet, and this had to be withdrawn and reissued without the FSC imprint. After the Yearly Meeting session, Graham was congratulated on his intervention by some of those who had been actively critical of the Society's peace witness during the First World War, and the Clerk, Harold Morland, happening to pass by, remarked 'Strange company to find thee in, John Willie!'[11]

But that was not the end of the matter. The day following, Young Friends' session in the Small Meeting House was dominated by responses to Tagore's address. C. F. Andrews spoke, and made a deep impression by his warm appreciation of Lord Irwin as well as Gandhi. Myrtle Wright, the Clerk of Young Friends, spoke of the tragedy of both Irwin and Gandhi doing what they felt was right, but still finding themselves in conflict. The final minute affirmed Friends' conviction that 'no race or nation has the right to impose its will upon any other. We wish to record our profound belief in the right of India to choose freely what is to be her relationship to Britain.' This conviction would have far-reaching consequences, but light would be given to carry out the necessary measures.

This minute was taken back to the main session of Yearly Meeting, and Myrtle Wright insisted that Friends must be ready to trust the spirit of God that dwelt in others as well as in ourselves. The meeting was able to come together on agreement to take risks for peace, urging the leaders on both sides to 'take some definite step towards reconciliation and thus release all the latent forces of goodwill which are now failing of expression'. A deputation was to go to the Prime Minister.[12]

Alexander felt that all this public drama was not in the least helpful to plans that were being formed behind the scenes. C. F. Andrews returned from South Africa to Britain at the end of April, and as he enjoyed the full measure of Gandhi's trust, and was genuinely respected by Lord Irwin, he seemed the obvious person to bridge the gulf that had opened between the two leaders. But Andrews felt he was too obvious. The task was one that had to be done quietly. Andrews was too well known: he would be dogged by reporters whose persistence would inevitably frustrate his mission. So he turned to Alexander and said, 'You must go'.[13]

Recalling this moment in 'Silence: An Indian Adventure', Alexander admitted that his first reaction was angry. Andrews seemed to think it was as easy for him to drop everything and book a passage to India as it was for Andrews himself. He apparently had no conception of what it meant to leave an invalid wife, and he certainly made no attempt to help Alexander talk it over with Olive. Left to Andrews, Alexander might well have remained in Britain, finding someone else to undertake the mission. But Amiya Chakravarty was more persuasive. He at least had some idea of what it was to be separated from wife and child, and showed that he understood Alexander's resistance. But surely, he said, everything that had gone before was leading up to this call. Alexander already enjoyed Gandhi's confidence; he could take with him a letter of introduction from Tagore. He was known as someone committed to reconciliation.[14]

Alexander capitulated. 'And so, in great agony of mind, I had to confess late one night to Olive that this burden was laid on me. And though it was harder for her than for me, she too accepted it.'[15] His colleagues in Woodbrooke accepted it too, promising to see that his work was done if he should be delayed in India. Thus released, he set about devising a strategy for his approaches to Irwin and Gandhi.

Since his return from India in 1928 he had become acquainted with the mother of Sir George Schuster, the Finance Member of the Viceroy's Council. Hilda Schuster was a Friend, and very much concerned to promote the welfare of India. She had contributed generously to Tagore's work at Santiniketan. Alexander was sure that she would help him to meet her son, and to discuss with him practical ways of improving the economic and social conditions in the sub-continent. Since Gandhi's first priority was improving the lot of the poor, this seemed a solid basis for cooperation. If Gandhi could be convinced that the Government of India was ready to meet his demands for reducing military expenditure, prohibiting drink and drugs, abolishing the salt tax and so on, this would be a great step towards political agreement.[16] Sir George Schuster himself was certainly a promising contact: he was politically in the Liberal camp, and after his return from India served as a National Liberal MP. After the war he played a crucial role in the setting up of Voluntary Service Overseas, and of the United World College of the Atlantic. An obituary in *The Times* described him 'a rare combination of the idealist, the intellectual, the man of action, the sportsman and the patriot'. Alexander was to find in him a powerful ally.[17]

Alexander's next step was to obtain support from the wider body of Friends. He had already received encouragement from such sympathetic correspondents as his old science master, Hugh Richardson, who saw in the non-cooperation movement a parallel with early seventeenth-century opposition to Stuart absolutism.[18] He was emboldened to approach the Indian Affairs Committee and through them the July Meeting for Sufferings, where he found favour to an extent that he hadn't expected.

> Margaret Sefton Jones, whose political creed is that of the *Morning Post*, gave the mission her blessing; and a member unknown to me said that he didn't suppose he agreed with my politics, but he was sure I was being led by God and that I should follow his leading.[19]

His old patron Frederick Merttens had independently reached the conclusion that Alexander should go to India, and he embarked on his mission amply assured of a great measure of goodwill from within the Society of Friends, and, even more, the encouragement of an atmosphere of cheerful hope. Carl Heath wanted him to report on his interviews with Gandhi in ornithological code: 'I saw a fine Paradise Flycatcher at Poona yesterday.' But, he told Olive, 'I think I had better not, really.'[20]

Alexander needed someone to go with him, given the political stresses and the sheer physical strain of travelling through the hot weather, and he found a companion in one of his friends in the Indian YMCA in Gower Street. This was Robin Rutnam, son of a Sinhalese father and a Canadian mother, a man who had little patience with the more facile kinds of nationalism, but who encountered racial insults with total self-confidence, and knew how to stand his ground without aggressiveness. At first he thought Alexander's project rather mad, but as he took in the details he exclaimed that he wished he could come too. Alexander accepted the offer, and C. F. Andrews gave it his blessing. Reginald Reynolds, when he heard about it, thought Alexander was demented to take a Christian and an Anglo-Indian, but then he didn't know Rutnam.

Through Philip Noel Baker, Alexander secured a meeting with the Secretary of State for India, Wedgwood Benn, and secured his blessing. 'I did not feel that he had much grasp of the situation', Alexander remarked, 'nor yet that he had much understanding of my mission.' Still, he agreed to write favourably to the Viceroy, and that was the main thing.[21]

At the last minute, Alexander received an additional commission, which proved to be of crucial importance. An elderly Westmorland Quaker, Harrison Jackson, who believed that from time to time he received very definite 'leadings' of the spirit, had received a leading that needed to be communicated to Gandhi. He had no idea how to do this, and then he read of Alexander's mission in a report of Meeting for Sufferings. So he travelled to London to press his message on Alexander. The message was not one that Alexander particularly wanted to deliver. 'It was friendly, but it told him he had gone wrong.'

> I was not sure that he had gone wrong. Could I honestly be the bearer of such a message? In the end I felt I could, for I believed that Harrison Jackson's 'leadings' were apt to be right; and though I was not clear that Mr Gandhi had gone wrong, yet I was not clear that he had not gone wrong. So I undertook this added burden.[22]

Much more welcome were the many written messages of support for his mission of reconciliation, which he carried with him to produce whenever it was helpful to show the extent to which he was genuinely representative of British Friends.

*

This particular mission is worth recounting in some detail if only because it helps one to understand the mode of operation that Alexander adopted in later work of mediation and conciliation. He certainly attached great significance to it himself, writing two extended accounts of it which were, however, never published.[23] The essential conviction that emerges from it is the willingness to endure continual disappointments, and the need to accept that a mission may have no apparent positive result, even when in the long run it turns out to have made a genuine contribution to solving a dispute.

*

Alexander and Rutnam set off on 23 July, Alexander himself having seen Philip and Irene Noel-Baker, the Parmoors and Srinivasi Sastri during the day. While Lord Parmoor had been encouraging, Sastri was 'quite pessimistic' about the mission – a foretaste of the distrust which Alexander was to find so depressing through much of this visit. The two men went to Paris, and then on to Marseilles, where they embarked on the P&O ship, the *Macedonia*. They arrived in Bombay on 8 August. The voyage had been uneventful if argumentative, they being of very different tastes and temperaments: Rutnam was frank and open, Alexander kept himself to himself in a way that irritated his companion considerably. Still, Alexander benefited from the intrepid way that Rutnam broke down the usual colour-bar in the second class, and had many conversations with his Indian fellow travellers.

From Bombay they travelled to Delhi and then on to Simla, where the Government of India was based during the hot weather. They were in Delhi for long enough to attend great demonstrations and a public meeting, where they were struck by the large number of women present.[24] They also met the Congress President, Dr Ansari, briefing him on their mission's purpose. It was a delicate moment, as the civil disobedience campaign had led to arrests on a massive scale, and the entire Congress Working Committee was in jeopardy: Dr Ansari was himself to be arrested only a week or so later. In spite of the acute tension, Ansari was interested in the thinking behind the mission, and indeed impressed by it. Alexander thought it clear that 'he would do everything in his power to persuade the Congress to accept peace with the Government on honourable terms'.[25]

Thus encouraged, Alexander and Rutnam went on to Simla, and found Sir George Schuster as welcoming as they could possibly have hoped. Admittedly they encountered the first really distressing instance of India's social divisions, in that Alexander was invited to stay with Sir George while Rutnam had to make do with a room at the YMCA. Here and subsequently Alexander's intention to have his companion accepted on equal terms was a complete failure, and it is clear that he almost despaired at the all-pervasive separation of the races, and the Europeans' unconscious condescension (at best) that went with it. Still, in respect of the mission itself, Sir George was very willing to endorse the idea of making a large allocation to fund an ambitious programme of economic development, with a proper emphasis on 'village uplift'.[26]

The next step was to see the Viceroy himself, and Lord Irwin invited Alexander to lunch on 19 August. Alexander found him disarmingly friendly and unostentatious, apparently quite unconcerned by his Quaker visitor's inability to punctuate his remarks with the obligatory 'Sir' at appropriate moments. They had half an hour's private talk after lunch, of which Alexander left no record either in his letters to Olive or in 'Silence', except to say that he was encouraged by it, and that Irwin seemed 'even less obsessed by administrative obstacles than Schuster'. He formed the opinion that the outlook wasn't hopeless, 'though it will be a stiff fight with the diehards in England, and in the Government here, perhaps also with the ultra-nationalist, ultra-Gandhi Congressmen here.'[27]

He had good reason to believe that the Congress President at least would be supportive, and Ansari was one of the people he was to see on returning to Delhi. Another was his fellow committee member Pandit Madan Mohan Malaviya. Alexander told Olive that he now realised why her father had disliked him so much (he was 'no economist', and given to wild and unconvincing assertions). But 'he is really a dear old man', evidently a charmer if not a persuader.[28] It was on the following day that they had an appointment with Ansari. They had to wait a little while, and Alexander explained his plan in outline to Ansari's secretary, who noted down the main points. At this very moment, however, large numbers of police converged on the house to arrest Ansari and other members of the Congress Working Committee there gathered. Ansari came out on the balcony to greet Alexander and regret that he couldn't offer him hospitality: 'Perhaps there will be another opportunity.' The committee members were then carried off to prison, with the utmost courtesy and 'rather an excessive show of armed police' – last of all Ansari and Malaviya: 'As they passed us they waved a gay farewell, like schoolboys off on a holiday.' Alexander was very moved by the self-restraint shown by all concerned.[29]

There was nothing more to be done in Delhi, so Alexander and Rutnam went on to Bombay. Obtaining an interview with Gandhi was far from straightforward, he being in the Yeravda prison in Poona, which was under the jurisdiction of the Governor of Bombay Province, Sir Frederick Sykes. The Viceroy had proposed that Alexander should be allowed to visit, but Sykes was reluctant, and the telegram authorising Alexander to meet Gandhi did not come. Alexander and Rutnam waited, and waited, until Rutnam grew tired of waiting and caught the next ship back to England. Alexander's patience snapped too, and he decided to go to Poona – the hot weather seat of government in Bombay – and present himself to the Governor. This tactic paid off: Alexander was duly invited to lunch with Sykes and his Home Member, Sir J. E. B. Hotson, where he had a surprisingly pleasant chat with Lady Sykes, a daughter of Bonar Law and familiar with parts of Kent well known to Alexander. Sykes himself was friendly, Hotson not. But neither could understand why Alexander should want to interfere at this particular moment. Gandhi was engaged in negotiations with two leading Indian liberals, Sir Tej Bahadur Sapru and M. R. Jayakar, to see if they could find a formula which would be acceptable both to Gandhi and the Government. Alexander explained that he was less concerned with formulae than with a genuine basis for cooperation. He added that he had a message from Harrison Jackson, which he felt bound to deliver. 'Of course', said Hotson scornfully, 'if there were something religious or mystical that you wanted to say, that is another matter.' Alexander, resenting the scornful tone, replied sharply that he didn't want *that* to influence the decision.

Still, it probably did. Alexander admitted to Olive that if he did see Gandhi it would be 'largely' because of that message. He had had to persuade the Governor that he was 'likely to be useful (or should I say harmless?)'. Reginald Reynolds, he remarked, would probably prefer the latter interpretation – 'and I am almost driven to it myself.'[30] While the Sapru–Jayakar talks were going on, the assumption was that Alexander would not be allowed in to complicate matters, and while Alexander himself had mixed feelings about this, he agreed that he was glad not to be involved with 'a game of political intrigue': while that was being played, 'it is far better that I should be brushed aside.' It is clear though, that he didn't actually relish being brushed aside.

While waiting in Poona, Alexander stayed with the head of a little Montessori school, Jehangir Vakil. Vakil introduced him to the editor of *Servant of India*, and through him Alexander was able to meet Sapru. Sapru proved to be quite willing to allow Alexander to accompany him to Gandhi, but by this time Alexander felt that he should persist in waiting to go by himself, and indeed these political negotiations came to an end within a couple of days.

Alexander was authorised to see Gandhi at 11.45am on Monday 8 September, and he duly went along to the prison in good time, carrying flowers tied together with yarn that he had spun himself, under the tuition of Mrs Vakil. He was received by the Superintendent, who was concerned to assure him that it had been most interesting to have these nationalists in his charge. 'Mr Gandhi', he told him, 'is really quite a sahib.' Motilal Nehru was rated even more highly: 'he is a real pukka sahib.'

So they met, and the first thing that Alexander learnt was that, until Sapru mentioned his name, Gandhi had no idea that Alexander was in India at all. Next, presumably on the principle that unpleasant business should be got out of the way as soon as possible, Alexander presented Gandhi with Harrison Jackson's message. Gandhi received it quite amicably: 'I suppose "taking the wrong course" means my march to the sea to manufacture salt.' Several good friends had said this at the time, but the decision was taken after prayerful consideration, and he had rarely felt so convinced of doing right. Alexander felt prompted to say:

> 'No, I am not sure that the message means that. Perhaps it means that you took a wrong course when you lost faith in the good intentions of the Government. Perhaps it was when you began to distrust their good faith that you went wrong.' And to this he replied: 'I must tell you plainly that I have been disappointed with Lord Irwin. We were told that he was a good man. But I find him less friendly to Indian freedom than one or two of his predecessors – Lord Hardinge for instance. I certainly have lost faith in him. And I have seen nothing so far that would justify me in trusting him.'[31]

Alexander told Gandhi of his own high opinion of Irwin, but this apparently made not the slightest impression.

They then turned to the proposals that had been agreed to by Schuster, and Gandhi liked them. They evidently prompted him to clarify some parts of Congress policy that had been misunderstood, in particular insisting that it wasn't true that he wanted to repudiate India's debts, but would like them to be impartially assessed. But he wanted Alexander to take the proposals to certain Congress people in Bombay, and to get the opinion of the two Nehrus, Motilal and Jawaharlal.

And that was it. Alexander duly reported back to Sykes and, after consultation with Sir Purshottamdas Thakurdas and others in Bombay, to Irwin himself. To the latter he pointed out that his aim throughout had been to re-establish confidence: 'If the leaders on both sides would show towards each other the confidence and candour they have so generously shown towards me, I am confident that an understanding could very quickly be reached.'[32]

While waiting in Poona, Alexander occupied himself with visits to the Christa Seva Sangha, the Christian ashram where Verrier Elwin worked, and to the Servants of India Society. He was pleased by the good social work carried on by the former, and intrigued to find that, though they did not reckon to proselytise, they were more concerned with theology than was quite comfortable for him. One member had heard one of John William Graham's innumerable lectures, and pressed Alexander on the importance of sacraments. 'I did not rise to his worms (or flies?)' he told Olive, 'as well as he hoped I should.' As for the Servants of India, he told them about the stirrings of sympathy in Britain for Indian aspirations, and felt that he had made a real impression on the group. A renewal of goodwill was a genuine possibility, but there was such a long way to go, and time was running out. 'But we must try to be patient and courageous.'[33]

Jehangir Vakil and his wife were sympathetic hosts, though Vakil himself was far to the left in politics, and thought his guest was suffering from pacifist delusions. This opinion was evidently shared by his three-year-old daughter,

> a small person of tireless energy, inexhaustible appetite, and somewhat uncertain temper, much too bewitching to be effectively crushed. In fact

> it is very certain that however long Britain may hold on to India, we shall have to give up when she comes of age. Already she struts around in a Gandhi cap, when she can find one, and does her best to 'boycott British goods'.

Assuming that coming of age means being 21, the prediction was remarkably accurate. She appeared to regard Alexander with deep distrust, but her mother told him that the young woman planned to travel to England with him, which he interpreted as a mark of esteem.[34]

Gandhi had told him to consult the Nehrus, and so Alexander now went to Allahabad, where they were held in prison. On his way he stopped in Nagpur, at the college where Jack Hoyland had worked. At dinner he was seated next to 'a dear old die-hard lady', a Mrs MacFadyen.

> Of course I did not attempt to argue [he told Olive], but rather encouraged her to run on, until she reached a point (as I expected she would: they nearly all do) where she had exhausted her power of invective, and then proceeded to tell me of the good and hopeful things in the country.

He felt more kindly to Mrs MacFadyen than he did to some of the Quaker missionaries, whom he met a day later in Itarsi. They appalled him by their contempt for the local people, and of course they were out of touch with their real feelings about politics. Alexander had a chance to talk to one of the Indian Friends when no missionary was present, and found that he sympathised with the national movement: 'The simple fact is that every self-respecting Indian, of every creed and caste, is sick to death of the bad manners and 'we know better than you' attitude of practically all Europeans, including missionaries, and Friend missionaries.' Still, even the missionaries appreciated that his was an important and difficult peacemaking initiative, and he went off with their blessing.[35]

From Itarsi he travelled to Allahabad, arriving there on 16 September. He immediately went to see Jawaharlal Nehru's sister, Mrs Pandit, but a letter of introduction from Bombay had not arrived: she had no idea who he was or what his intentions were, so he felt it best to book a room in a hotel and then come back and explain himself. In the interval the reassuring letter had arrived, and Mrs Pandit bestirred herself on his behalf, telephoning the prison to see if a visit could be arranged. It could not, and a little later a letter from Lord Irwin arrived regretting that, because Congress had been interpreting the Sapru–Jayakar talks as an intimation of capitulation by the Government, it wasn't appropriate to let Alexander visit. On the other hand, Motilal was being released on account of his poor health, and obviously he could go and see him.[36]

Mrs Pandit had been most friendly, but rather discouraging about Alexander's mission itself. 'I have no heart for peace', she told him, 'but if you can get it, it will no doubt be good for the country.' He was hardly surprised at her scepticism, considering that her husband was currently in prison just for making a speech (an inaudible speech at that), and her car taken to pay a fine – 'pure vindictiveness, as far as one can see, on the part of an angry government that is rapidly losing its head.'[37]

Motilal was taken by his daughter to their house in the hills at Mussoorie, so to Mussourie Alexander went too. Again he had to endure the now familiar experience of waiting, in this case waiting for the sick man to be well enough to receive a visitor. He stayed at the Savoy Hotel, where he met a number of Indians who held senior posts in government or were landowners. One, a Muslim magistrate from Lahore, was a Cambridge graduate. He had known Oscar Browning and J. M. Keynes, and remembered his time there with a warm appreciation of the kindness he had received. Another, G. S. Dutt, turned out to be the author of a book with whose publication Olive had been associated. This was *A Woman of India*, an appreciation of his wife who had died at a relatively early age. At the suggestion of C. F. Andrews the text was sent to Olive to have its English rendered more idiomatic. Now he appeared in Mussourie and Alexander and he went hill-walking together. When it became clear that Alexander would have to stay over the weekend, Dutt suggested that there should be a Quaker meeting for worship in the hotel.

He had, it turned out, a particular reason for doing this. A prison superintendent, who happened to occupy the next room to his, had shown him a private circular from Sir Malcolm Hailey, Governor of the United Provinces, warning all officials to have nothing to do with Alexander, who was going around spreading false stories about what high officers of the Government of India had said to him, and seeking unauthorised access to political prisoners. Dutt was indignant at this underhand slander, and in part simply wanted people like the superintendent to see for themselves the kind of person Alexander was.

And so the meeting took place. In retrospect it seemed to Alexander to be the high point of his expedition. Just ten people were there, all of them Indians apart from Alexander, all eminently 'reliable' from the point of view of the British Government, all deeply unhappy at the sharpness of the confrontation between Government and Congress. Dutt in particular was profoundly grateful to Alexander for trying to find a way out of the confrontation. But the meeting itself had no direct bearing on the political situation.

After about twenty minutes of silence, Alexander spoke a few words about the difficulties he'd experienced in maintaining his faith in the essential goodness of man, and the importance of remaining steadfast in that faith none the less. One of the judges present said he had been reflecting on how short he had fallen of his duty to God, and another remarked how unimportant religious differences were: the true religion was that of service. Others apparently added short testimonies in the same sense. And then it was over.

If it isn't immediately obvious why the occasion should have impressed Alexander so deeply, one must appreciate how insistently stressful the whole visit to India at this time must have been. The situation was extremely tense, and he must often have felt that the odds against making a significant impression were very daunting. The meeting for worship will have provided a rare moment of unconditional affirmation and trust, the more impressive because of its including both Muslims and Hindus. He had appreciated the goodwill shown by the Viceroy and Schuster, by Gandhi and Ansari, but meeting with them was inevitably complicated by the political objectives, the sense of bargaining. The meeting in Mussourie had nothing of that. It was a foretaste of the friendship that might be possible once India was free. It filled him, he said, with infinite hope.[38]

The remainder of Alexander's visit was something of an anti-climax. He did eventually see Motilal, but Motilal would agree to nothing while his son was in prison, and in any case he was less impressed by Schuster's proposals than Gandhi had been. He insisted on the British Government's acceptance of his own proposals for a Constituent Assembly based on universal suffrage. As for Jawaharlal, Alexander stayed long enough in Allahabad to meet him immediately after his release from prison. The younger Nehru impressed Alexander greatly by his fine, sensitive face, the face of a poet or a saint rather than that of a political leader. But their talk achieved little, except to confirm that Congress did not mean to repudiate India's debts in the Russian fashion, but wished to have them independently assessed, perhaps by the League of Nations. Finally, Alexander asked him if he had any message for the English people, or for the Government. No, he didn't. 'What would be the good of my concocting some fine-sounding message to send?' Alexander reflected that after all his life, his action, his renewed imprisonment were a sufficient message, and if anyone wanted more they should read his presidential address to the Lahore Congress, 'in which he sees a world of interdependent peoples, set free from political and social tyranny and maladjustment'.[39]

He was able to see the Viceroy again, and told him of Harrison Jackson's message, and of Gandhi's response. He felt that Gandhi's loss of trust made a deep impression on Irwin:

> He took it quietly and humble-mindedly. 'After all', he said, 'that sort of thing cannot be proved by demonstration. Trust is an attitude of mind.' I don't remember if he said it could only come by personal intercourse. Later events led me to believe that he meant that.[40]

One thing that Irwin said in this conversation struck Alexander very much. It evidently slipped out in an unguarded moment. 'Yes', he said, 'I do want to see the Indians running their own show.' 'Oh', Alexander responded, perhaps a little too fervently, 'I wish you would let me go to Mr Gandhi again to repeat that to him.' 'No', said Irwin resolutely, 'it is no use now. We must wait.' And Alexander saw that that was as far as he was going to get this time.[41]

One interesting fact emerged from this interview. Alexander mentioned the circular about him which had been seen by G. S. Dutt. Irwin said that a letter from Alexander had been found among Ansari's papers, detailing Schuster's proposals. This was sent to the Governor of the Punjab, who forwarded it to Irwin, saying he thought it scandalous that Schuster should be reported as putting such ideas forward. Irwin tore the letter up, and thought no more of it. But, he remarked to Alexander, 'it shows that in this country it is better not to write letters at all, when you are dealing with matters of this kind.'[42]

In fact it wasn't a letter at all, but Ansari's secretary's notes. Alexander was extremely indignant at these officials' willingness to blacken his name on such flimsy evidence, and without consulting Schuster. Such attitudes indicated the difficulties which a plan like Schuster's would have to overcome, and Alexander returned to England in no mood to do anything but support Gandhi with even greater vigour.

He might even have felt less confidence in Irwin himself if he had seen a confidential letter the Viceroy had written to R. R. Maconachie, the British Minister in Kabul. Things were looking up in India, he told him. Civil disobedience was slackening, and commercial people couldn't really want Congress to succeed.

> If we can defeat the Congress now, it will I am positive have been all to the good to have allowed them the full length of the rope this summer, and to have let people see what the logical conclusion of the Congress policy is. Not that we are out of the wood yet but I feel that we are getting nearer the edge of it.[43]

But of course it was natural for Irwin to write in this way to an official who probably shared the prevailing attitudes of British people working for the Government of India. In his biography of Lord Halifax, Andrew Roberts has indicated the complexity of the Viceroy's attitude to Congress in general and Gandhi in particular, but concludes that 'he saw himself as fighting a doomed rearguard action . . . Congress had the tide of history running with it.'[44] His willingness to act boldly and imaginatively in this rearguard action is shown by the so-called Gandhi-Irwin Pact of 1931, which, as we shall see, gave little satisfaction to anyone, but allowed Gandhi to justify to himself his attendance at the second Round Table Conference.

The Round Table Conference and the India Conciliation Group

The Labour Government in Britain and the Government of India hoped to advance a gradual process of constitutional reform in the first Round Table

Conference, which met in London from November 1930 to January 1931. It was billed as representing all sections of the Indian political scene, but as the Indian National Congress declined to accept the role of one party among a dozen others (including the discredited Indian princes), and as it saw no reason to call off its campaign of civil disobedience, leaving many of its leaders in prison, it did not attend, and the outcome was therefore necessarily inconclusive. None the less the conference was important in serving as the focus of a greatly enhanced interest in India in the British public generally. Friends had already been stirred by Tagore's intervention in Yearly Meeting, and the concern established then was followed up by an 'emergency conference' held in mid-November. Once again Alexander emphasised the importance of entering into the feelings of all parties to the conflict. *The Friend* reported him as saying that he had 'never been so profoundly impressed with the truth of the central principle of the Society about reaching out to the best in all men'. He particularly commended Lord Irwin, insisting that his unassuming Christian discipleship had made a deep impression in India. It was important to recognise the genuineness of his belief that, since there undoubtedly was a challenge to the Government's authority, he had to meet that challenge.[45]

Words like these evidently disarmed Alexander's mistrustful father-in-law, and Graham was moved to say that efforts to make the Round Table Conference a success was something on which all Friends could unite. Dominion status was going to be established anyhow, and all must be persuaded to cooperate for this end.[46] Since Congress was very much associated with *non*-cooperation, Alexander will have detected a glint of continuing antagonism here, but the recognition of the inevitability of Dominion status is a symptom of a widespread shift in attitudes. The British public was being left in no doubt that Indian national aspirations were not confined to a few irresponsible agitators.[47] After the opening formalities, the very first speech in the general discussion was by Sir Tej Bahadur Sapru, who asked emphatically whether Britain could expect a country 'brought into contact with Western ideas, vibrating with the new movement of the East', to remain content with a colonial government.[48] And, as Alexander put it in an unpublished assessment of the conference, 'one speaker after another insisted on Dominion status as a minimum demand'. There was also scope for useful work behind the scenes: Alexander particularly valued the contribution of one of the Indian Christian leaders, K. T. Paul, who was on familiar terms with the British Prime Minister, Ramsay MacDonald, and the Archbishop of Canterbury, and left them in no doubt about the state of feeling in India.[49] And the conference as a whole seems to have convinced even some sections of the Conservative Party that the hardline assertion of British rule was not a realistic option. Provisional plans for greater Indian autonomy were not, indeed, satisfactory from the Congress point of view: defence, external affairs, and much control of the finances, were all reserved to the Viceroy's officials – a situation which, as Alexander pointed out, 'Canada or any other British Dominion would instantly reject'. Still, much depended on the way that the new constitution was administered, and under the arrangements envisaged full financial control might well come in ten years. The continuance of a restricted franchise was a more serious problem, as was the autocratic rule of most of the princes, but here again there was scope for development and reform. If Congress had to fight for a general enfranchisement, it would be 'against the privileged classes in India rather than against a reluctant British Government'. Alexander ended his assessment with a vision of a post-colonial world:

> a future, not far distant, when a great United States of India, accompanied by a free Burma, a free Ceylon and perhaps a free Malaya, will sit beside the other free nations of Asia, of Europe and of America, perhaps of Africa too, in a world federation.

In any case, the world could ill spare the contribution that an India emancipated from political and social inferiority had to make.[50]

Alexander's paper may suggest the existence of a more positive attitude in Britain to Indian aspirations than was actually the case, but it was anyhow plain that some further initiative by the Government of India had to be attempted, if only because the Congress boycott of British imports had made a serious impact on trade at a time when the worldwide depression was already endangering the economies of all western nations.[51] Accordingly, just as the London conference was coming to an end in mid-January, Irwin made a strikingly conciliatory speech to the Legislative Assembly, acknowledging 'the spiritual force which impels Mr Gandhi to count no sacrifice too great in the cause, as he believes, of the India that he loves'. As Alexander had always insisted, Irwin agreed that the ultimate purpose of both Government and Congress had differed little, if at all, but that the difference in method had impeded the progress that both desired: 'On the wide basis of friendship and mutual respect alone can we confidently build the structure of a strong and self-reliant India, one with herself and one with the other partners in the British Commonwealth.'[52]

On 25 January Gandhi was released from prison, and shortly afterwards he and Irwin entered into a correspondence which led to a series of meetings in the second half of February. The outcome was the Delhi Pact, in which Gandhi agreed to call off civil disobedience and the Viceroy agreed to release all prisoners not convicted of violent crimes. As for the boycott of British goods, Irwin distinguished between campaigning to encourage Indian industrial products, and boycotting for a political purpose: the latter would not be compatible with the spirit of the agreement.

Neither Government officials nor Congress activists were happy with the Pact, the former feeling that it gave too much legitimacy to a rebellious movement, and the latter believing that Gandhi had conceded too much to imperial authority. When Nehru's sister, Vijaya Lakshmi Pandit, wrote to Alexander about her father's death in March 1931, she said that the Pact had come as a shock to her: 'I have no faith in it.'[53] Reginald Reynolds wrote an eloquent letter to Gandhi complaining that he had given up all the demands Congress had been making, and getting nothing substantial in return. In publishing Reynolds' letter in *Young India*, Gandhi responded that the British position had shifted significantly, and that there was an 'utter sincerity running through Lord Irwin's conversations'.[54] Clearly there was a long way to go as yet, and unsurprisingly there were many disputes about the interpretation of the terms of the agreement, particularly with regard to picketing and boycotts. With the departure of Lord Irwin at the end of his viceregal term, in April 1931, and the arrival of the far less imaginative Lord Willingdon, the prospects for a good understanding dwindled. Nor was the situation helped by the collapse, in August, of the Labour Government. It was replaced by a coalition, with Ramsay MacDonald continuing as Prime Minister, but with several Conservatives in the Cabinet, including Sir Samuel Hoare as Secretary of State for India. Still, a fresh agreement was eventually patched up between Willingdon and Gandhi, so that Gandhi could feel able, with considerable misgivings, to take part in the second Round Table Conference.

He came at a time when appreciation of the nationalist point of view was increasing, even though it was hardly apparent in some places where it might have been expected, such as Kingsley Martin's *New Statesman*. An organisation with which many Quakers were closely associated, the Friends of India, had organised a caravan to tour Britain in the first half of 1931 with posters, literature and speakers to press the case for Indian freedom.[55] There was a great public meeting in Friends' House on 4 July addressed by a wide range of speakers, including C. F. Andrews, Annie Besant, Fenner Brockway, and Indians like Shiva Rao and Srinivasa Sastri.[56]And one must not forget the many small local meetings of which there is necessarily only an imperfect record.

Gandhi arrived in London on 12 September, and was given a warm welcome at a reception held in Friends' House. This greatly disturbed people such as John William Graham, who had been assured by Alexander that there was no intention of using these premises, and who were greatly exercised by the thought that the Society might be officially associated with the rebellious mahatma. When plans for a reception were first mooted at a meeting on 22 July, ambitious admirers contemplated the use of a huge hall like the Crystal Palace.[57] This would have been expensive, and it was agreed simply to organise a public welcome for Gandhi when he arrived at Victoria Station. He would then be driven off to Kingsley Hall, in the east end of London, where he was to stay for the duration of the conference. But the police feared that there might be an imperialist counter-demonstration, with possible disorder resulting, and insisted on Gandhi's being driven to London in a private car. If there was to be a reception, it would have to be inside a building. The committee that had been planning the welcome had to make a rapid decision, and Friends House seemed the obvious venue. Alexander was in Birmingham, and thus in no position to exercise a veto. The people who oversaw the letting of Friends' House knew nothing of Alexander's scruples, and the reception went ahead.[58] The consequent correspondence in *The Friend*, much of it very indignant, went on for some weeks, and one may doubt whether Graham ever really forgave his son-in-law for what must have seemed yet another transgression. Alexander himself wrote defiantly:

> it was one of the most beautiful meetings I have ever attended; as a gesture of goodwill it seemed to me almost perfect. The doubts I had had about it beforehand vanished into smoke. I felt glad that I had not been in London to press my foolish scruples.

That was more than enough to infuriate Graham. A fortnight later, in its issue for 23 October, *The Friend* published an elaborate philippic from Graham entitled 'The Case Against Mr Gandhi'. Gandhi countenanced irresponsible proposals to demand from Britain a huge indemnity to pay for earlier wars – he wanted to drive out all Christian missionaries – his rejection of separate representation for the untouchables showed that his version of *Swaraj* still meant Brahmin rule – he wanted to destroy Britain's cotton industry. On this last point Graham said that Gandhi had made various contradictory statements by way of mitigation, such as his wanting to close Indian mills too. Graham evidently relied on his readers' perceiving the disingenuousness of any such attempt to gloss over Indian hostility, and permitted himself an unquakerly snarl: 'This is the trustworthiness of our charming friend round whom so much glamour is cast'. There were, of course, wholly admirable Indians, working in the Brahmo Samaj, the Arya Samaj, the Ramakrishna Mission, and so on: 'These all welcomed me as a lecturer, and I met delightful and consecrated people there.' Self-government will have to come, eventually. But 'the Simon Report goes courageously as far in that direction as is now for the good of India.'[59]

For good measure Graham also complained about Gandhi's 'ostentatious asceticism', which was certainly much in evidence during his residence in London. Muriel Lester, who ran the Kingsley Hall settlement in Bow, had visited Sabarmati in 1926, and it was she who invited Gandhi to stay with her while he was attending the conference. This was obviously appropriate as the nearest he could get to the voluntary poverty so central to his convictions, but it was not convenient for taking part in sessions in St James's Palace. So premises at 88 Knightsbridge were found, just opposite the Knightsbridge underground station, and backing on to Hyde Park. Alexander wrote that he could sometimes see the wings of white gulls flying over the Serpentine, 'a comforting reminder that streets and houses and governments and politics had not utterly banished carefree beauty from the world'.[60] This was where Gandhi's staff lived and worked, and from which statements to the press were issued. Alexander had permission from Woodbrooke to spend a couple of days a week in London for the duration of the conference, and in *Gandhi through Western Eyes* he has left a vivid account of the buoyant and rather chaotic atmosphere of the place. The quality in Gandhi which particularly impressed Alexander was evidently his affection for the people around him – an affection which kept the much-tried cook at her post to the end. Her food was often spoiled by people being late for their meals, and she could never safely take time off. She was always on the point of leaving, but never did. She and the young woman who answered the door soon found, Alexander says, 'that they were not just domestic servants but . . . personal friends, an essential part of his family'.[61]

On his days in London, Alexander evidently assisted with press releases and other publicity. Among his papers from this period is a corrected typescript, giving some account of Congress policy, and explaining its background. It looks as though one of Gandhi's assistants – Mahadev Desai or Pyarelal Nayar – composed the statement, and it was then typed by Mrs Cheesman in a form that could be revised by Gandhi himself. The revisions – in Gandhi's rather untidy handwriting – were quite numerous. One instance is the addition of a couple of sentences about the role of women in the national movement, pointing out that 'thousands came out of the purdah [and] picketted liquor shops, foreign cloth shops, did village work, organised khadi work, took part in processions braving all the risks with men. They occupied during critical times posts of the highest responsibility.'

To this Alexander has added an explanation that purdah 'means seclusion in the home' and khadi means 'hand-spinning'.The title also is in Alexander's hand, 'India and the National Congress'.[62] The typescript is evidence of the informal way the 'commune' (as Alexander called it) did its business, its easy collaboration. One can well believe that it was also more than a trifle exhausting. Alexander ends the sketch he composed at the end of term for the Woodbrooke 'Log Night' with the voice of a Sinhalese student, Bernard Aluwihari, whose job it was to answer the telephone. 'Mr Alexander, come down and let's go and get a decent lunch. I'm tired of all these saints.'

However disturbed John William Graham may have been by the spectacle of Friends House serving as the venue for a reception for Gandhi, he will have been comfortable enough with the initiative that Friends did take officially at this time, which was to have a regular meeting for worship to support the proceedings of the conference. The first such meeting, on 30 September, was attended both by Gandhi and by Lord Sankey, Lord Chancellor and Vice-Chairman of the conference. Then there was a break, but the meetings were resumed on 21 October, and continued once a week till 2 December; eight in all. Less publicly, a group of Friends, with one or two others, came together to form the Indian Conciliation Group. Carl Heath called a meeting in mid-October, and some consideration was given to how best to inform the British public about developments in India. On the eve of his departure at the end of the Conference, Gandhi met this group and encouraged them to put these arrangements on a firm footing. Agatha Harrison, who had been one of the team working at 88 Knightsbridge, agreed to make this her main concern, and was appointed secretary. The industrialist G. D. Birla, Gandhi's principal financial backer, subsidised the project, paying Harrison £6 a week for the rest of the 1930s.[63]

The Indian Conciliation Group (later the India Conciliation Group) built upon the achievement of Gandhi in reinforcing sympathy for the nationalist cause in the British public. Gandhi himself had been tireless in making contact with a wide range of people, with academics in Oxford and Cambridge, with mill-workers in Lancashire, with future rulers of the Empire at Eton College and Westminster School, with the Quakers at Woodbrooke. At Woodbrooke he met Olive Alexander, and was touched by her physical infirmity. He realised how difficult it must have been for her husband to leave her for extended periods while he laboured in the cause of Indian freedom.

Gandhi's insistence on complete independence could appal well-wishers who sought to persuade him of the necessity of some concessions. In Cambridge Lowes Dickinson and Ernest Barker consulted.C. F. Andrews about a possible toning down of *purna swaraj*, but with little hope of success. Dickinson told Alexander that at a meeting in Pembroke College Gandhi had said that he would rather see 'India drowned in blood than abate one jot of her claims for immediate independence'. As it happens, there is an account of this address in *Young India*, which makes it clear that he was trying to take on board the worst case that opponents of independence could imagine. He thought the fear of communal slaughter was exaggerated, but even if it were not, it would be better than the slow, ignominious death caused by British rule. But this made no sense to Dickinson. No British government, he said, could possibly accept such an outcome. He was confirmed in his reluctance to go along with Alexander's endorsement of Indian nationalism. As he had remarked in March 1929, the Indian willingness to take risks for independence was 'the sort of enthusiasm that sweeps over a country before a war, when what war means is not realised by anybody'.[64] Gandhi simply did not realise what he was talking about.

But although Gandhi may have perplexed and alarmed many of his British audiences, his personality made a deep impression. A. D. Lindsay, the Master of Balliol, with whom Gandhi stayed during his two visits to Oxford, shared Alexander's conviction that Gandhi was 'much more realistic about India than most politicians, whether British or Indian'.[65] He was warmly received, too, by working-class people – famously by the Lancashire mill-hands whose livelihood was threatened by the Congress boycott of British textiles. The General Election that took place in October endorsed the National Government in a crushing defeat for the Labour Party. Labour's natural supporters among working people had been bewildered by the formation of the National Government, and disheartened by the ensuing election result. For them Gandhi represented a power which had at least shaken the seemingly invulnerable Empire, and they got some pleasure from the spectacle of Winston Churchill and his friends writhing with frustration as they witnessed the deference accorded to this subversive character. 'There', said a Birmingham trade unionist to his five-year-old son, as they both watched Gandhi going into Woodbrooke, 'is a very great man: and the Tories *loathe* him.'[66]

Although the role of Friends associated with the India Conciliation Group inevitably placed them on the political left, many of India's champions felt that they were far too moderate. Reginald Reynolds, for one, was scornful of attitudes within the Society of Friends, telling Romain Rolland that Quakers were pseudo-pacifists, sly and cowardly, failing to understand that peace may be founded on violence and injustice.[67] Krishna Menon was at this time coming into prominence as a spokesman for Indian aspirations through the India League, and although he cooperated with people like Alexander, the alliance was an uneasy one. This is vividly brought out in the monumental work of Suhash Chakravarty on Menon and the India League. Chakravarty bases his narrative on the Menon Papers in the Nehru Memorial Library, and it faithfully reflects Menon's irritation with the 'missionaries of goodwill' of the India Conciliation Group. They

> sought to strengthen the moderates of all faiths in India, make them sit together, deny all possibilities of giving offence to one another, work out a mode of understanding between them, open all closed doors, soften the blows of unsympathetic official actions and make both sides appreciate the problems and difficulties of each other.

As for the 'prophet of Selly Oak', Alexander himself, he was 'far too keen to trace areas of conciliation and . . . avoid confrontation with the Labour leadership'. Menon even detected in Alexander's concern to promote an understanding of Indian aspirations a desire to defend the British Indian empire: any attempt to reconcile the dominant and the dominated 'would clothe imperialism in an ethical garb based on personal morality. Given the opportunity, it might turn out to be the most subtle mouthpiece of imperialism offering in liberal terms the alluring prospects of an uneven partnership.' For Alexander's father-in-law, of course, these prospects would have seemed less than alluring.[68]

Menon's irritation is particularly apparent in his dealings with the Birmingham Council for Indian Freedom, very much controlled by the local Quaker network. 'Soft and seductive', even 'malefic' in its influence, it was 'a strange combination of empty radical slogans, tepid sentimentalism and an overwhelming concern of the Quakers to leave the door open for an unending dialogue between adversaries'.[69] It was this group, aided by politicians Fenner Brockway, and countenanced by friends of Gandhi such as C. F. Andrews, who warned the Mahatma off 'extremists' like Menon in a political scene newly dominated by the Conservative Party. Chakravarty makes clear that Menon would have been much more at home with Irish republicans like Maud Gonne MacBride, who wanted him to speak in Dublin, and who, at a rally there in January 1931, declared that the Irish had no hand in the Empire, and that 'every enemy of that evil thing was a friend who it was their duty to help and support'.[70]

The India Conciliation Group embarked on its work by agreeing to support Gandhi's proposal that a fact-finding mission should go to India to assess the situation for themselves. Three Quakers, Percy Bartlett, Hilda Cashmore and Eric Hayman, did indeed spend several months in an India that was subjected to a period of harsh repression by Lord Willingdon. As Alexander explained to Sir Samuel Hoare, the visit was not an attempt at mediation but a quiet act of friendliness, which was essentially the nature of his own visit to India in 1930. Then, it is true, he had tried to bring Irwin and Gandhi together, and had no immediate success.

> But I learnt much which I believe hardly any official or journalist ever does learn, not as to particular events but as to hidden feelings and passions – and how terribly deep and amazingly widespread these feelings are. An experience of this kind gives one the almost despairing sense that those who are only concerning themselves with political understandings will never get near the root of the trouble. . . . You probably *know* Mr Gandhi and his friends who were here far more truly from your association with him in the free and equal give and take of the Conference than those who have had 'dealings' with him for years in the tense atmosphere of India, where everything becomes distorted.[71]

In addition to what the three Friends had to tell there was also evidence from C. F. Andrews, who had again been in India, and reported back to the Group in some detail. The first actual emergency with which the ICG had to deal was a report that Gandhi had given an interview in Rome on his journey back to India, declaring that the Round Table Conference marked a rupture of relations between India and Britain, that he was returning to India to restart the struggle, that the boycott would be total, and so forth.[72] Gandhi telegraphed an immediate denial of having said any such things, and the ICG did what it could to publicise this. But it was difficult to make much impression, because the Viceroy almost immediately had Gandhi arrested, for all the world as though the interview were indeed authentic.

From this time on, the ICG attempted to keep in touch with the Congress leadership and brief British ministers accordingly. Although militant protests were left to Krishna Menon, Reginald Reynolds and their colleagues in the India League, ICG activities created considerable anxiety in Whitehall. Carl Heath, as Chairman, wrote to the Prime Minister about the three Friends' mission, and their finding that there was a growing disenchantment with British rule, and with Sir Samuel Hoare in particular. There was a need for a 'reassuring and big-minded declaration *by yourself*', along with some release of prisoners, and a firm timetable for constitutional development. Ramsay MacDonald passed the letter to Hoare, who commented that it was evidence of 'very active propaganda' to suggest that MacDonald had one Indian policy and Hoare another. He hoped MacDonald would see his way to 'dissipating this myth' in his reply. The India Office, he went on, often restrained the Government of India, though this couldn't be admitted publicly as 'it is essential to preserve a united front'.[73] The governmental need to preserve a united front proved to be a serious obstacle to the ICG's endeavours on many future occasions.

Alexander was constantly in touch with Agatha Harrison and Carl Heath, but as 1932 drew to a close, other concerns competed for his attention. In an article in *The Friend* of 9 December, Alexander discussed the problem of the Polish Corridor, the strip of land that gave Poland access to the sea, and cut East Prussia off from the rest of Germany. It was, he said, the worst danger zone in Europe. It was not that the difficulties for Germany and Poland were insuperable, as was shown by proposals coming from both countries by parties not in government. The real problem was an absence of mutual respect. 'To ask a German to respect Poland is like asking an Englishman to respect India.' In general they don't.

In applying to the European scene what he had learned from his engagement with relations between Britain and India, Alexander had some difficult adjustments to make. They were the more difficult because of the scale and the immediacy of the crisis that developed early in 1933.

5

THE 1930s

Fritz Berber and the Nazi revolution

The scale of the impending European crisis was in no way unforeseen. On 8 October 1931, Jan Christian Smuts – the Boer general who became a member of the Imperial War Cabinet in the First World War – delivered the Basil Hicks Lecture at the University of Sheffield. His subject was 'the disarmed peace'. He pointed out that the armament situation that reached a climax in 1914 was unprecedented in history. This was the 'armed peace' that emerged after the Franco-Prussian war: 1871 marked the beginning of an 'unstable equilibrium of peace maintained through great armies and navies always ready to take the field or go to sea at short notice'. Each nation spurred on the others, and in 1914 the situation passed out of the control of statesmen altogether. Following the war, Germany's forces were reduced to a minimum, and assurances given that her disarmament would be the first step towards a general disarmament. No such thing.

> The armaments of the world are greater today than they were in 1914. . . . The present position involves an immense risk. It is a question whether the exceptional disarmament of Germany does not add to that risk. One-sided preparedness is even more dangerous than all-round preparedness. We dare not sit still and allow this perilous situation to drift.[1]

Smuts' ambition was modest. He accepted that it would take a long time to wean nations from their trust in armaments. The great thing was to make a start, to begin a process not of rearmament but of disarmament, developing the mutual confidence which the League of Nations had made possible. Well, the start was not made, the nations did indeed dare to sit still and allow the perilous situation to drift. In due course Hitler ended the anomaly of a disarmed Germany in an armed world, and the League of Nations began to disintegrate. Alexander and Smuts came from very different backgrounds, but both had invested heavily in the League idea. In the face of disaster, what was the right strategy for them to adopt?

In his Sheffield lecture Smuts had conjured up a picture of a Germany that he hoped might seize the initiative for a general disarmament. Like all his other hopes, of course, this came to nothing, but it remained just conceivable that Germany, from a position of equality, might go along with that aspiration. For such a thing to happen, sympathetic elements in the Nazi regime needed to be encouraged and reinforced. And that was where Alexander saw a role for Fritz Berber.

While he had been a Fellow of Woodbrooke in 1927–8, Berber had been greatly influenced by Alexander's approach to international relations, congenial as it was to his preoccupation with the politics of conscience. He had originally intended to pursue a career as a magistrate, and did serve as a district judge in Bavaria for a couple of years. But in 1930 he was invited to join the staff of the Hochschule für Politik in Berlin, a kind of German equivalent to the Royal Institute for International Affairs. He accepted this much less secure appointment because it enabled him to pursue his interest in international law.

Then, on 30 January 1933, Hitler became German Chancellor, and on 5 March an election to the Reichstag gave the National Socialists almost 44 per cent of the vote, by far the largest single party. It was a time of great confusion, which the Nazi leadership and their storm-troops (the *Sturmabteilungen* or SA) exploited ruthlessly. The climax of confusion was the burning of the Reichstag building on 27 February, allegedly by the Communists as the signal for an insurrection. Mass arrests of left-wingers followed, conveniently reducing the number of Reichstag members opposed to the Nazis. The day after the fire, Berber wrote an anxious letter to Alexander, confessing his inability to foresee the outcome of present events, and regretting that better use had not been made of the years since the war 'to create a center of constructive international thought'. He was 'ready to perform any kind of service I might be required to do. But it is late . . .'.

It certainly was. The Hochschule was not the kind of institution that could survive the Nazi regime in its original form. Berber's salary was stopped in April, and he wrote to Alexander asking whether he could come across to see him as soon as possible. Alexander was spending that Easter in Lowestoft, and invited Berber to stay there for a few days. Berber came on 15 April, and during long walks by the sea the two men discussed his future. Should he accept that the situation in Germany was intolerable and that he should leave, or should he try to continue his work in unfavourable conditions with a view to exerting a helpful influence from within? If he chose to take the second course, Alexander offered him the fullest possible support, and with this encouragement Berber felt able to return and await developments.

On 19 May he reported that he had been reappointed to the staff of the Hochschule, which had been taken over by the newly created Ministry of Propaganda. The new appointment was only part-time, and because he had not been paid for the best part of two months he was having to leave his house, and had no idea where he was going to stay. He was evidently suffering extreme stress, at times cheered by hope when he thought of the 'wonderful building of our work' that was conjured up in his talks with Alexander, and then lapsing into a feeling of loneliness and near-despair: 'all seems so impossible and far.'

> But always in the background is this vision with wonderful harmony, which even seems able to penetrate to the foreground because there are so many telling me that strength and consolation comes to them from it. Thus I live in the first words of the Sermon on the Mountain! I pray God may give me a spot where to breathe and to build before I may be drowned.[2]

Alexander invited Berber to visit England again in the summer, but it is hardly surprising that he declined. He was too concerned with establishing his position in the new circumstances, and he was able to tell Alexander when they did eventually meet in Berlin in August that he had been consulted by senior officials in the Ministries of Justice and of Foreign Affairs. He also believed that his advice had been useful to the German delegation at Geneva. 'If things go on in the same way', Alexander remarked, 'he may be called to more important work. It is, of course, a big "if".'[3]

Alexander paid an extended visit to Germany after the 1933 Woodbrooke reunion, which was held at Roudnice in Czechoslovakia, not far from the German border. He gives an account of it in a report which he circulated to several people who shared his concern that developments there should not jeopardise the peace of Europe. The report begins with a sketch of attitudes to the Nazi regime expressed at the reunion itself. Five Germans attended, two of them definitely opposed to the regime. The other three were not members of the Nazi Party, but felt moved to defend it against censorious and perhaps unfair criticism. In particular Alexander describes the long talks he had with Hans Buchinger, 'I might say "wrestlings", friendly but at times rather intense'. Buchinger said that it was one thing for an outsider to look critically at the regime, but quite another 'for a young German who has got to live in it, and must make the best of it'. Moreover, it had to be allowed that Germany had emerged from a mood of despair and now looked to 'a future which seems to offer purpose, work, hope – great things indeed!'[4]

Thus briefed, Alexander embarked on his tour of the new Germany, beginning with a three-day lecture-conference at Löwenberg, near Liegnitz, on the position of the *Auslandsdeutsch*, German minorities in central and east European states. The speakers insisted that Germany did not seek frontier revisions, but only full civil rights for these minorities. And these rights would not be conceded until Germany herself was strong enough to command respect. League of Nations guarantees were useless. This was a sensitive point for Alexander, for whom the League had always been the crucial champion of the people who had found themselves in minority communities created by the Versailles settlement. 'Some of us', he objected, 'want to get away from that old jungle law – we think that the real adventure for our generation should be the introduction of Christianity into world politics.' 'Oh yes', was the reply, 'we should aim for that, but it is a long way off. And Luther said . . .'. Alexander could not recall exactly what Luther said, 'but I suppose he may have been the inventor of that ingenious notion of the "Interim-ethik", which we heard so much about in 1914–15.'[5]

He moved on to Elbing in East Prussia, staying with an Old Woodbrooker whose schoolteacher husband had joined the Nazi Party. He had done so reluctantly, but felt it was necessary in order to exert some control over the Hitler Youth members in his classes. It was proving a strenuous commitment, with obligatory attendance at lengthy meetings. He was also required to support the 'German Christian' movement, of which he disapproved.

The school's drawing master showed Alexander round the primary school. He was a Mennonite, so was gratified to find that his visitor was a Quaker. He told a class of small girls that Quakers had been friendly to Germany after the war, and Alexander added that Quakers still wanted to be friends of Germany.

> I hope I spoke the truth; I am sure that any English Quakers who believe in the moral isolation of Nazi Germany would have changed their minds if they had listened to these smiling schoolgirls singing to the foreign visitor; for myself, I had no compunction at all in returning the 'Hitler salute' which they all gave me. My hostess had, indeed, already been assuring me that I need not regard it as in any sense a 'party' salutation.[6]

Alexander returning the Hitler salute to a class of little girls would certainly have made a fine subject for a cartoonist in the Woodbrooke log-book, but it demonstrates his sensitivity to friendly feeling, however disconcertingly expressed. And it would be a serious misjudgement to see this as evidence of a sentimentally favourable view of the regime. On the contrary, he absolutely refused to accept the excuses offered for concentration camps and the persecution of Jews, socialists and others – arguments that the country had been in a state of virtual civil war which one side or the other had to win, and then suppress its opponents, with consequent unavoidable injustice and oppression. There was no use denying that there was something vicious in the whole regime: its leaders seemed to be either monomaniacs or despicable characters. But, in spite of this, 'they have somehow evoked a spirit that has something great and creative in it'. As long as the evil things continued,

> we must indeed do anything we can to hasten their end; and for my part I see only one possible way of doing that: To seek to find what George Fox called 'that of God' in the instruments of this terror, and to understand what real desires for good may be in their hearts.[7]

His assessment was endorsed by a British member of staff at Königsberg University, T. P. Conwil Evans. He was one of the people Alexander met in East Prussia, and it is clear that they had much in common. Like Alexander, he saw the League of Nations as the most hopeful vehicle for a better world society, and like him too he argued that the emphasis on *military* sanctions was a source of distrust rather than a means of creating confidence. In fact, if a war crisis threatened, 'unless the League can in such circumstances bring hostilities to an end by means other than war, it had better refrain from action'.[8] Conwil Evans was closely associated with the pacifist peer, Lord Noel-Buxton, and had collaborated with him in a book on the problems of ethnic minorities created by the Versailles settlement, *Oppressed Peoples and the League of Nations* (1922). In 1932 he had published a study of Noel-Buxton's involvement in efforts to prevent the outbreak of the First World War, and to stop it once those efforts had failed: *Foreign Policy from a Back Bench, 1904–1918*. So it isn't surprising that he found Alexander's report 'extraordinarily fair'. He felt that the Nazi revolution had in some sense been necessary, and that it was quite wrong to regard the Germans, as some British commentators did, as 'something different from the rest of humanity'. Still, he was all too conscious of things that horrified and distressed him, and he hoped that the revolution would 'move into milder channels'. He had told Herman Rauschning, the Nazi President of the Free City of Danzig, that good relations with Britain would be impossible until the concentration camps were closed, the violence stopped, and the Jews rehabilitated. He assured Alexander that he was doing everything possible to get reforms, and indeed while Alexander was in Königsberg, Conwil-Evans told him of a Professor of History who was a Jew but still kept his post at the insistence of colleagues and students. For that matter,

Alexander's host in Königsberg was himself a Jewish professor, Theodor Spira. His position had been challenged, but he continued in quiet faith. He was an authority on Shelley, and was perhaps sustained, as both Alexander and Berber were, by the triumphant conclusion to *Prometheus Unbound*:

> To suffer woes which Hope thinks infinite;
> To forgive wrongs darker than death or night;
> To defy power, which seems omnipotent;
> To love, and bear; to hope till Hope creates
> From its own wreck the thing it contemplates;
> Neither to change, nor falter, nor repent;
> This, like thy glory, Titan, is to be
> Good, great and joyous, beautiful and free;
> This is alone Life, Joy, Empire, and Victory.[9]

These words acquire an almost intolerable poignancy when set in the context of the final degradation of German society under Nazi rule, but it is important to recognise that conditions in 1933 were much more fluid than they later became. The sense of purpose and hope so valued by Hans Buchinger could be summed up as an impression that the old world order was changing rapidly, and that Germany was somehow at the forefront of this change. From being a shattered and bankrupt nation she was now on the way to being a world leader. It has been impossible since the Second World War to set aside one's knowledge of where all this was leading, but some attempt must be made to understand what the prospects appeared to be in the early 1930s if one is to reach an adequate understanding of Alexander's initiatives.

*

While there have been innumerable accounts of how the Nazi Party came to power, few documents throw more light on the atmosphere in the early days of the regime than one of Hermann Rauschning's books, *Makers of Destruction*, first published in English in 1942. Rauschning, who left the Party in 1935, is chiefly remembered for his analysis of the Nazi revolution, *Germany's Revolution of Destruction* (1938), but its unpretentious sequel is in some ways a more remarkable work. Rauschning was of some importance in the Nazi Party in the early 1930s: Conwil-Evans was pleased to have had the opportunity of speaking to him as a Nazi with direct access to Hitler. *Makers of Destruction* simply records conversations that Rauschning had had with representative party members and with others who cooperated with the regime. A recurrent theme is that of 'the amazing vistas of boundless opportunity that seem suddenly to open' (p. 125). A young economics professor prepares maps that show sources of energy but ignore national boundaries. 'Boundaries? Frontiers? Don't interest us', he remarked brusquely. 'Chance, arbitrary interruptions in existing fields of energy; we've got to get rid of them' (pp. 192–3). Young army officers were developing theories of warfare in which each component could be exactly calculated, 'as the changes of energy can be calculated in an internal combustion engine'. 'Modern war consists of exact processes such as are implied in any industrial activity, processes in a system of co-operation and control hitherto inconceivable' (pp. 68–71). Above all, there is a pervasive sense that these dramatic developments are irresistible: 'All this will happen whether we want it or not' (Hermann Rochling, an industrialist, quoted p. 170); 'The tragedy will run its course' (a Prussian official, p. 75); 'This process has got to go on to its end' (a friend of Alfred Hugenberg, a conservative industrialist in Hitler's first cabinet, p. 224); 'Let things take their course' (Constantin von Neurath, Hitler's first foreign minister, p. 109).

Like Conwil-Evans, Alexander rejected this seductive insistence on inevitability. One topic that he and Berber had discussed at Lowestoft was the formation of a group that would keep in touch with developments in Germany, and do what it could to exert influence in a constructive and peaceable direction. Alexander was making contact with possible participants through the autumn, and on 11 December the group met for the first time, chaired by Charles Roden Buxton. Clifford Allen (Lord Allen of Hurtwood), Carl Heath, Walter Layton of *The Economist*, and Will Arnold-Forster were among those present, and Gilbert Murray and Lord Cecil were named as people who would probably be sympathetic. Lord Noel-Buxton, Charles's brother, contributed largely to the expenses of the group. Others who contributed to expenses were Alexander's friend and patron Frederick Merttens, the historian G. P. Gooch, the journalist Vernon Bartlett, and John Wheeler-Bennett, later to be an implacable critic of the German opposition.[10] On 5 January 1934 the group hosted a meeting for Berber at Lord Noel-Buxton's home in London. His talk was probably on the same lines as one he had prepared in the previous July, a text of which is among Alexander's papers. Hitler's appeal stems from his having unified a divided country, making it once again powerful. 'In the months since January 30th, there has been less bloodshed and more discipline than for many months before.' Like Rauschning, he testifies to the existence of a mood that the poet Wordsworth called 'shapeless eagerness'.[11] Germany had dared to take a new step towards a future

> dark, full of dangers, unknown in its consequences. It is not an old stuffy air coming back; it is a new wind blowing, a strong wind no doubt, a wind which takes away many things with elemental force; but it is a fresh wind at last.[12]

Additionally, in January, he was able to mention what impressed him as positive developments initiated by his new chief, Josef Goebbels. Goebbels had seen him on 13 December and authorised him to undertake 'the renewal or finding of all sorts of spiritual and intellectual contacts with other countries in the frame of the Hochschule für Politik.[13] His formidably well-informed audience will have cross-questioned him closely, and the occasion seems to have brought out the difficulties of what Berber hoped to achieve. Will Arnold-Forster, for one, felt him to be 'a most sympathetic, honourable and courageous man . . . enmeshed in a horribly false position'. He wasn't able to say anything that would displease his chief: he even removed the dust-jacket from a book he was taking home with him because of its 'compromising' title, *The United States of Europe*. Moreover, Arnold-Forster wondered whether Berber even *understood* the idea of collective security. He still seemed to think in terms of pre-war, pre-League, 'international anarchy' ideas. Still, he had no doubt of his good faith, and was deeply impressed by Berber's warning him, in private, of German war preparations.[14]

Others viewed Berber with less favour. He went to see Wickham Steed, formerly editor of *The Times* but now lecturing at King's College, London, who felt that he was engaged 'in Nazi propaganda of a more subtle kind than Nazi agents usually indulge in'.[15] And at his next visit, in March, when he had a session with Charles Roden Buxton, Buxton's wife Dorothy disturbed him with her 'continuous bitter interruptions' about concentration camps, anti-Semitism and the like.[16] Buxton himself, however, felt on this occasion that Berber's attitude had changed: there was less frankness, more 'holding back', and he sensed that Berber seemed '*rather* more Nazi. I'm not *blaming* him'.[17] Taken as a whole, these comments illustrate the extreme difficulties of the task Alexander and Berber had envisaged during those long discussions by the sea at Lowestoft. In order to sustain his position in the Nazi regime he had to go along with as much of its policy as he could accept, and there were indeed some things with which he could go along. No German was likely to object to Hitler's campaign against the hated Versailles Treaty, and most will have taken some pleasure in the thought that the new regime had once again made Germany a force to be reckoned with in the world. With a few exceptions, the opposition that developed furtively as time went on had no desire to undo that part of Hitler's work which had made Germany a Great Power again. They wanted, in fact, to hold on to what unsympathetic British diplomats were to describe as 'the Hitler loot'. Their position could easily be represented as little different from that of the Nazis, and their revulsion against the anti-Semitism and the repressive machinery of political control slighted. The fact that the repression was so pervasive meant that critics had to be extremely cautious to survive, and the caution was held against them by people who could comfortably denounce the Nazi regime from afar.

Berber did his best to adopt a coherent position that was compatible with both his status in the regime and with the internationalist ideas that he had absorbed in Woodbrooke. His first publication after the Nazi take-over was an introduction to the main issues of international law, entitled *Sicherheit und Gerechtigkeit* (Security and Justice; 1934).[18] It is a vigorous critique of the ideas sustaining the League of Nations, an institution flawed by its origins in the dictated peace of Versailles, and incapable of promoting peaceful change. He saw it as an exercise in soteriology, a doctrine of redemption that belonged to theological rather than legal or political discourse. It was not the result of compromise, reconciliation, treaty-making, but a one-sided enactment by victorious powers.[19] Alexander himself would have had much sympathy with some aspects of this critique, but he remained committed to the League idea, as Berber well understood. He therefore tactfully explained to Alexander that the book was concerned to combat the prevalent idea that military sanctions were a crucial guarantee of international law: the most potent guarantee was justice itself. At the same time he developed an exposition of Germany's alternative to the League of Nations, thus acting as an apologist for Hitler's withdrawal from the League.[20] The significance of this is vividly apparent from a letter in February from Arnold-Forster in which he reproaches Alexander for suggesting a disarmament conference outside the framework of the League, presumably with a view to keeping disarmament on the agenda in some form. But this, Arnold-Forster argues, would be a deplorable error, 'simply playing into Goebbels' hands'. Philip Noel-Baker added a supporting postscript, insisting that nothing but the League was practical politics, and that Goebbels must not be allowed to think that he could split Europe.[21]

Goebbels may or may not have been grateful to Berber for his efforts, but the book was deeply offensive to National Socialist theorists. Berber's autobiography, written late in life as a rather moving apologia for the extremely difficult course that he followed, relates how the book had been commissioned as a publication of the Kaiser-Wilhelm Institute of Public International Law. When Viktor Bruns, the Director of the Institute, read the manuscript, he felt that he couldn't possibly allow it to appear as a book from the Institute, and advised Berber not to publish it at all. Berber would not agree to this, so Bruns – evidently a man of some spirit – authorised a grant to support its publication elsewhere. It soon attracted unfavourable attention. *Deutsches Recht* published a notice – a denunciation rather than a review – in which the book's failure to contribute to the Nazi New Order was demonstrated at length. It was a re-hash of liberal ideas, and Berber had a bad habit of quoting non-Aryan authorities. This diatribe had immediate consequences for Berber. The University of Hamburg had appointed him to a chair in international law some time before, but the review amounted to a veto on the appointment, so that he had to continue his poorly rewarded labours in Berlin. Hamburg did what it could for him, however, and appointed him to a post in the University's Institute for Foreign Affairs, which he was able to hold in conjunction with his post at the Hochschule.

He had one other compensation for the trouble caused by the publication of his book: in the spring of 1935 it earned him an invitation to a conference at the Royal Institute of International Affairs in London on collective security. Here he met Arnold Toynbee, and one result of this was that Berber persuaded him to come and give three lectures in Germany on peaceful change. This was under the auspices of Viktor Bruns and his Kaiser-Wilhelm Institute. Both Berber and Toynbee have left accounts of this visit, with some interesting differences of emphasis. Toynbee's main concern was his unexpected interview with Hitler, where the Führer evidently gave an impressive demonstration of his grasp of history and his dialectical skill. Toynbee also had a good deal to say about the two non-Nazi servants of the regime whom he knew, Berber himself and Hans Dieckhoff of the Foreign Ministry: both, he felt, were in a false position, though he concedes that they both believed that they were acting for the best. But he describes Berber, rather disparagingly, as 'double-faced', and wonders 'how he can have justified his ambiguous behaviour to his own mind, and, still more, to his own conscience, which was, or had been, a Quaker one.'[22] Berber's account is to some extent a defence of himself against these severe judgements. His narrative illustrates the extremely precarious position he occupied, which forced him into 'Tarnung', camouflage. Toynbee could stigmatise this as double-faced if he liked, but it was hardly fair to do so. Anyhow, he was not above a bit of camouflage himself: Berber cites a passage from one of Toynbee's other lectures, of which he had a transcript, in which he seems to praise the great measure of national unity which Nazi Germany had achieved. This would have been music to the ears of a Nazi audience. If Toynbee, who was only in Germany for a few days, felt it necessary to be thus obliging, should he not feel some sympathy with anti-Nazi Germans who had to live with the regime all the time? Toynbee's own brief account of his main lecture only mentions that he teasingly quoted St Paul as an authority: very much a 'non-aryan author', but one who insisted that there should be no schism in the body (Romans 12.25). Whether the teasing or the flattery made the greater impression must remain uncertain, but Berber sensibly comments that the Toynbee visit was amply justified as an effort to build a bridge where bridges were badly needed.[23]

Bridge-building was certainly Alexander's main preoccupation, and Berber's role was always crucial to his efforts to check the drift to war. His strategy had some measure of success, inasmuch as Berber was always alert to identifying opportunities for lowering the political temperature, showing what would satisfy moderate German opinion, and educating, as far as he could, German policy-makers about the real state of opinion in other countries. After the reoccupation of the Rhineland in 1936 – Hitler's first act of defiance of the Versailles Treaty – Berber edited a collection of documents bearing on the issue under the title *Locarno*. This assembled the texts of a wide range of international agreements and policy speeches, and Berber reckoned that the book could just as well have been used in support of French or British positions as it could in support of the German action.[24] He made this claim for all his later document collections, even those published after the outbreak of war.

He secured a commendatory preface for the Locarno volume from Joachim von Ribbentrop, at that time Hitler's 'ambassador at large'. For the next few years Ribbentrop served as a kind of patron for Berber, although Berber insisted that this was no more than a recognition of his usefulness to Ribbentrop as someone who knew the British scene well, and was also possessed of an impressive general knowledge of history, which Ribbentrop lacked. With some humour Berber relates how Ribbentrop would phone him with a query about who Skanderbeg was, or the origin of the song 'It's a Long Way to Tipperary', or whether Portugal really had an alliance with England in the Middle Ages which was still in force. Ribbentrop was deeply impressed by the fact that Berber never had to look the answer up, but seemed always able to respond instantly. He called him 'a walking encyclopedia'.[25]

These phone calls from the minister impressed colleagues as indications of high-level consultation, a false impression which Berber never contradicted, such mistakes being an invaluable resource in a totalitarian state. But clearly Alexander's hopes that Berber might become an influential contact at the heart of the Nazi regime were never realised. His value as an interpreter was considerable, though, and it was a demanding role in itself which caused him almost intolerable stress. Without Alexander's moral support, on which he knew he could always rely, the stress *would* have been intolerable.

*

The experience of what was eventually called the Group for Anglo-German Understanding led on to a project to which Alexander devoted considerable time and energy in 1936–7. This was a community and a centre in the service of peace and justice. The inspiration for the idea was the Servants of India Society, which he had encountered during his visit to India in 1930. In a draft prospectus he quoted Ramsay MacDonald on that Society.

> Its membership is small because it calls for much sacrifice and renunciation, but its spirit is far spread. It is a very small band of men, who undergo a long period of probation and preparation, and who then enter upon a life-service of devoted work for the public good, profoundly influencing the lives of millions of their fellow-countrymen, and the whole outlook of their country.[26]

Alexander added that so far as he knew there was no such 'lay order' for the service of world peace. Members of the community would devote themselves to the study of international issues with a concentration on practical results.

They would be available for lecturing, and a nucleus at least would live in a residential centre. These members in residence would have funds held in common, with a salary of £400–500 a year (not lavish, but not far either from the Woodbrooke scales). Allowances would be made for children, and for travel. There would be a library and a periodical. Everyone would share in household tasks, though there would be domestic staff – first described as 'girls', but this unsuitable word was deleted, and 'men and women' substituted. All would appreciate the spiritual purpose of the community.[27]

A statement of aims prepared in 1936 makes clear how Alexander defined that spiritual purpose. The Centre's atmosphere would encourage an open-minded search for truth and a spirit of the broadest tolerance.

> But this is not enough. The members must be sustained by a faith in human destiny that can face defeat and disappointment undismayed: they must be impelled by the conviction that, come what may, man's task is to work for a vital harmony of man in the world.

These words indicate how much the accelerating arms race and the aggressive challenge to the status quo posed by the new dictatorships were testing Alexander's faith.

An inaugural meeting was held in October 1936 at the home of Mrs Bigland in the Quaker village of Jordans in Buckinghamshire. There were later meetings in the summer and autumn of the following year, one of them on 20 October in Friends House. But the project, demanding as it was in personal commitment, petered out, though it provided the framework for the continuing contacts with Fritz Berber, and was indeed referred to as 'the Berber group'. As relations between Germany and the western powers moved towards war, the link with Berber took on an enhanced significance.

R. A. Butler and India

During this period, although the disturbing situation in Europe clearly preoccupied Alexander, he was constantly drawn into the concerns of colleagues in the India Conciliation Group. The coalition Government under Ramsay MacDonald had exerted itself to push through Parliament the political reforms arising out of the series of Round Table Conferences (the third and final one being held towards the end of 1932). Unsatisfactory though this legislation appeared to Indian nationalists, it was vehemently opposed as too radical by a large section of the Conservative Party, most notably by Winston Churchill. So far as they were concerned, conciliation was a dangerous irrelevance. Tory loathing for Gandhi might give deep satisfaction to a working man in Birmingham, but it constituted a serious political obstacle for the Secretary of State for India, Sir Samuel Hoare, when he embarked on the Government of India Bill. When Carl Heath and Archbishop William Temple went to see

Hoare in the summer of 1932, urging the Government to adopt a more conciliatory policy, he reminded them of his political difficulties. 'Do you really mean', asked Heath, 'that the Conservative Party does not *want* peace with Mr Gandhi?' 'Certainly I do', Hoare replied, 'they hate him like the devil.'[28] If anything, the attacks on Gandhi and Congress became fiercer as the prospect of new legislation became more immediate. For the campaigners against the Bill, Gandhi became not merely an irresponsible and devious agitator but a criminal who ought to have been executed long ago. Indian national aspirations were clearly no longer confined to insignificant extremists, but the outcome was likely to be a cluster of fragmented and poverty-stricken succession states, at best resembling Latin America.[29]

Because this opposition was so influential, it was the more important for people such as Alexander himself, Agatha Harrison and Carl Heath to remind ministers of attitudes in India, where any policy would after all eventually have to be made to work. In a letter of 13 February 1933, Agatha Harrison spoke of the 'utter unreality' of debates in the House of Commons, solemnly discussing the pros and cons of the bill, when in India the Legislative Assembly was already preoccupied with its rejection. She felt, and this was to become the salient conviction of the ICG, that it was essential to send 'some important statesman' to cut through the tangle of misunderstandings, and in effect to bypass the obdurate British establishment in India.[30] This was a view shared by such sympathetic observers as the industrialist G. D. Birla, who used his business visits to Britain to lobby political leaders in the interests of a conciliatory approach to Indian aspirations. He constantly reiterates his regret that the atmosphere of friendship and goodwill that he found in England apparently could not be transplanted into India, where, as he told Lord Linlithgow before his appointment as Viceroy, the administration was 'stern and stiff'.[31] Personal encounters were all-important.

Agatha Harrison herself carried this approach as far as it would go, and several anecdotes in her letters vividly illustrate her strategy. On a ship going to Ceylon for a YWCA conference in 1936, for example, she was placed for her meals at the same table as a tea-planter and his wife. She dutifully bore the conversation: the planter was convinced that Nehru was 'a rank communist, by gad!' But then – she must have impressed them as a wise and discreet woman – they each confided to her something of their marital difficulties, and she evidently gave them satisfaction. Having thus secured their confidence, she said to the planter, doubtless in her smoothest and most winning tones, 'I want you to do something for me', and pressed a copy of Nehru's *India and the World* into his hand, having marked the order in which he should read the chapters. Read them he did, and the next day spent three hours talking with her. The outcome delighted her: he said he was going to ask the United Planters' Association to invite Nehru to speak to them.[32]

Figure 2 Agatha Harrison

She was equally diligent in cultivating Indian nationalists whom others gave up as 'extreme'. In 1933 she spent a fortnight in Geneva to have long conversations with Subhas Bose, the radical Bengali rival of Jawaharlal Nehru and future commander of the Indian National Army in the Second World War. She learnt about his expulsion from Presidency College and about his acceptance in another college by a Dr Urquhart: 'I shall always', Bose told Harrison, 'be grateful to him.' He also had good feeliings towards Sir Stanley Jackson, the Governor of Bengal between 1927 and 1932, who, when Bose was ill in prison, sent his own doctor to treat him. Bose was being excluded from Britain, and Harrison pointed out how counter-productive this was. If he were admitted he could renew his acquaintance with people such as Urquhart, Jackson and

Irwin, and this might change his feeling of hopelessness about better relations with Britain.[33]

One needs to bear in mind her mode of operation when considering a characteristic initiative after a meeting between a deputation from the ICG and Lord Zetland, Secretary of State for India, and his officials. This occurred on 2 April 1936, when the ICG made a formal complaint about the Government of India's official report, *India in 1933–34*. The report was extremely hostile to Congress, suggesting, for example, that money raised for work with untouchables and for earthquake relief had been diverted to political activity.[34] In a letter setting out their objections to the report, the ICG urged 'in the interests of conciliatory understanding and of constitutional development, that it would be right to put aside, once for all, such methods as distinctly unhelpful to the major end in view.' In a letter afterwards to Carl Heath, Harrison praised him for the way he had handled a difficult meeting, resolutely sticking to the main point at issue, but regretted that he and Alexander had not waited behind with her, when she had contrived to have a word with the Permanent Secretary, Sir Findlater Stewart, of whom she had heard from C. F. Andrews and G. D. Birla.

> I believe he is the 'power behind the throne'. So I thought I would take the bull by the horns and introduce myself to him. The result was even better than I expected. We talked for nearly 25 minutes. And in this talk I was able to clear up many things. I had a feeling after this talk that this is the man through whom we can usefully work.[35]

The ICG's subsequent contacts with Stewart suggest that he was a man of considerable tact whose real opinion was not always easy to discern, but that should not depreciate the audacity with which she disregarded protocol and went straight up to 'the power behnd the throne'.

Strenuous as the work of the ICG was, it was necessarily done out of sight. Putting the nationalist case before the British public generally was more the province of the India League, whose approach, as we have seen, was altogether more abrasive than that of the ICG. Relations between the two organisations continued to be rather strained, with League leaders like Krishna Menon and Reginald Reynolds expressing their impatience with the discretion integral to the ICG's strategy. Alexander was a member of the editorial board of the League's journal *India Bulletin*, but in June 1932 resigned because he was out of sympathy with the aggressive tone of some of the material published there. In May he had drafted a leading article to which Reynolds wanted to make unacceptable changes. Alexander, in withdrawing, complained that the journal had no faith in any statesmen, and attacked them unreasonably.[36]

In spite of this, though, Alexander himself was still regarded as an irredeemably hostile partisan of Congress by officials at the India Office. His activities in India in 1930 were viewed with great suspicion: had he perhaps been collecting Indian national and revolutionary songs and slogans for propaganda purposes in Britain?[37] His reputation as a trouble-maker was confirmed by the publication, in 1933, of a pamphlet for the Howard League for Penal Reform, *Indian Prisoners: A Case for Enquiry and an Opportunity for Progress.* Gandhi's imprisonment after his return from the Round Table Conference had been one of a great wave of arrests, which led to the detention of some 36,000 supporters of civil disobedience.[38] Alexander criticised the often degrading conditions in which these prisoners were kept, and the use of punishments such as whipping.

At London Yearly Meeting in 1936 there was some discussion of a minute from Yorkshire Quarterly Meeting which appealed for a new spirit of reconciliation in India, and advocated an amnesty for all political prisoners still held there, mostly suspected terrorists in Bengal. Detention without trial was a major grievance in India, the more so since the issue did not seem to make any impact on British public opinion. Jawaharlal Nehru visited London early in 1936, and speaking to the ICG on 4 February complained about the'amazing ignorance' shown on this subject in Parliament.[39] Yearly Meeting was thus taking up Nehru's challenge when it agreed to approach the new Viceroy, Lord Linlithgow, urging him to consider an amnesty as part of the general policy review to be expected when taking up his appointment. Six Friends were appointed to draft the request; in due course it was turned down.[40] The group then prepared a statement about the situation for circulation to Clerks of all Quarterly and Monthly Meetings in Britain.

Alexander, as the group's convener, drafted the statement, which was published as a short pamphlet in January 1937, *Political Prisoners in India.* While drafting it he had the happy idea of consulting the Under-Secretary of State for India about matters of fact, and about the Government's current attitude to the issues raised. The Under-Secretary was Richard Austen Butler, at the age of 34 one of the youngest ministers in the National Government, now headed by Stanley Baldwin. He had been born in India, the son of Sir Montagu Butler, an administrator who eventually became Governor of the Central Provinces. 'Rab' Butler always retained a keen interest in the affairs of the sub-continent, and as a minister showed himself to be a liberal-minded and intelligent advocate of official policy. He took a conspicuous part in the heated debates on the Government of India Bill, and proved to be one of the most sympathetic listeners to G. D. Birla in his visit to Britain in the summer of 1935.

Alexander seems to have persuaded a neighbour in Birmingham, A. S. Marshall, to write on his behalf to Butler, who was an old friend. Marshall told Butler that it would be useful to see Alexander, a man whose sincerity and ability he admired. Butler was interested, and asked his officials to make arrangements for a meeting. They warned him that Alexander had committed a whole series of 'misdeeds', which were enumerated at some length in his file.

Butler agreed that he had better read the file, but added that he would like to see him anyway.[41]

The meeting accordingly took place at the beginning of November. Butler's memorandum about it is distinctly cool, natural enough when it was to be read by hostile officials. He remarks that Alexander wasn't particularly well briefed about the situation in India, and was unduly proud of his association with the leaders of the Indian National Congress. But Butler appreciated the fact that Alexander found some Congress propaganda distasteful, held no brief for terrorism, and felt real distress at the 'stubborn and resentful' attitude of young people in India. He wanted to do all he could to improve the atmosphere, but lacked specific proposals that the Government might reasonably accept. He had indeed come up with the idea that people like Nehru might be persuaded to cooperate in a practical way in dealing with problems such as the aftermath of the Quetta earthquake, but Butler objected that Congress would exploit such practical work for its own purposes.

Alexander must have felt that little progress could be made with the degree of suspicion that this objection disclosed. A year earlier Birla had got Butler to acknowledge that the root problem was the bad atmosphere in India, but Butler could not see practical ways of working towards an improvement.

> He said he was at one with me but did not know how to translate the feeling into action. I said, 'I have given you half a dozen alternatives, now you should produce more, but you do not mean to say that Englishmen have gone bankrupt of statesmanship and that they have no formula for translating their feelings.'[42]

Perhaps Butler hoped that Alexander would help him to avoid bankruptcy, but given the premises of British policy that was hardly possible. As it was, the overall effect of the interview was a shade too sympathetic for the taste of the officials who looked at the report, one of whom commented that 'Mr. A. appears to have undergone some sort of conversion. But I doubt whether with his temperament it will last.'[43]

In December the draft text of the pamphlet was completed and sent to Butler. He questioned some details, such as allegations of corruption in the police, and (in part prompted by his officials) expressed regret about the lack of 'realistic' suggestions on the problem of 'the terrorist activities we both deplore'. Alexander's response was that the root problem was 'the mental attitude of each side towards the other' and that Butler's letter was, alas, an illustration of failure to see what things looked like from the Indian side.

> It makes me wish that you could go incognito and live in Indian homes for a few months, and see the other side of the picture. At any rate, I can tell you that some of the things I discovered at first hand in India

> nine years ago utterly humiliated me. And until we have felt that awful humiliation, I doubt if we can heal these wounds.[44]

There was some further correspondence in which Alexander thanked Butler for putting his time and knowledge at Friends' disposal, and Butler expressed appreciation of the spirit in which they had consulted him. This good feeling was emphatically not reflected in the comments of an official, R. T. Peel, who evidently felt that he had much to bear from a minister who sometimes questioned the factual accuracy of his briefing papers,[45] and who treated troublesome Quakers with needless deference. Writing to the Secretary to the Government of India Home Department, R. M. Maxwell, Peel remarked that the pamphlet was written by 'our old friend, Horace Alexander'. In civil service minutes, an 'old friend' is usually a long-standing nuisance of some kind. It suggests heavy sarcasm, not cordiality. Still, Peel thought that *Political Prisoners in India* could have been worse, and was certainly 'slightly less objectionable now than it was originally'. It remained an 'unfortunate production', with an obvious bias against Government. Happily it wouldn't attract much attention[46] – and indeed the Clerks of Quarterly and Monthly Meetings to whom it was sent were not very likely to stir up a political storm that would subvert the British Empire.

Butler was not only impressed by Alexander's manifest determination to be conciliatory, but knew also of his involvement with Quaker relief work at the time in Catalonia, then in the throes of the Spanish civil war. Alexander visited Barcelona between 13 and 20 December 1936 to see how the feeding programme for children was functioning, a mission which would have underlined, even for a Government minister less sympathetic than Butler, the vigour of Friends' humanitarian concerns.[47] This will have been in the background of Alexander's next meeting with Butler in May 1937. The immediate occasion for it was a political crisis that had followed Congress victories in several Indian provinces, in the first elections held under the Government of India Act. Congress ministries objected to the powers retained by the British-appointed Governors to overrule decisions taken by elected representatives. They refused to take office, a decision endorsed by the Congress Working Committee on 28 April. A day earlier Alexander wrote to Butler requesting a short meeting, it being easier to talk than to write. (He wished Gandhi were 'near enough for me to say a few things to him too'.)[48] They met on 6 May, and a letter of Alexander's dated 9 May makes clear that he saw the problem as one of convincing Congress that Governors would not vexatiously interfere, and of convincing the British that these ministries would not act in a provocative and irresponsible way. He expressed satisfaction with what the current Secretary of State, Lord Zetland, had said in the House of Lords in the afternoon of the 6th, as well he might, since Zetland had made exactly this point, insisting there was no intention to 'trench upon the wide powers which it was purpose of Parliament to place in the hands of ministries'. Zetland's speech was described by *The Hindu* of Madras as 'an earnest attempt to understand the Congress point of view'.[49] Since Alexander saw Butler at 12 noon that day, it is tempting to conjecture that, over lunch, Butler may have had something persuasive to say to his Secretary of State.

In the same letter of 9 May, Alexander told Butler that since their meeting he had written at length to Gandhi and Nehru in an attempt to interpret the British Government's attitude, and suggesting ways in which *they* might help to create confidence on the British side. The British themselves had an opportunity to cooperate with the new ministries to improve conditions in India's villages. Statements like Zetland's were helpful, but couldn't be expected to elicit an immediate response. 'I think they need cumulative evidence of goodwill, in their present mood.' Courteous as ever, Butler replied that he was glad to have seen Alexander: 'I should like to think over what you say.'[50]

A couple of weeks later Butler was transferred from the India Office to the Ministry of Labour, serving again as Parliamentary Under-Secretary. The Butler Papers in Trinity College Cambridge include some interesting tributes from friends and acquaintances on this occasion, such as a letter from Sir Mohammad Yakub, who regretted his departure at a time when his experience and commitment as 'an Indian by birth' were especially needed: 'the political atmosphere in India', he said, in words that E. M. Forster would have relished, 'is beset with dark clouds of complicated problems.' Butler reassured Sir Mohammad that his new post would enable him to be 'a better "Servant of India"' if the need should ever arise: a characteristic attempt, by invoking Gandhi's mentor G. K. Gokhale, to identify himself with an acceptable nationalist sentiment.[51]

The crisis of 1937 was resolved, the Congress ministries did take office, and in June 1938 Alexander published yet another pamphlet, this time offering an interim assessment of the ministries' work, *Congress Rule in India*.[52] He sent a copy to Butler, by now Under-Secretary at the Foreign Office, who said that he had enjoyed it, 'after removing the outside cover' (its colour was a brilliant red). He went on: 'As one of those who felt they would tackle their responsibilities, I am well pleased. I only hope they will continue with the good work they have started.'[53]

*

Alexander's preoccupations with Germany and India need to be seen against the background of his work in Woodbrooke. Teaching international relations absorbed much of his time and energy, and as a senior member of staff he had demanding responsibilities in helping to foster the Quaker ethos of the college. In this role Olive had a greater importance than Alexander himself. She knew all the students well, and kept in touch with them after they had left. She edited the *Woodbrooke International Journal*, and compiled its 'Personalia' section in which she gave an account of all the letters she had received from former students in the previous months. Reading these sections gives an impressive picture of a worldwide community, warmly supportive of each member. Throughout the 1930s people came from Germany, and subsequent items in 'Personalia' indicate that some of them became refugees. One conjectures that a term in Woodbrooke must have been a welcome escape from the oppressive atmosphere generated by the Nazi regime. There were Jewish students: one Hertha Israel attended in the 1936–7 session, and I have been told of a Jewish doctor who, listening to a broadcast of a Hitler speech denouncing the Versailles Treaty, observed that, when the Führer spoke thus, he spoke for every German.

Woodbrooke reunions in different parts of Europe were a characteristic expression of the college's ethos, and Olive did much of the preparatory work for them. Only occasionally does her animating activity achieve visibility, most memorably as a result of the residence in Woodbrooke of Jomo Kenyatta. At the prompting of C. F. Andrews this future leader of an independent Kenya stayed there from the end of November 1931 until the following Easter. He was in England on behalf of the Kikuyu Central Association to campaign against the expropriation of Kikuyu farmers from their land for the benefit of white settlers. He was preparing a memorandum to be presented to the Kenya Land Commission, chaired by Sir Morris Carter. Olive worked with him in the writing of this document to ensure that it was in the idiomatic English necessary to gain respectful attention. One of the people who read it was the Labour peer Sydney Olivier, who made effective use of it in a debate on the East African land issue in the House of Lords on 23 March 1932. He deplored an earlier report that started from the premise that 'whoever had any rights in these lands, the land did not belong to the natives'. On the contrary, there was a long-developed procedure for determining land ownership, and 'where you have a community which has sane and intelligent customs and laws it is the most stupid thing in the world to try to thrust the ram-rod of your British law into these works'.[54] It is pleasant to think of Olive's helping to make unmistakeably clear how sane and intelligent Kikuyu customs were.

Olive made a deep impression on Jomo Kenyatta. He said that he could hardly find words to express his gratitude to her,[55] but perhaps the words were found in the appreciation of 'the spirit of Woodbrooke' that he contributed to the spring term 1932 log-book. He writes of the qualities that distinguish it – its 'patience in trial, resignation in affliction, humility in success and virtue in whatever position in life it has pleased God to place us'.[56] Olive's character shines through this affirmation, and is a moving testimony to the kind of influence she exerted over those whose lives she touched.

6

THE SECOND WORLD WAR

War comes again

On 20 May 1937 Alexander opened the Peace Committee session of London Yearly Meeting. He reminded his hearers of the Gospel story of Jesus and the rich young man who could not bring himself to give up his possessions and enter a life of voluntary poverty. He applied this to Britain's position as an imperial power, protecting itself by maintaining tariffs against competitors, and holding on to outposts like Gibraltar, Malta, Cyprus and Hong Kong. Such clinging to possessions inevitably incited rival powers to make their own claims, and there was a need to break out of the whole predicament.

> It must not be a surrender to threats, or a surrender due to fear. It must be a surrender of Empire for something more glorious than any empire – that man may live at one with God in bonds of firm necessity. . . . Like Peter of old, we must pay heed first of all to what Jesus says to us: 'Follow thou Me.'[1]

Alexander was speaking ten days after the coronation of George VI, an event marked by profuse affirmations of loyalty from all parts of the worldwide British Empire, and followed by a month-long Imperial Conference in which the beneficent role of the Empire was reviewed and illustrated. It may well be that Friends felt they had had a surfeit of patriotism, and found Alexander's audacity refreshing. *The Friend* said that the address made a deep impression, and evidently Alexander succeeded in conveying something of the Gandhian confidence that a way forward would open up for Britain once the nation had resolved to 'get off the backs' of Indians and others.

None the less, with an international situation becoming steadily more threatening, Alexander and his colleagues found themselves preoccupied with attempts to lower tensions in particular crises rather than pursue a grand strategy of peace-making. Not that the grand strategy was forgotten: on 2 November 1938 the National Peace Council launched a petition for an international conference to remedy 'economic and political conditions likely to lead to war'. By the following summer they had collected about a million signatures, including those of leading figures in the arts, from John Gielgud to Emlyn Williams, from David Low to E. Phillips Oppenheim, quite apart from predictable names like Bernard Shaw and H. G. Wells.[2] But petitions, no matter how well supported, could not neutralise the impact of the all-too-evident drive to war. The continuing havoc created by the Japanese attack on China and the civil war in Spain generated an almost intolerable anxiety in the crises precipitated by Hitler in 1938 in Austria and Czechoslovakia, and left little energy for other concerns. Surviving correspondence is preoccupied with attempts to avert the supreme disaster of a full-scale war.

One of the group of Friends who dedicated themselves to keeping communications open between Britain and Germany was Corder Catchpool. He had been in charge of the Quaker Centre in Berlin from 1930 onwards, and had suffered arrest and interrogation after the Nazi seizure of power. He convinced his interrogators of his goodwill, and earned himself the privilege of continuing to question without interference the objectionable features of the regime: the anti-Semitism, the intolerance of political opposition, the concentration camps, and so on. None the less, like Alexander himself and Conwil-Evans, Catchpool believed that there had been benefits for Germany in this revolution, and it was right to concede this while challenging the warlike ideology and abuses of human rights that had accompanied it. He remained in Berlin until the autumn of 1936, and thereafter continued his work of relief and reconciliation from his home in Hampstead. In the spring of 1937 he accompanied the veteran Labour politician George Lansbury on his controversial mission to Hitler to appeal for support for a World Economic Conference, an initiative which earned him vehement criticism from friends who had no patience with anything that tended to legitimise the Nazi regime. In response, Catchpool wrote, in words that Alexander would have warmly endorsed,

> Sound internal spiritual forces which we know to exist in the German people and which seem to have been crushed, are not dead and will quietly rise and gradually modify and leaven the national life. Such home-made sanctions are better than economic boycott from abroad,

> or international war. . . . Though sometimes shaken I have come back standing in the old faith, a conviction that if the way of violence is rejected, a quite new vision and practice of another way is called for, showing a spirit of courage, endurance and patience, and also ability, which war cannot match.[3]

Among Catchpool's most characteristic enterprises was his involvement with the feeding programme for children in the Sudetenland on the borders of Czechoslovakia. The area suffered a severe economic depression, with devastating consequences for the children there. Funds were available from a German relief organisation, Brüder in Not (brothers in need), but German involvement was unacceptable to the Czech authorities. Catchpool arranged for the German funds to be channelled through Quaker relief, and since both Czech and German children benefited, everyone concerned was satisfied. In his account of this affair, William R. Hughes makes clear what impressive diplomatic skills Catchpool possessed, and more especially the extent of the goodwill he earned among his Czech contacts. He was actually awarded the Czechoslovak Order of the White Lion for his work in alleviating the sufferings of children in distressed areas – an award which stood him in good stead when all Britishers were in disgrace in that country at the time of the Sudeten crisis in September 1938.[4] But that crisis was an intimation of how overwhelmingly powerful were the forces making for a general war, and although Catchpool showed great courage in deliberately returning to Prague when the threat of war was imminent, his presence was felt to be unwelcome, and his approval of the Munich agreement organised by Neville Chamberlain over the heads of the Czechs was not easily forgiven.

While he was in Prague, he received a telegram from Joan Fry (another Quaker active in peace issues) urging him to join herself, Maurice Rowntree and Alexander in Berlin to make a plea to Hitler himself for a peaceful outcome to the dispute. The precedent eighty-five years earlier of the Quaker mission to the Czar to prevent the outbreak of the Crimean War was not encouraging, but in any case there was no opportunity to make the attempt, as the German army was mobilising and normal travel became impossible. With the easing of the crisis, though, Alexander made arrangements to go to Berlin to consult Fritz Berber, arriving at the same time as the so-called 'Kristallnacht', 9–10 November 1938, when Jewish homes and property were destroyed in a concerted attack on the entire Jewish population. He saw Berber twice, and transmitted a report of the meetings to Butler at the Foreign Office. At the first meeting, on the 12th, Berber left Alexander in no doubt about his extreme revulsion at what had happened: 'dark supernatural powers' were at work, and a spiritual power for good was needed in the same degree to cope with it. Alas, it wasn't apparently available. 'I doubt now whether it is not too late to save

Europe' he said, twice, during the conversation. Fanatical anti-Semitism would lead to further horrors: many deplored what was happening, but did not see how to oppose it. Moreover, protests from abroad did nothing to strengthen what was undoubtedly a 'growing abhorrence of Nazi methods' in Germany itself. People in the German army who disliked the regime would none the less feel that collusion with foreign intervention would be treasonable. The necessary spiritual power had to come from within Germany, or it was useless.

At the second interview, five days later, Alexander noticed that Berber seemed particularly nervous and weary: not surprising, since he had just spent seven hours with Ribbentrop, never the most comfortable of companions. Berber was (rightly) anxious that German policy was drifting towards further and unjustifiable demands on the Czechs, and seems to have reacted by pressing on Alexander the deficiencies in the British response to the crisis. Why had Chamberlain allowed a hostile Opposition to force on him a policy of accelerating rearmament? Berber felt that some good might be done if Foreign Ministry officials in Britain and Germany were to organise Hitler into making a conciliatory speech. Lord Londonderry might have a word with Goering, or Alexander himself might speak to Sir George Forbes, who then might speak to Woermann.[5] But he was evidently clutching at straws.

Through the winter Friends' preoccupation was very much with assisting Jewish people to leave Germany, and Roger Carter, who was then in charge of the Quaker Centre in Berlin, was deeply impressed by the help freely offered by non-Jewish Germans. They could have had no motive but sheer good-neighbourliness in their efforts to protect and support their Jewish friends, not to mention the risk of incurring the displeasure of the authorities. The same experience was reported by Muriel Lester in Vienna when she visited central Europe in the autumn of 1938. There were still groups working on behalf of the Jews, although they were risking liberty and employment by doing so. But far more needed to be done by British sympathisers.:

> Telephone calls, bus fares, meals out, take up a lot of money, and most of our keenest members [of the Fellowship of Reconciliation] are already out of work for conscience sake. I found some who, having provided themselves with a bit of bread-and-butter for their midday meal, were tramping about on errands of mercy, rather cold and a little hungry. A steady flow of support from us could make things much easier for them.[6]

There was some response to this plea, but the overall situation was steadily worsening. Efforts to avoid the ultimate catastrophe of war seemed more and more futile, particularly when in March 1939 the Germans marched into what was left of Czechoslovakia after the Munich agreement, and Italy made an easy conquest of Albania. I vividly remember the news of the latter enterprise coming through on Good Friday. I was staying with a friend (we were both twelve years old at the time), and one of his relatives came through to where we were playing some board game to tell us what Mussolini had done. He was very agitated, and thundered 'There *must* be a war, and the sooner we have it and get it over with the better.' My friend and I were petrified, said absolutely nothing, and then resumed our game to put thoughts of mass bombing and indiscriminate slaughter out of our minds. But the expectation of war was now pervasive.

Berber continued to exert such pressure as he could, and to inform his Quaker contacts about the state of play. Alexander saw him again in late May or early June, and in a report forwarded to the Foreign Office by Corder Catchpool he remarked that 'many thoughtful Germans' feared there was an ominous resemblance between Germany's relations with Czechoslovakia and Britain's relations with Ireland. Britain had had to concede independence eventually, and the lesson was one the Germans would do well to heed. Overwhelmingly, though, the current German preoccupation was with'encirclement', the frustration of her legitimate needs by British diplomacy. Germany would go to any lengths to extricate itself from this predicament: 'Rapprochement with Russia would be the answer, and a very dangerous situation result.' Berber made this warning nearly three months before the Nazi–Soviet Pact, and presumably reflects his understanding of the way Ribbentrop's mind was working.

Berber was clinging to the basic assumption of the policy of 'appeasement', the assumption that, as he put it, a prosperous Germany would be a peaceful Germany. Many people 'boiled with indignation' at the anti-Semitic excesses of the regime. Given prosperity there would be free movement between Germany and other nations, and this would be the best remedy for fanaticism.[7] He also evidently felt that it was still possible by diplomatic moves to avoid unnecessary hazards. There is a revealing glimpse of him at this time in the recollections of the British businessman Ernest Tennant, who met him on 26 July after they had both been with Ribbentrop when he was at a castle near Salzburg to confer with his Italian opposite number Count Ciano. Tennant described Berber as 'a mild young man, obviously alarmed at the outlook':

> He told me that, if he might venture to give me some advice on the present crisis, he would endeavour to urge on Mr Chamberlain the importance of making it clear to the Poles that they must without further delay come to a settlement with Germany over the Corridor and Danzig, even if that meant Danzig returning to the Reich. When I asked him, 'and then what would Germany demand of Poland next?', he replied, 'Your guarantee to Poland would still stand and would operate if Hitler went beyond what the Poles felt compelled to agree to concede. That should prevent any further demands on Poland.'[8]

Two days later Berber flew back to Berlin accompanied by Roger Carter, whom he had summoned from the Quaker Centre to brief him in the secure (if chilly) setting of a small aeroplane. He said that Hitler was 'resolved to solve the Danzig problem', and that a guarantee to Poland of access to the sea might be feasible, but no more than that. This was in effect a warning that Hitler had withdrawn his earlier offer, in April, of a formal recognition of Poland's right to the so-called 'Polish Corridor' that separated East Prussia from the rest of Germany, in exchange for the return of Danzig to the Reich and the concession of extra-territorial road and rail links across the Corridor. He added that there was currently no prospect of progress towards a more liberal regime in Bohemia and Moravia, and repeated his prediction of a 'surprise' about Soviet–German relations.

Alexander forwarded Carter's report to Butler at the Foreign Office, urging him to treat it as strictly confidential: otherwise it might have serious consequences for Berber, for whom contacts with his British friends remained extremely hazardous.[9] Presumably such intelligence did something to support the hope that there were some reasonable Germans with whom it might be possible to do business. And indeed a sixteen-point peace plan was drafted at the end of August that was much closer to Hitler's April offer than Berber had thought likely, proposing as it did that the future of the Corridor would be decided by a plebiscite. But the Polish Government was given no realistic time to react to the plan, and the first that the British ambassador, Sir Nevile Henderson, heard of it was at midnight on the 30 August, when Ribbentrop read it out to him, rapidly, in German. Little more than twenty-four hours later, German forces moved across the Polish frontier, and war had begun.

The sixteen-point plan was published in the British press on 1 September, and Alexander immediately telephoned Butler at the Foreign Office, suggesting that an effort should be made to induce the German government to keep to the plan.

> It seemed as though, if anyone could get at Hitler, even if he should say 'Now it is too late,' one might fairly reply, 'But if you thought this an inherently reasonable plan yesterday, it must be inherently reasonable today or tomorrow.'
>
> I found that some of my fellow-Quakers were inclined to regard it in much the same light, and that both Corder [Catchpool], who had seen Berber just before he left Berlin ten days ago, and I had thought we traced the hand of Berber in the proposals.
>
> It still seems to me that the time might come when the fact that such a reasonable basis of discussion was put forward by Hitler, even if he never intended it to be taken seriously, would be useful for negotiating a just settlement in those regions.[10]

Butler sent a courteous reply, saying that Catchpool and Carter had written in the same sense, and that their views were being considered carefully. This was clearly a polite fiction, but Butler treated his Quaker contacts with remarkable deference. He asked one of his officials, William Strang, to draft a response to Catchpool and Carter that was 'thoughtful': 'Reference might be made to our White Paper. These', he added, 'are important "friends".' The letter that resulted agreed that some elements in Germany wanted to settle matters by negotiation, 'but unhappily it was not with those elements that the decision rested.' Butler ended with a sentence which was almost certainly not in Strang's draft: 'I hope to keep in contact with you, since some years' experience with Professor Alexander has taught me to value your ideas and ideals.'[11]

*

Alexander may well have 'traced the hand of Berber' in the sixteen-point plan because of a single detail. Point 8 set out proposals for ensuring free access: between East Prussia and the rest of Germany if the plebiscite went against Germany; between Poland and the sea otherwise. The road and rail links should be constructed in a way that ensured that neither country's lines of communication were affected, '*i.e.*, they shall pass either over or under' the other's means of access.[12] This specific solution is not mentioned in earlier proposals about access, and it will have reminded Alexander of the ingenious formula devised by Hugh Richardson for preventing conflict between imperial Germany and imperial Russia before the First World War. Since it is most unlikely that Alexander failed to mention this example of diplomatic resourcefulness in the course of his many conversations with Berber, he can be forgiven for thinking that Richardson was the ultimate source for the German proposal.

It is clear that Ribbentrop had no intention of giving these proposals a chance to persuade the Poles to be more accommodating, and even if Berber did have a hand in drawing them up (which is quite possible) we know that at this time he was deeply despondent and apprehensive. There is a vivid account of an interview with him on 25 August by one Ulrich Noack, two days after the signing of the Nazi–Soviet Pact. Berber told Noack that belligerent propaganda had made any hopes of a moderate settlement with Poland impossible. The understanding with Russia would provide a probably transient opportunity to complete the revision in Germany's favour of the frontiers unjustly imposed in the Treaty of Versailles. Noack remarked that the pre-1914 frontiers would leave a lot of Poles in German territory. Berber gave the official reply that the Poles could be resettled elsewhere (e.g. in Siberia) – saying this with an expression that showed his revulsion at the idea. But by now clearly he felt quite helpless.

In order to understand the full significance of this interview, and its bearing on Alexander's next dealings with Berber, it is necessary to say something about Noack himself. He was an academic historian who had spent the summer term of 1927 at Woodbrooke, while Berber was still a Fellow there. H. G. Wood, the then Director of Studies, had introduced him to the work of the liberal Catholic scholar Lord Acton, and Acton was the subject of a book that Noack published in 1937. It gave as much offence to the Nazi authorities as Berber's had done, celebrating as it did someone who was obnoxious twice over: a liberal and a Catholic. Having thus disgraced himself, he found a less perilous enterprise in writing a politically innocuous history of the Scandinavian peoples. This was funded by an official research council, and he was given leave to work on it in Norway. It was on the eve of his departure for Oslo, in November 1938, that he met Berber for the first time since they were together at Woodbrooke. Berber affirmed that he remained true to his earlier ideals, and that the handling of the Sudeten crisis a few weeks earlier had shown that some parts of the Nazi leadership were more conciliatory than others. Goering and Hess, in particular, took a much milder line than Hitler himself, or Ribbentrop. Berber aligned himself with those – influential in the Foreign Ministry – who sought an enduring settlement with Britain.[13]

Noack departed for Oslo, where he not only embarked on his historical researches but found time to complete a study of a new European order, the foundations for which could have been laid by the Munich agreement. This book, *Das politische Ethos in der europäischen Diplomatie* (The Political Ethos in European Diplomacy), was published in March 1939, just as German troops were marching into Prague, thus subverting the assumptions on which Noack had based his argument. He had seen the four-power conference – Britain, France, Germany and Italy – as the starting-point for an international order more soundly based than the League of Nations, and one to which other powers such as the United States could adhere. Munich could have opened the way to a rationalising of central European borders, a renunciation of imperialistic domination. But the destruction of Czechoslovakia was just the kind of destabilising expansion that inevitably provoked a reaction from other states. Noack thought it possible that Germany might avert the consequences of this calamitous step by granting a genuine autonomy to Bohemia and Moravia. But with increasing tension over Poland and Danzig, magnanimous statesmanship on these lines seemed increasingly remote.[14]

Noack was in Berlin again in the summer of 1939, and the meeting with Berber on 25 August led to his taking on an official role. Berber asked him to serve as cultural attaché to the German embassy in Oslo, and had persuaded the head of the Information Department at the Foreign Ministry, Gunther Altenburg, to accept him. Noack did not welcome the idea, but allowed himself to be persuaded when he was assured that he could count on complete freedom to report back as he saw fit. He returned to Oslo on 4 September, one day after the Allied declarations of war, and was soon assisting the architects of a Scandinavian peace plan, based on a formula which balanced a German withdrawal from much of Poland and from Bohemia and Moravia against a reopening of the German claims for the return of its pre-1914 colonies. The story of how the Bishop of Oslo, Eivind Berggrav, took this plan to Lord Halifax and Herman Goering, makes an instructive chapter in the history of mediation in deadly conflicts, and Berggrav's own vivid account of it has, curiously, never been translated from the original Norwegian.[15] It is important to bear this hurry of activity in mind, and the parallel unease and restiveness of Hitler's army commanders,[16] when considering Alexander's initiatives in the autumn of 1939.

Although the outbreak of war might seem to destroy all hope of peaceful settlement, the fact that military action was at first confined to Poland and to some naval battles meant that it was still possible to think in terms of a resumption of negotiation. There was much discussion of 'peace aims'. A debate in the House of Commons on 3 October 1939 ended with a strong plea by the Labour MP Sidney Silverman for a diplomatic initiative: 'Now, while people are in the mood to talk, talk to them. It is not necessary to talk to them on their terms, but if you tell them what are your terms, and invite them to talk on your basis, you take the initiative out of their hands.'[17] In the same debate the veteran statesman David Lloyd George made a speech reminding his colleagues that offers of negotiation from the enemy or from neutral powers should not necessarily be rejected out of hand.[18] While the speech was fiercely condemned by several of Lloyd George's parliamentary colleagues, it drew a huge response in letters from the public, most of them fervently agreeing with him.[19] A few days later Alexander drafted a letter to the Prime Minister, signed by twenty four Friends from his local meeting, Cotteridge, which expressed confidence in Chamberlain's desire for peace, and urging him 'to express and to focus the longings of millions of men and women in this and other lands, including Germany, who are hoping for a better Europe and a happier world'.[20]

It was at about this time that Friends' Peace Committee organised a special 'Emergency Group' to take action on opportunities for peacemaking. The first recorded meeting was on 12 October, when a proposed visit of Percy Bartlett and Horace Alexander to Switzerland was welcomed, and the hope expressed that Alexander might have an informal talk with Butler with a view to opening the way to 'fairly regular contacts with neutral countries'.[21] During the 'phoney war', or what the French expressively called the 'drôle de guerre', it was still possible for non-official civilians to travel abroad, although only with permission. The visit to Switzerland (in November) was ostensibly to attend Swiss Friends' Yearly Meeting, but also to renew contact with people like the veteran pacifist Friedrich Siegmund-Schultze, Pierre Ceresole of Service Civile Internationale, and Visser't Hooft, secretary of the embryonic World

Council of Churches.[22] Alexander also attended a meeting of a committee of the Rockefeller Foundation in Geneva, where the Foundation supported the Graduate Institute of International Studies. Here Alexander had a private conversation with Berber, who had also been allowed to attend. So far as I am aware there is no written report of what Berber said on this occasion, but he will have been fully informed about the Scandinavian peace plan, and was well aware that when it had been put to Ribbentrop in mid-October he had rejected it outright.[23] Berggrav was determined to see if he could win support in Britain, and Alexander's report – presumably to Butler – may well have helped prepare the way for the bishop's visit to London and other British cities in December, when he won the wholehearted support of the Bishop of Chichester, George Bell, and a cautiously sympathetic hearing from the Foreign Secretary, Lord Halifax. But a debate in the House of Lords on 13 December showed how difficult it was to advocate the case for a negotiated peace in an atmosphere when any concession would be construed as weakness.[24]

Shortly after this debate, Alexander and some other Quakers were given permission to visit neutral capitals and form an assessment of how far the non-belligerents might have a contribution to make in the current situation. Alexander himself was concerned to advance the idea that there should be no question of 'war debts' but rather of a planned European rehabilitation, a 'healing of the nations', where funding for relief schemes would be sought from governments, but non-governmental organisations would actually carry out the work.[25] He went to the Netherlands, where he saw a former prime minister, Hendrikus Colijn. Their discussion (summarised by Alexander in a letter to Butler) ranged over the whole war situation. Colijn had several contacts with older German diplomats, and had formed the impression that the Scandinavian formula of a smaller but independent Poland and Czech republic was quite acceptable to them. He felt that German morale would be adversely affected by a perception of the war's futility, and that it might be all over in six months: no one victorious, and therefore all the more possible to make a better peace. Alexander agreed with this warmly, but speculated that perhaps a *more* reasonable Hitler might encounter a *less* reasonable Britain and France. Colijn agreed that while Halifax and Chamberlain might be relied on, Winston Churchill's influence was less satisfactory. And of course throughout the first six months of the war, it was Churchill, the First Lord of the Admiralty, who oversaw most of the fighting that was going on then. For good measure he made much more bellicose speeches than his colleagues, and in Cabinet promoted the idea of an invasion of the northern parts of Norway and Sweden to deprive Germany of its sources of iron ore. Indeed, this plan was about to be put into effect in April when it was forestalled by the German invasion of Denmark and Norway, which had the useful side-effect of preserving Sweden's neutrality.[26]

With hindsight it must seem inevitable that influences working towards a negotiated peace were too fragile to withstand the united determination of war leaders on either side to get on with the fighting. But at Christmas 1939 peace hopes did not appear unrealistic. In a late autobiographical note preserved at Woodbrooke, Alexander recalls how he returned to Birmingham from his visit to the Netherlands on a train that arrived after midnight on Christmas morning. He had to walk all the way back to Selly Oak, reaching his home at 1.30am. The weather was appropriately still and quiet. Apparently he heard no angels singing, but his mood was buoyant. And it was a moment when several positive influences for peace were converging. Alexander was aware of Berggrav's shuttle diplomacy; Bishop Bell's support for a possible negotiation may have been adversely received in the House of Lords, but at least a debate had been held; and President Roosevelt was sending a letter to the Pope affirming his belief that a new order was 'being built silently but inevitably in the hearts of masses whose voices are not heard but whose common faith will write the final hiistory of our time.' This message caused consternation in the Foreign Office, whose officials thought it signalled an American–Vatican 'peace offensive' which would be dangerously popular among the neutrals.[27] They were also concerned about a New Year broadcast by William Temple, then Archbishop of York. Temple had referred to the importance of constructive peace terms, and of the willingness to accept third-party judgements in a peaceful world order. Roger Makins minuted that this was 'admirable in theory but not very practical'.[28]

Not only were there influential peace pressures, but Alexander could reasonably feel that in Butler he had an important friend at court. His helpfulness to the Quakers was not restricted to facilitating quasi-diplomatic ventures like Alexander's. On 5 January 1940, Paul Sturge, secretary of the Friends' Service Council, asked permission for Myrtle Wright to proceed to the Quaker Centre in Copenhagen and for Margaret Collyer to the one in Amsterdam. He also reported on the outcome of previous permissions, allowing Quaker workers to help Polish refugees in Hungary. There was also a prospect of similar work in Rumania. Butler endorsed this letter with a note requesting facilities for these Friends, but the files also contain an anxious note from one civil servant wondering whether all FSC members had 'discretion', and another (H. L. Farquhar) remarking that such people 'when given an inch, take an ell; – and in this particular case the 'Friends' quite understandably want to take advantage of any pull they may have to short-circuit the procedure necessary in the case of the ordinary public.'

Butler took the point, and asked for a '*warm* and *melodious* rendering of Mr Farquhar's theme.' The warm and melodious draft follows: 'I should like to do anything I could to assist you', but the normal procedure is outlined, and perhaps they would be so good as to follow it. Paul Sturge responded (11

January) that of course they would be happy to do so.[29] Butler had to tread carefully, but was evidently interested in picking up any indications there might be of the possibility of limiting the war. In December he led the British delegation to the League of Nations session which expelled the Soviet Union because of its attack on Finland, and a London magazine, the *News Review*, picked up an odd story that '39 agents' of Dr Goebbels were in Geneva then to set rumours going about peace on the lines sketched in the Scandinavian plan.[30] Alexander mentioned this dismissively in a later letter to Butler, but expressed more concern about a report that the French secret service had got wind of his meeting with Berber in November. Butler reassured him: 'As you know, I have full confidence in you.'[31]

By now, however, there had been a discouraging development. On 6 February 1940 Butler summoned Alexander to the Foreign Office and, on instructions from Lord Halifax, formally notified him that 'the Government could not countenance even private and unofficial negotiations at the present time until the Germans have received some hard blows.' No further exit permits would be granted for journeys that might involve meetings with German emissaries, 'whoever the emissary may be'.[32] This evidently marks the point in time when the policy of 'absolute silence' in response to German opposition groups first took hold. It was taken up and rigorously enforced by Chamberlain's successor, Winston Churchill, but the policy itself clearly antedates Churchill's premiership, though it probably reflects his influence in cabinet. Butler softened the blow by requesting Alexander to prepare a memorandum outlining Friends' alternative strategy, and this he did, with the help of Carl Heath and others.

The memorandum argued that any attempt to destroy the German military machine by war would unite the Germans behind their government. A truce, on the other hand, would in itself be a check to Nazi dreams of domination. Admittedly any such truce would be precarious: could anything be done to stop people like Ribbentrop destroying it? Yes, he said,

> *a ceaseless and determined holding of the initiative* by the British and French (and let us hope American and other neutral governments). Hitler, let it never be forgotten, has feet of clay: he has no sure foundation for his action. His clever improvisations have succeeded again and again; he succeeds because he never pauses. Our pace must be as quick as his.

A new European political structure, economic agreements, disarmament measures, a fresh approach to colonial problems – all these could be kept in play with 'a clear sense of the way the world ought to be travelling'. Embarking on such a strategy there could be confidence that 'all that is decent in human society will rally behind you, and that you can rightly ignore the screamings of mob prejudice'. Who better to rise to the occasion than Chamberlain and Halifax? Alexander's peroration is eloquent:

> I believe the man who had it in him to fly to Munich (however disappointing the results of that heroic effort) and the man who had it in him as Viceroy to call the leader of 'rebellion' into conference (whatever may be thought of the results of that daring initiative) have it in them to undertake a still harder initiative, and to sustain it if need be through disappointment and seeming failure to final success.
>
> The salvation of Europe requires men who can outwit Hitler and his tribe in such a manner that they may conceivably even convert them.[33]

While this memorandum may well be ridiculed by those who see 'Munich' as the ultimate symbol of craven ineffectiveness, it manifests an appreciation of elements in the 1939–40 situation that the Churchillians slighted and wasted. The revulsion of senior German army officers against Nazi barbarity only once drew the attention of the British War Cabinet. This was on 17 January 1940, when Halifax communicated details of the attempted mediation of the Pope, who passed on the message from Josef Müller, acting on behalf of General Halder and others. Halifax's embarrassment as he outlines the proposals for peace with a reliable German government is almost palpable in the Cabinet minutes: clearly these were not matters over which a War Cabinet was going to waste time.[34] That the time would *not* have been wasted is shown by the unwilling testimony of Hans Frank, the Nazi administrator of Poland. In a notorious speech to the SS in Warsaw in the summer of 1940, he complained angrily about accusations that he ran 'a regime of murder', prompting interference by busybodies from the Foreign Ministry and the Ministry of Propaganda and even from the army itself. Opening up the war in the West would have the distinct merit of ridding him of this nuisance.[35] The worst evils of the Nazi regime were protected by the expansion and intensification of the war. The Holocaust depended on it. And the psychological consequences of that expansion and intensification had destructive effects on all the belligerents, fostering tolerance of mass bombing, and a general indifference to human suffering.

Two years of frustration

Hopes for a compromise peace persisted through March 1940. At the end of February President Roosevelt sent Sumner Welles as his special representative to Europe to find out what the current situation was, and what views the various governments, belligerent and neutral, actually held. British Foreign Office officials were alarmed. They wondered whether the United States might be playing with the idea that it could broker a settlement, and guarantee it. On the other hand, this possibility very much appealed to the National Peace Council, which urged the British Government to take seriously the opportunity for negotiation thus opened up, and secured an impressive list of supporting signatories, almost as representative if not as numerous as those secured for its pre-war petition for an international peace conference.[36] Insiders knew, however, that preparations were being made to extend the war. In a final dismissal of the Sumner Welles mission, written on 8 April, the fiery Robert Vansittart scorned the 'embarrassing rigmarole' of convincing the Germans of our good intentions. 'Let us', he wrote, 'now get on with *fighting* the war, which is the only effective form of propaganda.'[37] The following day both sides launched attacks on Scandinavia, the Germans just getting in first.

This extension of the war was bound to make any discussion of peace proposals seem irrelevant, although discouragement took a little while to take hold. As it happened, R. A. Butler saw Alexander and Francis E. Pollard on 10 April, the day after the invasion of Denmark and Norway. Pollard had visited the United States with a view to assessing the possibility of peace initiatives from that quarter, and there was a proposal to send Raymond Wilson, Peace Secretary of the American Friends Service Committee, to undertake exploratory discussions in Britain and Germany. Butler was evidently interested in all this, and Alexander commented that 'the invasion of Scandinavia did not seem to have modified the willingness of our authorities to consider first steps in the direction of an honourable peace'.[38] But when in May the Germans attacked the Low Countries and France, threatening Britain itself with invasion, the very idea of making peace an objective became a species of 'defeatism' or even treason. Warwickshire Monthly Meeting had been encouraging discussion of a constructive peace policy, but this was blighted by the new situation. When Alexander's own local meeting, Cotteridge, considered the issues on 5 May it was noted that 'a number of Friends . . . now . . . find it difficult to hold the traditional Peace testimony'.[39] Alexander, as might be expected, persisted in his endeavours to the last possible moment, proposing at the end of May to go to Rome with Raymond Wilson (Italy still being a non-belligerent), presumably to see what moves might be pressed on the Italian government and on the Vatican. But Butler, well briefed on Italy's impending entry into the war, dissuaded him, thus probably saving Alexander from prolonged internment as an enemy alien.[40]

Disappointing as Alexander's intrepid efforts to encourage a peace settlement must have been for him, he never abandoned the conviction that something of the kind had in principle been possible. When in December 1940 Lord Halifax was appointed ambassador to the United States, Alexander took the opportunity of wishing him well in his new work. He thanked him for the confidence he had shown in Friends in the autumn of 1939, and speculated that if people of greater weight and ability had been involved they might have been better able to use 'those opportunities to save the world from its present plight'. He conceded that war was almost inevitable, 'in view of the temper and mentality of the present rulers of Germany'. But something more fruitful *might* have been achieved.[41]

*

Although entirely frustrated in his concern for peace in Europe, Alexander could see some prospect for improvement in relations between Britain and India. In left-wing circles at least, Congress campaigning was seen as an integral part of the struggle against fascism, with objectives as acceptable as, say, those of the women's suffrage movement. Until the entry of Japan into the war in December 1941, there was no great sense that Indian independence would threaten the British war effort. Admittedly the strains and stresses created by German victories in May 1940 did have some impact on British attitudes towards Indian aspirations. Krishna Menon had for some time been one of the two Labour candidates in the Dundee constituency, where there was a significant Indian community. As the major parties had agreed to a political truce for the duration of the war, there was no question of Menon's contesting an election until peace was achieved. Even so, in the disturbed atmosphere of that anxious May the Dundee Labour Party decided to cancel Menon's candidature. Labour's National Executive endorsed this decision on the grounds that 'he represented an important section of Indian public opinion and that his first loyalty appeared to lie in that direction'.[42] Arguments about his standing in the Labour Party dragged on through the autumn, and eventually Menon resigned his membership, continuing his work as a London borough councillor in St Pancras as an independent. Alexander supported him in his conflict with the party, writing to Philip Noel-Baker to question the idea that someone devoted to Indian freedom couldn't also be a good Labour man. Noel-Baker, however, was disturbed by Menon's 'absolutely bitter hatred of everything to do with the British'.[43]

Menon's radical nationalism would necessarily set him at odds with anything that seemed to perpetuate British rule in India, and the coming to power of that arch-enemy of Indian nationalism, Winston Churchill, hardly encouraged him to believe in the good intentions of the Government. For Alexander and his colleagues in the India Conciliation Group, on the other hand, the unwelcome presence of Churchill was to some extent neutralised by the appointment of the new Secretary of State for India, Leo Amery. Although a thorough-going champion of the British Commonwealth, he was an enlightened and imaginative one. He was fully convinced of India's right to Dominion status, joining Canada, South Africa and the rest as soon as the war was over. This led to endless friction with the Prime Minister, who famously refused to preside over the dissolution of the British Empire.[44] Already at the end of May 1940 Butler had advised Alexander that he could hope for a good deal from Amery, and offered to introduce him to the new Secretary of State. 'So there is another door opened', Alexander remarked to Agatha Harrison.[45] The introductory note, sent on 5 June, said that Halifax had always found Alexander 'useful and well-informed', and a meeting evidently was arranged, as was one for Carl Heath, who found Amery 'an able little man with a mind very widely open'.[46]

Amery's first major speech as Secretary of State in a Commons debate on India (14 August 1940) was strikingly conciliatory in tone, emphasising, as Carl Heath remarked in *The Friend* (23 August), that India was to be understood 'not from the point of view of a superior dealing with an inferior, but as equal dealing with equal'. Alexander had seen Butler just before Amery made his speech, and once again one wonders what might have been said over lunch. Certainly Alexander was very gratified at the tone and temper of the speech, 'a big advance on anything said by his predecessors'. But he still felt more might be done to persuade the Congress leaders to join the Viceroy's Council, which hitherto they had refused to do. Could there not be more emphasis on the fact that while the Viceroy had the constitutional right to override the Council's decisions, in practice he would be reluctant to do so? It was the same argument he had used in relation to Provincial Governors and Congress Ministries in 1937, and illustrates his faith in the beneficial effects of practical cooperation. He contended also that Congress had a right to be recognised as the leading political organisation in India. It was unreasonable to put it on the same footing as groups that were less well established, less representative. Nor should anyone be surprised that Congress leaders mistrusted a government presided over by Winston Churchill. But there was a remedy. The Prime Minister could make a speech extolling the merits of democracy, applauding its growth in India, and looking forward to the creation of a constitution 'rooted in the aspirations of her silent millions'.[47] Alas, whatever effect Alexander may have had on speeches by Secretaries of State for India, his helpful hints to Churchill made not the slightest impression.

And in any case, while Alexander and Heath may have been impressed by the tone of Amery's August speech, in India the Congress Party saw it as a rejection of the terms on which they had offered to throw their 'full weight into the efforts for the effective organisation of the defence of the country'. Chakravarty Rajagopalachari glossed this as implying Congress's full participation in the war. Nehru was less accommodating, and insisted that it did *not* mean support for the war effort of British imperialism. Either way, the precondition was immediate independence and the formation of a provisional National Government at the Centre, this provisional government to be formed in such a way as to command the confidence of all parties.[48] The latter condition could not easily have been achieved, and manifestly it was well beyond anything that the British Government was disposed to contemplate, so that Gandhi did not after all have to endure a breach with colleagues less committed to non-violence than himself. Rejection of this Congress formula meant that the party unanimously refused to support Britain's war, not in a hostile sense, but like a conscientious objector. At a meeting of the All-India Congress Committee in Bombay on 15 September 1940, a resolution drafted by Gandhi and Nehru called for the practice of non-violence by a free India with a view to achieving world disarmament and a just political and economic order. It commended the courage showed by the British nation in its hour of peril, and declared that the spirit of *satyagraha* 'forbids the Congress from doing anything to embarrass them'.[49] There was to be no mass civil disobedience.

The India Conciliation Group quickly secured a text of what Gandhi himself had said in support of this resolution, and Alexander transmitted a copy to Butler, remarking that it gave a striking insight into the way his mind worked: his speeches were an unguarded thinking aloud.[50] Alexander was also anxious to convince Amery that Gandhi was far from unreasonable. The Mahatma's concern was, overwhelmingly, to end the poverty of the Indian masses. 'The moment he is convinced that this vast burden of India's poverty is really the concern of any individual Englishman representing the Government in India, that man has won a place in his heart.'[51] Alexander went on to say that Gandhi's view of the war was like that of the Quakers. Nothing could justify the ghastly destructiveness of war, but their sympathies were wholeheartedly with the resistance to Hitler's bid for world domination. Amery, however, insisted that Gandhi's opposition to the war *was* decidedly political, and must be treated appropriately.[52] So, at this time, as more and more Congress supporters engaged in 'individual *satyagraha*' by making speeches against the war, they were duly imprisoned. Nehru himself was the most conspicuous example, arrested at the end of October and sentenced to four years' imprisonment. Carl Heath tried to keep doors open, urging Gandhi to appreciate the impossibility of any British government's allowing propaganda against a struggle which for Britain was a matter of life and death: 'we are bombed here day and night.' To Amery at the same time he advocated the sending of a strong mission to seek a Treaty of Peace, 'in the big spirit you have personally shown'. But the big spirit did not appear: Agatha Harrison was deeply disappointed at Amery's negative response to all this, and Heath explained it by suggesting that he had been 'overridden in the Cabinet'.[53] Whatever Amery's position might be, Alexander thought it worth his while to remind Butler that Gandhi and Nehru utterly detested Hitlerism. Failure to agree with them suggested that no one in Britain was 'big enough to win them over'. And Butler was willing enough to concede that this was so, though he wished that Congress could come a little nearer to meeting British concerns. He added, though, that he 'would like a longer opportunity of thinking over what you have written, since your views either rejoice or disturb me, and on this occasion I am disturbed.'[54]

Over Christmas 1940 Gandhi declared a truce in the *satyagraha* campaign, and Alexander hastened to remind Butler that this was not a sign of weakness.

> He is not that kind of a man. He is always wanting to find a way of understanding and he is strong enough to ignore the fact that his gestures may be interpreted by others as weakness. It is really a sign of his strength. It will be evidence of our weakness if we are too faint-hearted to respond.

The letter went on to propose that a delegation should go out to India to cut through the misunderstandings that prevented the settlement that was surely possible. Could not Malcolm MacDonald go, or Butler himself? The Viceroy, Lord Linlithgow, seemed incompetent, and people in the India Office were bent on distorting Congress utterances. In this respect it was a pity that Halifax was going to the US, inasmuch as his advice on Indian affairs was good, and badly needed. In response, Butler encouraged Alexander to continue writing about India, as indeed it was one of the great issues of the time. He added, cautiously, that he was 'not averse from any suggestion such as you make in your letter'.[55] Alexander's reply led him to formulate his larger strategy, a strategy deliberately contrasted with the Nazi idea of a *Herrenvolk*, a master race.

> The issues we are facing today in our relationship with India are as decisive not only for the British Empire but for the world as the issues Chatham was facing over America in the eighteenth century.[56] I sometimes think that the main issue before the British Empire to-day is, Can a non-European section of the Empire – a section inhabited by coloured people with such a different tradition and history as India has – be brought into the same kind of harmonious relationship that we have been able triumphantly to establish with the main elements of the French and Dutch populations of Canada and South Africa? It is a much harder task, and I believe it can only be accomplished by men who genuinely regard Indians as their spiritual equals.[57]

Alexander lived to see both his imperial precedents brought into question by the stresses of a post-colonial world, but as an argument in 1941 it was persuasive. It certainly reinforced the reasoning behind his concern that an effective mission should be despatched to India. Apart from Butler and MacDonald, he also suggested Agatha Harrison – 'a most determined reconciler' who had the confidence of Congress leaders and might gain that of Jinnah as well. In conjunction with the widely respected Chief Justice of India, Sir Maurice Gwyer, she might prove irresistible. But Butler remained his preferred candidate, 'a man of singularly attractive personality, broad-minded, tolerant and imaginative', resilient and able to cope with apparent failure. He if anyone had the flexibility of mind and the imagination to win over Gandhi and Nehru to a scheme that would allow public opinion in India to have 'strong and effective representation in the Viceroy's Council'. There was no need for 'vast electoral machinery' or even for conceding a majority position for Congress. The crucial thing, he told Agatha Harrison on 21 February, was to make representative Indians feel they were being offered something of substance *now*, not just in the future. Still more was it necessary to convince them

> through personal contact with some real representative of the Government that the kind of suspicion that Nehru, for instance, has of British motives is quite unfair. I do not see anybody but Butler who is likely to be able to do this.[58]

His enthusiasm for Butler, it must be said, was not always shared by friends and colleagues. Even Carl Heath felt he had something of an obsession on the subject, 'a kind of "King Charles's head"', he told Agatha Harrison, his mind straying towards Dickens' Mr Dick in *David Copperfield*.[59] But Alexander was surely justified in feeling a certain confidence in a minister who could appreciate that the situation in India could not be allowed simply to go on as it had been since the outbreak of the war. This was said in an interview with Alexander on 26 June 1941, just four days after the German attack on the Soviet Union. Butler hoped that this turn in the war would dispose left-wingers in India to support the Allies. Alexander rejoined that he couldn't see them rallying to the cause while they were all in prison, and he wished he'd had Agatha Harrison with him to reinforce his concern. He felt, however, that Butler had been at the receiving end of some strong advice 'to cool him down' from the principal official at the India Office, Sir Findlater Stewart, described by Butler as 'a pretty hard nut to crack'. Alexander had seen him the previous day, and found him relying on the new German aggression to exercise its salutary effect on Indian opinion unaided.

> This led him incidentally to an amusing digression on his Presbyterian upbringing, and how it had led him to recognise the importance of fear as a motive in human actions; so we had a slight and rather entertaining discussion of the Christian estimate of the comparative importance of fear and love. He admitted that this was a somewhat pessimistic line to take, and he was prepared also to believe that if one or two private people such as members of the Conciliation Group and who know Mr Gandhi and other Indian leaders personally, could go out with the goodwill of our Government, it might help.

But Alexander wasn't sure that he really meant this. Still, since he'd said it, it should be followed up.[60]

The British Government did in fact make some positive response to the new situation created by Russia's enforced entry into the war. Exactly one month after the German attack, Amery announced a substantial enlargement of the Viceroy's Council, so that there was for the first time an Indian majority there of eight to four. Of course there was no Congress presence, but Alexander, as always, sought to encourage the Secretary of State in well-doing.

> It is certainly my sincere hope that these new arrangements may quickly prove themselves so valuable that both Congress and Muslim League will see their way to co-operate in them, and that they will find in them the machinery for the full self-government of India.

A fresh effort should be made to come to such an understanding with Congress as might make possible the release of all political prisoners.[61] In the following months, Alexander spared no effort to press his case. He had the support of Yearly Meeting, held in York that summer, which agreed to send a memorandum to the Prime Minister urging him to welcome India's desire for freedom and affirm Britain's acceptance of that aspiration.[62] And he was tireless in his efforts to educate his correspondents in Indian realities. As he told Amery, it was a complete misconception to suppose that Gandhi's and Nehru's initiatives could be explained as mere political astuteness.

> At bottom both men are following, according to their lights, principles that they hold with great intensity. If only we could convince them that our country is to-day standing for a high principle and not just using this principle as a device in order to preserve the empire, I think we should have taken a big step towards a real understanding with India.[63]

For whatever reason, the Government did find it possible soon afterwards to authorise a release of prisoners, and on 4 December Alexander wrote to Amery to congratulate him on this account. He requested a meeting with Amery to make a few suggestions about how best to follow this up with an approach to Congress. The meeting took place on 17th, and Amery was, as always, approachable and willing to listen. He wished that Congress were more willing to accept that he *had* made some advances, though he found it 'easy to understand that they were in no mood to be polite'. But Alexander found the meeting somewhat depressing, in that Amery clearly underestimated the hold that Gandhi and Nehru had over people in India. As he left Amery's office he saw the pelicans in St James's Park, and thought that he had 'left a still odder bird in the India Office'. But he felt better after seeing the Upland Goose and the beautiful plumage of the gulls – and after having tea with Agatha Harrison.[64]

By this time Japan had entered the war, and embarked on its rapid conquest of colonial territories in south-east Asia. From being remote from the fighting, India now found itself in the front line. Even India Office staff had to concede that things could not just be allowed to drift. Early in January 1942 Alexander wrote to Findlater Stewart suggesting that Sir Stafford Cripps, now on the point of leaving his post as Ambassador to the USSR, might return by way of India. Because of his past support for Congress claims, he was 'the one man in British public life who might induce Nehru to regard those August 1940 proposals in a new light'.[65] And it was to Cripps that the Government turned to take fresh proposals for an agreement with Congress.

The India Conciliation Group had great expectations of Cripps, and were encouraged by his concern to consult them before he set out. In *Gandhi through Western Eyes* Alexander refers to a meeting between Cripps and the whole group, presumably to explain his objectives and elicit their comments.[66] On what seems to have been a later occasion, shortly before his departure, Cripps consulted Agatha Harrison at a dramatic midnight meeting. She told Carl Heath that the telephone rang just as she was going to bed: it was Cripps's wife asking her to come to their house immediately. After a hasty cup of cocoa she found a taxi and arrived at the Cripps's home in Whitehall Court at 11.00 pm. He asked her to read the short three-page statement about the mission that he had prepared, and to give her reactions. The statement was presumably essentially the same as Cripps actually presented to Indian leaders after he arrived in Delhi on 22 March, and the obvious problem with it was its emphasis on post-war constitutional development, with little that was new in what could be offered immediately. It was, as Gandhi put it, a post-dated cheque. Still, Cripps assured Harrison that it had been difficult enough to get Cabinet agreement even to what the document conceded. While Harrison must have seen the force of this, she felt compelled to reiterate that the situation required the taking of a risk – the risk involved in granting power *now*. She was also convinced that the personal contact between Cripps and Gandhi might have borne fruit, and she did not want Cripps to leave India until he had had far more extended talks with him than were planned. She had cabled Gandhi on 11 March that C. F. Andrews' legacy could now be implemented – referring to Gandhi's belief that it was possible for the best Englishmen and the best Indians to meet together and never to separate till they had evolved a formula acceptable to both.[67] After Cripps's return, empty-handed, he had a talk with Alexander in which the latter tried to convince him that Gandhi might still be willing to cooperate in efforts to save the poor of India from the worst effects of the war, which might lead on to other forms of cooperation. 'In the case of the Irwin–Gandhi agreement', Alexander told Agatha Harrison,

> it was not fundamentally a question of a satisfactory political or constitutional compromise. It was simply that Irwin went on and on until he convinced Gandhi of his fundamental trustworthiness: – just what might have come from that talk that you wanted Cripps to have with Gandhi at the very end.

As always, there was a failure to take on board the larger significance of Gandhi in India. Alexander doubted if Cripps realised that even for those who rejected Gandhi's leadership, 'in the bottom of their hearts they know that he is still the Mahatma – the man whose moral and religious instincts are in the end nearly always right'.[68] It was no doubt an awareness of this limitation in Cripps that led her to come away from that midnight meeting in Whitehall Court with a feeling of resignation.

> I got home at 2 a.m. Walking down a deserted Whitehall – happily there was a moon and I did not need my torch – I pondered over this talk. . . . It is no light thing to be faced with this brilliant mind. But I knew I had something, through these years of work. A sense of the *minds* of the men to whom this statement was going, and that the best I could do was to try and interpret this.[69]

*

At least it was fair to assume that Sir Stafford Cripps would be interested in the minds of those whom he was addressing. The policy of 'absolute silence' meant that there was officially no interest in the minds of German people, even those who were anxious to overthrow the Nazi regime. Naturally this policy was rejected by Friends, and indeed by those churchpeople who had been in contact over the years with German evangelical groups, notably George Bell, Bishop of Chichester, and William Temple, Archbishop of York. In the 1941 Yearly Meeting, not only was there a strong concern to conciliate Indian opinion, but also an insistence on the need to make contact with Christians in all the warring countries, urging them to unite in continuous prayer in order to realise their common service to the Prince of Peace. It was only thus that the atmosphere needed for a just peace could be created. Temple was sympathetic to the idea, and a delegation of Friends – Alexander among them – met him on 25 September. By a remarkable coincidence, Temple had just received a letter from Friedrich Siegmund-Schultze in Zurich, informing him that a significant German opposition group was in touch with him about possible peace terms. In particular they wanted to know if Britain would still stand by former declarations (in Chamberlain's time) of willingness to deal with an anti-Nazi German government. They indicated the terms on which they were prepared to negotiate. Very properly they accepted that Germany would withdraw from Czechoslovakia and all neutral states occupied in the course of the war. Rather hopefully they indicated that Germany should retain control of Austria, the Sudetenland and Memel. Astonishingly they thought that the frontiers of 1914 might be restored in France, Belgium and Poland. They repeated the claim for the return of German colonies. They also proposed to work for a European Union and for general disarmament. It is evident that this group – almost certainly Carl Goerdeler and his circle – were still influenced by a sense of Germany's military preponderance: Siegmund-Schultze's letter had been despatched on 24 July 1941, and he speaks of consultations 'some weeks ago': presumably just after the German attack on Russia.

Writing to Sir Alexander Cadogan at the Foreign Office on 25 September, Temple said that he welcomed the initiative. Its detail would have to be carefully defined, and he would of course be willing to take advice about his response to Siegmund-Schultze. In a postscript he said he had just received a Quaker delegation, who assured him that Siegmund-Schultze had been very sceptical of earlier peace moves, so that his endorsement of the present inquiry carried considerable weight. R. A. Butler would be able to confirm this account: 'I feel sure that he would be found to remember what took place.'

Fortunately for himself, Butler had by this time been promoted to a Cabinet post, as President of the Board of Education. When the Foreign Secretary, Anthony Eden, read Temple's letter, he was evidently very angry, and one can only guess what he might have said to a mere Under-Secretary in his department.

> I am much astonished to see this letter. I had read a minute somewhere that Schultze's letter had not been forwarded to the Archbishop, which was in accordance with my view. My recollection is that I so reported to P.M. In no circumstances can we have anything to do with this or any other peace negotiation.[70]

Roger Makins carefully explained that the minute had only said that the letter had not *yet* been forwarded to the Archbishop, and in self-defence remarked that Temple's response had struck him as 'quite sensible', though naturally any reply to Siegmund-Schultze would have to have any references suggesting encouragement to negotiations deleted. But William Strang found Temple's reaction to the letter 'very disturbing', and complained that there were church-people, like the Bishop of Chichester, 'who might like to think of making peace on these insidious and disastrous terms'. Eden added a marginal comment: 'Of course.'[71]

So Temple was instructed to send a simple acknowledgement to Siegmund-Schultze, and had no alternative but to acquiesce in this negative reaction. Even so he was willing to support Friends in their concern to appeal to Christians everywhere to create the atmosphere needed to build a just peace, and was ready to make a broadcast on these lines. But for this Foreign Office approval was needed. As ever, Alexander sought the advice of R. A. Butler, who agreed to put in a word of support to his successor as Under-Secretary, Richard Law. 'I am seeing Richard Law tonight, and will tell him about our long and happy association.'[72]

Nothing came of this, of course. No relaxation of 'absolute silence' could be tolerated. At best, Anthony Eden was willing to be informed of any peace initiatives that came to the attention of the embassies in Stockholm and Berne. 'They are', he noted in a minute, 'a rather interesting psychological study, and they won't do any harm' – no harm, that is, while they stay out of the hands of such as the Archbishop of York.[73] Even in time of war, though, the churches had their own networks, and the peace message signed by the Archbishop on behalf of the Commission of the Churches for International Friendship and Social Responsibility did eventually get transmitted, after a fashion. In March 1942 Meeting for Sufferings took note of the fact that the church organisation was not itself prepared to distribute the message, but was happy for Friends to do so. Peace Committee was then authorised to send it to all ministers of religion in Britain, and to selected people abroad.[74]

*

All this time Alexander was carrying on the routine of his work at Woodbrooke, encouraging students to write dissertations about international institutions, and taking his usual classes on political developments in different parts of the world. He was a leading figure in his local meeting, Cotteridge. One of its younger members, Assistant Clerk for a time, recalls regarding him with awe, almost as a kind of divinity.[75] It was Alexander who proposed that, when air raids made evening meetings impracticable, there should be regular Sunday after-meeting picnic lunches to hear about Friends' concerns.[76] And when, in May 1941, a by-election had been fought in Birmingham with an independent peace candidate (Stuart Morris, General Secretary of the Peace Pledge Union), Alexander played a firm if unpublicised role. H. G. Wood had written to the *Birmingham Post* in critical terms about the peace candidate. As a leading Birmingham Quaker, and Director of Studies at Woodbrooke, he could have been seen as expressing the official view of the Society of Friends. At Cotteridge PM on 11 May, it was agreed that he did *not* necessarily speak for Friends as a whole. Alexander was appointed to *visit* Wood and convey to him the views of Cotteridge Friends. No doubt he did this with tact and clarity.

All through his time at Woodbrooke, Alexander worked in collaboration with Olive. In spite of her physical infirmity, she was the one who sustained the worldwide community of former students, and played a quietly painstaking part in support of the causes with which Friends were in sympathy, notably, as we have seen, in the assistance given to Jomo Kenyatta when he was preparing a case against the 'White Highlands' policy in Kenya. She was remarkably active throughout the 1930s, and her condition seems to have been stabilised to some extent by the diet she followed. But wartime shortages had an adverse effect. Some foods may have become impossible to obtain. Whatever the reason, her health deteriorated in the autumn of 1941, and on 14 January 1942 she died.

The obituary notices in the *Woodbrooke International Journal* overflow with appreciation of the warmth of her personality. As Winifred Wilkinson put it, 'it has never been, and is not now, an ill person of whom I think and see: but somebody full of life'. Another friend said that he thought most of her happiness – 'which always goes with bravery, doesn't it? And I think I never knew anyone with so fine a courage.' Bertram Pickard was deeply impressed by her strong and vivid personality, which found expression in a humour that was somehow both caustic and kind. 'I can still hear her say: "Go on, Bertram," when quite rightly she was fed up with superfluous introductions in one of my Woodbrooke talks last winter.' It was he who found perhaps the most telling metaphor for her activity:

> It was as though she was a really nice kind of spider who sat at the middle of a web of fellowship she had spun across the world, so that flies from every continent and clime were caught, and delighted in the catching – which presumably is the kind of spider–fly relationship there is in the Entomological Heaven.[77]

There is touching evidence of this in a letter Alexander received – with what sadness one can only imagine – from one Traute Riedel in August 1946. She was an Old Woodbrooker who lived in Bayreuth, and this was her first opportunity to write to the United Kingdom since 1939. The letter was addressed to 'Mrs Alexander', and she wanted all the Woodbrooke news. For herself she said that her family had had terrible experiences during the war, but that miraculously they had all survived, her husband turning up unexpectedly in January 1946. Evidently it never occurred to her that Olive might *not* have survived.

The beginning of 1942 was a low point in Alexander's life, what with the loss of Olive, the British refusal to respond to peace initiatives from the German opposition, and the continuing saga of mutual incomprehension between the Congress leadership and the British Government. But the threat to eastern India from triumphant Japanese forces unexpectedly created an opportunity for renewed and fruitful action.

7

TO INDIA WITH THE FRIENDS' AMBULANCE UNIT

With the Japanese entry into the war, and their rapid conquest of a great part of south-east Asia, it seemed only a question of time before an attack was mounted on India itself. The Executive Committee of the Friends' Ambulance Unit, active in the Second World War as in the first, was quick to realise the scope this situation gave for putting experience acquired in the London Blitz to use in the cities of India most threatened by air raids. By the end of 1941 there had already been some discussion of ways and means. Harold Loukes, a British Friend who had been in India since 1934, was asked to assess the prospects.[1] His initial reaction was discouraging, but the Executive was attracted to the idea and unwilling to let go of it. On 21 January 1942 Ralph Barlow wrote to Alexander inviting him to spend the following Saturday night (24th) in the FAU hostel in London with a view to finding out what *he* thought of it all. Although it was barely a week since Olive's death, Alexander was exhilarated by the possibilities, and after his weekend meeting wrote a letter to Loukes asking him to think again. Simply as a gesture of goodwill the project would have great value. Moreover, although conditions in London were very different from those in Calcutta, experience in Britain would be helpful in working with Indians engaged in air-raid relief work. Agatha Harrison had suggested that the Unit might collaborate with the Servants of India Society, thus avoiding the impression that 'they were just acting for the Government, or that they were just acting for or with the Congress'.[2] The Cripps mission in March provided an opportunity for an offer to be made to the Viceroy: a member of the mission's staff, David Owen, conveyed the proposal to send an experienced FAU group there to help and advise on civil defence matters, and the offer was accepted.

It was agreed that the team should consist exclusively of men and women familiar with air-raid relief work, and half a dozen such people were chosen. This experience, though crucial to the team's effectiveness, was not in itself sufficient. Any effective protection of the civil population in India would require a high level of local trust and goodwill, and in the troubled political conditions of 1942 this was not easily achieved. Gandhi's secretary, Mahadev Desai, had been invited to address the Yearly Meeting of Friends in India in December 1941, and he expressed sympathy with the idea of organising Quaker ambulance units in the event of a Japanese invasion. But these should serve with the voluntary organisations that would be set up by the people of India rather than with the alien Government.[3] This speech reflects Gandhi's conviction that only the Indian people themselves could mount a successful resistance to invasion, and demonstrates the difficulty that the Unit might well have found if simply acting under the supervision of the Government of India. But if there was anyone who could persuade voluntary organisations that they would not be compromised by contacts with Government, it was Horace Alexander. It must have been evident to a number of people that his presence would be extremely helpful. It is not clear when his name was first mentioned as a possible recruit, but it was at a relatively late stage that he was added to the team. He agreed to act as leader. Richard Symonds, a young Oxford graduate who had been in charge of work in London air-raid shelters, was to serve as his deputy.

Woodbrooke gave him a year's leave of absence and, since Olive had died, he had no other responsibilities to rearrange. Clearly he and his colleagues in the India Conciliation Group will have seen this as the opportunity for which they had long been waiting. Ever since the outbreak of war, the mutual incomprehension of Congress and the British Government had caused the ICG increasing frustration. Alexander had always seen practical cooperation for human welfare as the most effective way of creating a good understanding, and here was work that urgently demanded cooperation by all concerned. It would also allow him to make direct contact with Gandhi and his colleagues. As Agatha Harrison reported to a meeting of the FAU's Joint India Committee on 27 July 1942, the ICG saw this as an opportunity 'to keep the way open for negotiations between Mahatma Gandhi and the Government'.[4] Alexander appreciated that the ground for this would have to be prepared carefully, and went to the India Office to assure Amery of his discretion. He put it to him that

> obviously he could not escape contact with his old friends including Gandhi, and that if he did find there was any work of conciliation to be done behind the scenes he hoped it would not be taken amiss if he attempted it.

Amery told him that he saw no objection to Alexander's visiting his personal friends provided he took no *overt* part in politics.[5] There may indeed have been some feeling that Alexander might just conceivably do some good. It will be recalled that in September 1941 Findlater Stewart had suggested to Alexander that there might be value in a member of the ICG going to India, and while Alexander did not quite believe that he meant it, the concession was at least worth noting. And it is evident that some India Office officials saw Alexander's Congress associations as of direct practical use. Because of the political situation in Bengal, the Congress Party was not cooperating there with measures of civil defence. But Congress was the only party able to organise enough volunteers for the purpose in this emergency.[6] While they were unwilling to assist a non-Congress government, they might feel differently about a group led by a friend of Gandhi's. The reasoning was sound, but the India Office tactfully failed to inform the Government of India about Alexander's participation in the FAU team. Stewart probably guessed that the Viceroy would have vetoed the arrangement if he had known about it, while Amery had sufficient confidence in Alexander's moderating influence on the Congress leaders to give him some quiet scope.

Early in May 1942 Alexander and Symonds travelled ahead of the main party, leaving Glasgow on a ship bound for Lagos, from which West African port they flew to India, arriving in Gwalior in the following month. On the long sea voyage their fellow passengers were, appropriately enough, civil defence instructors. Alexander dismissed them as 'NCO types', but noted that Symonds managed some 'friendly intercourse' with them.[7] Symonds himself recalls that he and Alexander had endless conversations, greatly appreciated by the latter, rejuvenated (it seemed) by this association with a young man who reminded him so much of his own time at university. Many years later Alexander recalled one of the topics they discussed. The ship's captain asked for volunteers to keep a look-out for the periscope of a submarine.

> As I had my binoculars and liked to sit on deck looking for sea-birds, I volunteered, and spent some hours on the job. One of my FAU colleagues was rather shocked. 'But if you had spotted a submarine, and it had been sunk, you would have been responsible', he said. Yes, I agreed. But also, if I refused to look, if I shut my eyes, and the submarine sunk our ship, I should also have been responsible . . . In other words, in war-time, you cannot totally separate yourself from what is happening around you. I do not say that what I did was right, but it was the best I could see, and in the same circumstances I think I should do the same again.[8]

Symonds' comment when I asked him about this was that he doubted that he *was* shocked, but he would certainly have been curious to know how Alexander reconciled such a military duty with his pacifist convictions. It is in any case arguable that if an interesting bird had coincided with the periscope, the ship might well have been in mortal danger.

On arrival in Gwalior they went first to the Quaker missions nearby in the Central Provinces, around Itarsi. They were given a warm welcome by sympathetic expatriate Friends like Geoffrey Maw, Edith Backhouse and Donald Groom. Their leading Indian colleague, Ranjit Chetsingh, had already written to a number of influential figures explaining the purposes of the FAU initiative – to Maulana Azad as President of Congress, to H. N. Kunzru as President of the Servants of India Society, and to the General Secretary of the YMCA in India, a helpful start to the quest for cooperation by voluntary organisations.[9] On a rather less exalted plane, however, Alexander was disconcerted to find that the local Indian Quakers were mainly interested in gaining his support for a fair share of employment in the local munitions factory.[10] The monsoon broke while the two visitors were there, causing serious damage to the Friends' hospital building, but they had to move on to Gandhi's ashram in Sevagram, not far away near Wardha. Alexander felt that it was important to explain to Gandhi at first hand what the FAU had come to do, before he read about it in the newspapers.

Gandhi welcomed his visitors as Englishmen who had come in a spirit of friendship and not as members of a ruling caste. He explained that it was actually in a letter to Alexander himself that he had first formulated his recent demand to the British to 'quit India', but Alexander had left Britain before the letter could reach him. Gandhi emphasised that this did not mean the expulsion of people, only the ending of the imperial regime: 'every Englishman in India can convert himself into a friend – as you have come as Friends – and remain here.'[11] The same point was made in the Congress Working Committee's 'Quit India' resolution a couple of weeks later: it 'was never intended to mean the withdrawal of all Britishers from India', and envisaged the stationing of Allied forces in India to resist the Japanese.[12] And indeed Gandhi had despatched Mirabehn (the name adopted by Madeleine Slade when she became Gandhi's disciple) to eastern India to initiate measures of popular resistance to the expected invasion.[13]

Since Alexander had not received the letter, Gandhi enlarged on its significance in a long session, and finished with a statement that, as Symonds recalls, profoundly moved and awed his colleague. 'So', Gandhi said, 'you have now to do what [C. F.] Andrews did – understand me, pitilessly cross-examine me, and then if you are convinced be my messenger.' Mahadev Desai's report in *Harijan* remarks that Alexander 'felt overwhelmed and said: "We dare not assume his mantle. We can but try."' His sense of insufficiency was understandable. Andrews, who had died two years earlier, was one of Gandhi's oldest friends, and had long worked devotedly to support Indian aspirations and interests. He was also someone to whom the imitation of Christ seemed second nature, and this could hardly be said of Alexander. But Gandhi's words were a challenge he could not evade, and will have encouraged him to exploit the latitude allowed by Amery to the limit, and perhaps beyond it.

The report in *Harijan* proved to be of great importance in ensuring a friendly reception for the Unit in nationalist circles. Desai himself was privately rather patronising about the visitors, describing them to G. D. Birla as 'goody-goody fellows like all Quakers', and moreover perhaps holding a brief for Cripps – for otherwise why should Amery have his permission to Alexander to see Gandhi and others? He wanted them to stay with Birla, for Horace needed educating, and Birla could do this.[14]

So Alexander and Symonds proceeded to Delhi, staying with Birla as suggested, and for that reason alone giving the Viceroy's staff an unpleasant shock. Symonds relates how they were received by the Viceroy's secretary, Sir Gilbert Laithwaite,

> to whom a senior official in the India Office had written commending me because he had been at Rugby School with my father. The India Office had neglected to inform the Viceroy that Horace had been added to the party. When in addition to the expected politically innocent young man from a sound family and school he was confronted with Horace, arriving via Sevagram, emerging from Birla House, and wearing the mantle of C. F. Andrews, he was somewhat disagreeably surprised, as was his master, Lord Linlithgow, who did not receive Horace either then or later.[15]

Still, they were there to do useful work, and Laithwaite referred them to the Civil Defence Department, where they made arrangements for cooperating with the Bengal Government. They arrived in Calcutta on 4 July 1942,[16] settling into Buchanan's Hotel in Sudder Street. There they found another member of the FAU, Alex Horsfield, who had come to India on his way to work with the China Convoy, but was held up by the fall of Burma to the Japanese. The three men set about assessing the preparations made so far by the Bengal Government for coping with air raids, and benefited greatly from the Friends' good standing with nationalist leaders. They gained the confidence of the Bengal Civil Protection Committee, an organisation associated with the Congress Party. It was managed by some distinguished medical men, in particular Dr B. C. Roy, later to become Prime Minister of West Bengal. Amiya Chakravarty, who was now Professor of English at Calcutta University, helped them by contacts with students, anxious enough to join in defence against air raids, 'so long as it was not labelled "Government".'[17] Symonds recalls that the work of the House Protection Fire Parties was reliably supported by the local prostitutes, 'alert at all hours and greeting me as I made the rounds with the cry of "Long live our Commander"'.[18] The Unit's practical experience of the London Blitz earned them the respect of the provincial administration. At this time there was a coalition government in Bengal, with whose ministers, as well as the Governor, effective collaboration was soon established. The India Conciliation Group had long been conscious of the importance of contact with the Muslim community, and Agatha Harrison had secured an introduction for Alexander to the Muslim League politician H. S. Suhrawardy, who was then in opposition to the government: when it fell, in April 1943, he was to become Minister of Civil Supplies.[19] As an opposition politician he was at first not exactly helpful to the Unit's work. At one point he put down a motion in the Provincial Assembly noting that few Muslims had been recruited for air-raid defence work, and demanding that none but Muslims should be appointed for several weeks. For all that, Suhrawardy soon became very friendly to the FAU and to Alexander in particular, partly no doubt because his brother Shahid Suhrawardy, Professor of Fine Art in Calcutta University, was a man after Alexander's own heart: a friend of Lowes Dickinson, E. M. Forster and other members of that King's College elite with whom he always felt at home. Alexander was very taken with the politician's genial cynicism and amused by his explanation of why the Quaker community remained so small in numbers: they gave so little scope for human vices.[20] Symonds describes him as 'a man of great imagination, with whom we would sit up until all hours building castles in the air for a better, juster society in Bengal'.[21] Suhrawardy found Alexander equally congenial.'No praise', he told Symonds, ' can be too high for that man. You have no idea how much we all admire him.' Symonds attributed this to Alexander's 'gentleness, almost saintliness, which in India means infinitely more than executive ability', and is unexpected in an Englishman.[22]

Alexander's connection with King's College paid one further dividend. *The Statesman*, India's leading English-language newspaper, was edited at this time by another Kingsman, Ian Stephens. Stephens encouraged Alexander to visit him after the day's work was over so that they could exchange impressions. He was very ready to publish articles by members of the Unit, and indeed Alexander later acquired some notoriety as a regular contributor. One Unit member, Clem Alexandre, recalls that on more than one occasion, when an English stranger on a train learnt his name, he was asked 'You're not related to that fellow Horace Alexander who writes that terrible stuff in *The Statesman*?' Alexandre says that he would respond at once that he was not related, 'and then have to add that I did indeed entirely agree with what he wrote.'[23]

*

Alexander was not long in India before he began to feel the full weight of C. F. Andrews's mantle. Ten days after his arrival in Calcutta, the Congress Working Committee, meeting in Wardha, agreed to its 'Quit India' resolution. It demanded an orderly withdrawal of the British administration, making way for a provisional national government which would be able to give effective support to the United Nations against the Axis powers. This political formula had the merit of appealing to a wide range of Indian opinion. Throughout the war there was a certain undercurrent of sympathy with the Axis powers inasmuch as they were fighting the British: my enemy's enemy is my friend. This undercurrent was strengthened by Japan's overthrow of a succession of colonial regimes. Her victories discredited the colonial rulers' comfortable conviction of total superiority – the conviction so graphically conveyed in Somerset Maugham's short story 'The Door of Opportunity' (1933), where a couple of Dutchmen casually put down an insurrection of 200 Chinese coolies. On the other hand, Japan had also engaged in an unjustifiable and cruel war against China. Congress leaders, Nehru especially, had long been emphatic in their opposition to the fascist regimes of Italy and Germany, more than ever now that they were at war with the Soviet Union. Congress policy statements had always been careful to emphasise that they looked forward to an Allied victory. As we have seen, Gandhi was concerned to resist any Japanese onslaught, and even the official – and secret – report on the August 1942 disturbances conceded that Gandhi genuinely believed that only a free India would have the stamina to stand up to an invader.[24] Moreover, he assured Alexander that he had never, 'even in the most unguarded moment', expressed the opinion that Japan or Germany would win the war.[25] The 'Quit India' resolution continued this political strategy, but the starkness of the demand for withdrawal reflected the perceived weakness of the British position. Moreover, Subhas Chandra Bose, whose radical Forward Bloc had always been impatient with Gandhi's moderation, now had a policy of gaining Indian independence through an Axis victory. He was soon to take on the leadership of the Japanese-backed Indian National Army. Congress had to take account of the appeal which this exercised, particularly in Bose's native Bengal, where the possibility of a Japanese attack was greatest.

The British authorities took little account of claims that Congress supported the United Nations, dismissing them as 'eyewash'. They had no conception of the state of mind which Alexander articulated so vehemently at this time:

> You just have to know the daily sense of frustration that influences almost every Indian of every party, faced as he is by the presence of a cold, aloof and unimaginative Government, to realise how much force there is behind the Congress decision. . . . I am sure they are fully convinced that only a free India, free now, not at the end of an endless war, can really give the allied cause the moral drive and the physical backing that it needs for victory. . . . Government will not talk while the 'threat' remains. How childish statesmen are! Do they not realise that the threat is always inevitably there while *they* remain.[26]

The inclusion of civil disobedience in the Wardha resolution obliterated everything else in it. At last the 'threat' had taken a palpable shape. The Viceroy and his advisers planned a massive pre-emptive strike to be made as soon as the 'Quit India' resolution should be endorsed by the full All-India Congress Committee meeting in Bombay on 8 August. The Government might well calculate that removing the leaders would cripple the campaign, and that other sections of the population would view the Congress strategy with sufficient unease to acquiesce in repressive action. As Alexander himself puts it, in *Gandhi through Western Eyes*,

> the Delhi establishment of officialdom had disliked Cripps and his mission, and were eager to have another go at the old enemy, the Congress, with Gandhi as enemy number one .This time they would demonstrate finally that Gandhi and Nehru really counted for nothing in India.[27]

Even that senior Congressman Chakravarti Rajagopalachari objected to the campaign on the ground that it was politically ill-prepared, and would provoke repression that could only help the Japanese.[28] As for the Muslim League and the Hindu Mahasabha, they saw their interest in terms of supporting the Allied war effort, while the Communist Party of India's support for the beleaguered USSR inevitably put them in the same camp. Back in Britain, the Congress action was seen as a disastrous mistake even by those sympathetic to Indian aspirations. The National Executive of the Labour Party, for example, expressed acute anxiety at the prospect of civil disobedience, which might 'imperil the fate of all freedom-loving peoples'.[29]

Alexander went to Sevagram again almost at once after the publication of the resolution to learn more clearly what was in Gandhi's mind in proposing it. He was accompanied by Ranjit Chetsingh. They found some reassurance in Gandhi's evident concern to have a friendly discussion with the Viceroy to find a way through the differences between India and Britain: civil disobedience was not an immediate prospect. He went on to Allahabad to see Nehru, whose anti-Fascist credentials were, after all, so impeccable. He found not only Jawaharlal but the rest of the family: his sister Mrs Pandit was there with her daughters; the newly- married Indira Gandhi had just returned from her honeymoon in Kashmir, and Jawaharlal himself and his brother-in-law R. S. Pandit appeared from their morning walk 'wearing remarkable wine-coloured shorts. . . . We had a merry party. Within a month nearly all were in jail.'[30] Nehru made it clear that he wholeheartedly supported the 'Quit India' call. British rule in south-east Asia had collapsed before the Japanese, whereas China steadfastly resisted. 'The only effective resistance to the Axis would come from a people fighting for its own freedom.'[31] But he accepted that it was unrealistic to expect or to wish for the withdrawal of Allied troops from India, and the 'Quit India' resolution acknowledged this. None the less, its concluding anticipation of civil disobedience impressed Alexander as a serious mistake. He wrote an anguished letter to Gandhi, saying that even the staunchest friends of

India in Britain, given the threat posed by German forces, were bound to see the resolution as 'a most cruel stab in the back'.

> I don't for a moment doubt that those men and women in Bow or Lancashire who were your friends in 1930, and who have always been friends of Indian freedom, are saying hard things about you today for apparently giving them still one more blow in a vital spot just when they are in mortal danger from relentless foes. And they are not saying those hard things because Churchill or even Cripps tells them to, but because it looks just like that to them.[32]

He urged Gandhi to show his friends in Britain that he wasn't blind to the damage that the 'Quit India' campaign might do to the Allied cause, 'that it is for you, as it is for them, a terribly painful step to take – a real agony'. In responding, Gandhi paid a warm tribute to Alexander and to Agatha Harrison for their tireless championing of Indian aspirations, but insisted that he was acting 'in the spirit of pure friendship'. Some form of conflict was inevitable to bring about British conversion. Success will 'enable Britain to acquire a moral height which must secure victory for her and her Allies. . . . The movement is designed to help Britain in spite of herself.'[33]

Gandhi intended to publish the correspondence in *Harijan*, but he was arrested before this could be done. It was indeed later published in *The Hindu* of Madras, but the vigour of Alexander's presentation of British attitudes would probably have made little impact on nationalist opinion, and certainly failed to earn the gratitude of the Government of India. The Viceroy did not appreciate Alexander's efforts to mediate. After all, an ordinance against revolutionary activities had been drafted as long ago as 1940, with a view to 'smashing' the Congress Party for good when occasion arose.[34] Now that the occasion had arisen, the Viceroy had no wish to find well-meaning conciliators getting in the way. 'Had I known', he told Amery, 'that there was to be any question of any political activity by these people I would not have agreed to their coming, and I am bound to say that I shall take very strong exception to it if Alexander develops on these lines.'[35]

This particular letter coincided with the somewhat feverish activities of the India Conciliation Group following cables from Alexander indicating that there was still scope for negotiation. As Agatha Harrison and Carl Heath told Stafford Cripps, Alexander's concern was to 'keep doors ajar in an effort to break the deadlock'. They went to see Leo Amery on 27 July, an interview, Harrison wrote, that was 'difficult beyond words, though at the same time friendly and very frank'. They managed to extract from him a promise that if Gandhi asked for a talk with the Viceroy, Amery himself would not oppose this. It was not much of a concession, but from Stafford Cripps they had more comfort. He had always seen the value of intervention by unofficial people like

Alexander, and they urged him to reassure Amery about this. He promised to do so, and Harrison cabled Alexander to advise him that Gandhi should seek a meeting with the Viceroy without delay. She also cabled Gandhi himself, making the same point.[36]

It was all in vain. The Metropolitan of India, Bishop Foss Westcott, had written to Linlithgow to tell him of Alexander's recent visit to Gandhi, suggesting that a meeting with Alexander would be informative. The Viceroy did not think so. In the same letter to Amery in which he reported the bishop's intervention, he had rejected any idea of conciliating Congress or appealing to their better nature.[37] A week later he wrote rather sternly to Amery complaining that Alexander was 'busily engaged in endeavouring to act as an intermediary to Mr Gandhi and has been having conversations with him, Nehru, etc., and according to intercepted correspondence has found Nehru's point of view conclusive.' In a letter to Linlithgow himself, Alexander had claimed that Amery had assured him it would be 'entirely in order' to undertake conciliation work, provided he didn't go around making speeches. Was this true?

An evidently embarrassed Amery responded on 10 August, after the flurry of business attending the arrest of the Congress leaders had subsided. Yes, Alexander had been persuaded to join the Unit – because they needed someone with them who had a knowledge of India – and, yes, Alexander had pointed out to him that if he went to India he could not escape contact with old friends, and there might thus be scope for some discreet conciliation behind the scenes. Amery emphasised his confidence in Alexander's sincerity and good intentions, but appreciated that he had probably become 'involved with Gandhi more deeply than he can have anticipated'. Alexander had been keeping Agatha Harrison abreast of developments, and his telegrams to her had been passed on to Amery. Amery told Linlithgow that he had already warned her that Alexander 'might be exceeding our understanding with him', and Linlithgow could pass this message on himself.[38] In reply, the Viceroy accepted that Alexander had good intentions, but his 'unwise zeal' had made him a nuisance. Not that it mattered now: most of his friends were out of reach.[39]

Linlithgow may have thought that that would be the end of the matter, but unfortunately Alexander wrote to him again on 22 August, defending his activities. Had he not asked Nehru how he reconciled civil disobedience with his strong support for Russia and China? Had he not explained why English opinion was so hostile to Congress, and had he not pleaded for delay in launching civil disobedience? His sole purpose had been to find a way of averting the threatened campaign, and bringing the parties in dispute together.[40] This did not please the Viceroy at all. In fact, he was extremely irritated. 'It would be the greatest mistake', he told Amery, 'to have people wandering about here playing at politics as they think fit under the cover of humanitarian activities.' And Alexander *was* engaging in politics. The *National Call* of 17 August had published a statement by him.[41] Linlithgow evidently felt he would be much better out of the country, and it looks as if it was only Amery's goodwill towards Alexander that saved him from deportation.[42] A few weeks later, though, he made his peace with the Government. He had an interview with Laithwaite in which he insisted on his concern to cooperate with the Government for the good of the Friends' Ambulance Unit. Any contacts with political persons would not be used for political purposes.[43] Laithwaite was unlikely to have believed this, but allowed Alexander to continue on probation. He may even have been a little reassured when Alexander demonstrated his detachment from Congress associations by spending an hour with the leader of the Muslim League, M. A. Jinnah.[44] (His reassurance would have been less, though, had he known that the meeting had been arranged by Devadas Gandhi.)

A few weeks after the arrival of the other members of the FAU team at the end of July 1942, a permanent base for the Unit had been found in a quiet part of south Calcutta, 1 Upper Wood Street, and they moved in on 1 September. Alexander lost no opportunity of developing useful contacts. Perhaps through Shahid Suhrawardy he came to know Calcutta University's Vice-Chancellor, Shyama Prasad Mookherjee, and at his invitation gave a set of lectures in the university appraising the achievement of the League of Nations.[45] Mookherjee was also leader of the Hindu Mahasabha in the Bengal Legislative Assembly; and Finance Minister in the coalition government then in power. Relations between the politicians and the British administration were often difficult, and on one occasion Alexander sought to help matters by inviting Mookherjee and the Congress leader Kiron Shankar Roy to dinner at the Unit's house with J. R. Blair, Chief Secretary to the Government of Bengal. Although Blair had served in Bengal since 1935, it was the first time that he had met either man. The encounter of Blair and Mookherjee will have had some piquancy, as in 1941 the latter had censured Blair for failing to take strong enough measures against a threatening mob in Dacca. Blair's claim was that he had dealt with the situation by patrolling the streets shouting 'Hindu-Muslim ki-jai!' – long live Hindus and Muslims alike. He evidently had no great faith in mere force, and was quite willing, after a glass or two of wine, to propose a toast to the good health of the FAU people in Bengal. 'I never thought I should be grateful for the arrival of a group of pacifists in Calcutta.'[46]

The Unit had quickly established itself as a competent and experienced body, whose advice was respected. At the prompting of the Governor of Bengal, Sir John Herbert, the Unit devised a simple khaki uniform with Quaker Star shoulder badges, which Alexander often wore himself. This was obviously appropriate in Air Raid Precaution (ARP) work. Anxiety about the possible impact of air raids was considerable: Alexander himself reflected, after taking possession of 1 Upper Wood Street, that 'this house and all its inhabitants may all be bombed to bits any day'.[47] As it turned out, Japanese attacks on

Calcutta proved to be few, the most serious being on Christmas Eve 1942 and 15 January 1943.[48] Based on their experience in the London Blitz, FAU personnel helped the Indian local authorities to complete their preparations for every branch of ARP. They helped in organising relief centres, first-aid posts, emergency information centres, fire-fighting services, rescue and ambulance services, including a mobile dispensary. They were also involved in the training of government personnel and volunteers, including a corps of Indian women. One recommendation by the local authorities proved fallacious. Symonds remarks that they had been advised to recruit stalwart non-Bengalis for the volunteer fire parties, not timid citizens of Calcutta. But when the bombs fell, the up-country stalwarts went home while the Bengalis remained, having nowhere else to go.[49] Their timidity may in any case have been exaggerated, as Symonds recalls that Sujata Mookerjee, one of the student volunteers, cheerfully went round the Calcutta slums with him during the raids, inspecting the shelters and 'explaining at the same time that I was really totally in error in my respective judgments of the poets Auden and Day Lewis'. Her 'fine disregard for danger' was indeed exceptional.[50]

But it was not air-raid relief work that proved to be the Unit's main contribution. Well before any raids occurred, Bengal was visited by a far greater calamity, a devastating cyclone that particularly ravaged part of the Midnapur district south-west of Calcutta. The cyclone struck on 15/16 October 1942, breaking the dyke that protected a large area of rice-growing land, and destroying that season's crop. About 11,000 people were killed, and towns and villagers battered and smashed. News of what had happened came through slowly, as all communications had broken down. On 22 October Alexander and Symonds were conferring with a member of the Bengal Secretariat when Blair, Chief Secretary, accompanied by B. R. Sen, Secretary of the Revenue Department, came in. They had only understood the scale of the disaster within the last couple of days, and were now trying to organise immediate relief, both food and medical aid. Could the FAU help? Alexander and Symonds withdrew to the passage, and after a rapid consultation agreed that they ought to do something. So three members of the Unit were released for this work, and were in fact the second relief party to go to the stricken area, on 24 October. They went with two doctors and two assistants from the Bengal Civil Protection Medical Committee, whose presence was invaluable in reassuring the local population that the Unit members were not part of a British punitive expedition. The FAU had a special role to play in this situation, because the area had been particularly rebellious in August 1942, and clashes with Government forces continued. Bengali doctors and relief workers were not allowed to enter the stricken area unless the Unit guaranteed their non-political conduct, and FAU members accompanied them. Alexander was pleased that it had been possible to achieve 'co-operation between official and unofficial agencies of the very kind that we visualised before we left England, and in a situation of exceptional tension and complexity'.[51]

Alexander paid only brief visits to the affected areas, but was active in supporting cooperation between the various relief agencies. The Government set up a Cyclone Relief Committee, in which all the agencies involved were represented, and Alexander attended regularly. On one occasion he helped to keep the committee functioning after some of the nationalist members felt that they had been insulted, and stormed off threatening not to return. Alexander 'ventured to follow them to the car and finally induced them to come back'.[52] This supportive diplomacy, reinforcing the many contacts that the Unit made in the course of its work, proved invaluable when, later in 1943, the dreadful Bengal famine began to take hold.

*

In February 1943 Alexander once again risked irritating the Viceroy by a further attempt to play the part of a conciliator. Early in 1943 Gandhi and Linlithgow had been corresponding with each other over Government claims that Congress was responsible for the violence that followed the arrest of the leaders in August 1942. Gandhi argued that these claims were ill-founded and unjust, but Linlithgow saw no reason to withdraw them. In these circumstances Gandhi felt it appropriate to mortify the flesh and embark on a 21-day fast. He described it as 'an appeal to the Highest Tribunal for justice'. The Viceroy understandably saw it as 'political blackmail'.[53] It certainly created an atmosphere of near-panic in Government circles. There was a widespread impression that at his age and with his uncertain state of health he was unlikely to survive a three-week fast, and his death would cause serious disturbances. While Linlithgow claimed that he himself was willing enough to allow Gandhi to put his life at risk if he so insisted, the Indian members of the Viceroy's Council felt no such insouciance, and intensive consultations and negotiations were needed before a procedure to deal with Gandhi while fasting could be agreed. There was no unanimity, but it was eventually decided that Gandhi's detention should be suspended for the period of the fast, and that he should receive the fullest possible medical attention. Visitors were to be allowed, though undesirables would be excluded.

As soon as Gandhi's intention to fast was made known, Alexander wrote immediately to Laithwaite offering to make himself available 'if Lord Linlithgow thought he could be of any service'. Unsurprisingly Laithwaite responded that the Viceroy did not wish to trouble him in this matter, though he courteously accepted that the offer was well-intentioned.[54] It became clear, however, that the freedom allowed Gandhi to receive visitors opened the way for Alexander to see him anyhow, and accordingly he left Calcutta for Poona, where Gandhi had chosen to remain in detention in the Aga Khan's palace.

Whatever the Viceroy might think, the Bengal Government accepted that this visit might be useful. Before his departure, Alexander arranged with Blair to see Government files about the disturbances in August 1942, so that he could take Gandhi an independent assessment of the information which had led to the charge of Congress responsibility. Symonds accompanied him, with the hope that any interview would be witnessed by a sympathetic observer, but he was unable to remain because, as Gandhi's condition was deteriorating, Alexander's visit was inevitably delayed until there was some improvement. He actually saw him for some twenty minutes on 23 February and sent a report of the conversation to the Governor of Bombay, Sir Roger Lumley. In contrast to the Viceroy, Lumley had warmly welcomed Alexander's visit, hoping that it might contribute to some formula by which the fast might be ended. He was greatly exercised by the possibility of serious disorder should Gandhi die in detention. The formula was not forthcoming, however. Alexander emphasised Gandhi's real distress at the accusation that he had instigated violence. He would welcome a judicial inquiry into the evidence. He also reminded Lumley that if Gandhi were released from detention,

> he would naturally deal with all the forces of violence in the way he knows, and he would also naturally plunge into the task of bringing relief to those who are suffering from the present scarcity of food and other necessities.[55]

These words could only have struck Linlithgow as further proof of Alexander's fellow-travelling role, demonstrating that the fast was a blackmailing manoeuvre to gain release. Alexander was well aware that his efforts would be discounted in this way, and tried to meet inevitable suspicions by remarking that Gandhi himself wasn't much interested in such manoeuvres. He would only welcome release if he thought that the Government positively desired his assistance as a free man. But this notion was so alien to Government thinking that it is doubtful that it made any impression. What did make an impression, though, was Alexander's comment that Gandhi seemed confident that he would survive the fast, playfully referring to it as a 'fraudulent fast', as he was now, on medical advice, taking a little orange juice. This phrase was very welcome to Linlithgow and his colleagues when they felt assured that Gandhi would survive, enabling the Viceroy to say that those whose heart-strings had been plucked should realise that their legs had been pulled.[56] This was a natural enough comment if the fast were simply perceived as a suicide threat, but as Alexander was to point out in his assessment of the fast in *India since Cripps*, there was more to it than that. The fast had indeed failed in its primary aim of touching the Viceroy's heart so that he would be willing to reconsider the allegation that Gandhi had actually stirred up violence. But it was also a reminder of his absolute commitment to non-violence, an 'appeal to the people of India to discipline themselves, to purify and quicken their minds, to find ways of serving their fellow-men'. It also had a tonic effect on Gandhi himself.

> People who came to Poona angry and pessimistic, after visiting Mr Gandhi's bedside went away cheerful, hopeful, courageous. One seemed to get a sense of renewed sanity; the world was seen in juster proportions. Evil was still big and noisy on every side; but good, though it might be hardly visible or audible, was known to be the conquering force.[57]

On the most mundane interpretation, Gandhi will have been inspirited by the liberty given him to receive and encourage his friends. And he would have been less than human if he had not relished a little the unconscious tribute paid to his power by the acute anxiety his fast so evidently caused the Government of India. If this was blackmail, it was surely one of its more innocent manifestations.

The fast lasted its full twenty-one days, and ended with an impressive act of interfaith worship. Alexander himself contributed a reading from Paul's Epistle to the Romans, the passage in the twelfth chapter that ends with an exhortation to overcome evil with good.[58] Thereafter Gandhi was again detained without access to visitors, but he had the satisfaction of knowing that he had publicly rejected the charge of inciting violence, and had discouraged further violence as far as he could.

*

Alexander returned from Poona to Calcutta early in March 1943, and remained there for three weeks. Then, at the end of the month, he embarked on a month-long visit to the south-western provinces of China not under Japanese occupation. Friends here were engaged in two kinds of work. A Friends mission had long been established in Chengtu, based in the West China Union University, with outposts elsewhere in Sichuan, and a large secondary school in Chungking.[59] Then, in the Second World War, the FAU had undertaken its China Convoy operation, one of whose principal tasks was the distribution of medical supplies to civilian hospitals, some (perhaps half) maintained by Christian missions, the rest by the Chinese Ministry of Health.. Two members of the China Convoy, Duncan Wood and Parry Jones, have written detailed accounts of Alexander's month in China, and these are the basis of the following narrative. (Duncan Word's narrative remains in private hands.)

Alexander's presence in India meant that it was possible for him, as a senior Friend, to pay a kind of pastoral visit to this remote area of Quaker work. But there was a further motive for his expedition. Although the FAU was organised and administered by British Friends, the China Convoy received important financial support from the American Friends Service Committee, a member of a fund-raising consortium called United China Relief. The AFSC decided to send staff member John Rich to China to gather some of the first-hand personal impressions so important in fund-raising. But he was also mandated to pave the way for the arrival of American conscientious objectors recruited for service with the Convoy. This assignment arose out of efforts to give American COs more satisfactory expression to their convictions than their government was allowing them. When the United States entered the war in 1941, the Peace Churches – Brethren, Mennonites and Quakers – were put in charge of all registered COs, who were despatched to Civilian Public Service camps where they were engaged in forestry and other 'work of national importance', well away from the mainstream of public life. Many COs chafed at these limited opportunities, and the AFSC had seen in the China Convoy a possible opening for such active-minded pacifists. Indeed, they had begun the selection of a group of seventy American reinforcements for the China Convoy, and an advance party had already set out when John Rich was in China preparing the way for their arrival. The project caused some anxiety at the London headquarters of the FAU, because the China Convoy was already troubled by divisions over leadership, and the scope for further difficulties if there was significant American recruitment was all too apparent. John Rich, moreover, was felt to be 'impulsive', and someone needed to 'keep an eye' on him. Alexander might well have seemed the obvious person to do this.

But Duncan Wood remarks that Alexander did not relish this assignment, nor was he well equipped for it. As we have seen, he was drafted into the FAU's India work because of his unique qualifications for being of assistance there. But he was in no way a typical FAU member, and was not well informed about the internal problems of the China Convoy. Moreover, he found John Rich distinctly uncongenial. Rich was younger and more ebullient, and, says Wood, tended to monopolise the attention of the young men in the Convoy.

Rich had joined Alexander in Calcutta, and they flew from there to Kunming on 26 March. According to one Unit member, the flight at high altitudes was something of an ordeal, causing Alexander considerable physical pain, and making Rich lose consciousness.[60] They then travelled by rail to Kutsing, where the FAU's China Convoy had its headquarters. There he shared in the discussions about the Convoy's future plans, and took part in devotional meetings. One evening there was a failure of the power supply, and according to Wood, who was present, 'we took the chance to hear Horace talk about India, which he could do in the dark'. He not only described the work of the FAU, but also assessed the political situation, and the reasons for Gandhi's fast.

The medical supplies carried by the Convoy were delivered to Kunming by the US Air Force, which maintained a continuous service for goods and personnel over the mountains separating Yunnan from Assam and known as 'the Hump'.

> From Kunming [Wood writes] these goods could be taken by rail to Kutsing, but then had to be transported by road. The roads, though well engineered, were very ill-paved and traversed much mountainous country. The trucks had increasingly to be powered by charcoal gas as petrol supplies ran short.[61] So the Convoy was engaged in an arduous and sometimes hazardous task. Rich and Alexander decided to sample it for themselves by travelling on a truck taking a load to Luhsien on the Yangtse River and due to leave on 7th April.

The experience left a deep impression. Alexander wrote afterwards,

> Day after day for eight hours or more, these men are driving over mountain roads with endless blind corners, no wall to save them from plunging into the abyss, up and down mountain sides round numberless hairpin bends, and every hour they drive means a hundred gear changes.

Even so, 'our Welsh driver broke into song at his wheel'.[62]

The Welsh driver was Parry Jones, who remembers that the songs included 'Dafydd y Garreg Wen', about an old harpist who on his death-bed 'called for his harp so that he could just once again play the songs of his youth'. Another was 'Myfanwy', 'a love-song in which the love-sick youth pines for the beautiful dark-haired maiden awaiting his return from distant places': a theme doubtless of considerable poignancy to members of the China Convoy. Jones sent me a vivid account of his journey with Alexander and Rich, written in 1997, which deserves extensive quotation.

> I told my passengers we would leave at 2 a.m. and that they should go to bed early. This way, I hoped to make Suanwei, 60 miles away, in time to get some breakfast there because the next chance for a meal would be in Weining. It was in Suanwei that a small accident occurred. My two passengers had taken comfortable seats on top of the medical cargo, which we had loaded carefully above and behind the cab so that they could see the countryside. Unfortunately by the time we reached Suanwei they were cold and somewhat stiff. I helped them down over the cab and the bonnet, but Horace, who was older and not so nimble, managed to protrude his derriere through the windshield, which was completely shattered on his side. What saved Horace from serious injury was the tough British raincoat he wore; his dignity suffered only from the fecund ribaldry of John Rich's mind. We covered that half of the windshield with cardboard until I got it repaired in Luhsien for my return trip.

The reason why Alexander and Rich had to travel on top of the cargo was that, until Weining, there was at least one more passenger, Ellen Ling, who sat beside Parry Jones in the cab, but evidently made so little impression on him that by 1997 she had altogether dropped out of the story. She wrote to Alexander in 1962 with a contribution to the fund to support the anti-nuclear protest of the small ship *Everyman III*, of which Alexander was the treasurer. She reminded him that

> when the truck stopped you were benumbed and stiff with cold – and following others descended via the bonnet of the truck – but you slipped and crashed through the windscreen giving me a shower of bits of glass – and no cuts![63]

It appears that after this incident Alexander will have joined Ellen Ling in the cab. As we shall see, there was room for two passengers beside the driver.

> Suanwei to Weining was the most difficult section of our route, partly because of the great distance, 200 miles of mountain road, with only a small village – Tse Cho – where a bowl of soup was sometimes to be had and one might find sparse lodging for a night. Stopping there was not recommended, however, because of the reputation of the village as a bandit hide-out. The aim was to make Weining before dark, which was possible in good weather, without rain or snow, and assuming no mechanical troubles arose.
>
> After Weining we were once again in mountainous country, with beautiful valleys and an occasional good restaurant offering fish and vegetables, heading for a 10,000-foot pass, the highest point on the trip. The approach was via the notorious Tsewantien Por, a long and stiff climb that became steeper toward the summit. On a clear day one could see the snow-capped mountains of Tibet to the west, but it was dangerous in winter because of icy conditions with many hairpin bends. The next stop was the town of Pichieh, where we would spend the night as guests of the Lutheran sisters of the Friedenshort Mission.[64] Their welcome was so warm, and their table so rich in home-made dishes, good bread, and a famous walnut cake that a visit there was always a luxury.
>
> Since my passengers and I were crammed on a bench seat in the cab of the truck, I had time to study them by the time we got to Pichieh. John Rich was voluble, full of stories about the joys of living in Philadelphia and tirelessly loquacious. He was appalled at the dirt and poverty of the people we encountered and seemed unable to grasp the reasons why they were so backward after two thousand years of civilisation compared to three hundred years for Philadelphia. Horace was very quiet. His binoculars hung on his neck like part of his person, and his eye was on every bird we saw. He identified most of them, but the excitement lay in the possibility of recording two or three birds that were rare, and which he had been informed might be seen on our route. He caught sight of one

> bird as we negotiated a steep S-bend; he had his binoculars on it until it flew away, then relaxed with the triumphant smile of one who had made a successful Klondike strike and looked for the next bird. All the birds seemed to perch on S-bends. Going downhill into the gorges it was difficult to stop on his request; with a heavily-loaded truck it could be even harder to start again when going up the other side, sometimes requiring rolling back to take a run at the bend. We lost a lot of time but learned much about the birds of China.
>
> John Rich had an encyclopedic fund of jokes, many of them risqué and all of them funny. I laughed with him, but Horace put on a great stone face and ignored them. John was not fazed by this but babbled on. The tedium of long hours of driving never developed on this occasion.

The rest of the ten-day journey to Luhsien[65] was no less picturesque but not so hazardous, and Alexander and Rich were safely delivered to their next FAU minder, who arranged the next stage of their journey to Chengtu. Being across the Sichuan plain, it took less time and was less exhausting than what had gone before. Nevertheless, that sample of wartime travel in China occupied nearly half the time the two visitors had to spend in the country, most of it on the road but some in recuperation since, according to Parry Jones, at some point both of them needed hospital treatment for exhaustion and exposure.

Wood's narrative continues:

> In Chengtu Alexander was much more in his element than he had been in Kutsing. He was there as the representative of the Friends Service Council with whose personnel, programmes and principles he was familiar. FSC had inherited from the Friends Foreign Mission Association the Quaker share of responsibility for West China Union University, founded and maintained by a group of missionary societies. Some, at least, of the Friends then at work in Chengtu will have been former students at Kingsmead, the Friends' Missionary training college across the Bristol Road from Woodbrooke, so they shared some of Alexander's background. His visit was an important personal link between these Quaker workers and their London headquarters from whom they were increasingly isolated by wartime restrictions. He was able to bring them the support of FSC, to listen to their problems and act as their messenger.

He was also able to speak about India to people with an intelligent and sympathetic interest in Indian affairs. Chinese leaders had always supported Indian aspirations, and a visit to India by Chiang Kai-shek had perhaps given Lord Linlithgow some of his most embarrassing moments. Alexander must have found the political atmosphere a refreshing change from that prevailing in India.

As always, he carried out his regular practice of getting into touch with local Friends, A Yearly Meeting had been established in Sichuan in the early 1930s, and there were local meetings in Chengtu, Chungking and other places.[66] It was Chungking that he and John Rich visited after leaving Chengtu, and there a Friends' school was maintained, situated on the south bank of the Yangtse, overlooking the city. The headmaster was F. L. Yang, a leading Chinese Friend who, unfortunately, was later to suffer in the Revolution. His wife recalled meeting Alexander's father in 1906 or 1907. In Chungking, too, Alexander again encountered Duncan Wood. If his bird-watching had been an irritation to Parry Jones, for Wood it was an exhilarating pleasure. Alexander had initiated him into the art when a schoolboy, and now he had been able to take his mentor to the wetlands near Kutsing and the hills around Chungking. These two excursions were almost certainly the occasions in China on which Alexander will have looked back with most gratification.

*

After his final round of discussions in Chungking, it was time for Alexander to return to Calcutta. He arrived back in the city in the early hours of a late April morning, and was shocked by the huge numbers of starving people sleeping in the streets. The food shortage had worsened considerably while he had been away, and villagers were flocking into the city in the hope of finding imported food. The Unit was transferring such resources as it had from cyclone relief to famine relief. One of its members, Pamela Bankart, had organised a corps of women emergency volunteers to engage in air-raid relief work, in particular to help other women, and they now devoted themselves to this new emergency. Eventually there were eight milk canteens, feeding about 1,100 children. The work was initially subsidised by a few wealthy Indian friends of the Unit, enabling the FAU to buy up supplies of dried milk in the bazaar.[67] The project was, as Symonds later remarked, 'infinitesimal in the vast relief operations which have been and are still necessary',[68] but was as much as the Unit could accomplish on its own initiative. It was clear that immensely greater resources were needed. Alexander realised that his most useful role now would be to return home and bring his first-hand appreciation of the emergency to arouse people there. John Rich was to do much the same in Philadelphia.[69] In Britain an appeal was launched by the *News Chronicle* which raised considerable funds, and the help of the Red Cross was enlisted. Supplies of tinned milk came flooding in from both Britain and the US, and milk distribution was taken over by the Red Cross in Calcutta, assisted by one FAU member, reaching a daily total of some 3 million children.

Alexander did not lose sight of his concern to help forward constitutional reform. Before he left India he travelled around from Madras to Bombay and then to Delhi, interviewing people as diverse as Rajagopalachari, Dr

Ambedkar, and civil servants Sir Frederick Puckle (Director of Information) and John Sargent (Commissioner of Education).[70] He also paid a final visit to Laithwaite, who remarked acidly that he seemed to have been gadding about a good deal. The fruits of his 'gadding about' were soon to appear in his short book on recent events, *India since Cripps*, and Laithwaite may have guessed that some such publication was contemplated. Anyhow, Alexander returned to Britain by air with a mind full of projects and purposes, and arrived there on 15 September.

8

CAMPAIGNING IN BRITAIN AND THE USA

Six months in Britain

Alexander's return to Britain was of course partly dictated by the fact that his year's leave of absence from Woodbrooke had expired, and he could in any case feel very reasonably that he had done all that he could to see the Unit well established. And, as the Viceroy remarked, all his Congress friends were in detention where he could be of little service to them as a conciliator. There was much to be done in Britain. The scale of the Bengal famine had not yet been sufficiently realised, and Indian political aspirations were understood even less. Alexander was particularly dismayed by the Government's continued refusal to acknowledge Gandhi's essential goodwill. The first thing he did on his return was to seek an interview with Amery in order to brief him on the situation as he saw it, and in particular to urge him to enlist Gandhi's help in coping with the famine. Amery was too busy to see him. He could see P. J. Patrick instead, and did so on Thursday 23 September.[1]

Meanwhile Agatha Harrison lost no time in organising a programme for him. In a letter of 19 September, just four days after his arrival, she proposed meetings with concerned Members of Parliament, with journalists such as Crozier of the *Manchester Guardian* and Kingsley Martin of the *New Statesman*, with representatives of the religious press, and with the various groups working on India who would have had a sense of great grievance if Alexander's knowledge had not been shared with them too. She imagined Gandhi saying to himself,

'Horace is now back in England – he will do what Andrews would have done.'[2] While Alexander was willing enough to bestir himself in this way, what chiefly preoccupied him at first was his frustration with attitudes in the India Office, in particular their refusal to accept that he might actually be useful to the British Government. In a letter to Harrison, written on 27 September, he remarked on the fact that, at that moment, he was the only person in Britain who had been

> in close and intimate touch with Indian leaders of every shade during the past year. . . . It does not seem to occur to those India Office people that if they are ever going to get anywhere with a settlement, they must pick my brains.

Moreover, like Harrison, he had the confidence of those who were going to matter most if any attempt was made to achieve a settlement. Any negotiations would always be at risk because of misconstructions by either party. 'The right people have to be behind the scenes to prevent a breakdown of any talks that may begin.' And who were the right people?

> So far as M. K. G. [Gandhi] is concerned the simple fact is that there are only two English people now living who really have his confidence enough to give the help from the English side that Rajaji and Devadas [Gandhi] and the other 'peacemakers' on the Indian side will need. They are you and I.[3]

This, Alexander admits, may all seem 'horribly conceited – perhaps it is. But there are times when a man knows his destiny'.

His experience in government circles was not altogether discouraging. R. A. Butler remained a warmly supportive presence in the background, although inevitably preoccupied with piloting his Education Bill through the Commons. He told Alexander that India was never out of his mind, that when he saw a Catholic deputation about the Bill, he thought of the Hindus, and when it was a Protestant deputation, he thought of the Muslims.[4] Presumably Butler hoped to reconcile these conflicting interests, and if it could be done in Britain, why not in India? More specific than such diffuse goodwill was the reception of an idea that he put to Stafford Cripps's colleague, David Owen, and through him to Amery. This was the possibility of forming a group in Britain who would explore ways of developing contacts with Indian liberals. The model he had in mind was Alfred Milner's 'kindergarten', the young men who had worked together in the reconstruction of South Africa after the Boer War, and had created the Round Table movement that sought a new role for the British Empire. Amery had been closely associated with this group, and its thinking informed his own relatively liberal approach to Indian constitutional issues. Amery was mildly interested in the idea of an 'Indian kindergarten', and David Owen agreed with Alexander that Wavell would be greatly assisted if he could turn to a team acceptable to people like Sir Tej Bahadur Sapru. Alexander had drawn up a list of possible recruits, but in the end nothing seems to have come of the proposal.[5]

As Alexander's destiny was not going to be fulfilled through the India Office, he turned to the press. He had quickly established his authority after his return by writing to *The Times* and other newspapers about the famine, its causes and the measures needed to deal with it. He gave a short talk on the overseas service of the BBC on 7 October 1943. An article in *The Spectator* for 15 October provided a clear account of what had happened, and ended with a sharp reminder that those best able to deal with the crisis were held in detention. But his main preoccupation was with writing his assessment of the issues in a short paperback volume commissioned by Penguin Books, *India since Cripps*. He wrote this with a vigour commensurate with his frustration.

It should be remarked here that while Alexander was in India his house at 144 Oaktree Lane continued to be occupied by Winifred White, who had cared for Olive, and by others with a Woodbrooke connection. Among these was Dorothy Hogg. She had visited India with Agatha Harrison and, like her, had come to know Gandhi well. Her account of Gandhi in her *Memories for Tomorrow* (1981) is exceptionally sensitive and understanding. On Alexander's return she agreed to act as his secretary, and in her letters to Harrison at this time she has left a vivid account of the writing of *India since Cripps*. It has to be said that Dorothy had a distinctly imperfect sympathy so far as Alexander was concerned, detecting in him more self-indulgence than was proper in a disciple of the Mahatma. When she learnt that Woodbrooke gossip had made a match between her and Alexander she was not well pleased. As she said to the Warden's wife, Edith Richards,

> 'Can you imagine any two people more unlikely to "fall" for each other?' and I fear our conversation ended in merry laughter. I am convinced that Horace would drive me crackers, and equally that I should drive him to drink![6]

But Dorothy's irritation with his foibles enhanced her descriptive powers, and it is tempting to quote the letters she wrote to Agatha Harrison about Alexander at disproportionate length. The first draft of the book was evidently quite uninhibited, 'very hot' as she put it.

> I really was staggered. I went into his room late one night when he was rounding off a chapter. He was like an over-excited schoolboy and he just rolled his tongue round the juicy bits as he read them aloud to me. 'Well, really, Mr Alexander', said I, 'you're a fine Quaker! You'll make even the outspoken George Fox turn in his grave.' Of course I loved the bits all the same, but I really did not think he should put them in. What he first wrote about the Secretariat at Delhi was the limit.[7]

One can glean some idea of what this sensational version was like from Alexander's comments to Agatha Harrison about Sir Gilbert Laithwaite – a man who separates religion and politics absolutely, so he doesn't have to be too scrupulous in winning a trick. Alexander wanted an honourable agreement between Congress and the Government. To Laithwaite 'anyone who wants that is an enemy, who must be crushed by any means'.[8] Alexander was evidently much refreshed by such dissection of his adversaries, and his zest was infectious. As Dorothy Hogg remarked to Agatha Harrison, being Alexander's typist was as exciting as racing in the Derby.

> As fast as he forges ahead with a chapter, I race with the typing, but so far he manages to lead all the way. Thrilling. I am enjoying it. Don't ever let him think that it has been anything but a labour of love bringing to me a thrill and joy which far outweighs any energy expended.[9]

Her most serious disagreement with Alexander was in her assessment of Rajagopalachari. While evidently an important player in any attempt to reach an accommodation in India, she was unhappy with, for example, the sneering way she had heard him speak of the Chinese resistance to Japan. Moreover, Alexander's insensitivity to Rajagopalachari's limitations seemed to her a sign of his own inadequacy. She later complained to Harrison that Alexander was tactless and often blind to the reactions of others. The idea of his returning to India as a mediator between the British Government and the Congress alarmed her. 'I don't think Horace is safe on his own. He says and does such extraordinary things.'[10]

These critical comments must, however, be seen in the context of the letter in which they occur. Dorothy Hogg was bent on persuading Harrison that Harrison herself had a better claim than Alexander to being a useful emissary to Gandhi, and one can see that Harrison's more direct and emphatic mode appealed to her more strongly than the quiet and sometimes unpredictable approach that came naturally to Alexander. In the same letter, she conjures up a dramatic if implausible vision of Harrison in operation.

> How good it would be to hear that *you* were forging straight ahead, irrespective of whatever anybody else thought you ought or ought not to do and that you had swept that bewildered little man [Amery] off his feet with the announcement that you must now go to India because you must, and he must give you a plane because he must, and you must see Mr Gandhi because you must and that was all there was to it![11]

Such fantasising was not at all how Harrison saw herself, although she did think that Amery had sensitivities that might be touched, and that were at odds with the Government's current odious policy. Had he not agreed to forward a letter from herself to Gandhi, and to send the new Viceroy a copy of C. F. Andrews' pamphlet, *The Indian Earthquake*, as a reminder that Congress leaders might conceivably cooperate with Government on constructive projects?[12] Harrison's irrepressible goodwill to all may well have been a contrast to what Dorothy Hogg found uncommunicative and unapproachable in Alexander in some moods, but she was cheerfully ready to forgive nearly everything after an evening's merry conversation with him and Elizabeth Fox Howard:

> You know what she is like when she really gets going. We had Horace literally weeping with laughter at our ribald renderings of some of the less inspired hymns, and E's fund of funny stories of course never comes to an end.

Even so, she was uneasy at what Alexander told her about his answers to questions about Gandhi: 'It seemed to me that he had just missed the point.'[13]As she did not enlarge on this criticism, however, it isn't clear what point he was missing.

She would no doubt have agreed that others were missing the point far more comprehensively, and that Alexander did well to confront the more grotesque misunderstandings of the Congress position at every opportunity. *India since Cripps*, published in February 1944, was – in its final version – a scrupulously fair analysis of the overall situation in India. India Office officials conceded that it might have been worse, and Krishna Kripalani, in a rather scathing review in the *Visva-Bharati Quarterly*, was offended by what he saw as an excess of Christian charity.

> Gandhiji and Lord Linlithgow were almost equally good men and well-wishers of the Indian people, if only they could have understood each other. Presumably if either of them had had the wisdom and tolerance of Mr Alexander, the Indian tragedy could have been averted. Jinnah, Jawaharlal, Suhrawardy, Nazim-ud-Din, Dr Ambedkar, even M. N. Roy, seem all excellent patriots, if only the Indian politics were free from the poison of mutual suspicion! The author, however, has not lost all hope. For Lord Wavell is there. If only he and Gandhi learn to understand each other, all may yet be well. How nice and simple it all seems, and how truly Christian![14]

Certainly when Alexander addressed a private meeting of the Royal Institute of International Affairs on 9 March 1944, he was at pains to emphasise the latent goodwill that might be mobilised to build a united India, an India that would 'feel itself part of the present world struggle'. This was something that Rajagopalachari was trying to achieve, and more could be done to help him from the British side. Alexander tried to explain the motives that underlaid the utterances of Gandhi and Nehru, describing 'the real human being, a composite mixture of conflicting motives and tendencies, just as we are, behind the mask which almost all public men wear when they make public statements'. But his attempt to show Congress as a potential ally in the war, provided that independence was conceded, seems not to have carried conviction. Even a sympathetic listener like Penderel Moon told him afterwards that he felt Alexander hadn't disproved the claim that Gandhi thought that the Japanese would win.[15]

For many months after his return to Britain, Alexander laboured to lessen the mutual incomprehension that bedevilled relations between Britain and India. Besides alerting the press to the appalling scale of the Bengal famine, he was at pains to insist that the governing coalition ministry had not shirked its responsibilities. In a letter to *The Times* of 2 October 1943 he praised H. S. Suhrawardy for his efforts to achieve effective food distribution, though he hoped that fresh efforts would be made to put the ministry on a broader basis, 'in order to ensure the fullest co-operation of every section in the province'. This was a continuing preoccupation. Ten months later he wrote to Shyama Prasad Mookherjee urging him to work for a new coalition ministry in Bengal, achieving which would silence critics who complained that you could never get Indians to agree with each other. Hindus, said Alexander, were in a position of strength in Bengal, and could afford to make concessions to the Muslims. 'I do trust that a supreme effort will be made'.[16] Alas, the supreme effort was not forthcoming, and Alexander was hardly in a position to influence events several thousand miles away. Even his mild commendation of Suhrawardy in *The Times* caused anxiety in Calcutta. Glan Davies wrote that Pandit Kunzru was unhappy at reports, based on this letter, that Alexander was backing the Muslim League ministry.[17] Davies tried to explain that Alexander was simply saying that Suhrawardy had put his back into the job, an endorsement he may well have judged necessary for British readers, all too ready as they were to assume that Indians were invariably slack and incompetent.

By far the most difficult task of interpretation, though, was created by Gandhi himself. Suffering from poor health, and from the distress caused by the death of his wife in February 1944, he had been released from detention in May of that year. Almost the first statement he was reported to have made after his release was that he could not 'withdraw the August [l942] resolution'. As soon as this report was received in Britain, Alexander wrote to Rajagopalochari urging him to persuade Gandhi to say that his main concern – and Alexander was sure that it *was* his main concern – remained the ending of Indian poverty. As it was, he was only on record as saying that he still stood by the August resolution, which was a source of perplexity to his well-wishers in Britain.[18] Towards the end of June, Alexander wrote to Gandhi himself about a number of matters, including his own assessment of the violent resistance to the British in Midnapore in 1942. He described the efforts by the Friends'

Ambulance Unit to help in the work of dealing with the Bengal famine, and doing so 'in happy comradeship with everyone – Government people, Congress people, Ramakrishna Mission, Moslems, missionaries and all.' This led tactfully up to the main point of his letter:

> May it not be that the needs of Bengal, and of other provinces, too, provide the real foundation for a new understanding between Government and Congress, not to mention Moslem League and everyone else? Perhaps you doubt whether the need of the starving millions is really the serious concern of the Government; or perhaps you suspect that their expressed concern in the matter is due to a desire to side-track the political issue. . . . Far from side-tracking the political issue, an effective joint campaign against famine might surely prove the royal means to its solution. . . . Can you offer unconditional assistance in fighting the food shortage? If you can, I believe you may find a response.[19]

Alexander recalled that Gandhi, during his recent fast, had said that if he were free he would wish to give all his energy to fighting the famine conditions that were then spreading over India. Lord Wavell had manifestly shown his determination to deal with the famine as well as he could, and Alexander was glad that Gandhi had been in correspondence with him. But there needed to be a meeting. 'The mutual trust that is needed can surely never come through correspondence.'

How right he was. If any letter could have influenced Gandhi, Alexander's surely would have done. But it seems to have had no effect. Gandhi's reply, sent on 12 July, was warmly affectionate so far as Alexander himself was concerned, but he could not accept his arguments.

> Your anxiety that I should offer co-operation at least for the alleviation of hunger I fully understand. My difficulty is that I cannot, for the reason that the alleviation is only apparent. The Viceroy's good intentions in the matter are not to be doubted. His promptness in rushing to Bengal on arrival was worthy of the soldier that he is. The agency through which he had and has to work is not designed to carry out the work of alleviation. . . .. Sufficient to say that at no time has India been so bound down as now. The remedy is liberty consistent with the movements of Allied troops. But there is deep mutual distrust. Authority distrusts the Congress and every public body including the Muslim League. Public opinion is flouted at almost every turn. In this state of things voluntary co-operation becomes impossible.[20]

Discouraging though this letter was, it did not close the door altogether. It was evidently written in a mood of depression, and there had not, after all, actually been any meeting with Gandhi. If only this could be accomplished there might be progress. Perhaps, as in 1930 and again in 1942, the Society of Friends might exercise its influence in support of a fresh initiative. Its executive body, Meeting for Sufferings, was to meet on 2 September in Manchester, and Agatha Harrison pointed out that India was on the agenda. Alexander should go to explain the context of Gandhi's letter, and underline the importance of some kind of mission to him.

Now, as it happened, just at this time Alexander was looking forward to a week's bird-watching in South Wales. Strong though his commitment to India's aspirations was, the pleasures of bird-watching sometimes tempted him from the path of duty. So it was on this occasion. Once again, Dorothy Hogg has painted a vivid picture. She had agreed with Harrison that Alexander must go to Manchester on the 2nd, and told him so.

> 'But it is my holiday.'
> 'Yes, and I'm sorry this has come just now, but events won't always wait.'
> 'There are other people who can help on this.'
> 'Who? Anna Barlow?'

This was a shrewd blow. Anna Barlow was one of the most conservative members of Friends' Peace Committee, and as strong a critic as William Graham might have been of anything that suggested appeasement of Gandhi.[21] Alexander tried to brush the objection aside, but then realised it had some weight.

> 'Shouldn't think she'd go. Oh yes she might, she's got relatives in the area.'
> 'Then how can you leave things to anyone else? You've had the letter [from Gandhi] and you can speak with an authority that no one else can at the moment. Here's a practical job for the Society of Friends to tackle, but you'll be needed to show them how.'
> 'Agatha might go herself.'
> 'Agatha won't spare herself . . .. But what can Agatha do really as far as Meeting for Sufferings is concerned? They'll listen to anything you've got to say, but if Agatha says the same thing the weighty friends won't listen. And Carl [Heath] not there either.'

Still, Alexander insisted that he was not going to have his holiday interfered with. So Dorothy Hogg pointed out that he could both have his holiday *and* go to Manchester if he travelled by a night train. She then got a 'terrific diatribe' about how he *could not* travel by night: 'His legs were the sort that got pins and needles and that made him fidget, disturbed his own rest and other people's.' She next suggested he might travel first class, but that idea did not commend itself.

> There was a pause, and then he ventured,
> 'Anyhow, I couldn't go up to Manchester from Haverfordwest because it would mean wasting my return ticket.' That was supposed to be final.
> . . .
> 'What on earth does that matter? India's happiness against a mouldy half ticket from Haverfordwest. You're not even hard up! Besides, you could get part of the money back from the railway.'
> 'No, I couldn't.'
> 'Who said you couldn't? You can fill in a form and get part of it back anyhow.'

She eventually wore him down, and when, next morning, he left for his holiday, and she asked when he would be back, he replied, 'Not before last thing Thursday night, perhaps Friday, but it all depends on Manchester.'[22]

It is not clear whether he curtailed his holiday or whether, setting pins and needles at defiance, he travelled through the night, but to Manchester he went, and on 1 September convinced Meeting for Sufferings that something had to be done about Gandhi's state of mind. His intervention silenced Anna Barlow: Alexander told Harrison that 'she lay low in Meeting for Sufferings, and only whispered to me as I was going out of the meeting, "You've put it across them again".'[23]

The following day Alexander wrote to Gandhi once more, pleading with him to go to Bengal and 'bring new strength to the work of Dr B. C. Roy's committee,[24] and other such voluntary efforts, cooperating, not with the Government perhaps, but with all the voluntary societies, in the spirit that you showed in Bihar after the earthquake'. Such a move might produce incalculable results. Public opinion in Britain had been deeply stirred and shocked by the Bengal famine, and Alexander wanted them to learn that Gandhi and his friends were 'bending every energy to rescue the people from this menace of famine'. He ended: 'How I wish we could talk it all over; or better, that Agatha could be with you soon'.[25]

Gandhi's response came in the form of a telegram: 'YOU AGATHA MURIEL WELCOME. LOVE.'[26] It arrived, opportunely, just in time for the October session of Meeting for Sufferings, which accordingly agreed to approach Leo Amery for permission to despatch Agatha Harrison to India. Amery was not willing to allow this, so the idea petered out.[27] The India Office would certainly have been deeply suspicious of anyone as closely associated with Gandhi as she and Alexander were, and there was probably little awareness of the extent to which they attempted to interpret British concerns to Congress representatives. So the negative decision was almost inevitable. But it was shortsighted. As Alexander assured R. A. Butler, 'if once she were there the official attitude would very soon be that her influence behind the scenes was most useful.'[28] Agatha understood Gandhi to an extent that few people could match, but she also understood the point of view of the British Government, and thus was uniquely qualified to restore confidence between it and Gandhi. She had, too, an unusually sure grasp of the wider implications of the conflict between Britain and India, enabling her to encourage Gandhi to look beyond the depressing frustrations of the present. In September 1944 she attended a National Peace Council conference on the post-war settlement, and in a letter to Alexander complained about the inadequate attention paid there to India and China. She had broken into the discussion a few minutes before it ended, pointing out how unwise it was to think that, after the ending of the Japanese empire, there would just be an .improved colonial administration. The 'Far East' must be taken in on the ground floor of thinking and planning, otherwise we were heading for disaster. 'The trouble is [that] the Far East's contribution is never really recognised – save temporarily. If they could only get a knowledge of the intense irritation people like Nehru feel, Above all what the West is missing.'[29]

Alexander was certainly doing his best to raise awareness of the Indian perspective on current events in his travels round Britain, speaking to groups of all kinds. In the second week of March 1944, for example, he spoke to three meetings in Manchester: a public meeting on the famine, a meeting for Friends on the political situation in India, and a repeat of his talk in London to the Royal Institute of International Affairs, given to its Manchester branch. He told Symonds that the local 'progressives' had heard that the 'imperialists' were boycotting this last meeting, 'so they rallied round and it was a very good attendance'. Doubtless a more sympathetic one, too, than he had found in London. Letters from colleagues in Bengal kept him up to date with developments and picturesque details. Speaking to an audience of businessmen in the Rotary Club in Bilston, Alexander quoted Symonds' 'account of the Indian children as chipmunks in a Walt Disney film'. This moved them extremely. In another letter, Pamela Bankart illustrated the hazards Unit members had to cope with in travelling through the Ganges delta. Returning from a milk canteen by country boat, she found herself in the middle of a fierce storm. The sail broke loose, and nearly turned the boat over.

> It was just like a vision of Hell (except that it was very cold – but why should Hell necessarily be hot?), seeing the figures of the three boatmen wrestling with the sail, silhouetted grotesquely in the flashes of lightning against an apparently solid sheet of water.

But this was a mere detail. She was chiefly concerned to emphasise her admiration for the local people's competence, shown in the way the canteens were organised. Hindus and Muslims were treated alike: there was no discrimination. 'I feel there lies the real hope for India – in the peasant class.'[30]

The competence of Indian voluntary organisations was an important issue when raising money in Britain for famine relief. It was affirmed very strongly by Richard Symonds in person when he was recalled home for two months in the summer of 1944, in order to help with discussions on the future of the FAU in India. At a meeting on 26 July in the House of Commons, organised by the India Relief Committee, he thanked that committee for the £1,000 recently despatched to India, and sharply criticised people who said such funds were not well used. They *were* well used, and voluntary efforts created more confidence than those of the Government.[31]

Symonds was in fact about to accept an invitation from the Governor of Bengal, Richard Casey, to join the Government to help with its relief programme. There was a good deal of correspondence between Symonds and Alexander about the way the Unit worked and the suitability of various people for its activities. Symonds remarked of Duncan Wood that he had clearly acquired 'the appropriate qualities for high command in the Unit', being an ornithologist and therefore having 'long experience of what has always seemed to me a pretty dreary occupation in which nothing ever particularly happens'.[32] There seems to have been a kind of family joke that morale in the Unit was sustained by large quantities of alcohol. When it was proposed to despatch Christopher Taylor to India, Alexander did not feel happy at the idea, thinking his manner might be too cold and forbidding. A talk with him, however, was reassuring; 'and then Ralph [Barlow] joined us and asked C.B.T. [Taylor] how he would get on with a section whose members were more often drunk than sober. He did not seem to mind at all.' Symonds, for his part, welcomed the opening of the Mediterranean to Allied shipping because it had slightly improved the drink situation. He hoped that Meeting for Sufferings, edified as it had been by letters from him, appreciated 'how much of our grand strategy has been planned in the Park Street Restaurant'.[33] This kind of manly badinage was one aspect of Alexander's continuing identification with the convivial Cambridge ethos of King's College.

Alexander had returned to Woodbrooke with some thought of galvanising the place into new life. He said that he felt about ten years younger than he did when he left England, chiefly as the result of working with men and women more than twenty years younger than himself. 'I had to try to become young again too, and to some extent I seem to have succeeded'.[34] But the demands of the work he had left behind in India were too unremitting for him to insist on the 'wild revolutionary changes' he had in mind, and he concluded that it was only right for him to withdraw. On 25 February 1944, the Woodbrooke Council accepted his resignation from the post of Director of Studies, to take effect 'within the next twelve months'. It became clear that one useful task he could perform would be to go to the United States to speak about the work in India and China, and to consult with American Friends about the shape of post-war Quaker initiatives in Asia. As early as November 1943 the Executive Secretary of the American Friends Service Committee, Clarence Pickett, had warned him that he would be invited soon, and in December a formal invitation was made to him to come to the USA in the summer of 1944.[35] In March 1944 Alexander wrote to Leo Amery pointing out that a visit of this kind would be helpful in enhancing American interest in Indian relief. Amery, who by this time had come to feel that the FAU was a political asset, was sympathetic, but sympathetic in vain.[36] An apologetic official in the Ministry of Information told Alexander that new regulations had made it more difficult to authorise private visits abroad, so the whole project had to be cancelled.[37] But by the end of the year the regulations must have been relaxed again, for Alexander started making preparations for an Atlantic crossing, and the meetings and committees with which he was associated prepared supportive minutes to accompany him. After a brief bird-watching holiday in the island of Jura, off the west coast of Scotland, Alexander set sail, arriving in New York in the morning of 26 March.

USA 1945

Alexander spent four-and-a-half months in America, and during that time he was almost always either attending meetings or travelling between meetings. It was only during a fortnight in early July, when he visited Mount Desert Island off the coast of Maine, that he had an extended period of rest. He arrived from Britain just in time to attend four Yearly Meetings, two in Philadelphia, one in New York, and another in Baltimore. He was impressed by the amount of business transacted in a short space of time. Friends there 'said what they had to say in three sentences, or even two, and then sat down again' – a striking contrast this to the longwindedness which speakers in London Yearly Meeting seemed to feel was indispensable. A sign too of a quicker pace and more energetic temper than Alexander was to find altogether congenial. At some later date Dorothy Hogg told Agatha Harrison of a letter in which he complained that he sometimes wanted to say to kind friends, 'Oh can't you just be *silent* for a moment, and stop and listen and think.' And he often felt more at home with servicemen he encountered on his train journeys than with some of the vociferous pacifists he was with when he arrived.[38] In retrospect, though, he saw himself as fulfilling the concern that Olive had always had to visit America at some time:

> Once I got into the swing of your life I discovered that Olive's companionship was very close – above all when I met her old friends in State after State, all across the Continent. It was to me a very moving circumstance that I was with friends of hers, in the silent beauty of the woods by the Brandywine river, when the distant sound of sirens told us of the

> end of the war in the East; and as we bowed our spirits in thanksgiving and fresh resolve, I pictured in mind the little home where we spent our first year of married life in Kent, and how on November 11th, 1918, we resolved together, though no word spoken, to work for the healing of the nations.[39]

In many ways he found the well-filled days exhilarating, encouraged as he was by reports that large sums of money were being raised for medical supplies and rehabilitation programmes in India. And there were many congenial meetings in the first few weeks, some with old friends like Bertram and Irene Pickard, others with notable American Quakers like Rufus Jones, Henry Cadbury, Robert Yarnall and Clarence Pickett. He came across Mrs Pandit in New York, and was pleased by the warmth with which she spoke of Pamela Bankart and Richard Symonds. 'She said she had never met an English girl who had such a sure touch and genuine understanding of the way to work alongside Indians.' As for Symonds, she was confident that his working for the Government would not undermine his natural friendliness to India. Alas, he also found that Mrs Pandit had not made a good public impression in the US. She had lost her temper with the ebullient English politician Robert Boothby, and had compared Churchill to Hitler.[40] She was having to learn the hard way that what passes as commonplace in one culture may be mortally offensive in another.

Although Alexander was in America primarily to win financial support for Indian relief and rehabilitation, his visit coincided with the major international conference in San Francisco which set up the United Nations Organization. He had in any case to visit California in order to carry out his fund-raising mission, and by doing so in the last week of April and the beginning of May he was able to attend a number of the initial sessions. Hubert Peet, editor of the London Quaker weekly *The Friend*, organised press credentials for him, so that he had the advantage of facilities provided for journalists. His reports appeared in *The Friend* for 4 and 11 May.

The San Francisco Conference attracted immense interest in North America, stimulated in part by the report from the Dumbarton Oaks meetings the previous year. Representatives of the three major allies had met at this centre near Washington DC from 21 August to 28 September 1944, and drafted proposals for a post-war world organisation. These proposals were the focus of much discussion by civic and religious groups. In January 1945 the US Federal Council of Churches held a study conference in Cleveland, Ohio, which agreed to recommend fourteen amendments to the Dumbarton Oaks plan. These amendments sought to limit the privileges of the Great Powers and to strengthen the role of international law. Similar amendments had already been outlined by the Friends Committee on National Legislation, which saw Dumbarton Oaks as 'opening the way for progress', an opportunity to develop 'a democratic and satisfying system for achieving international peace, justice, and good will'.

Such resolute hopefulness was an American rather than a British phenomenon. At its March 1945 session, Meeting for Sufferings in London agreed a statement about the forthcoming conference in which it spoke of a 'current cynicism' about the United Nations idea, a cynicism which saw it only as a step towards a precarious and transient peace. The statement admittedly rejected this cynicism, but made no commitment to anything like an endorsement of the Dumbarton Oaks proposals. It called for the building of a new world on moral foundations, and saw the hope of peace lying in 'mutual co-operation in international reconstruction'. A month later, in early April, Carl Heath formulated a series of questions for Alexander to keep in mind when he represented *The Friend* in San Francisco. He was, he said, 'not exactly the smiling optimist as regards this gathering'. Pooled sovereignty didn't seem to be on the agenda, the Security Council idea was apparently taken for granted, Switzerland and Sweden played no part and the vanquished were altogether excluded. 'Is there', he asked, 'anything basically *democratic* in the whole "frame-up"?' – a rhetorical question to which the answer was clearly 'No'.[41]

Even among internationally minded Americans there were those who saw no good coming out of San Francisco. The veteran pacifist A. J. Muste saw the Dumbarton Oaks proposals as radically flawed. He published a vigorous attack on them in *Fellowship*, the journal of the American Fellowship of Reconciliation. He wanted the US to offer an immediate end to the war with Germany and Japan, and, for good measure, to renounce imperialism and power politics as well. (He added, with a refreshing touch of realism, that he was 'well aware that what we have proposed cannot be accomplished at one stroke'.)[42]

Sympathetic or hostile, there was a high level of interest in these issues in North America which generated a non-governmental involvement in the conference proceedings that greatly impressed Alexander. As he wrote to Paul Sturge,

> the presence of large numbers of representatives of independent organisations, most of them keen to get a really effective peace charter out of the conference, had real value. The public galleries and press galleries were well filled every day, even through the dullest speeches.

The American delegation in particular paid considerable attention to these organisations, arranging frequent briefings and consultations.[43]

The visiting Quakers from the eastern states, together with Alexander, stayed with William and Anna James in Berkeley, across the Bay. This meant a daily journey across the eight-mile bridge and back again. At night they could gaze down from the heights of Berkeley to the twinkling lights all round the

Bay. In the morning they woke up to the twitterings of strange birds – which could hardly have made it easy to drag Alexander away to the conference proceedings. It was clear from discussion among themselves that American Friends held views as various as the statesmen about what should be the outcome. Alexander, for his part, tried to indicate where British Friends stood, and indeed what he thought some continental Friends might have to say on some issues.[44]

Alexander's main despatch to *The Friend*, published on 4 May, is a reminder of how different the international scene looked before the advent of the atomic bomb. He took for granted that the USA and the USSR would be nearly impregnable to an invader. 'Neither USA nor USSR could destroy the other. Therefore a war between them is unlikely.' But that other Great Power, the British Empire, might well come into conflict with the USSR, in Iran or in central Europe. In that event, would it make sense for one party to be declared the aggressor, with sanctions to be enforced against it? Alexander argued that it would be unrealistic to expect anything of the kind. The Great Powers had to be unanimous. But if a Great Power proved recalcitrant to measures recommended by a majority of states not party to the dispute, then it was still possible to mobilise 'a steady pressure of world opinion. . . . If there is a vigorous minority opinion inside the guilty State, demanding a change of policy, such a change may soon happen and justice will thus be vindicated.' The crucial element in a successful world order would thus be 'a constantly informed, wakeful, vigorous world opinion'. Without this, even the wisest and most ingenious arrangements would not work.[45]

In the letter to Paul Sturge, mentioned earlier, Alexander remarked that 'the Russians were on the whole more co-operative than had been feared', and that the press had tended to exaggerate tensions between Russia and the West. But even if Alexander were too sanguine in this assessment, it is clear that substantial hopes were embodied in the UN Charter, and these were dealt a severe blow by the destruction of Hiroshima and Nagasaki, with the message it contained of America's overwhelming military power. Still that catastrophe did not happen until just before Alexander's departure for Britain. For the greater part of his visit he was able to speak in an atmosphere of some confidence about the future. After San Francisco he spent a few meeting-packed days in Los Angeles, and then travelled eastwards. He visited a Quaker school near Iowa City, invited by Hans Buchinger with whom he had had strenuous discussions on Nazism in 1933. Now Buchinger was a political exile, and the conversation was about the environmentally friendly practices adopted on the school farm. The next stop was in a rain-soaked Chicago, where he spent three nights, one of them with his old colleague in anti-opium campaigning, Tarini Sinha. Sinha chaired a meeting for him at the International Club, and evidently organised some much-needed laundering. Alexander told Paul Sturge that 'when he discovered the rather sad condition of my underclothes his comment was "There is another likeness between you and C. F. A. [Andrews]".'

After Chicago Alexander travelled south-east to Richmond, Indiana, where he spent a few days in the neighbourhood of Earlham College, a major centre of Middle West Quakerism. Amid the usual round of meetings and discussions, he found time to reflect on what he hoped to do with his life after Woodbrooke. He set down his reflections in a long letter to Ralph Barlow, a sympathetic and knowledgeable listener whose judgement he respected. In the immediate future he had been promised Friends Service Council funding to support a return to India as a kind of 'Quaker commissioner' to involve himself in and advise on the development of Quaker work in India and elsewhere. (He facetiously described the role as one of 'chaplain-general of the Quaker forces in the East'.) Of course, Quaker work might come to an end, or restrict itself to the rehabilitation schemes in eastern India. But Alexander also found himself 'dreaming strange dreams'. He foresaw the possibility of an unprecedented *expansion* of Quaker work, with centres in the major cities of India, and in Burma, Malaya, Siam and so on, right through to China and Japan. The reason was this:

> Because the whole 'Orient' will be in revolt against western politico-economic domination after the war, and Quakers *as a body* are about the only people who are fairly generally trusted (where they are known) by even the most nationalistic leaders in those lands as disinterested friends and servants, reliable, trustworthy, without racial arrogance. Therefore we have a *duty* to go into new territories, if we can find the man for the job.

Alexander had the temerity to suppose that he just might *be* the man, although he lacked confidence in his ability to 'give the spiritual support needed to men struggling with impossible technical jobs among an often stiff-necked and irresponsive populace'. Still, he felt that his experience with the FAU in India had some relevance to the task he envisaged., in particular his ability to identify work that would be useful and then to get people to do it without quite realising that it was his idea. His return to Bengal to act as an adviser in Quaker work there might be the beginning of a more ambitious project. But at this point in the letter he was evidently overcome with self-doubts. What after all *was* he going to do with the rest of his life? 'I gad about to Geneva, to the Saar, to Berlin, to Spain, to Poona, to San Francisco – and what does it all lead to? Nothing, so far as I can see.'

The kind of fulfilment which he sought might be found in political action, 'a big job if you are fit for big responsibilities' (which he seems to have felt that he wasn't); or in influencing minds, as he had been trying to do at Woodbrooke for the past twenty-five years. He regretted that his energies had been dissipated in writing pamphlets and articles to meet an immediate situation. He was haunted by the desire to do something of more 'permanent' significance, a biography of C. F. Andrews or of Gandhi perhaps.

> But in the back of my mind I have for years had other things lurking. I believe, for instance, that the Indian genius and culture (by which I don't just mean 'Hinduism', or Gandhi, or Tagore, or any of the usual subjects, but that curiously elusive quality in Indian life which somehow captivates nearly every European who lives in India for a time – Ralph Barlow excepted) has something to say to the world, to a world perishing of falsehood and expediency and power-politics and the worship of bodily comforts, and that a rather matter-of-fact person like myself, who won't go all sloppy and sentimental about it, might in the course of years work out a volume of 'Indian Essays' which really would have some value for the world – not only for 1950, but for 3000 even.

Once again his confidence failed him. He thought it most unlikely that he would ever 'head up a great Quaker drive into the "Orient", or write a book of "permanent" significance in the re-shaping of the world'. But still he wanted Barlow's advice on which dream seemed the more appropriate for him.[46]

It is not clear what, if anything, Barlow would have said to Alexander on his return to England. By then he was so taken up with the immediate problem of how he should secure a passage to India, and take part in the rapidly developing situation there, that these long-term reflections were pushed to the back of his mind. But it is interesting that he was evidently already thinking of the ideas that were to find expression some fifteen years later in *Consider India* (1961).

He continued his journey eastwards through Indianapolis and Ann Arbor, pausing in Pittsburgh to look at a coal mine and see the remarkable housing project in the model village of Penncraft undertaken by unemployed miners during the depression. Back in Philadelphia he continued his unremitting programme of meetings and conferences. Day by day he sat in on committees of the AFSC and other Quaker groups. He addressed large audiences at Friends' schools. He had to do so on one occasion without warning, when he attended the George School commencement ceremony to witness the graduation of the youngest daughter of the Pickards. Sitting quietly in the audience, he was startled to find himself summoned up to the platform to make an impromptu speech. Apparently the Principal's father had been put through a similar ordeal by John William Graham when he visited England in 1903, and at Graham's urging had attended the Bootham 'speech day'. Now, forty-two years later, the son took his revenge on the son-in-law. Alexander began by assuring his audience that 'J.W.G. would certainly have been equal to the occasion' – a slightly barbed remark when one recalls the many lectures that Graham gave in the Indian sub-continent, thus shutting himself off from what was actually happening there.[47] Alexander may well have felt that he was giving too many lectures for the good of his own understanding of the American scene. He complained to Paul Sturge after nearly three months in the country that he understood no more about American political life than he did before he arrived.[48] He was constantly on the move – up to New York City for a Fellowship of Reconciliation event, and down to Nashville, Tennessee, to give the commencement address at Fiske Negro University (its President, Tom Jones, was an Old Woodbrooker). Then at the end of June there was New England Yearly Meeting and Canada Yearly Meeting. One experience stood out when he looked back on his travels – a visit, on 6 June, to Byberry Mental Hospital in north Philadelphia. The staff there included conscientious objectors, who were working under the Civilian Public Service scheme, and Alexander felt that their experience could lead to a complete reform of mental health treatment. He gave his usual talk on India, and was surprised by the warmth of the men's appreciation. 'Can it be, I wonder, that India has some special gift of healing to offer . . . ?'[49]

As always there were the occasional days of bird-watching, one in particular in the John Woolman country in New Jersey at the beginning of June. He was accompanied by several fellow Quakers, including one Rebecca Bradbeer, the widow of an English Friend, Frank Bradbeer, who had died some ten years earlier. Frank Bradbeer had taken part in famine relief work in Russia in the aftermath of the First World War, and had later been in charge of the Quaker centre in Frankfurt am Main. Bertram Pickard met him in Philadelphia in May 1935, and remarked that his wife was 'a fine looking girl of 30 odd'.[50] She came from the Biddle family, very much part of the Quaker establishment in Philadelphia. She and Alexander had met soon after his arrival at one of the Philadelphia Yearly Meetings, and were to meet again when he visited Washington towards the end of July. In that holiday month she was temporarily in charge of the Davis House, a Quaker centre in the capital where he stayed overnight. Her daughter Cecilia was fifteen at the time, and mentioned the visit in her diary. He was, she wrote, a wonderful person with 'an amazing equilibrium (according to Mum) and is very objective about India and England and the problems of the world'. That was on Monday 23 July, and the following morning there was a lively conversation over breakfast. Since the diary mentions Nehru, who had been released from detention a month earlier, the talk was evidently of post-war developments in India. Later in the morning Alexander was taken to the British Embassy to see a Major Lockhart, almost certainly about the prospects for travelling to India.[51]

Rebecca Bradbeer's friendship proved to be of greater significance than any other of his American encounters. Fourteen years later she was to become his wife.

9

INDIAN INDEPENDENCE AND ITS AFTERMATH

India again

Alexander was back in Birmingham in the latter half of August 1945, and for the next few months was preparing, rather fitfully perhaps, for his intended return to India. The political atmosphere there was tense, with the Muslim League staking its claim for the creation of a Muslim state, and Congress insisting that it found this claim totally unacceptable. To complicate matters further, there was a general disinclination to believe that the British had given up their imperial pretensions, even though their General Election in July had resulted in a Labour administration, far more sympathetic to India than its predecessor. As Dorothy Hogg pointed out in a letter to Agatha Harrison at this time, if she were one of the Indian leaders she would be concerned about the high-handedness of the India Office. 'People here are continuing appointments to the civil service and planning this and that as if our sojourn in India as masters were assured for many years yet.'[1] Harrison herself was sufficiently uneasy about Labour's policy to seek an interview with her old friend Sir Stafford Cripps (now President of the Board of Trade) to make sure that all was well in that quarter. She and Alexander met him on 14 November 1945, and suggested that, as a gesture of good faith, Gandhi should be asked to meet the Viceroy, provided that the Cabinet were willing to advise Wavell that 'extraordinary powers' would not be used unless all other measures had failed.[2]

One proposal that had Alexander's support was to send out a small group of experienced and knowledgeable people, sympathetic to Indian aspirations, ostensibly to consider the terms of a treaty between Britain and India, but more importantly to create the right atmosphere for a peaceful transfer of power. This was in effect a revival of the 'kindergarten' idea which Alexander had championed after his return from India in 1943, but which at that point had come to nothing. It was, however, taken up by one Major John McLaughlin Short, an officer in the Indian Army who had been transferred to the Ministry of Information in Britain, and who corresponded at length with Alexander on Indian affairs. Short prepared a memorandum for Cripps making the case for such an initiative, and suggesting Penderel Moon, Richard Symonds and H. V. Hodson as leaders of the group. At the beginning of December Cripps passed the memorandum on to Lord Pethick-Lawrence (now Secretary of State for India), and it was given some consideration. In the end, though, creating the right atmosphere was left to a delegation of MPs who visited India in January 1946, and whose final press conference made clear that, in their judgement, independence was imminent.[3]

Agatha Harrison, for one, was pleased with the reception that the MPs had had. She had been permitted to return to India to attend the All-India Women's Conference, and was now engaged in renewing contacts with Gandhi and his Congress colleagues. She accompanied Gandhi on one of his speaking tours, and was reassured by the tone of what he said to the huge crowds who came to hear him. She told Pethick-Lawrence that he spoke very simply, 'with no trace of bitterness, denouncing no one, telling them freedom cannot be won through violence or through slogans, urging on them a simple disciplined life.'[4] She looked forward to going on to Allahabad to stay with the Nehrus, and a letter to Rajkumari Amrit Kaur suggests that she made an equally reassuring contact with Jawaharlal himself.[5]

Although Harrison was determined to sustain a positive view of the situation, it was difficult for most observers not to be daunted by its immense complications. Penderel Moon strongly agreed with Alexander that he was right to keep 'pegging away' at Pethick-Lawrence about the need for a 'kindergarten', but thought that there were some things that Alexander himself was best qualified to do. In particular some 'wholesome influence' needed to be brought to bear on Nehru. His uncompromising attitude to Britain, to the Muslims, to the Communists defeated his own objects. He was wilfully blind to the growing power of the Muslim League. 'Cannot you do something with him?'[6] Alexander may well have doubted his ability to achieve much, though assured of the need, as he told Pethick-Lawrence, for 'endless tact, patience, imagination and courage' in dealing with the problems. In this the Quakers had a distinctive contribution to make, as he had told Ralph Barlow in his letter from Earlham College, and as he now reiterated to the Secretary of State.

Figure 3 Horace Alexander with Rajkumari Amrit Kaur, Gandhi, Agatha Harrison and Pyarelal Nayyar, 1946

> Quakers have been known in many lands as peacemakers . . . [who] try to gain the trust of men on both sides or all sides of a conflict, drawing out and interpreting what is best on each side and so helping mutual understanding.

Gandhi might yet be brought to cooperate with the Government in dealing with poverty, but at present he did not feel the ground for cooperation existed. Each suspected the motives of the other. And that was where Alexander felt he might indeed achieve something.

> It was once my privilege to 'betray' the noble mind of Lord Irwin, as he then was, to Mr Gandhi. I am looking forward to 'betraying' the good-will of the present government not only to him but to many others whose mind is poisoned by suspicion.

He hoped that Pethick-Lawrence could trust him to serve in this way.[7]

Pethick-Lawrence might have trusted him, but that did not mean that his trust was shared by his officials. The India Office had its well-tried procedures for controlling subversion, and Alexander chafed at the constraints that seemed to encompass his well-meant initiatives. For one thing, he would be returning to India, not as the leader of a relief organisation, but as a representative of the Friends Service Council, and thus in some sense a missionary. On the face of it this burdened him with the so-called 'missionary promise' – an undertaking to observe all due obedience and respect to the Government of India. While FSC workers had never been formally required to bind themselves in this way, it remained in the background, and, as P. J. Patrick of the India Office reminded him, might be invoked by the Indian authorities if his activities were felt to be incompatible with 'due obedience and respect'.[8] Alexander felt, reasonably enough, that this was putting him in a false position. There were other things too, he told Agatha Harrison. 'Somehow I still don't feel quite *ready* to go; but perhaps I never shall.'[9] The censorious Dorothy Hogg had little patience with what she called this 'mournful bleat'. She told Harrison that she found no sense of direction in Alexander. He had made almost no attempt to make preparations for a mission to India 'in spite of various attempts by members of this household to encourage him to stop playing around'. If self-sacrificial service were required, it was pointless to expect it from *him*: 'I am glad you were not born a Friend with all the deep craving for security and respectability that that entails. Nor was C.F.A[ndrews] nor Carl [Heath]. I believe it makes a lot of difference.'[10]

While this is an interesting if ungraciously expressed observation, the fact remains that the obstacles to Alexander's return to India were far from merely subjective. Although at the end of October P. J. Patrick had assured him that he should be able to get a passage to India soon, he was still waiting at the beginning of December. Then on 5 December he was told that he could occupy a hammock on a slow boat leaving on 24 December. On the 7th he was informed there might be something on the 27th, but this was almost immediately denied. Alexander reminded Patrick that people might well put this down to 'India Office prevarication', and urged him to make clear that this was not the case. 'I am most ready to attend to your advice – indeed any suggestions you may offer, *except* that "There is a shortage of shipping",' – this being the standard justification for the exclusion of undesirables from India.[11]

In the end, though, a passage was found, and he embarked from

Southampton on 28 December 1945.[12] On arrival he found the country still involved in elections which gave Congress a massive endorsement, and, in the Muslim reserved seats, a strong showing for the Muslim League. In contrast to Agatha Harrison's relatively optimistic assessments, the atmosphere depressed him. He contributed an unusually gloomy report for *The Friend*, published there on 1 March.

> The depths of suspicion and mistrust and defeatism are indescribable and seemingly incurable. . . . It seems as if no human wisdom, none of the actors of this last scene of the drama, is great enough to find the way to the goal which, I believe, nearly all genuinely desire. How, one asks, are we to learn the divine wisdom that can destroy fear, suspicion and arrogance? Nothing but the piercing light of truth can release Indian and Briton alike from the chains that bind them.[13]

He wrote a letter to Clarence Pickett of the American Friends Service Committee on 11 February which sounds a good deal more positive than this, though it must have been written at about the same time. He was pleased that the AFSC was likely to support projects in India for some years, and greatly appreciated the work that Julia and Harry Abrahamson from the AFSC were currently doing at the Calcutta Centre, he wise and urbane, she a perfect hostess.[14] Certainly the Centre had done as well as Agatha Harrison in making a friendly connection with Nehru. One of the Indian Friends Service Unit members, Swarn Sarin, was the daughter of a friend of Motilal Nehru's and had known Jawaharlal from her youth. He had a meal at the Centre early in September 1945, when she insisted on serving him, 'all in a flutter', according to an AFSC report. This was just a couple of months after his release from detention, and his hosts were impressed by his reasonableness. It would take time, he said, to work out the details of the transfer of power, and so far as the Pakistan issue was concerned a plebiscite in Muslim majority areas would be fair enough. Through the autumn of 1945, however, the political atmosphere became much stormier, what with the trial of former members of Subhas Bose's Indian National Army, and mounting distrust of the Labour Government. This evidently had no direct effect on the Unit's standing. Early in December Swarn Sarin was with a group of Unit members in a Calcutta street, when she saw Nehru and went up and spoke to him. They were evidently just outside a Congress Party office, and, as one American member of the party related, he invited them all in.

> Swarn protested to Nehru that he was undoubtedly very busy and that we didn't want to take any of his valuable time, but he told her to stop fussing and sit down. He sat at the head of the table while we sat on either side. Dr B. C. Roy came out at this juncture and wanted to know what

was going on. Nehru replied that we were having a business meeting and we proceeded to the interview.

He was chiefly interested in hearing about the Unit's current work.[15]

An urgent problem confronting the Government of India at the beginning of 1946 alongside the constitutional issue was the real prospect of famine, perhaps worse than the Bengal famine of 1943. There had been a failure of the winter rains, and the food-grain imports needed were 4 million tons rather than the 1.5 million previously estimated. But this was in a world where the devastation of war had created a general food shortage, and it was difficult to see where imports on the scale needed would come from. In the event the situation was brought under control. The world shortage was tackled by the Food and Agriculture Organization of the UN, bread rationing and the running down of stocks in relatively privileged countries like Britain eased the situation in war-ravaged areas and in India. Although food shortages continued to overshadow the political scene for several months, moves towards independence rapidly came to preoccupy politicians, officials and the press in the subcontinent to the exclusion of almost everything else. On 19 February 1946, the British Prime Minister, Clement Attlee, announced in the House of Commons that a delegation of three Cabinet Ministers would go to India to negotiate the basis for an independent India. Here at last was serious evidence that Britain was determined to end her empire in the East.

The three Ministers were Pethick-Lawrence himself, as Secretary of State, along with Sir Stafford Cripps and the First Lord of the Admiralty, A. V. Alexander. On 1 March Horace Alexander wrote to Cripps welcoming the mission, observing that reasonable people 'are pretty sure that the Government would not send three of its best men to India for a fairly prolonged term unless it meant business. But' – he added in terms that suggest his patience must have been much tried in recent weeks – 'I need not tell you that very few Indians are reasonable.' Suspicion of British motives was widespread. He had one specific suggestion, namely that the Major Short who had proposed the Indian kindergarten should accompany the mission. This was because of the influence he had acquired with the Sikh community: he could be very helpful in inducing the Sikhs to accept an unpalatable solution of the Punjab problem. Whether or not because of this recommendation, Short did indeed act as a personal assistant to Cripps in contacts with Sikh representatives.[16]

The Mission arrived in Karachi on Saturday 23 March, and gave a press conference in New Delhi on the 25, at which they emphasised that the issue of freedom and self-determination was settled. What remained to be done was deciding the form of the new institutions 'with the minimum of disturbance and the maximum of speed'.[17] But of course the Mission was burdened with the task of reconciling radically incompatible aspirations, and from the outset it was clear that the creation of an agreed constitution was an almost impossible goal. Almost, but not quite. In an assessment of the prospects published in *The Friend* for 19 April, Alexander saw the most satisfactory outcome as 'a new central Government composed half of the Congress and half of the Muslim League' – that is to say, accepting the League's demand for parity as a necessary confidence-building measure that would enable both communities to work together.

> Some people seem to think that if the Congress leaders, who represent the great majority of the total electorate, would generously say: 'We are willing to recognise an independent Muslim State for those parts of India in which the majority of the population is Muslim, provided the elected representatives wish it', then all would quickly be settled. Personally, I hope the Congress can see its way to making an unqualified declaration of this kind.

He accepted, though, that there was too much bitterness for such a gesture to be made at once. The British themselves could help by being less cynical about the Indians. 'Until we can root out this kind of poison from our minds (the poison is called "political realism") we have no right to expect a settlement.'[18]

Agatha Harrison and Alexander had been in Delhi since the beginning of March. Alexander's main concern was to work with B. R. Sen of the Food Department in developing strategies for coping with the food crisis. He had come to know Sen well in Bengal in 1942, and was gratified to find him now a senior official in the Central Government. Alexander always felt that political difficulties were most readily overcome in the context of cooperation to deal with a common danger, so that impending famine represented an opportunity as well as a threat. Certainly the obstacles to efficient food distribution had more to do with the anxiety of food surplus provinces to guard their stocks than it had with communal loyalties. Alexander was appalled by the attitude of the Punjab's finance minister to supplying famine areas in the south. The minister was, Alexander learned, closely connected with the food-grain trade, and 'thinking more of traders' profits than of the urgent needs of starving people'.

> Or perhaps it would be fairer to him to say that he is one of those people who I think are fairly common in America and elsewhere who still believe that the best policy for Government is to interfere as little as possible, and let trade find its own channels.[19]

Thus, in the first phase of the Cabinet Mission's work, Alexander was less preoccupied with their activity than Harrison was. As soon as the ministers arrived, she made arrangements for having a regular Sunday morning silent meeting for worship, at first in the Modern School in Barakhamba Road, and later in the YWCA where she was staying.[20] These meetings did not suit the jovial A. V. Alexander, the Minister of Defence, who wanted a hymn or two to liven things up. He felt much more at ease in the YWCA's social occasions, at one of which he played the piano for a sing-song, ranging from 'What Shall We Do with the Drunken Sailor,' to his favourite hymns, and then taking part in 'Auld Lang Syne' with such vigour that Harrison nearly had her arm wrenched out of its socket.[21] For Cripps and Pethick-Lawrence, however, the meetings represented an opportunity to affirm their good faith as negotiators in a way that transcended the intractable complexities of day-to-day diplomacy. Sudhir Ghosh recalls some ministry he gave in one of these meetings about the work of C. F. Andrews, witnessing to the 'silken bond of the spirit' between what was good in Britain and good in India, and how these words prompted warm testimony from Gandhi about Andrews' labours in the cause of Indian independence.[22]

Sudhir Ghosh was a Bengali who had encountered the Quakers and the India Conciliation Group when an undergraduate in Cambridge in the mid-1930s. He came to know Agatha Harrison well and, through her, Horace Alexander. As a result he organised a university society to make Indian aspirations better understood and, when back in India, joined the Friends' Ambulance Unit after its arrival in Calcutta in 1942. His work there brought him in touch with Leonard Elmhirst, the agricultural economist who founded Sriniketan, the village development project associated with Santiniketan. It was with Elmhirst that he first met Gandhi in the early summer of 1945. Ghosh's temperament was one of affable and buoyant goodwill, and with his easy command of flawless English he was manifestly well qualified to be an intermediary in discussions between Indian and British people. Gandhi was quick to notice this, and recruited Ghosh as a fellow worker. It was through Ghosh that the Governor of Bengal, Richard Casey, was persuaded to support the idea of Gandhi's visiting Bengal, and subsequently Gandhi made regular use of him as a negotiator and messenger.[23] His autobiography, *Gandhi's Emissary*, is an important source of information about the Cabinet Mission's proceedings as they appeared to the Congress participants. It should be added that the Viceroy took an intense dislike to him, describing him variously as 'a snake in the grass' and 'that little rat', reacting against a deferential fluency and, it has to be admitted, a certain vanity that grated on his soldierly plainness. Wavell's suspicions of Ghosh's genuineness as an intermediary were, however, ill-founded.

Wavell was equally irritated by the presence of Alexander and Harrison in the background of the negotiations. Both of them were, of course, well known to Cripps and Pethick-Lawrence, so it was natural for them to be in regular contact with them. But as they were closely associated with Gandhi and the Congress, in the current situation this created difficulties in relation to the Muslim League. One can understand Wavell's perception of them as a nuisance. He felt that they were 'completely sold to Gandhi', and since they saw

Pethick-Lawrence almost daily it was inevitable that Jinnah and his colleagues would feel that the Cabinet Mission was biased against them. He regretted not having been 'more vigorous' about their presence.[24]

They were the more conspicuous because, when the negotiations were being conducted for a week or so in the relatively cool climate of Simla, Gandhi's party consisted only of Sardar Vallabhbhai Patel and his daughter Maniben, Acharya J. B. Kripalani and his wife Sucheta, the 'Frontier Gandhi', Khan Sahib Abdul Gaffar Khan, Sudhir Ghosh, together with Alexander and Harrison. These all stayed in a house called 'Chadwick' which had been provided by the Government. Pandit Nehru, Maulana Azad (the Congress President), Sarojini Naidu and Rajkumari Amrit Kaur stayed elsewhere, but came to Chadwick regularly. The two Quakers thus made up one-sixth of the Congress team.

In letters to her sisters, Harrison gave a vivid account of the atmosphere in Chadwick. She herself made the house more presentable by going round with a duster and arranging 'massed flowers'. It was she who presided over the serving of tea in the intervals of negotiation, and reflected on the wide range of preferences revealed in this way.

> Amrit likes one spot of tea, the rest water and milk; Azad likes it milky and sweet; the Frontier Gandhi likes it to have 'body' in it; Nehru likes it weak with lime; Patel likes it strong; Mrs Naidu likes it hot. I was kept busy.

She reckoned to carry messages between Chadwick and the Viceregal Lodge, picking up a good deal of information in the process, and assured her sisters that she was getting a great deal of good vegetarian food, and from time to time wandering down to the lower part of the garden to have a cigarette. 'Horace and I', she remarked, 'have brought a normal atmosphere into this motley crowd in the house. They tease us a great deal but take us for granted and make us part of them'.[25]

One may conjecture that Harrison's care for her appearance may have been one element in the teasing. Earlier in the year, when she had had a fall in Delhi, and an anxious bystander asked if she had hurt herself, her immediate response was 'I have ruined a perfectly good pair of silk stockings'.[26] Alexander was notoriously negligent in this respect, but even he rose to the occasion sartorially, because his friend Sir Malcolm Darling lent him some good suits to equip him for Viceregal encounters.[27] This evidently had no adverse effect on his diplomatic skills: looking back on the Simla negotiations in *Gandhi through Western Eyes*, he emphasises the easy informality of the contacts between himself, Harrison and Ghosh on the one hand, and the Cabinet Mission team on the other.[28]

> After breakfast each morning, armed with my binoculars, I would set off down the 'wrong path', leading away from Simla; if any of the patiently waiting journalists accosted me they would say: 'Are you going to look

> for birds?' 'Yes' was my truthful reply. But having reached the lower road, I turned along it towards Simla; and unless the birds delayed me, as they sometimes did, within thirty or forty minutes I found myself at the hotel where Bill [Short] and Woodrow [Wyatt] were living, and would try to review the progress made the day before, as it had appeared to their chiefs and to mine. Sometimes they dropped some useful tip, which I could take back to share with Gandhi later in the day.[29]

This retrospective narrative makes clear how wrong Wavell was in seeing Alexander and Harrison as 'sold to Gandhi' in the sense that they were uncritical Congress supporters. And this is equally apparent in the account of the negotiations that he wrote immediately after his return from Simla. As between Congress and Muslim League there was no doubt where their sympathies lay, and to that extent Wavell had a fair point. But it was equally true that Gandhi needed to have critically minded people round him, 'people who, he knew, at bottom were 'on his side', that is wishing for India's freedom immediately, without reservation, and friendly to the Congress: but beyond that, critical of this step and that step, day by day.'

The Viceroy might have been surprised to find how stubbornly Alexander and Harrison had to insist on the good faith of the Cabinet Mission in the face of the almost ineradicable disbelief felt by some members of the Congress team. Alexander recalls an argument he had with Patel and Kripalani about the necessity of taking Muslim League concerns into account. The two men refused to be moved from their conviction that British anxiety about communal strife was 'sheer cant and hypocrisy', a mere excuse for holding on to power. In the same vein it was impossible to get the Congress people to see that, when at one point Jinnah had conceded the principle of some kind of union, this represented in his mind a big shift in the League's position. No doubt to some of Gandhi's colleagues the usefulness of the two Quakers consisted simply in the light they threw on the Cabinet Ministers' reactions to any move that might be contemplated. But clearly they did a good deal to maintain a friendly atmosphere. Harrison told her sisters how she had found Pethick-Lawrence exasperated with Gandhi at a difficult moment in the negotiations, and she tried to infuse a note of hope in the gloom.

> At one point he put his hand on my arm and said 'You are a darling trying to make me see the best of things'. And at the end – when I said goodbye – he put his arm round me and said 'Good night darling' and kissed me. Turnbull [his secretary] the complete civil servant – seemed to take it as quite natural to see his chief bidding me this farewell. And I was deeply touched – for he is a very contained man and does not show his feelings. But of course through the day he had seen what Horace and I had done and was grateful. What a book one could write of these days.[30]

On one specific occasion at least Alexander felt they had contributed directly to sustaining the negotiations. Gandhi had been disappointed in his efforts to get the Viceroy to abolish the Salt Tax, and this contributed to his negative view of Jinnah's acceptance of the idea of a loose union. Harrison and Alexander had an hour-long session with the ministers after this, and they were able to assure them that Gandhi himself held fast to his belief in the Mission's good faith, whatever his concerns about many of the issues under negotiation. Afterwards Alexander composed a written note emphasising three or four points where compromise might be acceptable, and despatched it to the Ministers for them to consider before their next meeting with Gandhi. Alexander says nothing of the content of the note, but apparently it was well received.

One other characteristic initiative proved abortive. Among the many visitors to Simla in that week was another Alexander, a Travancore Christian recently returned from a long sojourn in the USA, working for the World Congress of Faiths. He had several ideas for promoting agreement, one of them being to highlight the value of mutual sacrifice as a spiritual force. He succeeded in obtaining an interview with Jinnah, who received him cordially. Horace Alexander took the opportunity of sending a message of friendly greeting to the Muslim leader, and it seems that Jinnah spoke appreciatively of the talk he had had with the FSU in Calcutta two months earlier. His interviewer thought he had persuaded Jinnah to join Pethick-Lawrence and Gandhi for a time of silent prayer together, doubtless in the hope of obtaining divine guidance. Alexander introduced his namesake to Gandhi at his 6.00am walk on Sunday morning, and the idea was put to him, but 'his report of the Jinnah talk was more negative than it had seemed when he told Agatha and me about it'. Other people were waiting to meet Gandhi, and no more was heard of the proposal.

The only direct encounter between Wavell and Alexander was unpropitious. He and Agatha Harrison had been invited to the Viceroy's place for lunch with the Ministers, and afterwards Wavell had politely asked Alexander about the current work of the Unit, but seemed rather bored with what he was told. In order to keep the conversation going, and pretending to be more ignorant than he was, Alexander then asked Wavell about the food situation, and how much the scarcity was due to cyclone damage.

> He began to tell me. Lord Pethick-Lawrence had drawn up his chair on my other side, and asked Wavell about cyclones in general, and Wavell replied by talking about the Midnapore cyclone and the 'tidal wave' that did the damage. . . . I intervened to explain that I was in the devastated area a few days after the cyclone . . . and that I was quite satisfied that there was no tidal wave – still less the two tidal waves of the Woodhead report. After I had thus (a) told the Viceroy things about the F.S.U. that did not interest him, (b) professed an ignorance that was unreal in order

> to get him talking, (c) explained to Pethick-Lawrence that Wavell was all wrong about the Midnapore cyclone, the Viceroy had to rise up and go to a meeting.

Not, Alexander remarked, the happiest of ten-minute talks.

Whatever Wavell might have thought of Alexander, Alexander had a great respect for Wavell, particularly after listening to the broadcast he made in the aftermath of the Simla talks – 'grander than anything Pethick-Lawrence or Cripps or any of the politicians have done'.[31] Because negotiations hitherto had failed to produce agreement, the Cabinet Mission had put forward a scheme that they believed went some way to meeting the aspirations of all parties – giving a large measure of autonomy to the Hindu and Muslim majority areas, to be linked by a central government with responsibility only for matters of all-India concern. In commending this scheme in his broadcast the Viceroy sought to remind his listeners that they were about to embark on 'the greatest and most momentous experiment in Government in the whole history of the world', an experiment that would have a profound influence not only on India but on the wider world community. The experiment required concessions from everyone – 'a hard thing and not easily palatable. It requires some greatness of mind to recognise the necessity, much greatness of spirit to make the concession.'[32]

Well, the kind of greatness of mind and spirit for which Wavell was calling was certainly not forthcoming in the weeks that followed. Nehru was convinced that old British attitudes were still frustrating the demand for independence, Jinnah had no doubt that Congress demands were incompatible with Muslim well-being, the Sikhs felt betrayed by everyone. The Cabinet Mission and the Viceroy were setting out various unpalatable alternatives for the consideration of the British Government in the event of a breakdown in the negotiations, such as the granting of independence to the Hindu-majority provinces only. The threat of widespread violence meant that there needed to be a plan to evacuate British nationals from the sub-continent.[33]

Towards the end of this phase Agatha Harrison jotted down an extended account of the negotiations as they appeared from her vantage-point. It begins on Sunday 9 June, Whit Sunday as it happens, and Harrison reminded Gandhi of the story of the coming of the Holy Spirit in a rushing mighty wind – something of the sort needed 'to clear all our minds'. Gandhi may have been thinking about this when the same day he wrote a short editorial for *Harijan*, 'The Unknown': certainly he asked Harrison to type it for him, and to send a copy to the British ministers. The article is distinctly enigmatic, declaring that the Unknown God 'had often confounded man's wisdom and in the twinkling of an eye upset his tin-pot plans'. If the safety of a political agreement was unreachable, then he would invite the parties to join with him 'in saying that it was as well, and that safety lay in unsafety'.[34] Typing these words gave Harrison what she called a 'bone feeling' that she should go back to Gandhi again, and she found that the Congress Working Committee was in a negative mood, Maulana Azad feeling that their latest talk with the Viceroy had made things worse, and Gandhi being distressed that the Ministers did not trust him better. She, Alexander and Sudhir Ghosh then went to see the Ministers again, trying to persuade them of the wisdom of seeing Gandhi directly. They did not succeed in this, but evidently Ghosh in particular elicited a suggestion from the Ministers which was taken back to Gandhi, and encouraged him to make 'valuable suggestions for formation of Government'. This will have been the proposal Gandhi made in the afternoon of 9 June to Woodrow Wyatt (along with Major Short, from the Cabinet Mission's staff), that Nehru and Jinnah should draw up a list of members of the Interim Government in consultation together.[35]

Mildly encouraging developments on the Monday were followed by renewed gloom on the Tuesday. Sardar Patel wanted them all to go home. Harrison appealed to him to do her a favour: 'what was the use of going when things were at crisis – wasn't that the time to stand steady?' 'What is the use?' he asked; 'had we known they were going to insist on parity – I should not have come back to Delhi.' But grudgingly he said he would reconsider going, and then Alexander followed up this advantage with what Harrison felt was some good persuasion. Later, she was gratified to learn that the Viceroy had asked to see Patel as well as Gandhi, but an entry in Wavell's journal makes clear that the two Quakers had laboured in vain. Patel was hostile, uncompromising and voluble in his denunciation of the Muslim League.[36] Alas! that Harrison was not present to deploy her beautifully modulated, mournful reproach – 'Now, Vallabhbhai . . . '

Meanwhile Gandhi was making his views known to the Viceroy and the Cabinet mission members by letter. What Harrison and Alexander learned of their contents disturbed them, and having been asked to read one to Pethick-Lawrence they agreed to urge Gandhi to withhold it until they had seen him. This they did, along with Sudhir Ghosh, and Gandhi accepted their advice, to the consternation of his entourage who marvelled at their presumption. ('They did not say it – but it was apparent.') On the Friday (14 June) the three of them – Harrison, Alexander and Ghosh – had a long talk with Pethick-Lawrence about the unsent letter, and why they felt Gandhi had been moved to write as he did. 'Pethick-Lawrence's comment as we came into the room was "Faint yet pursuing" – and asked if it came in the Bible.[37] I said I would ask Gandhi who was supposed to be expert on the Bible.'

Another Sunday came, and another silent meeting in the YWCA. 'Horace read a passage from Thomas à Kempis that "fitted" the tense atmosphere',[38] and afterwards he and Harrison had breakfast with Rajkumari Amrit Kaur and Major Short. They had a very 'heavy' time, presumably because Amrit adhered firmly to the Congress position. Short and Alexander both worked in some useful observations, but Harrison, 'having had this all these weeks – was silent and smoked'. Later in the day there was another meeting with Gandhi: 'We tried to instil faith and belief in spite of lack of outward proof for this. For we are so close to both sides we often feel the truth of that saying "how little it is that divides men".' By this time Rajagopalachari had come to Delhi in the hope that he might be able to help break the deadlock, being the one Congress leader who was not altogether unacceptable to Jinnah. Harrison remarked that, like Alexander, he didn't feel that the Muslim League demand for parity with Congress should stand in the way of a settlement, but he couldn't persuade Gandhi, and far less other Congress leaders. Harrison's last diary entry is for Monday 17 June. She still felt that there were good men trying to find a way out: 'we live in hope. But – oh – if it only weren't so hot and sticky . . . '.[39]

Although by the end of the month both Congress and League had contrived to reach an uneasy acceptance of the Cabinet Mission's proposals, the objectives of both parties remained incompatible. This became almost immediately apparent when Nehru, in a press conference on 10 July, insisted that Congress would enter the new Constituent Assembly 'completely unfettered by agreements.'[40] Although it has been remarked that Nehru here was reacting to critics who thought him too subservient to the British,[41] in the overheated atmosphere of the time it was predictable enough that Jinnah should see these words as a repudiation of previous negotiations, justifying the renewal of his campaign for the establishment of a wholly independent Pakistan. Alexander's frustration at the inability of the politicians to achieve some form of united sub-continent was extreme. As he put it in a journal letter dated 20 July 1946, if only some form of administration could have been established, the task of government itself would have created a better atmosphere. 'There would develop a spirit of compromise, of give and take, which might soon make the passionate communal disputations of today seem absurd.' As it was, it seemed impossible to make effective contact with the politicians' minds. He found himself unable to say what he wanted to say either to the Cabinet Mission or to Gandhi. The British ministers never seemed to feel that he himself or Agatha Harrison had any wisdom of their own to offer. He had made an attempt on Pethick-Lawrence,

> but somehow I just could not get round to the things that were on my mind. It just simply did not make sense to talk impertinently to him. The Friends of 1800 would have known how to do it in love and humility, but I failed completely.

Gandhi was equally inaccessible. With him Alexander had 'a kind of thwarted sense, as of one who believes he sees light on what needs to be done, but cannot see the way to make it clear to those who are deciding things'.[42] Looking back on these events over twenty years later in *Gandhi through Western Eyes*, he still felt baffled by the lack of rapport between the parties to the negotiations. Pethick-Lawrence in particular had so much in common with Gandhi, having been a veteran of the women's suffrage movement who knew what it was to suffer imprisonment for a good cause. But his overriding concern to satisfy both Congress and the Muslim League put him so often at odds with Gandhi that their relationship was put under a severe strain.[43]

Agatha Harrison had returned to Britain with Isobel Cripps as soon as the Cabinet Mission had ended its work, and it was in a letter to her that Alexander expressed his exasperation at the way Congress was refusing to act with statesmanship in its dealings with the Muslim League.

> Authority must be put fairly and squarely on the Congress to make and mar the future independence of India. *They* must now win the League to a policy of co-operation both in the Interim Government and in the Constituent Assembly. Put responsibility on them, and I believe they will immediately begin to speak and act responsibly. Go on treating them as if we think them incapable of generosity and restraint, and we shall go on getting deplorable utterances such as some of Nehru's latest utterances seem to me to be.[44]

The political manoeuvring continued, but the mistrust deepened. August 1946 saw an unprecedented outbreak of violence, which, as it happens, Alexander witnessed at first hand.

Partition

Alexander spent much of July 1946 travelling round India, and then stayed in Delhi for three weeks, resuming his work with B. R. Sen in the Food Department. He had been accompanying an unofficial American mission, led by Dr Theodore Schultz of Chicago University, to assess the food situation. They travelled by air, and as it was at the height of the monsoon there were many hazards, in particular enormous cloud belts that were too high to climb over, too low to fly under, and dangerous to fly through. Moreover, on the flight from Calcutta to Madras one of the two engines blew out and the pilot had to make a forced landing, creating great interest among the local population and a splendid opportunity for the photographer from *Life* magazine. The group found that in the United Provinces in the north of the sub-continent, in Madras Province and in Bombay there was an excellent system of food procurement and rationing. Famine still threatened, particularly in the south, but the local officials were allowed by their political masters to tackle the problem with some effectiveness. This was not, alas, the case in Bengal, which was 'so riven with political partisanship that politicians, instead of closing ranks in support of drastic measures to meet the peril, rent the air with accusations and counter-accusations'.[45] Still, Alexander felt some confidence in the Chief Minister, H. S. Suhrawardy, who was present at the ministerial conference on food supplies which took place in Delhi on 9 and 10 August, and with whom he had some pleasant conversation.

Jinnah announced that 16 August would be a day of 'direct action' to enforce the Muslim League's demand for Pakistan. Suhrawardy supported this by declaring the 16th a public holiday. Demonstrations in Calcutta quickly turned into murderous attacks, with Muslim rioters soon prompting retaliation by Hindus. For two days the violence continued without effective opposition. Suhrawardy himself was censured by British officials for his too-evident anti-Hindu attitude.[46] The Governor, Sir Frederick Burrows, said that the damage to property and the sight of streets littered with corpses was as bad as anything he had experienced thirty years earlier in the Battle of the Somme.[47] A member of the Friends' Service Unit, Hallam Tennyson, described conditions in these terms:

> The dark deserted streets filled with corpses that were just beginning to decompose, the burning buildings, and everywhere the uncanny sense of terror paralysing the very fibres of the City's life gave an effect more hideous than can be imagined. It was as if the great Plague and the worst of the London raids had coincided.[48]

The Bengal Red Cross did what it could to rescue victims of the violence, and Alexander himself, with one of the Unit members, Mae Alexandre, toured the city in a jeep to bring families under threat into safe areas. His own report on events noted that one family was reluctant to leave without an armed escort. Happily they regarded him as equivalent to an armed escort, and came along.[49] Eventually British troops were called in and the butchery ended, but a sinister threshold had been crossed. The violence, Alexander told Agatha Harrison, was far worse than anything experienced hitherto, 'more sustained and systematic'.[50] It had left a devastating aftermath of human misery, and he himself felt 'almost unspeakably weary'. It was as if something were sapping one's roots all the time: 'It's no fun living in a revolution.'[51] The effects were not altogether negative. A Muslim daily paper, the *Morning News*, insisted that for generations 'the two communities have lived as friends, they must live as friends again'. Trying to reinforce this hope, Alexander sought out people from all parts of the political scene, proposing that Suhrawardy should give way to some other League member who might then form a 'ministry of peace', a coalition of Leaguers and Congress members, to begin a healing process.[52] He managed to interest Kiron Shankar Roy in the idea, and even Shyama Prasad Mookherjee. They encouraged him to enlist the support of the Governor. But Burrows fobbed him off, although he was soon thinking along similar lines.[53]

Alexander felt frustrated: 'I thought he might like to have someone doing a bit of exploratory work first.' He longed to have Richard Symonds back in Calcutta. He at least would understand what was at stake (and, one infers, have some influence in government circles). Leslie Cross and Mae Alexandre had some understanding, but Harry Abrahamson, the Unit leader, 'was as much a child in politics as many of the best American Friends are'.[54] He was evidently finding his life in 1 Upper Wood Street a strain on his patience, and it was with obvious relief that he told Agatha Harrison on 27 August that he had just moved into a room of his own in the house of two former Unit members, Glan and Sujata Davies, in the Ballygunge Circular Road, a short distance away.[55]

Not that he remained in Calcutta much longer. In September he was again touring the south of India, primarily to assess the food situation. For a couple of weeks he was based in Madras, travelling from there to villages in Mysore and elsewhere, and spending the weekends in the city with his old Cambridge friend Arthur Happell. Happell was now a justice in the High Court, and even more conservative in his views than he had been in 1928. He was distressed when Alexander arrived on the pillion seat of a motor-cycle: 'He assured me I looked "most undignified"', and he insisted on Alexander's using his car thereafter. The motor-cycle belonged to Parry Jones, who had driven Alexander across China and was now working on the Quaker food programme in Madras. He appreciated Happell's good beer, but this was insufficient to win Alexander's heart. Happell, he wrote, was 'one of those ageing men who deludes himself into thinking he is still a "liberal" when in fact he has become a hard-baked Tory'.[56] His stay with him was, he admitted, 'good fun', but he found more satisfaction in his meeting here, on 8 September, with Rajagopalachari. He urged him to encourage Congress to forego their claim to the inclusion of a nationalist Muslim in the Cabinet, and to offer the Muslim League coalition arrangements in Congress-majority provinces. Coalitions might be difficult to work, but if they could somehow be kept in being it could hasten the day when politics were about Left and Right rather than fixed in communal divisions. Rajagopalachari pointed out the difficulties in the way of any such initiatives, but Alexander had the satisfaction of learning that, later, the Madras premier had been adopting these ideas as his own, commending them to his closest associates.[57] But in other quarters there was less willingness to be persuaded. Gandhi could not yield on the nationalist Muslim appointment unless he could persuade Khan Abdul Ghaffar Khan that this was the right thing to do. And, more intractably, there was an underlying – and perhaps unconscious – refusal to regard the Muslim community as an equal partner in free India. As Alexander complained to Agatha Harrison in a letter written late in November 1946, there was 'no generosity on the Congress side', and India did so need generosity at that moment.[58]

It certainly did. In October, in the Noakhali district of east Bengal, where there was a large Muslim majority, the Hindu community was subjected to murderous attacks. This led to riots on a larger scale in Bihar, where Hindus turned on the Muslim minority. All this happened at a time when that veteran pacifist Muriel Lester was visiting India in the course of a world tour renewing contacts with peace activists after the war. She and Alexander went to see Suhrawardy, and had the satisfaction of hearing him dictating a message to be dropped as a leaflet in the riot areas, condemning the violence, describing it as treachery to the cause of freedom. Suhrawardy also took the opportunity of describing Gandhi as an old humbug. Muriel Lester simply said, quietly, 'I have heard that before.'[59]

Humbug or not, Gandhi felt strongly moved to meet the challenge to his vision of a united and non-violent India, and at the end of October he set off for Noakhali to see what he could do. His patient determination to restore confidence to the Hindus and disarm the antagonism of many in the Muslim community is a story that has often been told, and there is no need to repeat it here. He was in East Bengal from the beginning of November 1946 until the beginning of March 1947, and for much of this time he went on foot round villages that had been attacked during the riots. The Indian Red Cross and the Friends Service Unit (as the FAU in India had been renamed) were already working in the area, helping with the rehabilitation of riot victims, and establishing a dispensary. It was a project which set an example of cooperation between Hindus, Muslims, Scheduled Caste people, Britons and Americans, and naturally enough secured Gandhi's blessing.[60] It also provided Alexander with a reason for making a visit, and then joining Gandhi for a few days in January as he went on his pilgrimage of reconciliation. That made an opportunity for leisurely discussion of two projects that Alexander had been thinking about for some time: a meeting in India of pacifists from around the world, and the establishment of an interreligious fellowship among those who had united in witness against communal violence. In describing his visit in *Gandhi through Western Eyes*, though, it is not these projects that come to his mind but Gandhi's practical interest in house-building ('as if he were a professional builder'), and his warnings to the Hindu community that it was only right that they should accept a less privileged position than they had been accustomed to. Alexander was surprised, too, by Gandhi's preoccupation with a somewhat embarrassing moral problem. Because of his determination to give the least possible trouble to his village hosts, Gandhi insisted on occupying only a single room, and having his granddaughter Manu, who was accompanying him, sleeping there too. He saw this as an experiment to prove that 'sexual feeling can be totally conquered', but others did not see it in the same light, and it was an occasion for cynical gossip. Gandhi asked Alexander for his opinion 'as a Christian'. After due reflection Alexander remarked that one of his mottoes had always been 'Moderation in all things'. Gandhi's experiment perhaps too much resembled that of Simeon Stylites, who, not content with merely withdrawing from the world, insisted on doing so at the top of a pillar. Gandhi agreed that Simeon Stylites was not an admirable character, but that was because his action did not have the practical motives that influenced himself. Still, he took note of Alexander's opinion, and after consulting others as well agreed to end the experiment.[61]

While Gandhi was doing what he could to encourage good relations between Hindus and Muslims in rural Bengal, elsewhere the political manoeuvring between India's various communities went on in an increasingly disturbed and violent atmosphere. Following the Cabinet Mission an Interim Government including representatives from Congress and the Muslim League had been formed, but in practice they were unable to work together, and the Viceroy was perforce put in the position of overruling his ministers. In November 1946 Alexander wrote to Agatha Harrison that he wished the British Prime Minister Clement Attlee would clearly state that authority was definitely being handed over to the Interim Government, as they would do better if they were really convinced that they were essentially on their own.[62] The wish was at last granted on 20 February 1947, when Prime Minister Attlee announced in the House of Commons that a transfer of power to a responsible Indian authority would take place not later than June 1948. Wavell was to be replaced as Viceroy by Lord Mountbatten.

Alas, the effect was hardly what Alexander desired. The British Government was in no position simply to ignore the Muslim League's demand for a separate state. Attlee's first option was indeed a transfer of power to a central Indian government, but it would have been unrealistic to exclude his second option, that of transfer ('in some areas') to the existing provincial governments, 'or in such other way as may seem most reasonable and in the best interests of the Indian people'. It is difficult to see what else he could have said, and the censure by some later historians of the British Government's abdication of responsibility for keeping the peace in the sub-continent takes insufficient account of how uncontrollable the situation had become. Andrew Roberts, for example, in his very severe assessment of Mountbatten's performance as Viceroy, argues that no transfer of power should have been allowed before law and order had been established. But even in his own narrative there are intimations of how impracticable this line of conduct would have been. He censures Mountbatten for at first intending to suppress the first signs of communal warfare, but then failing to do so because of 'the public relations consequences' of British pilots bombing Indians. It would have been more than a public relations disaster: the British would have become one more belligerent in a region plagued by belligerency. [63]

The failure of negotiations after the efforts of the Cabinet Mission set the scene for a trial of strength between competing communities, at least in the

Punjab, where the Sikhs constituted a complicating third element in the struggle for territory. A fortnight after Attlee's statement there was major violence throughout the Punjab, which lasted for about a fortnight. After a lull it was renewed early in May. The hostilities, or more accurately the massacres, were ferocious. Nehru said that he had seen ghastly sights and heard of behaviour by human beings 'which would disgrace brutes'.[64] These outbreaks were mere preliminaries to the dreadful events that followed partition in mid-August. I was myself working in the neighbourhood of Amritsar in the early months of 1949, and even then the former Muslim quarters looked like First World War battlefields, or cities subjected to indiscriminate bombing in the Second World War.

Alexander clung to the hope that partition would not lead to total separation as late as May. Writing to Agatha Harrison on 5 May he suggested that there was much scope for common action in matters of defence, communications, trade, currency and food, on the model provided by relations between British India and the princely states. These common purposes, though, could only be found by '*agreements* between the sovereign States of India, and not by Central decisions'. There was, he added, no reason for any exchange of populations, 'as Hindu and Moslem have lived peacefully side by side for centuries and doubtless will continue living so'.[65]

He can hardly have held this belief for much longer, and his ambition that India might become a beacon of hope in a wartorn world was to be cruelly tested in the coming months. One event that did sustain him, though, happened at the end of March., 1947. It was a reassuring glimpse of the role that Alexander and Harrison had long hoped for India. Nehru convened the first Asian Relations Conference in Delhi, a gathering of representatives from many countries in Asia, from Jews and Arabs in the west to Chinese and Indonesians in the east. It was an impressive affirmation of the existence of a new power in the world, one that was not content to line up behind the established Great Powers, but with the potential of taking its own initiatives. Alexander wrote an enthusiastic assessment of the conference for *The Friend*, particularly impressed as he was by the success of the Indian delegation in making peace between the Arab and Jewish representatives. (The two leaders shook hands to tumultuous applause.)

> My mind [he said] leapt forward to picture an Asia in which the tired white man gracefully and modestly retires from the scene, and leaves it to an Indian to solve the conflict between Jew and Arab in Palestine, whilst an Arab finds the way to peace between Congress and Muslim League in India.[66]

The vision was sadly premature, but anticipated the strategy of 'non-alignment' that was to be increasingly influential as the Cold War between the US and the USSR developed through the 1950s and 1960s.

It was at this time that the new Viceroy arrived in India. Shortly after he and Lady Mountbatten were settled in New Delhi, the latter invited Alexander to see her about the prospects for relief work and other related activity. She astonished him by saying, 'You know, we think that Gandhi's demands are quite right. Our job is to meet them as quickly as we can.' She was evidently thinking of the general demand for independence as soon as possible rather than of the specific positions adopted by Gandhi as opposed to those advocated by Nehru, Maulana Azad, Sardar Patel or Jinnah. What struck Alexander was her tone. One way and another all previous viceroys had found him, at some point, an impossible man to deal with. 'For His Majesty's Viceroy (and cousin) to declare that Gandhi's demand was right and proper was new language.' Looking back at this time a few years later, Alexander insisted that it was impossible for anyone who did not witness it to appreciate the total change of atmosphere achieved by the Mountbattens after their arrival.[67] It has been argued that Mountbatten's preoccupation with favourable publicity contributed significantly to the carnage that accompanied partition, but this surely underestimates the power of the motives for violence that were already terrifyingly evident. Once the cycle of murder and arson was under way it became almost completely irresistible – *almost*, not entirely, as Gandhi and Suhrawardy were to demonstrate in Calcutta. The new governments did what they could to keep a measure of control, and for this Mountbatten's unswerving determination to gain the confidence of Indian leaders could only have been helpful. Whatever criticisms may be made of his tactics, he at least avoided a situation where Hindus, Muslims and Sikhs fought each other while they all fought a British Government perceived as exploiting the strife as an excuse for maintaining imperial rule.

Edwina Mountbatten was certainly a new kind of Vicereine. She called a meeting of Governors' wives to see what could be done to bring all the social welfare organisations, Indian and British, into a common effort. Alexander was present, discreetly in the background.

> You could almost hear these experienced women breathing their contempt at such naïve talk. Some of them were vocal: 'We have tried all that sort of thing again and again', they said, 'but it never works. The Indians refuse to co-operate.' 'Then', replied Lady Mountbatten coolly, 'we must try again and see to it that it does work.'

She did succeed, and in a few weeks had organised a coordination committee that proved its worth in the terrible events that followed partition.[68] She achieved a similar result as chair of the Indian Red Cross, until her time very much the preserve of the British establishment. She visited leading Indian women members of organisations which had never before cooperated with the Government, and invited them to join the Red Cross Committee, 'saying that she did not want to be chairman, but would be glad to serve as an ordinary member if her experience were considered to be useful.' An invitation in these terms was difficult to refuse.[69]

During the early weeks of the Mountbatten regime Alexander visited Friends' work in the Central Provinces, and spent some time in Delhi, keeping in touch with people in the Food Department, and advising on the allocation of supplies. He was due to return to Calcutta early in May, but was taken ill with a stomach infection and forced to remain in the capital. Gandhi came there for talks with Congress colleagues and with the Viceroy, and, learning of Alexander's illness wrote him a note:

> My dear Horace,
> Naughty of you to be ill. I must make a desperate effort to see you in your bed and make you laugh.
>
> Love
> Bapu

Alexander recalled that Gandhi did indeed pay him a visit that evening, spent some twenty minutes with him, and made him laugh. : 'That was the way he always treated his innumerable friends.'[70]

The illness was serious enough to make a holiday in the Himalayas desirable, and Alexander spent some time in Naini Tal where Mrs Pandit had a house. Then, towards the end of July, Alexander wrote to Gandhi expressing the hope that he could be with Gandhi on the day that power was at last to be transferred, 15 August. Gandhi replied that he would then be present, as promised, in Noakhali, and encouraged Alexander to join him.[71] Alexander met him in Patna, and then they went together to Calcutta, intending to go on to East Bengal. In *Gandhi through Western Eyes*, Alexander tells the story of how Gandhi was persuaded by Suhrawardy to remain in Calcutta to help him keep the peace. There was a serious danger that Hindu rioters would create a situation in which it was impossible for Muslims to remain in West Bengal, which would mean that Hindus would be driven out of East Bengal – with consequences as catastrophic as those that followed partition in the Punjab. By conspicuously working together, and with the aid of Gandhi's prestige as the mahatma who had made independence possible, peace was preserved and in the end Independence Day was celebrated in Calcutta with moving affirmations of communal solidarity. But it was not an easy achievement. Alexander relates how, two days before independence, Gandhi and Suhrawardy deliberately chose to stay together in a house in a Muslim quarter of Calcutta as a symbol of the Muslims' right to remain. It was soon surrounded by an angry crowd, anxious to lynch the man they regarded as the inspirer of the Calcutta killings in the previous year. When they tried to break in through the windows, Alexander and others managed to close the shutters, but not before they were showered with broken glass. A deputation from the crowd was admitted to talk with Gandhi, and there was some fierce argument. Gandhi insisted that a way must be found for all Calcutta's people to live in peace and security, and he evidently made some impression, as the following day the same people returned expressing willingness to support Gandhi's peacemaking efforts. The conversion was not complete, however. In the evening Gandhi held his usual prayer meeting in the grounds of the house, and made a strong plea for communal peace. Suhrawardy had prudently remained inside, and Alexander stayed with him. Some young men deduced that Suhrawardy was there, unprotected by Gandhi's presence, and once again tried to break in. Alexander and a police officer closed the shutters against a hail of stones, and thus temporarily kept the crowd at bay. Suhrawardy lay on the floor and, for Alexander's benefit, coolly translated the abuse that was being hurled at him. Eventually Gandhi returned, apparently not noticing that anything was amiss. But the shouting continued, so he went to a window and confronted the crowd outside. He soon quietened them, reproving them for not accepting his partnership with Suhrawardy, whom he beckoned to come to the window. Suhrawardy began to speak, but was interrupted by people challenging him about his role in the riots of the previous August.

> 'Are you not ashamed of yourself?' they shouted. 'Yes', replied Suhrawardy without hesitation, 'I am ashamed of it. We must all be ashamed.' And he continued by pleading that now all should support the Mahatma in his great mission of peace.

At this point news came that elsewhere in the city Hindus and Muslims were collaborating in making preparations for independence celebrations, and the tension eased. Later, Gandhi explained to Alexander that the crucial step had been taken by Suhrawardy himself in his frank expression of shame. 'Public confession is always good. This time it has changed the hearts of these young men.'[72]

Although there was a recurrence of communal rioting later in the month, Gandhi was able to bring it to an end by embarking on an unlimited fast. Bengal's peace may have been precarious, but it endured, thanks not only to the combined efforts of Gandhi and Suhrawardy, but also to a rather widespread revulsion against communal hostility., which found expression, for example, in the communist newspaper.[73] The same revulsion, alas, was not felt in the Punjab, and when the new boundary of partition was made public after 15 August large-scale attacks on the minority communities led to a complete breakdown of civil society.

*

With the violence in the Punjab becoming worse every day, there was pressure on the Friends Service Unit to join in efforts to cope with its consequences.

Swarn Sarin, whose work in Bengal has already been mentioned, had just returned from her home city of Lahore with dreadful stories of communal violence there. Sardar Patel, now Home Minister and thus responsible for law and order, sent an urgent appeal to the Unit to send assistance to the Punjab, and his appeal was backed by Lady Mountbatten. Gandhi felt he had to remain in Calcutta for the time being, but urged the Unit to help. A cable from Friends House in London informed the Unit that Richard Symonds had offered his services, and could soon be on his way. On 29 August the Unit held a meeting in the home of Glan and Sujata Davies (where Alexander was still based), and it was agreed that Alexander himself and a few others should leave the work in Bengal in order to meet the emergency in the Punjab. A letter from Alexander to Agatha Harrison indicates that American members of the Unit were reluctant to accept the disruption thus caused, but were overruled by 'the recklessness of the headstrong Britishers'.[74]

In a few days Alexander and some others, including two Americans, Russ Curtis and Bob Pittenger, as well as Swarn Sarin, managed to reach Delhi. Gladys Owen, a Quaker living in Lucknow, also appeared, as did others who had been associated with Friends' work in earlier years.The vengeful violence that had already devastated the Punjab was creating havoc in the capital itself. Richard Symonds arrived on 11 September, and found a city 'physically and nervously shattered. Stabbing and looting had spread from the narrow streets of Old Delhi to the broad boulevards of Lutyens' New Delhi', where the shops were either plundered or boarded up.[75] Another observer said that no food was procurable, most telephones out of action, no buses or taxis at all.[76]

The first task to which Alexander and his colleagues addressed themselves was helping the thousands of Muslims who had taken shelter in the old Mogul fortress of Purana Qila. They found that one useful role was acting as an unofficial post office, delivering letters, enabling family members to communicate with each other, and even securing the payment of salaries. The other task was reporting the needs of the refugees to the Government, and seeing to it that supplies were brought in. Richard Symonds relates how medical supplies were loaded into their hired car. 'It broke down outside the Irwin Hospital from which emerged Lady Mountbatten who, in her element as former head of the British St John Ambulance, was delighted to have the supplies transferred to her car', which then proceeded to Purana Qila.[77]

As a trusted associate of the Congress leaders who were now running the Government of India, Alexander was in a fair position to undertake initiatives that struck him as useful. He had, indeed, to exercise all the tact of which he was capable. Soon after Symonds' arrival the two men agreed that it would be helpful to travel to Karachi to assess relief needs on that side of the border. Sardar Patel was much displeased by this proposal: the Government of India had paid Symonds' air fare, and he took strong exception to his deserting India for Pakistan.[78] Symonds did not know till then who *had* paid his fare, but in any case it seemed high time to consult Gandhi, who appreciated that of course Quakers would want to work on both sides, and promised to mollify Patel. It would be as well, though, not to go to Pakistan just then.[79]

Symonds spent the latter half of September visiting refugee camps in the East Punjab, informing the central Government authorities about needs in a chaotic situation where the new provincial administration had barely established itself. Alexander continued to base himself in Delhi, and was increasingly anxious about the deteriorating relations between India and Pakistan. Gandhi himself was affected by the hostile atmosphere, and Alexander told Paul Sturge that on the 25th September he had 'pleaded and argued with him to be less "belligerent"'. He was accompanied on this occasion by Agnes Maclean and Sir Fulque Agnew, who gave a vivid account of the meeting in a letter to his wife. Agnew was disappointed that Gandhi seemed as biased and partisan as everyone else:

> 'Pakistan started the trouble [Gandhi said]. India has and is doing her best to re-establish order, Pakistan to make more trouble and bloodshed.' . . . He waxed more and more angry and began to talk about war with Pakistan. Then Horace cut in and began a terrific argument against war or talk of war. Horace continued to plead a doctrine of peace while several of Gandhi's followers entered to argue in favour of a 'just' war.

Next day, however, there was a change of heart. Agnew said that he was in a more reasonable frame of mind and 'appeased' Alexander by substantially qualifying the position he had expressed the day before.[80]

Early in October Alexander and Gandhi's personal physician, Dr Sushila Nayar, accompanied twenty St John Ambulance volunteers to the hugely overcrowded refugee camp in Kurukshetra, 100 miles north of Delhi. Symonds was there, having been appointed to help the Camp Commander, and doing so with characteristic vigour and initiative. But although the needs of the camp were daunting, the state of the refugee camp for Muslims nearby was even worse, and no one was taking any responsibility for them. Symonds suggested to Alexander that what they could most usefully do at this time was to act as observers or liaison officers, 'reporting on the situation of minorities on each side, Hindus and Sikhs in West Punjab and Muslims in the East, and in helping to protect them'.[81] As a trusted neutral presence they would counter the rumours of atrocities which did so much to perpetuate violence, and also encourage the local authorities to treat minorities fairly. They put the idea to Gandhi, who warmly supported it, and this eased the way to negotiations with the two central governments and the two provincial governments. The negotiations involved wearisome journeys back and forth between India and Pakistan, but eventually agreement was reached and the two men embarked on further tours of investigation. Symonds has left a detailed account of his activities in

Pakistan in his *In the Margins of Independence*.[82] Alexander sought the assistance of two Indian women, trainees from the YWCA's Social Training School in Delhi. Together they travelled about 1,000 miles over dusty roads filled with processions of refugees, through countryside littered with the bodies of people drowned by the terrible floods that had added to the chaos at the end of September. The stench was horrible. They visited some twenty camps, and Alexander undertook an investigation of a recent attack on a Hindu refugee train that had taken place near the border. He was gratified by the willingness of the authorities to pay attention to what he recommended, and always felt able to report that 'this matter is receiving attention'.[83]

By now the situation was much exacerbated by events in Kashmir, the princely state north of the Punjab.The population was mainly Muslim, but the ruler, Maharaja Hari Singh, was a Hindu, and cherished dreams of independence. He did not follow the example of most of the other states and accede to one or other of the new dominions. He was hardly in a position to maintain this policy, as he found himself unable to control the territory. The riots in the Punjab stirred up similar disorder across the border. Incursions from Pakistan were reported from September 1947 onwards, and killings of Muslims on a large scale occurred in the Jammu district in the south of the state. On 24 October a substantial force of Pathans invaded Kashmir and advanced towards the capital, Srinagar. Hari Singh called for military assistance from India, but before this was granted he had to accept India's conditions. These were that he must accede to India, and then install Sheikh Abdullah, leader of the Kashmir National Conference, as chief minister.[84] Indian forces just managed to prevent the capture of Srinagar, and drove the invaders back to a line which has since become the effective border between the areas controlled by India and Pakistan. At the time the Indian Government saw this as the first step towards clearing Kashmir of outsiders, thus making possible a plebiscite to determine the future of the state.

Alexander and Symonds offered to extend their investigations into this disputed territory, and Alexander took a joint memorandum to Nehru on the evening of 15 November.

> He kept me nearly two hours, and was particularly friendly and frank. He has given me all facilities for the Kashmir and Jammu visit, which will only occupy 4 or 5 days, I expect: and although he did not agree to the proposals for mediation that we suggested, I think he might welcome a UNO mediation for seeing fair play in the plebiscites, if no one from any other great Powers is included.[85]

As he left, Nehru told him that he would enjoy Kashmir. 'You will find that even one day there invigorates you.' Alexander found this to be true. 'None of the things written or spoken of Kashmir are exaggerations.'[86]

Symonds had a good deal more difficulty in getting access to western Kashmir, since the Pakistani authorities denied that they had any control over the area. His diplomatic skills eventually secured him an introduction to representatives of the Azad (free) Kashmir government and he then embarked on a hazardous and exhausting expedition, of which he has left a vivid account.[87] While his main concern was to report on the condition of non-Muslim refugees, he was also regaled with first-hand accounts of risings against oppressive measures by Hari Singh's regime. He returned to Lahore early in December, and with Alexander saw Pakistan's Prime Minister, Liaquat Ali Khan, who made a number of proposals about Kashmir, in particular suggesting that the UN might set up an interim neutral administration, pending a plebiscite. The two men then returned to Delhi, but found that Nehru was in no mood to listen to any proposals from Liaquat Ali. By this time Symonds was feeling very ill, and it turned out that he was suffering from typhoid fever. Gandhi insisted on taking him into Birla House, where he was cared for by Dr Sushila Nayar. He was there for a month, and had an enviable opportunity to witness Gandhi's routine at close quarters.[88]

Alexander's visits to Jammu and the Kashmir valley, were less strenuous than Symonds', but were fairly hazardous too. His first visit confirmed the truth of reports of massacres of Muslims in Jammu, and Nehru sent him back to investigate further with the full cooperation of Sheikh Abdullah's administration. This second visit, in December, included travel into a border area in an armoured car, and when fighting was reported, the officer in charge of Alexander went forward leaving him under a tree hoping no stray bullet would come his way. A second armoured car took him back to safety and a little quiet bird-watching. Early in January 1948 he went again with Agnes Maclean and a representative of the International Red Cross, Dr Wenger, to Jammu, and again found himself in the middle of a frontier skirmish. Even in these circumstances he was unable to repress his interest in the birds of the region, and wandering off alone was intercepted by an Indian soldier, whose suspicions were aroused by Alexander's binoculars. He told Agatha Harrison that the soldier 'threw me on the ground and tied my arms tightly behind my back. I thought my last hour had come.' In due course the prisoner was delivered up and the misunderstanding explained. 'I told Jawaharlal of this incident, he was much amused.'[89]

Although Alexander did not suffer any acute illness, he was not in good health, and had some kind of trouble with one of his fingers, which required hospital treatment. He planned to travel to England in February, and on 12 January returned from Delhi to the Calcutta headquarters of the Friends Service Unit in preparation for this. Symonds had gone to Calcutta a few days earlier, and Gandhi asked Alexander to take a letter to his convalescent patient. Alexander collected the letter on the morning of the 12, and in *Gandhi through Western Eyes* describes Gandhi's amusement on this occasion at seeing a snapshot of a little girl poking her nose into his cheek while he was writing. It was the last time that he saw him.[90] The following day Alexander learned that Gandhi was embarking on what proved to be his last fast for communal harmony. The necessary undertaking from Delhi's community leaders to guarantee peace was achieved five days later, but on 30 January he was assassinated by an unrelenting Hindu.

Writing in December 1947, Alexander said that he had come to feel very close to the Indian people and their leaders, 'sharing the horror and the shame of the brutal deeds of September and October. Mahatma Gandhi was a very sick man in October, with little will to live. But some deep faith within him has lifted him out again.' Alexander saw him often, and they would speak of the Punjab and Kashmir, or of C. F. Andrews and the plans for a World Pacifist Meeting. 'Always he brings laughter into the talk, and wisdom and sanity.'[91] No doubt Alexander was glossing over occasions like the 'belligerent' conversation on 25 September, but they counted for nothing in the abiding impression made by Gandhi's personality. Richard Symonds catches it deftly in speaking of 'that twinkle behind his glasses which made us all not only revere but love him, even if sometimes we felt unable to follow his teaching'.[92]

Gandhi was gone, which placed all the more responsibility on those he had left behind to carry out his commissions. He had wanted Alexander to visit the North-West Frontier Province – now in Pakistan, with Gandhi's disciple Abdul Ghaffar Khan in detention. So Alexander put off his departure for Britain to enable him to do this. Before going to Peshawar he spent some time bird-watching with his fellow ornithologist Salim Ali. The visit to Peshawar produced no immediate results, but gave Alexander the satisfaction of meeting some receptive young people, students at two of the colleges in the city. Perhaps, he told Clarence Pickett, one of his services in the next few years

> might be, as a known friend of Gandhi, to try, through educational work (seminars, etc.) to get some of these fine young men really thinking along Gandhian and Quaker lines. You can see what an exciting job it might be! But of course that is only a dream at present.[93]

His duty done, and his head full of such dreams, he was free to fly back home, and to treatment at the Acland Nursing Home in Oxford.

After Gandhi

Alexander's poor health had an unfortunate effect on his temper. Confidential correspondence with colleagues mention angry outbursts, and it seems that some letters home were unreasonably fierce. Paul Sturge wrote to Agatha Harrison that Alexander urgently needed the refreshment of a sea voyage: 'if he comes home in this state he will be no use to himself or anyone'. It was a matter of great concern that being in India should have had such a disturbing effect on his personality.

> Here he is, with an unparalleled position and influence – and his whole service may be spoilt (if true I fear it is already) by his growing inability to see other points of view, or to accept opposition or differences. It is tragic. . . . No doubt there *are* grounds for some of his complaints – but they are far overshadowed by this personal weakness (I have the greatest sympathy – I know how hard pressed one's temper gets – and I fail often), and in his position – and for the work he is wanted for – these things are crucial.[94]

As the fierce letters seem to have been destroyed, one can only conjecture what exactly the complaints were. No doubt he was easily irritated by the caution of those who did not share his vision of a great Quaker opportunity in post-war Asia, and he was certainly indignant at the failure of many Quakers to understand his view of interreligious fellowship. A paper from Hugh Doncaster at this time prompted a particularly strong reaction.

> The whole document seems to me to stink (I can use no gentler word) of spiritual arrogance, and I find in it a curious academic remoteness from the problems that are crying out for our help. . . . The exciting thing, which experience verifies, is that, in spite of all the differences of theology, the *experience* of God is the same, whenever it is authentic.[95]

Many incidents served to reinforce his belief that Friends were being culpably obtuse in this matter. In 1946 he had supported an application for membership of the Society of Friends from Gurdial Mallik, a Hindu who had for many years been associated with the powerful Christian witness of C. F. Andrews. The Foreign Membership Committee of London Yearly Meeting had declined to accept the application on the ground that it wasn't *explicitly* Christian.[96] The same problem had arisen with *The Clash of Loyalties* by a Swiss Friend, Edmond Privat. It was a lecture on interfaith issues commissioned by the Swarthmore Lecture Committee to be given at Yearly Meeting in 1948. Again, it was felt to be insufficiently Christian, and the Swarthmore Lecture imprimatur was withdrawn from it.[97] When in 1949 Alexander initiated the Fellowship of Friends of Truth, letters survive which deplored the insensitivity of colleagues who wanted to set up a Christian test. 'They really are a terribly old lot', he complained to Donald Groom. And when Marjorie Sykes wrote a letter to the emphatically Christian Ranjit Chetsingh suggesting that his objections to the Fellowship were not really justified even on his own terms, she sent a copy to Alexander: 'Result: a perfect storm from Horace', who thought that Chetsingh would twist the letter into a weapon against him. Clearly the 'perfect storm' was excessive, but is evidence of how beleaguered Alexander felt at this time.[98]

It was not that he ever lost sight in principle of the importance of patient understanding of other points of view. Agatha Harrison appreciated the quiet way he conducted himself in interviews, generating a more positive approach to the issues.[99] His old friend Philip Noel-Baker was now Commonwealth Secretary in the Labour Government, and was thus directly involved in discussions of Kashmir. Writing to him before he left India, Alexander expressed his understanding of the awkwardness of his position. 'It is difficult not to become unwittingly a partisan of one side against the other.'[100] When he later saw Noel-Baker in London, he had just been withdrawn from the complex negotiations at the UN in New York over Kashmir, apparently because Nehru had complained to Prime Minister Attlee that he was insufficiently sympathetic to India's position.[101] Attlee did not just take Nehru's word for this. According to Symonds, Agatha Harrison had arranged for Alexander, soon after his return, to see the Foreign Secretary, Ernest Bevin, about Kashmir. She and Symonds went too. When they arrived at the House of Commons, it was not Bevin that they saw but Attlee himself, 'who, as he puffed his pipe, asked searching questions as to what we had seen and heard in Kashmir'.[102] Noel-Baker may well have felt that Alexander was part of a pro-Indian bias that had had adverse effects on his standing in the Government, and his hostility at this first meeting was extreme. 'He said all sorts of fierce and wild and irresponsible things about "my friends", and they (the Indians) have, I fear, treated him very badly and foolishly to bring about such a result.' Alexander eventually managed to give the conversation a more constructive turn, and Noel-Baker asked him to come and talk again when he was in better health.[103]

One source of discomfort was eliminated at the beginning of May when he had an operation at the Acland Nursing Home in Oxford on his troublesome finger. The following month he visited Scandinavia with Douglas Steere, mainly with a view to persuading the Nobel Prize Committee to award the 1948 Peace Prize posthumously to Gandhi. The committee was not persuaded, but Alexander had a personal triumph in a lecture on Gandhi that he gave in Oslo. The audience was so moved that when he finished there was a profound silence – and only then the applause.[104]

By this time the United Nations had agreed to send a commission to India and Pakistan to encourage the two dominions to reach a settlement of the Kashmir dispute. At Vijaya Lakshmi Pandit's suggestion, Richard Symonds was appointed as an adviser to Erik Colban, a Norwegian diplomat who was to act as the representative of the UN's Secretary-General.[105] This personal contact could have been what prompted Alexander to make a flying visit to the sub-continent, which he undertook at the end of July and through to early September. Before he left, he and Agatha Harrison were able to meet Ghulam Mohammad, the Pakistan Government's Governor-General, who was briefly in London and may well have thought that Alexander could exercise a valuable influence on Nehru. According to Symonds, Ghulam Mohammad believed that great progress had been made in negotiations with Mountbatten while Nehru was ill, but Sardar Patel had then come along and thwarted a settlement.[106] Nehru was in his own way equally difficult, but Alexander may have seemed uniquely placed to remind him of India's responsibilities in the emerging world order, setting an example of commitment to internationalist principles.

Alexander arrived in Delhi on 27 July, attended a conference in Calcutta on the work of the Friends Service Unit on 1 August, and later, back in Delhi, made contact with Symonds and Erik Kolban. At the end of August, at Ghulam Mohammad's invitation, he and Leslie Cross were in Karachi. He told Paul Sturge that he was reminded of his experience in 1924, when he passed from France to the German Rhineland – then occupied by the French – and found himself in two utterly different and hostile worlds: 'that in itself will give you some idea of how intense feeling is at the moment.'[107] Reporting back to the Friends Service Council he described his technique as a mediator:

> In a country where people are so sensitive to atmosphere, I imagine that it quickly strikes them that when they start on tirades against the wickedness of the other side, they get little response but a sorrowful silence, whereas the moment they become reasonable and constructive, the light of hope kindles in our eyes.[108]

Although he had a long talk with Rajagopalachari, he evidently had little opportunity to exert any influence on this visit, but after his return Agatha Harrison hoped that he might have a useful meeting with Nehru himself, who was passing through London on his way to the United States. She was to be sadly disappointed. Alexander was taking a much-needed holiday on the east coast. At 10.00am on 19 October Nehru agreed to meet the India Conciliation Group people at breakfast the following day. An urgent telephone call was made to Alexander's hotel, but he had gone out. When he did eventually return, at 7.30 in the evening, he would not consider making the late-night journey that would by then have been necessary. Harrison was stern: 'I was unprepared – quite unprepared for this, Horace my Friend. Perhaps all I need say is that never before – at least recently – have I stood so much in need of Gandhi's non-violence of thought!' Of course, at the meeting she saved his face as much as she could: he was staying in the wilds, there were travel difficulties and so on. But she knew that they knew that the invitation had gone out twenty-four hours earlier, and it did not look well.[109] It certainly was a lost opportunity.

Alexander himself could well have felt that he was already at the limit of his capacity. He was returning to India in the following year to develop Quaker work generally, and more specifically to prepare for the World Pacifist Meeting. This had originally been conceived as a consultation of peace activists with Gandhi, and was now belatedly seen as both a tribute to his memory and as an inspiration to his disciples. Before that it was felt necessary that Alexander should once again visit the United States to discuss the objections he had made to some of the AFSC personnel in India. He wrote a vehement letter to Clarence Pickett in Philadelphia because he felt that the return to India of one couple in particular would be a 'complete disaster'. This kind of problem, Agatha Harrison remarked sagely, is best dealt with face to face: 'I always doubt the wisdom of putting them on paper *in the first instance*.'[110]

Anyway, Alexander did travel to Philadelphia 'to have it out with them', and early in 1949 was back in India. Preparations for the World Pacifist Meeting were well advanced, with an office in the FSU headquarters in Calcutta. Alexander himself was based in Delhi, and was much preoccupied with the other project that he had discussed with Gandhi in East Bengal, the interreligious association eventually known as the Fellowship of Friends of Truth. As we have just seen, its development drew him into controversy with many fellow Quakers, in particular with his former colleagues in Woodbrooke.

The basis of the Fellowship is anticipated in Edmond Privat's lecture to the 1948 Yearly Meeting of British Friends, *The Clash of Loyalties*. In the seventeenth century, Friends deliberately rejected all sacraments and rites.

> Such men as Tagore and Gandhi have done the same in the East and also put emphasis on the inner light perceived in silence. Christian Quakers and Quaker-minded men of the East are brought very near together as soon as they go deep and forsake exterior trappings to listen to the same voice, away from names and labels.[111]

'The same voice' is the crucial phrase. For Alexander what came to him as the deepest Christian experience was beyond any theological formulation. Those who might want to join the Fellowship of Friends of Truth could share the experience but not call it Christian. Theology was like a language. If you were in France you wouldn't speak German. To insist on Christian formulations in non-Christian cultures was to erect an unnecessary barrier. He was saddened and baffled by the assumption that the Fellowship

> somehow hampers us from expressing our full religious convictions. It does not do so in the least. . . . I make it my task to try and put the same thing, yes, I repeat, the *same* thing in a different language, one which will really go home to their hearts.[112]

He saw the Society of Friends as a group 'that has really abandoned the idols and who can help to reveal the God of life and truth and love to all men whatever their name or sign or label'.[113] This, however, was not a conviction shared by his Woodbrooke colleagues, or indeed by some of his fellow workers in India. A journal letter from Eric and Joyce Baker, dated May 1948, insisted on the need for a 'clearly thought out *Christian* message'. Without this there might be success in social work and even, to some extent, in reconciliation, 'but there cannot be success in the essentially *missionary* task of bringing people into the church through the power of the message'.[114] And this was the assessment eventually endorsed by the Friends Service Council in London, in a minute adopted in March 1950. The Fellowship, it said,

> cannot, in our view, become the future expression of Quakerism in India. We are convinced that the work and witness of our Society are still based on our knowledge that 'there is one, even Christ Jesus' that can speak to the condition of men.[115]

Disappointing though this undoubtedly was to Alexander, the Fellowship made a genuine appeal to those who had worked with Gandhi, or been touched by his influence. As Alexander explained to his niece, Lucy Brown, Gandhi himself was an admirable illustration of what the Fellowship was about. Though refusing to call himself a Christian, the Sermon on the Mount had stirred him to the depths.

> To the day of his death, he loved to include in his prayers the singing of Watt's hymn 'When I survey the wondrous Cross'. To him 'the Cross' meant as much as (or even more than) to many Christians. . . . If you live in such a religiously minded country as India and call yourself a 'Christian' you soon find that your Hindu neighbours expect you to be 'Christ like'. They do not ask: 'Do you believe in the divinity of Christ or the Virgin Birth or the resurrection of the body?' but rather 'Do you live according to the Sermon on the Mount?' – and of course we/you don't![116]

The Fellowship continued for many years, but never attracted a large membership.

The Fellowship of Friends of Truth may have been inconspicuous, but the World Pacifist Meeting had a considerable impact, at least in India. From its modest beginnings as an opportunity for western pacifists to confer with Gandhi, the project had developed into something less intimate and more ambitious, a gathering in India representative of those who had been inspired in many ways by Gandhi's example. It was an event which had the blessing of eminent figures like Albert Einstein and Thomas Mann, who saw it as expressing an idea whose time had come. This was evidently over-hopeful, but it remained an opportunity to meet, if not Gandhi himself, at least some of his fellow workers. Many of those fellow workers were now governing India, and the difficulties of applying nonviolence in that situation were one major theme of the conference. In a characteristically uninhibited address, Jawaharlal Nehru admitted that he had to compromise all the time. He had to work with people who were under the influence of all kinds of passion and prejudice. They may not come with one all the way, he said, but some of the way, perhaps. 'Ultimately one merely goes step by step, not knowing exactly what the next step will be.'[117]

The conference met in Santiniketan in the first nine days of December 1949, and at Sevagram for the last week of the month. There was also an open-air public meeting in Calcutta, attended by 3,000 people, and addressed by some twenty delegates from all parts of the world. It was an occasion that gave Alexander a rare sense of public acceptance and encouragement, but, alas, the acceptance was superficial and the encouragement transient. Early in the New Year reports began to circulate in Calcutta of attacks on the Hindu minority in East Bengal. In February there were corresponding attacks on Muslim areas in Calcutta itself. A huge movement of refugees from one side of the border to the other began, and there was some prospect that the dismal 'exchange of populations' that had accompanied partition in the Punjab might be repeated in Bengal. Furthermore, the crisis seemed to open up the possibility of ending partition itself, and reincorporating East Bengal into the Indian Union.

One feature common to the crises in the Punjab and Bengal was the incitement to violence caused by exaggerated rumours. The facts were often bad enough, but reports lost nothing in the telling. The Friends Service Unit attempted to cope with this by sending its own members to trouble-spots to make as objective an assessment as possible. These assessments were sent to that veteran of the Punjab disturbances, Mridula Sarabhai, whom Nehru appointed to head the United Council of Relief and Welfare in West Bengal. She thus acquired the information needed to give useful instructions to officials on the Indian side of the border, and provided reliable grounds for the Government of India to complain to the Pakistani authorities. When, early in April, an Indo-Pakistan agreement was reached, these and similar assessments formed the basis of practical measures of protection.

During the period of extreme tension, in March, Alexander was in Bengal, giving moral support to Unit workers and keeping in touch with people who were trying to counter the prevailing enthusiasm for war. Agatha Harrison was there for a time too, and as a young Unit member then I vividly remember her dignified presence and splendid assurance.[118] 'The tensions here are probably greater than anywhere else in the world just now', she said, and we could positively feel ourselves rising to the occasion. She visited jute mills north of Calcutta where Muslim workers had been attacked, and introduced herself as one who had worked with Gandhi, and was dedicated to peace between the communities. She made a powerful impression, and probably did some good. She then went to East Bengal, and spoke to the English Governor, Sir Frederick Bourne, who was still in post, though about to retire. She saw him just before the arrival of the Pakistani Prime Minister Liaquat Ali, and insisted on the desperate importance of getting the two Prime Ministers to meet and sort out the situation. 'I never left the point and kept coming back to it like the importunate widow.'[119] She felt that her importunity had done something to make the summit meeting happen, and, having witnessed her in action, I can believe it.

Alexander did not have her histrionic talent (a former colleague described her as a 'tragedy queen'), but he laboured effectively in his own quiet way. He spent some time in East Bengal to form his own impression of what was happening there, and in particular visited Barisal in the south of the province, an isolated area where some of the worst attacks on the Hindu community had taken place. At the time of Gandhi's peace mission there in 1946 Alexander had come to know the then District Magistrate, Edward McInerny. McInerny was now back in his old district as a lay worker with the Catholic Mission, and was in an exceptionally good position to assess the causes of violence and the role of the authorities. In Calcutta it was generally assumed that Pakistani officials were themselves organising the murder or expulsion of Hindus, or at least conniving at it. McInerny was quite clear that this was not the case, and although his successor as District Magistrate was not exactly welcoming, he gave Alexander every facility to explore the area under the guidance of his predecessor. It so happened that I was with the Unit in Dacca at that moment, and accompanied Alexander on this excursion. Barisal could only be reached by river steamer, and the journey through the Ganges delta was pleasant enough. Alexander was evidently a well-known figure, and fellow passengers were eager to discuss the situation with him. He was a patient listener, but used his bird-watching concerns as a device for breaking off conversations that were becoming tedious: 'I'm so sorry', he would say, turning from his interlocutor while peering intently through his binoculars, 'but that seems to be an unexpected kind of tern.' In Barisal itself he made efficiently systematic inquiries. We went to the European club, where three rather depressed employees of the steamer company told him what they could while, as if to emphasise that he was a normal fellow Englishman, he sipped a gin and tonic. McInerny took us to villages that had been attacked and were now deserted, and to a makeshift refugee camp where Hindus had some protection. It became clear that the current District Magistrate had the confidence of the local community leaders, and to the extent of his ability was trying to get looted property returned and security restored. But difficulties of communication were intractable, and it was clear that he was in no position to assert his authority effectively.

A few weeks later, after Nehru and Liaquat Ali had met and drawn up the agreement with Pakistan that ended the immediate prospect of war, I witnessed a further example of Alexander's mode of operation as a mediator. One of the most influential critics of Nehru's conciliatory policy was Dr Shyama Prasad Mookherjee, sometime Vice-Chancellor of Calcutta University. Although a leading member of the Hindu Mahasabha, he had joined Nehru's post-independence cabinet, but in April 1950 resigned in protest against the policy of 'appeasement'. Alexander had come to know him well in 1942–3, when he was a minister in Bengal's coalition government, and now wrote to him urging him to make clear in his public statements, as he had to Alexander privately, that he was above all concerned to restore peace and order and goodwill. He could do this more effectively in Calcutta than in Delhi. In reply, Mookherjee assured him that peace and goodwill remained his objective, but that there were disagreements with the Government about Indo-Pakistan relationships in relation to Bengal. 'I hope I shall have the pleasure of meeting you again while I am in Calcutta.'[120]

Peace may have been his intention, but he soon became the spokesman for those in Bengal who thought the April agreement a betrayal. He told Alexander on 6 May that the condition of Hindus in East Bengal remained intolerable. Look at what happened at the Dhakaswari cotton mill in Narayangunge (near Dacca), when Hindus were deliberately murdered.[121] Alexander at once wrote to me in Dacca, asking me to find out what I could about this incident. So I went along to the mill and asked the Hindu managers for their side of the story. They did not behave at all like frightened people, insisted that the killings were the deeds of criminal elements, and said that they were currently urging the Government to authorise the formation of an Ansar unit in the mill to protect it in the future. The Ansars were quasi-military police auxiliaries, and had a reputation in India for unbridled atrocity, so it was interesting to hear them described by a Hindu as an agency for good order. I sent a report to Alexander, and was dismayed to find, on my return to Calcutta, that he wanted me to give a verbal account of the affair to Mookherjee himself. I was quite unwilling to do this, as I was sure that he would seize upon anything I said that supported his point of view, and would dismiss the rest as the naïve illusions of an inexperienced and credulous observer. Alexander was disappointed by my lack of confidence, and said that the fact that I accepted much of Mookherjee's bleak assessment of the situation in East Bengal might make him more ready to listen to me where I disagreed. I felt that Alexander himself might carry this off, but that I was most unlikely to achieve anything of the sort.

Looking back on the affair after half a century, I think I was probably wrong, and that I had not quite appreciated the extent of Mookherjee's respect for Alexander, a bit of which might well have rubbed off on to me. And in fact the following September Alexander was able to report that Mookherjee's attitude had completely changed. He told Agatha Harrison that Mookherjee was making constructive proposals to implement the April agreement, and was conceding that that agreement was better liked in East Bengal than in West Bengal. He was 'quite different from the man we saw four months ago'.[122]

Although Alexander was encouraged by such developments, and was impressed by the exertions people in Indian were making to establish their new nation on a sound basis, a note of disappointment sometimes came to the surface in his correspondence. He was particularly concerned that the Gandhian heritage was no longer adequately valued. In a letter to Amiya Chakravarty, written in August 1949, he confessed that he sometimes felt very depressed. 'The forces of unreason and passion are terribly strong, here as in other parts of the world.' He was particularly troubled by attitudes towards Pakistan. An opportunity for better relations was being lost, for although governments were never willing to admit that they had done wrong, 'sometimes they show that they would like to begin a new chapter. I believe that is the mood of all the wiser men in Pakistan today.' This feeling was not being reciprocated. 'Here, even amongst those I most love and respect, the underlying attitude is one of impatient resentment at the continued existence of Pakistan.' Things would have been better if Gandhi had lived. He would, for one thing, have found a way to true reconciliation over Kashmir. Not, Alexander conceded, that India didn't have noble and selfless men and women to guide its destinies – people like Vinoba Bhave and Rajagopalachari. But it was a terribly thin line.

Although Alexander did not mention Nehru in this context, it is interesting that the Prime Minister expressed himself in similar terms in the middle of the Bengal crisis in March 1950. Writing to Rajagopalachari on the 10, after he had spent a few days in Calcutta, he said that he didn't doubt that reasonable people could stop the drift to war but they were unable to exert much influence over the far larger number of unreasonable people. He was disturbed by the feeling that war was inevitable. Still, he had some hope that the possible consequences of war were being realised.[123] The hope was not very confident, and he might have had a wry comment to make on the way that, eight months earlier, Alexander had concluded an exhortation to Amiya Chakravarty:

> The country that has given birth to Gandhiji is a country from which the world has the right to expect very much. No ordinary second best, merely on the level of the current public morals of the West, will satisfy that exacting demand.

That letter, admittedly, was written in an unusually buoyant mood, and ended on a particularly cheerful note.

> Next week I am expecting to be in Calcutta. I get a very good impression of the Unit at present. They are rather young and fresh, but they have their feet set well on the ground, and their heads well up towards the stars.[124]

This may or may not have been a justifiable assessment of the Friends Service Unit at the time, but it throws some light on how, when not unduly depressed, Alexander saw himself.

Last years in India

Alexander remained in India until the middle of July 1951. He was based in the Quaker Centre in Delhi, at 24 Rajpur Road, but made a number of visits to different parts of the sub-continent. He was gathering material for his book on the resettlement of refugees, *New Citizens of India*, which was published in October 1951. It amounted to an assessment of the prospects for India's future development, for, as Alexander remarked in the final chapter, the direction in which the economy should be moving needed to be clearly visualised if the millions of refugees were to find satisfactory employment. He was cautious about the then prevailing enthusiasm for developing great river-damming schemes, and insisted on the importance of reforestation, arresting erosion and promoting land-reclamation and improvement. He conjured up a splendid vision of refugees becoming 'men of the trees' in their thousands. He named several people who had shown an outstanding combination of idealism and practical competence, contending successfully with 'the inertia of routine officialdom'. This was no easy achievement, and one of them, S. K. Dey, had described himself as 'a madman'. 'Probably', Alexander remarked, 'Mr Nehru, like the elder William Pitt, wishes he would bite some of the other officers. Perhaps he will.'[125]

One of Alexander's excursions, in the late summer of 1950, was to Dacca in East Pakistan. An international Quaker seminar was to have been held here in October, but to his surprise he found that this would no longer be acceptable. The Quaker label had become a liability because of its involvement with alleged attempts to undermine East Bengal's links with the rest of Pakistan. This was the unintended result of a visit to Dacca in June of the poetry society that met in the Friends' Centre in Calcutta. The poet Buddhadev Bose accompanied the group (most of them students) , and there was a meeting with the contributors to a slender volume of Bengali poetry that had recently been published in Dacca. I was one of the organisers, and we simply saw it as a daring gesture of goodwill in support of the rather precarious agreement between the two dominions. We knew that people in Calcutta would view the project with suspicion, but had no idea that anyone in Dacca would find fault with our peace-making efforts. The emphasis on Bengali poetry, however, was perceived by some as betraying a hankering after a reunited Bengal, and was thus distinctly sinister. Alexander had to exert himself to convince his hosts that the initiative had no ulterior political purpose apart from a desire to promote good-neighbourly relations, and a correction duly appeared in the local press. All the same, it was thought prudent to cancel the seminar, and it was held later in the year in Rasulia.[126]

The other visit was a bird-watching expedition to the Naga Hills, near the frontier with Burma. An article Alexander wrote for the Calcutta *Statesman* conveys the excitement with which he entered a region so rich in bird life. There were hornbills which first made their presence known by a noise like a wheezy steam-engine 'that put on wings and was flying through the jungle. Looking up I saw a flight of six great birds, flapping across from one hill to the next. . . . They flap and then glide, and again flap and glide.' On the way down from the hills, and stopping at a resting place, Alexander took out his bird book with coloured plates, and his porters crowded round to see what he was looking at. 'Whenever they recognised some local bird, they ejaculated "oh" or "ah" with much satisfaction' – and he took the opportunity of learning their local names. This was one illustration of the friendly atmosphere he found in this part of the world, and it led him on to an account of his meeting with people who were campaigning for independence from India. The Nagas were, of course, culturally and racially linked with other hill peoples, and not with the Indians of the plains. Their aspirations had to be taken seriously, but Alexander believed that the link with India was in Nagaland's best interests, and would protect them against predatory multinational companies. 'If', he wrote, 'during the next few years, the Nagas can see that Shillong and Delhi are their true friends, no doubt their loyalty to India will grow.'

On his return to Delhi Alexander wrote to V. P. Menon, whom he had come to know well, and who was responsible for the government's dealings with the former princely states, requesting a meeting about the situation in Nagaland.[127] Presumably he was anxious to express his view that the Nagas would respond to sympathetic treatment but not to repression, and there was certainly reason for anxiety. When he proposed that he should return to Nagaland to have further discussions with the Naga National Council, the Chief Minister of Assam, Jairamdas Daulatram, firmly discouraged him. Such a mission would give them a legitimacy they did not deserve. Alexander's *Statesman* article had done enough damage already. It had 'elated' them simply because it had mentioned their movement.[128] Alexander responded that he was glad they had been elated by the article, because that showed that what the Nagas chiefly needed was understanding friendship even when it rejected their political claims. The article had argued that their destiny was bound up with that of India, and he had made this point even more forcibly in his conversations with the Naga leaders. Daulatram seemed to regard them as naughty children, in the same way that the British had regarded the Congress Party. 'I think it is short-sighted and that it plays straight into the hands of Moscow.'[129]

Daulatram was evidently hurt by this reproach and insisted that he did *not* regard the Nagas as 'naughty children'. The Government was doing its best to find a *via media*.[130] Alexander did not press his request, and the Naga independence movement, under the leadership of A. Z. Phizo, continued to reject Indian sovereignty. Matters came to a head in 1960 with open warfare. As we shall see, Alexander then returned at that point to his efforts at mediation.

But meanwhile, during the first half of 1951, he was in Delhi observing and reporting on the deteriorating food situation in some parts of India – Bihar, he reckoned, was threatened by famine on the scale of Bengal in 1943 – and attending to Quaker matters like the proposed union between the evangelical Friends in Mid-India Yearly Meeting with the Oriental Missionary Society. In spite of initial misgivings, he was happy enough with the arrangement after meeting the people involved. He had found them to be fairly tolerant of those who didn't share their theology, and as Mid-India Yearly Meeting was not in a healthy state something had to be done about it.

Agatha Harrison kept Alexander in touch with events in Britain, and told him of how annoyed she had been by an article in *The Friend* by Gerald Bailey on the Kashmir conflict. He was arguing that India's failure to resolve it undermined its efforts to halt the drive to war. The smug tone was just what would have outraged Indian readers.

> I just went off the deep end, and took up the phone and said what was in my mind. . . . Ruth was sitting in the room, and after I put down the phone she said I ought not to speak to anyone like that – like a school teacher, or to get so angry. SO – I typed out a letter of regret to G.B. there and then, but stressed the fact that those quotations were unnecessary and unhelpful.

Bailey wrote a kind letter back, but said that perhaps her knowledge of and caring for Indian leaders sometimes made her judgements unbalanced. 'So be it', was her firm response, and for good measure added that she was about to see the Commonwealth Secretary, Patrick Gordon Walker and tell *him* what was in her mind. In June 1950 the Korean War had broken out, and was to dominate the international scene for three or four years. India had early attempted to work cautiously towards a truce, and its independent line had not pleased the Americans. Harrison was in no doubt that India's policy deserved British support, and was going to be 'VERY VERY FRANK WITH GORDON WALKER TOMORROW'. Alexander was greatly entertained by her vehemence. 'You really are superb', he wrote; 'though I must add that my sympathy goes out to both Gordon Walker and Gerald Bailey.'[131]

One other event at this time that deserves notice is Alexander's meeting again with Fritz Berber. Through the war Berber had managed to maintain his position – just – in the service of the Nazi government, and with the end of hostilities found himself in the zone occupied by the French.[132] Here he worked as a defence counsel in a military court, and later became a legal adviser to the French military government in Baden-Baden. Meanwhile the Government of India was seeking an expert in international law to advise it on the legal status of the irrigation canals in the Punjab which ran through the territories of both India and Pakistan, and which had already led to disputes

Figure 4 Caricatures of Horace Alexander and Agatha Harrison by William Ewart Carnall, *c.*1951

over access to water. Alexander had already mentioned Berber's possible availability to Rajagopalachari, who recommended his appointment to the Cabinet.[133] Corder Catchpool had already raised with Berber the possibility of undertaking this work, and in the spring of 1951 he received an invitation to spend three months in India to examine the problem.[134] In April he visited Simla with Alexander, where they talked about the possibility of a new book on Gandhi – perhaps the first time that Alexander contemplated the writing of *Gandhi through Western Eyes*.[135] Nehru was impressed by Berber, and invited him to stay on as a permanent adviser, and in fact Berber continued undertaking this work until September 1954, when he was appointed to the Chair of International Law and the Philosophy of Law in the University of Munich.

Alexander had felt that he did not want to leave India until he had seen a real improvement in India's relations with Pakistan, and he felt that Berber's presence in the sub-continent at least contained the promise of better things.[136] He travelled back to Britain by way of France, where he attended the Old Woodbrookers' Reunion in Bièvres, near Paris. A report in the *Woodbrooke International Journal* describes him as quoting Fénelon's petition 'for delivery from the self-regarding spirit which identifies itself too much with the success or failure of work undertaken for God, instead of leaving the issue with Him'.[137] He was evidently in no very confident state of mind about the outcome of projects from which, in 1945, he had hoped so much.

Immediately on his return to London in August it was the food situation in India that preoccupied him, though in due course it seemed that an acute crisis had been averted, thanks to generous contributions from governments, aid agencies and individuals. He undertook his usual round of activities, visiting his sister-in-law Agnes Yendell in Devonshire, bird-watching with his brother Wilfrid in Scotland, taking part in the Woodbrooke Summer School and, in November, joining the Quaker observer team at the session of the UN General Assembly in Paris. At the end of December he embarked on a speaking tour of the United States.

This visit seems to have been uneventful, but he evidently experienced a sense of confident growth among American Friends which will have contrasted strikingly with the tentative initiatives in the Indian sub-continent. In *The Friend* of 7 March 1952 Elton Trueblood gave a report of the opening of a new Friends Centre in Dallas, Texas – new territory so far as Quakers were concerned. Alexander was one of the speakers, along with Elizabeth Gray Vining, the Friend who had been tutor to the Crown Prince of Japan. A similar buoyancy informed the World Conference of Friends held in Oxford in the summer of 1952, where Alexander made a passionate plea to his hearers to *listen* to people in Asia and Africa, and take seriously John Woolman's 'pure principle', a principle that 'in different places and ages bore a different name, but wherever it took root and grew, men of every nation became brothers'.[138]

The World Conference had been greatly exercised over the continuing war in Korea, and London Yearly Meeting's Peace Committee was encouraged to prepare a peace plan, presented to Meeting for Sufferings by Alexander, and with its endorsement taken by a deputation to the Minister of State at the Foreign Office, Selwyn Lloyd. This was Alexander's final piece of Quaker service in Britain before leaving once again for India. A photograph in *The Friend* shows an unusually large Quaker party about to catch the boat train at Waterloo (Alexander modestly in the back row) setting out to undertake various kinds of work in India.[139] During the next eighteen months he was constantly on the move, visiting the various Quaker projects in India and giving encouragement when needed. He found Fritz Berber in a depressed state and wanting to leave, so he took him to see the reliably cheerful Rajagopalachari, who provided some characteristic comfort:

> We are all living in a jungle together, a jungle of frustration and inefficiency – in a country that is trying to be democratic without any training or understanding of democracy. But there is rich life in the jungle, and each of us can but do his best.[140]

Berber stayed.

Alexander kept a discerning eye on political developments in the subcontinent. He was in Kashmir after the arrest of Sheikh Abdullah, and wondered what the eventual outcome would be, since Kashmiris were more pro-Abdullah than pro-India. He had been welcoming the possibility of better relations between India and Pakistan as a consequence of Ghulam Mohammed's becoming Pakistan's Governor-General, but such hopes came to nothing when Pakistan formed an alliance with the US in the South-East Asia Treaty Organization. On the other hand he was heartened by Vinoba Bhave's land-gift mission, initiated in 1951 and by now achieving remarkable results. He saw this mission and the Planning Commission's Five Year Plan as complementary contributions to the ending of the abject poverty which was still India's most intractable problem. He expressed his hopes in an essay written in January 1953, 'India Looks Ahead', in which he spoke warmly of the 'hundreds of dedicated men and women . . . who are determined to achieve a democratic economic and social revolution in India in this generation', people single-minded and undaunted by difficulties. 'It is a thrilling experience to live among such servants of God at such a time.'[141]

His most memorable visit to such dedicated people was to Laurie and Kuni Baker in Pithorigarh, a small town in the Kumaon Hills near the western border of Nepal. Baker was an architect who had worked in the China Convoy of the Friends' Ambulance Unit, and had met Gandhi while waiting in Bombay on his way home towards the end of the war. Partly through Gandhi's influence he developed ideas about the use of local materials in buildings, and found

Gandhi's concern for service to the poor very congenial. He married an Indian Christian doctor, and they had settled in Pithorigarh to provide a hospital and clinic for the local community.

Back in September 1948 Duncan Wood had written to Alexander expressing concern that Baker would 'quite happily go on living in real want because he feels that this is the level at which God wishes him to live'. Someone needed to visit him from time to time to find out what his real needs were. He might be given such things as cloth – surgical instruments – a primus stove. As Alexander was then about to return to India, perhaps he might look him up.[142] This did not prove possible at that time, and it was in other ways that Baker's work came to be supported by his home meeting of Sutton Coldfield in Warwickshire.[143] But now in 1953, even though it was perilously close to the onset of the monsoon, Alexander had an opportunity to make the long-deferred visit. He set out for Pithorigarh towards the end of June. He travelled by road to Almora, and then had to trek some fifty miles eastwards on foot. He was accompanied by his servant Sammy and several porters, but set out by himself early in the day to avoid the worst of the heat. Unfortunately at one point he took the wrong track and had to retrace his steps. By the time he had corrected his mistake it was late and he needed to find somewhere to spend the night. He was directed to a nearby ashram, and to his astonishment found it was in the care of three English Hindu monks, two of whom were graduates of his old college in Cambridge. To meet Kingsmen in these circumstances gave him extreme pleasure: 'I spent the most delightful evening with them.' They discussed their spiritual journeys, one of them, Nixon, saying that he had 'discovered religion' through friendship with a Mrs Chakravarty, wife of the Vice-Chancellor of Lucknow University. Through her he had come to find the same treasures in the Anglican ritual that he found in Hinduism: previously it had meant nothing to him. Alexander remarked that Gandhi had not made him want to be a Hindu but a better Christian. Privately he noted that the group resembled a high Anglican or Catholic brotherhood: 'I for one found more of Cambridge in them than of Hinduism' – a slightly ungracious comment, perhaps, after such delicious hospitality, talking 'much as we might have talked in Cambridge senior common rooms'.

The next day he found his companions and they continued on their trek together, finding the last part, down and up the sides of a deep valley, particularly exhausting. They reached Pithorigarh with no time to spare, for the monsoon then broke dramatically, and there was no way they could have used the paths by which they had come. In spite of the torrential rain, Alexander managed to see something of the Bakers' work, and then, since he could not stay for long, he had to return to his car in Almora by an exceedingly roundabout route. A bus took him to the railhead at Tanakpur, a journey that would normally have taken a few hours, but in monsoon conditions required three days. The state of the road was evidently worse than he had experienced in China: the drivers had to go for long distances in bottom gear to get through knee-deep mud, and the back wheels were constantly skidding out towards the edge of precipices. His admiration for these drivers was unbounded. He called them the most skilful and heroic workers he had ever encountered. The one compensation for this ordeal was the opportunity for bird-watching when the bus was halted. At one overnight stay he found himself in superb jungle. 'The place seemed alive with unknown bird cries and songs, and I had beautiful views of several species that I have very rarely seen before.'[144]

The train from Tanakpur took him down to the plains, and from there he made his way back to Almora. In the journal letter from which this account is taken he does not mention Sammy as a companion on this journey: he may have returned direct to Delhi at a later date. Alexander himself resumed his visits to individual Quakers and Quaker projects, but he is unlikely to have come across anything of greater long-term significance than the work of Laurie Baker, who has perhaps had more solidly based and enduring success in the application of Gandhian principles than anyone. From 1963 he and his wife moved to Kerala in the south of India, and his practice has continued well into the twenty-first century.

Alexander decided that in future he would base himself in Britain, though he was to revisit India on several later occasions. So in March 1954 he set off on a leisurely journey by sea and land, first to Basra and then through Iraq and Syria to the Friends School in Brummana in the Lebanon. From Beirut he travelled to Marseilles, and so to London. Among his fellow travellers was a woman from Texas, who expressed strongly 'McCarthyite' views – meaning, presumably, that she discovered Communist conspiracies everywhere. Alexander developed some admiration for her pertinacity, but asked himself how one could allow such people scope without also allowing an infinity of mischief. He was unable to resolve this problem.[145]

There was a farewell party for Alexander in the Quaker Centre in Delhi on 20 February. It was attended by Jawaharlal Nehru, who in a short speech expressed warm appreciation of what Alexander and his Quaker colleagues had done for India. Nehru must have been as aware as Alexander that there was a great deal more to be done for India in Britain, and back in Birmingham Alexander lost no time in settling into his role as champion of India's foreign policy at the height of the Cold War.

10

INDIA AND THE QUEST FOR A SUSTAINABLE WORLD ORDER

After India

It was Philip Noel-Baker who presented Alexander with his first challenge on returning to Britain. In a letter of 15 April 1954 he told Alexander that Nehru's reputation had suffered badly over the previous two years. Ninety-nine per cent of the population (he claimed) supported the North Atlantic Treaty Organiation, and were disturbed by Nehru's neutralism – a policy that was not only unwise but immoral. As for Kashmir, only Kingsley Martin in *The New Statesman* supported India's line in that dispute. Nehru's recent outburst on US aid to Pakistan was the last straw. Even the well-disposed Clement Attlee could not agree with him here.

As Alexander had only just come back to Birmingham he took his time in responding, but did so on 4 May. He accepted the importance of the principle of collective security, but suggested that the devastation in Korea showed the urgency of working for disarmament and the abolition of the war method. He had no radical objection to NATO, since it was genuinely supported by the people in member countries. Such support for a similar organisation did not exist in Asia. Those who *said* they wanted it did so because they thought it would help them get the aid they wanted – in Pakistan against India. Nehru's 'dynamic neutralism' deserved to be better understood. He and his colleagues were thorough democrats, and had no illusions about the difficulty of negotiating with the USSR.

> To describe his policies as immoral is a reflection, not on him, but on your own powers of understanding the Asian world. I hope you have forgotten that you said it. And with that Quaker thrust of faithfulness from an old friend I think I had better stop.[1]

Over the next few years Alexander engaged in much explanation and reproof of this kind, entering on his mission with a report on his experiences in India to Meeting for Sufferings on 7 May. Three days later he was to learn that his most effective ally in this work, Agatha Harrison, had died in Geneva, while involved in efforts to elicit greater cooperation from the Chinese in stopping the war in Indo-China. It put an even greater burden on friends of India who remained, and in September of the same year an Indian Affairs group was formed by Alexander and Ranjit Chetsingh with a view to securing a fairer treatment in the media of events in the sub-continent. Alexander had already published an article in *The Friend* on the foreign policy of India. It was a very carefully developed exposition of the factors entering into the formation of that policy, including the geographical remoteness of India from the US/USSR conflict, the suspicion of the USA as a successor to Britain as an imperialist power, and awareness of the diplomatic advantage created by the Soviet leaders' perception of India as somehow 'different' from the other non-Communist powers. This asset would enable India to assist in the task of positive peace making, and in no way compromised her determination to achieve social and economic change without violent upheavals or totalitarian direction. It was an honest endeavour and deserved the fullest possible support.[2]

Alexander became increasingly frustrated by the way this 'honest endeavour' was misrepresented in the western media, which for the most part insisted on seeing international relations in terms of Communism and anti-Communism. What were they to make of a politician who said, as Nehru did at the Bandung Conference of Asian and African nations in April 1955, ''We do not agree with the communist teachings, we do not agree with the anti-communist teachings, because they are both based on wrong principles.'

> Has it come to this, that the leaders of thought who have given religions and all kinds of things to the world have to tag on to this kind of group or that and be hangers-on of this party or the other carrying out their wishes and occasionally giving an idea? It is most degrading and humiliating to any self-respecting people or nation. It is an intolerable thought to me that the great countries of Asia and Africa should come out of bondage into freedom only to degrade themselves or humiliate themselves in this way.[3]

The simplest way to deal with such a refusal to accept the premises of the Cold War was to treat it as simple hostility, and accordingly when Nehru reminded the Soviet leaders visiting India that he and his country were good friends of

Britain, this was the part of his speech *The Times* failed to report. Or again, in a parliamentary debate Nehru had answered attacks on India's membership of the Commonwealth by pointing out that it did not compromise India's independent foreign policy: for example its refusal to countenance the 'deplorable' Baghdad Pact (allying Pakistan to the US). *The Times* chose to give this story the headline 'Baghdad Pact Deplorable. Mr Nehru's Attack'. Alexander used these examples, and others, to argue in *The Friend* that there seemed to be a kind of conspiracy in some quarters 'to destroy the new ties of friendship with Asia which have been so laboriously woven by men of patience and imagination'. His protest had evidently been provoked by an article in *Time and Tide* by John Connell in which the writer had criticised India for receiving Soviet leaders, and reminded his readers of the dreadful massacres that had accompanied the independence of India and Pakistan. Connell responded in a letter to *The Friend* complaining that Alexander's own article was perverse, disingenuous, uncharitable and extremely selective, and alleging that Nehru was a politician in the mould of Lloyd George, 'tough, sly, unscrupulous, able and courageous, . . . as chauvinist as he is personally ambitious'. It might be necessary for governments to flatter and fawn on one another, but journalists had a higher duty. 'My job is not to appease powerful and vindictive enemies of this country, but to expose – so far as I can - their hostility and their hypocrisy.' Alexander was eager to respond, but the editor, Bernard Canter, was rather appalled at the prospect of a long-running correspondence on this issue and refused to allow its continuance. So John Connell had the last word.[4] But by a neat piece of editorial juxtaposition, Connell's letter was immediately preceded by an article by Hallam Tennyson on the Soviet leaders' visit to India, trenchantly re-stating Alexander's argument. 'British newspapers suppressed Nehru's firm and open references to India's continued ties with Britain', so that large sections of the British public were now convinced that India had abandoned her policy of neutrality. In effect, the western response was that 'if the Soviet leaders behaved like bulls in a china shop then we would behave like a whole herd of bulls.'[5] It is not clear what Connell made of this.

*

These particular exchanges took place at the end of 1955, by which time the way in which Alexander was organising his life after India was becoming well established. He was soon to be moving from Birmingham to Dorset, 26 Bon Accord Road in Swanage, where he could be near his brother Wilfrid. Earlier in 1955 he had spent seven months in Pennsylvania on the faculty of Pendle Hill, among other things developing his acquaintance with his future wife, Rebecca Bradbeer, who lived nearby. In a diary entry for 22 January she described how they reflected on his feelings when he received a letter to Olive from a German friend – presumably Traute Riedel – who did not know that she had died. 'It was amazing to him to read this letter. I said "How beautiful: it would make her seem so alive".' Her own bereavement, Frank Bradbeer having died years previously, gave her a sympathetic appreciation of his state of mind, and it is clear that there was already a good understanding between them.

> Then he said 'It is so much easier to talk of these things in India than here. – If one gets into conversation here, and someone asks whether you have a family and learns the situation the subject is immediately changed, but there, when the situation is learned, they are not afraid to show an interest and draw you out' – and he kept saying 'It is such a pity that here people are afraid to talk.'

She spoke of the teaching of the *Bhagavad Gita* that joy and pain are equal, in contrast to the Western pursuit of happiness, and he agreed that this was superficial. She went on that

> if we are afraid of anguish we experience less healing . . . I said 'People here are so unaware that one person can be whole, aren't they?' He said 'Yes' – and I said this must be much less pronounced in India' and he said 'O *much* less.'

They were associated in other ways. Alexander had once accompanied Frank Bradbeer on a train journey in Germany many years before, and Rebecca at the age of ten had been allowed to stay up late to hear a lecture by John William Graham (who was staying with her parents). All things considered, the wonder is that they did not get engaged to be married there and then. But Alexander was content to take things slowly. ''Then I had to leave', Rebecca wrote, 'and he helped with my coat.'[6]

*

Around this time he was engaged in a rather heated correspondence with Ian Stephens, who had been editor of the Calcutta *Statesman* in 1942, and came to know members of the FAU well. Stephens took exception to Alexander's defence of the Indian position in the canal waters dispute, but did remark – quite amiably – 'How you do dart around! Switzerland, India, Birmingham, now northernmost Scotland [Alexander had been on a bird-watching expedition to Fair Isle] – with the USA in the offing.'[7] For the next sixteen or seventeen years this was to be a fair description of his way of life, and to relate his movements in detail would try the patience of most readers. What may be helpful is to attempt a broad summary of the landmarks in his later life, and then to consider some of the issues that preoccupied him in those years.

Through the latter half of the 1950s and much of the 1960s Alexander was an active member of committees in London Yearly Meeting, and was often heard in Meeting for Sufferings. He contributed many letters and articles to

Quaker publications, and wrote two books relating to India, *Consider India* (1954; reissued in 1961) and *Gandhi through Western Eyes* (1969; reissued in 1984). He made a helpful contribution to AFSC seminars for diplomats, attending one in Switzerland in 1954, and again in Ceylon in December 1957. He included the latter in the first of his return visits to India, this one lasting from the end of October until the middle of March 1958.

It was at this point that his friendship with Rebecca Bradbeer, whom he had come to know so well in visits to Pendle Hill, led to their marriage. It is not altogether clear by what stages they finally came to an understanding, but the ground was well prepared, and the wedding took place on 29 November 1958, at the Friends Meeting House in Media, Pennsylvania.[8] India's blessing was manifested in the presence of Krishna Menon, who as Minister of Defence was attending the UN in New York.

The marriage was a happy one, giving them both congenial companionship and for Alexander a welcome extended family. Like him, Rebecca had a good sense of humour (every thirty years, she said at the wedding, I marry an Englishman). Alexander was conscientious in initiating her into his Indian concerns, and in the early months of 1960 they actually travelled to India. Alexander spoke of his pleasure at seeing the country through her eyes, and it is clear that his many friends received her with great warmth. They attended an open-air meeting of the Fellowship of Friends of Truth in Delhi, and, just as it was starting, a large official car appeared and out of it stepped Krishna Menon. Alexander spoke of the campaign against nuclear weapons in the West – by this time the Aldermaston marches had become a national institution in Britain.

> Krishna brushed this aside as more or less irrelevant, saying that he was convinced that the Powers would agree about the bomb, but that what interested him was 'the bomb within all of us' . . . Did we look inside and see the explosive force of our own fears and ambitions?[9]

As Krishna Menon had a notoriously explosive temperament himself, this must have struck his hearers as a remarkable piece of self-analysis.

The Alexanders had originally intended to spend some time in Japan and in the western part of the United States, but Rebecca cracked a bone in her ankle during the Holi celebrations in March and they returned directly to her home in Moylan, Pennsylvania. Back in England again Alexander resumed his participation in Quaker and peace movement activities, becoming (for example) treasurer of a World Peace Brigade project to send a boat to Leningrad to protest against Soviet bomb tests. Then, from the middle of October until early December 1963 the AFSC encouraged Horace and Rebecca to visit India again to make contact with those whose support of peace initiatives had been cruelly tested under the impact of China's attack on the north-eastern border.

Figure 5 President Rajendra Prasad greeting Rebecca and Horace Alexander, 1960

They spent a week with the Friends Rural Centre in Rasulia, and, in Delhi, saw Nehru himself and other old friends. The most memorable encounter was with Mridula Sarabhai, whose championship of Sheikh Abdullah had estranged her from Nehru and had for a time led to her detention. Horace found her still the totally committed campaigner, abrupt in manner and fiercely single-minded. But there was another side to her.

> We saw her several times. One day we sat at her house for hours, listening to one of her Kashmiri friends. Then we all had lunch. Quite another Mridula appeared. She put us both to rest, thinking of every detail for our comfort; she would not let us be disturbed till she was quite sure I was fully rested; she mothered us with gentleness, understanding and what I can only call sweetness. How can one forget such an experience?[10]

Her activities led to her arrest again in 1965, but Amnesty International took up her case and she was released in 1968. She then started the first Amnesty group in the sub-continent, and this was her main preoccupation until her death in 1974.

During the present visit Alexander remarked that when they saw Nehru he seemed considerably older than he had done eighteen months previously, hardly surprising when the Chinese attack had destroyed one of the main bases of Indian foreign policy, which had always counted on the solidarity of

Asian nations against their former oppressors. He had been compelled, too, to dismiss his old friend and ally, Krishna Menon, who as Minister of Defence was in an impossible political position after the exposure of India's military weakness. Physically weakened by all that had happened, Nehru suffered a stroke in January 1964, and died the following May.

Alexander was moved by Nehru's death to recall the exhilaration of being part of India's freedom struggle. His letter of condolence to Nehru's sister, Vijaya Lakshmi Pandit, was evidently a real comfort to her. It brought back, she said, 'so many things from the past, which, looked at in retrospect, seems to have been such a fruitful one'.[11] For Alexander, nothing could ever allow him to forget the unique role in world affairs which India owed to her Congress leaders.

On returning to England he continued in his role as Quaker elder statesman, a role subjected to a severe strain during the first open warfare between India and Pakistan over Kashmir in 1965. The editor of *The Friend* invited him to write a guest editorial on the conflict in the issue of 10 September 1965, and he produced a concise and carefully balanced outline of the issues as perceived in the two countries. He concluded, however, by in effect endorsing the view of Sheikh Abdullah (still in detention, of course) that Kashmir should become a condominium, with India and Pakistan sharing responsibility for its security. Alternatively there was Jayaprakash Narayan's idea of a loose confederation between India, Pakistan and other countries in the region. The final paragraph appealed to 'the higher law of the spiritual world', which showed that 'the way to gain all is to surrender all. By surrendering an Empire, Britain has gained a Commonwealth.'[12]

Such counsel was unlikely to commend itself to most Indian sentiment, and Ranjit Chetsingh contributed a 'Letter from India' to *The Friend* in which the writer's irritation was all too apparent. 'Ably led seminars and a few calls on selected top politicians, Prime Ministers and Presidents, may under certain conditions be useful, but in the face of the immense tasks before us their value is negligible.'[13] Even Mrs Pandit was outraged. In a debate in the Indian parliament she observed that before independence 'India could count on the support of a small group of people in Britain, but today even this group seemed to have deserted India'. This reproach from someone for whom he felt such affection hurt Alexander very much, as is plain from the letter he wrote in response to what she had said. He assured her that if some Indian attitudes and actions had been criticised by people in his circle it was because they had such high expectations of India. They 'feel especially deeply when they have doubts about the wisdom of any of her actions'. He agreed with Lal Bahadur Shastri, Nehru's successor as Prime Minister, that India and Pakistan would have to learn to live together, and 'it is on this positive affirmation that we should concentrate all our thoughts and efforts.' He concluded with a splendidly diplomatic presentation of feelings that might have been perceived as at best ambiguous in their commitment to India:

> We in this country remember with gratitude the many kindnesses we received at the hands of Indians in the old days before partition. Many of our old friends now live in Pakistan, and our feelings for them are no less strong than for those in the new India. We want our friends in both countries to live happily and at peace with each other.[14]

This tactful reminder of Alexander's regret that partition had to happen at all evidently restored good feeling, as eighteen months later the two of them were conferring on ways and means of bringing the war in Vietnam to an end. She saw him in London on her way to New York. 'I would very much like to meet you', she said in a hand-written note beforehand, 'as there are so many things I want to discuss with you.' After the meeting Alexander wrote to Colin Bell at the AFSC urging him to encourage her to go to Hanoi to persuade Ho Chih Minh to make a gesture to help the US leave Vietnam without loss of face.[15]

*

In 1966 Wilfrid died, thus removing an important reason for Horace's basing himself in Britain. He had, indeed, found good friends in Swanage, dedicated bird-watchers like Ilay Cooper and Trev Haysom, but Rebecca had closer family ties in Pennsylvania, and it was a natural move for them to settle there. In 1969 they took up residence in Swarthmore, at 305 Rutgers Avenue.

Alexander's last visit to India took place in November 1971, when the Government of India, with the support of the Gandhi Peace Foundation, invited him and Rebecca to take part in the C. F. Andrews centenary celebrations there. They, along with others who had known and worked with Andrews, were honoured guests at meetings in Delhi, Ahmedabad, Bombay and Madras. Ironically these events took place when strife in East Bengal was reaching a climax, with the Pakistan Government's increasingly savage attempts to suppress the revolt against its regime there. On 3 December Indian forces moved in, precipitating a mercifully brief war by which the new state of Bangladesh was established.

Again and again, Alexander remarked, they were asked 'whether we considered the Gandhian or Andrews principle of non-violence relevant to the present situation. I could only reply: "Of course it is relevant".' If a nation relies on armed force, then it will find itself obliged to use that force. That does not mean that there isn't a better way, but it can only be found if one tries to see what would be a good outcome and then work towards it, 'even if the world does for the moment dismiss us as simpletons'. It is important to allow for the possibility that political leaders, 'struggling amid almost unimaginably complex forces, are striving to bring some rules of morality into the jungle of power politics'. What ordinary people of goodwill can do, he went on,

> is to try to keep their own hearts and minds as clear as they can of all harsh thoughts, free from bitterness and wrath and anger and malice. 'Create in me a clean heart, O God, and help me to bring healing to the world.' This, I think, is where Charles Andrews would invite us to begin. [16]

This conviction was severely tested in 1975 when Indira Gandhi proclaimed the 'Emergency' which led to nearly two years of autocratic rule, with the arrest of thousands of people associated with the political opposition. Soon after it began he remarked to T. N. Kaul, the Indian Ambassador to Washington, that he was reminded of the behaviour of the British in the old days, 'upholding law and order' by mere repression. He mentioned the occasion, back in 1932, when Lord Willingdon had taken over as Viceroy from Lord Irwin and was jailing the entire Congress leadership. Irwin said to Horace that it was 'much easier to get into this sort of thing than to get out of it'.[17] Earlier Congress leaders had been much more wary of this kind of procedure: even the tough-minded Sardar Patel hadn't liked detaining RSS people after the assassination of Gandhi. Kaul retorted, 'He should have done it sooner.' Then, he concluded, Gandhi wouldn't have been killed.[18] Alexander eventually wrote directly to Indira Gandhi, regretting (in the friendliest possible way) that so many devoted servants of the poor had been arrested. She replied rather coolly – addressing him as 'Mr Alexander' – that many 'old Gandhians' had had no scruples about joining with Naxalite Communist and other disruptive elements.[19] He responded that Jayprakash Narayan, for one, might have associated himself with Naxalites, but wasn't that with a view to converting them to non-violence?[20] Alexander was moved to endorse the US-based Committee for Freedom in India, and he and Rebecca turned out to support the setting off of the protest walk organised by the Committee in September 1976, from Independence Hall in Philadelphia to the UN in New York. He was greatly relieved when in the spring of 1977 the emergency ended and Indira Gandhi was defeated in the ensuing election. His old friend Morarji Desai presided over a coalition government, and in a letter of congratulation he took note of the fact that people were saying (disapprovingly) that he was 81 years old: 'I am nearly 88, so you seem quite young to me.'[21]

He had not quite agreed with Jayaprakash Narayan that it seemed as though Indian independence had led to dust and ashes.[22] But he was undoubtedly more and more disappointed with the performance of India in international affairs. In November 1977 he set out his views to Narayan Desai about the forthcoming special UN session on disarmament. People like Mrs Pandit and Krishna Menon had to be attended to.

> The voice of India was different from any other voice. They spoke with conviction and with authority. They had things to say that no one else was saying. For some years now, the voice of India in the UN has counted for very little. It has been no more than the echo of its more dynamic neighbours.[23]

Desai thought it worth making copies of this letter and sending them to members of the central Cabinet, as well as twenty other selected friends who he knew would be interested.

By the end of the 1970s the Alexanders felt that they should move to Crosslands, a retirement home which was within reach of Rebecca's son and daughter, Jim Bradbeer and Cecilia Sibinga, and from which it was still possible for him to be taken on bird-watching expeditions. He continued to take a strong interest in international affairs, and in particular the aftermath of the UN Special Session on Disarmament in 1978. In the early 1980s he wrote a powerful letter to the *New York Times* deploring the tendency in some quarters to attribute peace concerns to a paralysing fear. On the contrary, people were realising that 'if you constantly talk of war . . . war will certainly come'. Governments should rather begin to report what progress they are making in disarmament, and what the obstacles actually are.

> Let President Reagan begin to talk about these matters, and let him encourage the experts to talk . . . and we shall all begin to believe that he really cares about peace, and is working for it and thinking about it. We may even find that some of the Soviet leaders are thinking along parallel lines. The whole atmosphere will change. Hope will begin to replace fear. World harmony will begin to be possible.[24]

Over the years Alexander's relations with his old friend Philip Noel-Baker had sometimes been very stressful, but, in their closing years, campaigning for world disarmament was something which they could both support enthusiastically.

Marriage to Rebecca had brought Alexander five grandchildren, and the concerns about the future that grandchildren inevitably prompt. It gave a sharper edge to his lifelong peace convictions. He entered into his grandfatherly role with zest in other ways too. There is a splendid tape-recording of him reading from A. A. Milne's stories of Winnie-the-Pooh. His rendering of the lugubrious donkey Eeyore is particularly felicitous, and would surely have been appreciated at a Walpole Dinner in King's College seventy years earlier.

It was at this time that he organised the transfer of many of his most important papers to Friends House Library in London. This was related to his attempts to set down memories of his early life, typescripts which are now deposited in Woodbrooke. He looked back on his experiences in another way

Figure 6 Horace Alexander receiving the Padma Bhushan Medal, 1984

too. He had been consulted about two of the various scripts submitted for the Richard Attenborough film on Gandhi, which was finally released in 1982. Its remarkable success made possible a 1984 reissue of *Gandhi through Western Eyes* and the publication, in the *India Digest*, of some of Horace's memories of Gandhi. This may have been a factor in the decision by Indira Gandhi's Government to present Alexander with the Padma Bhushan medal – 'the Order of the Lotus' – the highest honour that India can award to anyone who is not an Indian citizen. The presentation, by Deepak Vohra, First Secretary of the Indian embassy in Washington, took place in Crosslands on 1 June 1984. Mary Hoxie Jones recalled that although Alexander – now 95 years old – had to be helped to the podium to make his acceptance speech, he spoke in a strong voice, and 'received a standing ovation from the large audience of fellow-residents, his family and many friends'.[25] He was someone who had always kept himself in the background, and a biographer may be permitted a feeling of satisfaction that on this occasion, at least, he took centre-stage.

By now he was physically frail, and his sight and hearing became increasingly impaired – though he remained mentally alert. Towards the end, indeed, the borderline between the past and the present became a little indistinct. His stepdaughter Cecilia visited him regularly, and on one occasion he said he would like to dictate a letter to Gandhi ('Mr Gandhi', of course), in which he asked after his health as though he had survived the assassination more than forty years previously. This seems less an indication of failing powers than a proof of how vividly Gandhi remained a living presence for him. Subsequently he composed a few letters to friends who were still alive, thus keeping in touch with them almost to the end of his life.

Unfortunately, Rebecca suffered a severe stroke in 1982, which left her unable to walk, and with no use at all in her right arm and hand. She suffered almost complete short-term memory loss, and did not read. They watched television together: the 1984 Olympic Games provided hours of entertainment, although Horace admitted to Ilay Cooper that he got tired of it sooner than Rebecca.[26] She survived him, dying on 4 March 1991. He himself died nearly six months after his hundredth birthday, on 30 September 1989.

Contentious issues

The following sketch of Alexander's later life mentions in passing a number of issues that preoccupied him, and the picture would not be complete without some attempt to present his approach to a few of the more significant conflicts in which India was involved in the second half of the twentieth century.

One conflict where India had to face particularly strong criticism in the West was that with Portugal over Goa and the other Portuguese enclaves in India. When at the end of 1961 the Indian army occupied these enclaves, Alexander admitted that it was a disappointment, considering that Nehru was 'still striving to live by the principles he learnt from Gandhi'. He was at pains to point out to readers of *The Friend*, however, that Portuguese colonial regimes were brutal, and that some previous non-violent attempts at subverting that regime in Goa by Goans living in India had been savagely repressed. But he ended his article on a note of self-reproach. He recalled that some years earlier he and some other Friends were trying to persuade some government or other to offer mediation between India and Portugal. Had they persisted 'they might have prevented this disaster to peace. Perhaps the Goan affair may serve as a reminder that we have all fallen short'.[27] He was here referring to the activities of the Goa sub-committee of the Friends Peace Committee in London in the first months of 1956. The incursions to which Alexander had referred took place in 1955, coming to a head in August. Alexander had written to R. A.

Butler (at this time Chancellor of the Exchequer) to find out if there was any possibility of the British Government's acting as a mediator between India and Portugal. Butler replied that the Government might do so if asked, but that its position in the matter wasn't easy. He was glad that Nehru seemed determined that there would be no extreme measures.[28] After the formation of the committee, which 'consisted of Friends with experience of India like Hallam Tennyson and Eric Baker, they had talks with the Portuguese ambassador, with the Brazilian ambassador (a possible mediator), and with people like Mrs Pandit and Morarji Desai. Approaches were also made to the Vatican and to Canada. There was some talk of sending a couple of Quaker representatives to Goa to report on the situation there, but little or no progress was made, and the committee lapsed.[29] With hindsight Alexander might well regret that this had been the outcome, but after all there was much else to be concerned about, and energies are limited. The beginning of the nationalist revolt against the Portuguese in Angola was in 1961, and an international anti-colonial conference in India increased pressure on Nehru's administration to take action. He did so, but with a clear sense of its negative side. At a press conference on 28 December 1955 he described it as 'the lesser evil'. From India's point of view, the ending of a colonial enclave was satisfactory. But, 'looking at it from the world point of view, which we should in such a matter, it had certain possible evil consequences' – for example undermining respect for international law.[30]

The fact that, as Prime Minister, Nehru was inevitably constrained by what his public opinion would tolerate was something that an effective peace-maker had to keep in mind and respect. For Alexander Nehru remained an example of the kind of leadership that had been so tragically lacking in the League of Nations. The non-aligned movement that he fostered so energetically provided a force on the world stage that had to be reckoned with. Even in dire situations like that created by the coincidence of the Suez crisis with the Soviet repression of the reform movement in Hungary, the presence of the non-aligned nations had a limited but positive role, making possible the UN force that provided cover for the withdrawal of UK, French and Israeli forces. The inability of the outside world to do anything about repression in Hungary was discouraging, but Alexander felt that Nehru's response showed a deeper understanding of the nature of the crisis than appeared in most comments at this time. Nehru had expressed a sense of deep foreboding, the twin crises indicating a catastrophic departure from the struggle 'to pull the world up out of the international anarchy which had resulted in two world wars'.

> 'Perhaps' (Mr Nehru seems to be thinking) 'our nations are not ready yet to undertake adventures involving such heroism, such self-discipline. . . . If this is the verdict that must be passed on mankind, what hope is there that man will ever build a city of peace on earth?'[31]

The same question pressed even more cruelly on him when, towards the end of his life, the war with China undermined so much of what he had been attempting. Although the Cuban missile crisis, which coincided with the border war, demonstrated the importance of maintaining the non-aligned movement, the confidence had gone out of Nehru's statesmanship. India, indeed, continued to intervene helpfully at the UN as long as Mrs Pandit was representing it, but during the 1970s Alexander's own confidence in India's role faltered. Still, even at the worst moments of Indira Gandhi's 'Emergency' he persisted in claiming to have faith that 'India will help to save the world from the suicide through violence that seems still to be our possible destiny'.[32]

To some extent this was a conviction that simply reflected the ineradicable impression made by Gandhi, but the thirteen or fourteen years when Nehru's foreign policy was most fully effective remained for Alexander a model, even if a flawed model, of the approach needed to create a sustainable world order. I say 'flawed' because there were a number of aspects of Indian policy with which Alexander was not satisfied. But even what he saw as imperfections drew attention to the kind of limitations within which any practical politician would have to operate.

The most conspicuous issue that troubled Alexander was the handling of the dispute over Kashmir. As we have seen, he had first-hand experience of the earliest phases of the conflict in Kashmir, always from the Indian side (Richard Symonds was his colleague on the other side). He took great pains to understand and represent both Indian and Pakistani interpretations of the situation as it developed, and attempted a definitive summing up of the position in his pamphlet *Kashmir: a Statement of Facts and Problems*, published by Friends Peace Committee in London in 1952.[33] He had considerable sympathy with the idea that both sides in Kashmir itself could resolve their differences on the basis of Kashmiri autonomy, with India and Pakistan sharing responsibility for its external relations. He had in mind the 'free zones' of Haute Savoie between France and Switzerland, an arrangement that had worked well for several decades. He remembered a friend at Cambridge saying that

> he thought the ideal solution for places like Alsace would be a condominium. 'But', he added, 'I am afraid it is too idealistic for this wicked world.' Perhaps so, but sometimes we realise that this world is rather more idealistic than we had supposed.[34]

With Kashmir, the difficulty with Alexander's idea was not so much the absence of idealism as the presence of global strategic interests. He remarked in one journal letter that the only conversation on Kashmir he'd had in Pakistan which wasn't utterly frustrating was with a government information officer who happened to be a refugee from Srinagar.

> After my talk with him, I concluded once again that if only every kind of Kashmiri could be put in a room together for a week, they might come out with an agreement – probably an agreement that would not suit either India or Pakistan. But I suppose this is an idle dream.[35]

Not only would it have failed to suit India and Pakistan, but Britain and the USA also would hardly have cared for it, because of Kashmir's geographical situation. As Indira Gandhi insisted in a letter to Alexander, it would become a hotbed of intrigue involving China, the USSR, Pakistan and India.[36] The only practicable way forward was through agreement genuinely acceptable, even if reluctantly so, to the two dominions. Outsiders could do little to help in attaining this desirable objective. Alexander told John Linton that Nehru resented *any* non-Indian intervention on Kashmir, such as Alexander's idea of a condominium. 'Don't forget his fifteen years (or whatever it was) in British jails.' He also thinks, Alexander added sadly, that Friends are 'dreamers and unrealistic', and should stick to their humanitarian initiatives.[37] Constructive ideas were indeed being produced in India. In the same letter he told Linton of Jayaprakash Narayan's idea for getting the two nations used to the idea of working together. A joint commission to supervise water supplies in the Indus valley could be a model for other areas of economic cooperation.

There was a characteristic series of letters on Kashmir in *The Friend* in the winter of 1956–7. A correspondent had argued that Nehru's claim to moral leadership was undermined by India's defiance of a UN order to decide the future of Kashmir through a free plebiscite. Alexander responded by pointing out that the correspondent had reproduced the Pakistani case, and that there was also an Indian case. 'For some reason', he continued, 'the Indian case on Kashmir is never given in the British press, or scarcely ever. So here it is.' There followed a summary of India's view that Pakistani troops must be withdrawn from Kashmir before a plebiscite could be held, and so on – Alexander emphasising that this *was* the Indian case. He added that in visits to Kashmir he had formed the impression that in a straight choice between India and Pakistan, a plebiscite would favour Pakistan, though other observers believed that in the Kashmir valley, at least, India would gain a majority. He conceded that Nehru's determination to accept the effective partition of the state and stop renewing legal claims and counterclaims, while not wholly unreasonable, was perhaps 'a serious blind spot'. That, however, did not disqualify him from playing a useful role in the international scene.

One might have supposed that this letter would have given more satisfaction to partisans of Pakistan than of India, but evidently the mere rehearsal of the Indian case was too much for some. Philip Noel-Baker wrote to Alexander saying that he was 'horrified' by the letter: had not Nehru gone back on undertakings to hold a plebiscite *six times*? And S. M. Haq, the Press Attaché at the Pakistani High Commission in London, wrote a long letter to *The Friend* giving a detailed account of moves made at the UN in the early stages of the conflict to show that India had not cooperated with them. In a further letter Alexander corrected a couple of details in Haq's letter, and then added the following paragraph:

> These unhappy wranglings about what did or did not happen years ago do not get us much further. May I make one final comment which I hope will appeal to Mr Haq as well as to others? It is surely clear that the real deep trouble is that neither India nor Pakistan trusts the other. Both produce what to them is convincing evidence that the other Government has acted in ways that are utterly deceitful. 'How can you expect us to trust them?' Well, I believe that the only way these things get solved in the end is through acts of, if you like, reckless trust. I wish that India, the stronger neighbour, could show this reckless trust in Pakistan.[38]

In responding to Noel-Baker's letter, he managed to find common ground in an odd but characteristic way. He deplored Nehru's 'appallingly patronising attitude' towards Pakistan, which reminded him of the way elder brothers speak of younger brothers. As a younger brother himself he *knew* how galling it was to be treated like a younger brother for ever. Treating people on the level was a fundamental axiom of peacemaking. A letter he wrote to *The Friend* in 1982 recalls a meeting of the Woodbrooke Council in the early 1920s when James Douglas sent his apologies – he was helping to draft the constitution for a newly independent Ireland. Alexander proposed that a message of support and encouragement should be sent to him, and this was agreed. But when he made the suggestion someone laughed, evidently in mockery at the very idea of an *Irish* constitution. Such a display of contempt indicated something as poisonous as hatred, and Alexander feared that even in 1982 it was still present in Anglo-Irish relations. The British had to learn a proper respect for the people of Ireland, and stop thinking of Ireland as a 'problem'.[39]

A similar concern informed Alexander's involvement with the conflict between the Nagas on the north-east frontier and the Indian Union. As we have seen, his encounter with Naga aspirations went back as far as 1950. During the following years unrest increased, and broke out into open conflict in 1956. Michael Scott, an Anglican clergyman who had championed the Herero people of South-West Africa at the UN, and was a leading figure, with Bertrand Russell, in the radical anti-nuclear Committee of 100, now turned his attention to the cause of Naga independence. He had helped the leader of the movement, A. Z. Phizo, to settle in London, and approached various people who might be sympathetic, such as David Astor of *The Observer* newspaper. It was probably his initiative that encouraged Friends Peace Committee to concern themselves with the issue. Alexander produced an account of the situation as he saw it in April 1960, in which he regretted the tendency of some Indian officials to treat the Nagas 'as inferior people who are a nuisance and should be put in their place'. He saw the need for a mediator who had the confidence of the Nagas, and who could be given authority to negotiate.[40] The Gandhian Sarvodaya movement in India, led by Jayaprakash Narayan and Vinoba Bhave, had already shown willingness to intervene, and the secretary of Friends Peace Committee, Stella Alexander (no relation), suggested that Vinoba Bhave and Alexander might usefully head an inquiry into the problem.[41] Another Gandhian, Asha Devi Aryanayakam, saw Mrs Pandit about peacemaking possibilities, and found herself subjected to an angry outburst about 'saints in politics' like the Quakers and Michael Scott. She added, however, that in spite of the trouble he caused she loved and respected him, and as for the Quakers, 'You may not know it', she told Asha Devi, 'but I am a Quaker too'.[42] Anything, of course, that pointed in the direction of secession from India was anathema to most Indians. Stella Alexander remarked that when Ranjit Chetsingh heard of a (false) press report that Michael Scott had led a delegation of Quakers to see Mrs Pandit about the Nagas 'he gave a passable imitation of Etna in eruption'.[43] Scott himself came to find the Quakers quite inadequate in their support, complaining that 'the peacemakers, for fear of being contaminated by violence, range themselves on the side of the big batallions'.[44] Certainly Alexander, with his long connection with Nehru and Mrs Pandit, was unwilling to adopt the confrontational approach that Scott felt was necessary. Early in September 1963, some three weeks after Scott's fierce letter to the Peace Committee, Alexander expressed his understanding of the Indian Government's concern that if there was to be a Quakerish visit to Nagaland it should be a *quiet* one.[45] Nehru himself was well aware of the obstacles to peace created by official attitudes, and accepted that it was unreasonable to expect them to feel that they were undoubtedly part of India.[46] He had been disappointed that the decision to make Nagaland a fully-constituted state of the Indian Union had not had immediate results, but it prepared the way for an acceptable peace mission, consisting of Scott himself, Jayaprakash Narayan and the Chief Minister of Assam, B. P. Chaliha. This led to the declaration of a cease-fire on 24 May 1964, just two days before Nehru's death. The cease-fire was monitored by a small team including Marjorie Sykes. She remained there till 1967.[47]

Four years later, in September 1968, Michael Scott was ready to concede that Friends had done some good, if not enough. He wrote to David Astor that Marjorie Sykes and the Quakers had indeed tried to bring 'some balm of goodness and healing' into the Naga situation, but Sykes herself had been constrained by the threat of exclusion if she took too strong a line. It was essential to point out that the Nagas *had* been victims of injustice, oppression, corruption. Alexander had said that Scott's approach would not bring results, but what was the alternative? He was frustrated that the Quakers did not do more as they 'have always had more influence with India than anyone else'.[48]

It is doubtful whether anyone was in a position to bring more influence to bear on the situation in Nagaland, particularly after Nehru's death. Armed forces remained in place after the cease-fire, and conflict continued to resurface The issues remained unresolved as India entered the twenty-first century. What can be said is that these mid-century efforts to deal with the situation showed what needed to be done, even if the political will to carry it through was insufficient.

Action for peace

Although Alexander was always pre-eminently concerned to encourage peaceful developments in the Indian sub-continent, he played his part in the wider peace movement, and welcomed the advent of the Campaign for Nuclear Disarmament and the opposition to American intervention in Vietnam. He was impatient with what he saw as misrepresentations of the peace movement between the wars as a way of discrediting peace movements in the atomic age. He had, of course, been a League of Nations Union supporter rather than a member of the Peace Pledge Union, and few things irritated him more than slipshod assertions that the LNU's 'Peace Ballot' of 1935 was a symptom of appeasement of ruthless dictators. A contributor to *The Friend* in 1976 had made just this claim, and he responded by pointing out that on the contrary it was 'a great effort to persuade the British government that the people wanted it to take the League of Nations seriously'. Ninety per cent of those voting supported the use of economic sanctions against an aggressor, and while only 70 per cent supported military sanctions, to regard this as a pacifist vote was perverse. But when Italy attacked Abyssinia the League machinery was not effectively used. It was surely the inaction of the British and French governments, not the massive popular support for collective security, 'that led Hitler to believe that he could go ahead with impunity'.[49]

Alexander was always painfully conscious of the complexity of international relations, and he was careful to avoid expressing his dedication to peace in simplistic terms. But if he felt that some specific initiative might work in the right direction, he was eager to support it. One such initiative, to which he attached great importance, was the formation of the World Peace Brigade. The project was first mooted at a conference of the War Resisters International held in India in 1961. It was actually launched the following January in Beirut, supported by Gandhian organisations, by western peace groups and by movements for independence from colonial rule, particularly in Africa. Alexander observed that it was an exceptional organisation in being truly intercontinental from the start. 'It will not always act in the Anglo-Saxon manner. But it may also mean that it can be a truer instrument of healing for mankind than a more hastily improvised and less world-wide instrument could ever be.'[50] Its first major action was to give support to the campaign to secure independence for what was then Northern Rhodesia, an integral part of the white-dominated Central African Federation. A nonviolent 'Freedom March' was prepared but never actually deployed. It remained as a possible sanction in case of need, but Zambia gained its independence anyhow in 1964.

The World Peace Brigade acquired office space at the Peace Pledge Union's London headquarters, and Alexander agreed to serve as Treasurer, making an effective appeal at the British launch meeting on 2 August 1962. By this time public concern about the poisonous effects of huge nuclear test explosions in the atmosphere was becoming irrepressible. The USSR was as guilty as the USA, Britain and France, but because of its closed political system it was harder to make protests against its actions effectively. In 1958 Albert Bigelow had attempted to disrupt US tests in the Pacific by sailing his ketch *The Golden Rule* into the test area. He described this action in a book published in 1960, with which Alexander was so impressed that he bought a number of copies to send to friends such as Morarji Desai and Rajagopalachari.[51] Now in 1962 several activists developed the idea of sending a boat to Leningrad to make a conspicuous protest against Soviet tests, and this was made a project of the World Peace Brigade. A ketch was bought, given the name *Everyman III*,[52] and registered in the name of the editor of *Peace News*, Hugh Brock. The skipper was an American Quaker, Earle Reynolds, who had previously conducted a protest voyage against US tests in the *Phoenix*. Alexander, as treasurer, set about appealing for funds. The *Guardian* newspaper doubted whether he would succeed, but his standing in the Society of Friends ensured that in that quarter at least donations would be generous. Even Anna Barlow, who disapproved so strongly of the way he was mixed up with Indian nationalists, gave him £100. His old colleague in the FAU, Leslie Cross, sent £5, remarking that he couldn't feel that the wise and prudent had made a great success of our world: 'Perhaps an injection of some sort of divine craziness is needed.'[53]

The *Everyman III* set sail from Gravesend on 26 September, and called at Ostend, Hamburg, Amsterdam, Copenhagen and Stockholm on its way to Leningrad, which it reached on 20 October. The Soviet authorities had already indicated that they would not allow the crew to land. Bertrand Russell issued an appeal to the Soviet Peace Committee to get this decision reversed, and indeed the Committee sent a strong delegation which had many hours of talks with the crew. But the boat had arrived just as the Cuban missile crisis was entering its most alarming phase, and there was never any likelihood that visas would be given. In the end some crew members tried to swim ashore, others tried to scuttle the ship. They were tied up until they undertook to attempt no more acts of disobedience, and then they set out on a return voyage.

At first sight this might seem to have been a rather futile exercise, except for the opportunity to reinforce opposition to nuclear testing in the cities they visited on the way. They altogether failed to make direct contact with ordinary Russians. But they *did* meet the Soviet Peace Committee, very much an organ of the establishment in those days. They were thus a reminder to that establishment that there was a public in the West ready to applaud a Soviet retreat and not gloat over it in triumph. Khruschev signalled his willingness to withdraw missiles from Cuba in response to an open letter from Bertrand Russell in *The New Statesman* appealing for sanity. Russell's eminence was a guarantee that the Soviet leader had a sympathetic gallery to play to. Those long discussions with the crew of the *Everyman III* may not have affected the issue at all, but clearly they will have done no harm.

For Alexander any political impact the *Everyman III* might have had was a secondary consideration. The protest was important in itself, regardless of consequences. His attitude is explained in a letter he wrote to Gerald Bailey in 1961, commenting on the Campaign for Nuclear Disarmament, whose call for unilateral action by Britain had been criticised by people such as Bailey himself and Philip Noel-Baker.

> Today I find myself in the curious position that I am a sponsor of the Direct Action activities in regard to the abandonment of nuclear weapons; and yet when I hear you or Bertram [Pickard] or Sydney [Bailey], or Philip Noel Baker, putting the case for general disarmament as against unilateralism, I find that my political judgment is in almost full accord with you. But note the 'almost'.

The Aldermaston marches, he suggested, were not a political move but a moral gesture. They expressed a revulsion against power struggles that could lead to world suicide. There was a great danger that ordinary citizens would feel that they were mere ciphers, pawns, so that they just cultivated their gardens until the final catastrophe occurred. The demonstrations were a protest against leaving decisions to high-level, important people.

> It is very understandable, and indeed right, that they should, under present circumstances, do something a bit more costly to themselves, than simply sending resolutions to the Government. . . . When the whole 'Aldermaston' type of activity is called in question, I feel inclined to say: 'If these hold their peace, the very stones would cry out.'[54]

Writing this letter prompted Alexander to develop his thoughts in an article in *The Friend*, published on 7 July. Near the end he recalled an idea suggested to him by Neave Brayshaw over half a century earlier, that of a 'martyr nation', witnessing to its Christian faith by disbanding its army and navy. It was an idea expressed by Dr McKennal, a former President of the Evangelical Free Church Council in March 1900, at the height of the Boer War.[55] Alexander admitted that he could see no prospect of any nation's renouncing armed protection, but if there ever was such a prospect it could change the course of human history. Meanwhile the determined witness of individuals to the need for a radical change of policy would help the statesmen to overcome their inevitable frustrations along the thankless, dusty road to an agreed disarmament'. And these statesmen did so need our understanding.

> Judging from the few political leaders and high officials whom I have met through the years in Whitehall and elsewhere, I have no doubt that some of them are striving for peace and disarmament as honestly, according to their lights, as any pacifist. It is only if we hold to our faith in them that we are likely to be able to help them.

This, Alexander reminds us, is a Gandhian idea: 'Always think the best of the man you are dealing with, however misguided he may seem to be.'[56]

*

A late example of Alexander's approach to peacemaking can be found in his correspondence about the negotiations that eventually brought an end to the war in Vietnam. Over the summer of 1970 there had been a vigorous discussion in *The Friend* about opposition to the US presence in Vietnam, Gerald Bailey, for one, claiming that it had encouraged almost total Communist inflexibility, since they believed they could gain their political ends 'without making any of the concessions which any true, negotiated peace demands'. Alexander responded a fortnight later with a letter that quietly endorsed American opposition to the war – the younger generation in particular finding all war 'obscene, absurd, ethically outrageous'. But he tactfully supported Bailey's insistence that everything possible should be done to get the negotiations going more effectively in Paris, 'and this, as he rightly says, means getting concessions from both sides'.[57] In December 1970 he wrote to Duncan Wood, who was then in charge of the Quaker Centre in Geneva, about the negotiations in Paris which seemed to be getting nowhere. Each side would issue prepared statements of their position, and showed no willingness to compromise on anything. Alexander felt that his friends and associates had been too ready to accept the position as hopeless, and to assume that it would be 'a waste of effort for anyone to sit around in Paris trying to be helpful'. He had been greatly encouraged by an article in a recent *New York Times* Sunday magazine, written by Averil Harriman. Harriman had been President Lyndon Johnson's representative at the beginning of the Paris peace talks in 1968, and in the article he maintained that a breakthrough had almost been achieved by the end of that year. He suggested that 'if the right invisible intermediaries had been present while he was in Paris, something might have happened then.' At this point, however, Richard Nixon was elected President and Harriman was withdrawn.

Alexander thought that if a breakthrough had seemed possible once, it might well be possible again. There was a need for someone prepared to go to Paris 'on an indefinite, probably quite long, probably very frustrating assignment, in the conviction that this is required of us'.[58] He felt that Gilbert White of the AFSC might be the right person, and three days later he wrote to him suggesting that the present dialogue of the deaf was not insurmountable.

> Someone who can speak to the deaf – not just on one side but on both – with some understanding of the causes underlying the deafness, might help both sides to find that they are not so far apart as they think they are.

Referring to the Harriman article, he claimed that 'the presence in Paris of one or two invisible people of intelligence and goodwill, trusted by both sides, or by all sides, might just make the difference'.[59]

In fact it was Duncan Wood who went to Paris to take soundings, and his initial impressions were depressing: both sides were insisting on their full war aims, and all decisions were being made in Washington and Hanoi. Still, there might be value in a Friend becoming *known* to the negotiators in Paris, which might provide the basis for intervention in the future, but an appointment of this kind would be frustrating.[60] Wood later wrote an account of a meeting with the South Vietnam representative, Le Van Loi, which Alexander found quite encouraging.

> Here is a man who knows Duncan well, and obviously has confidence in him. He accordingly finds an opportunity to him along lines that are not just the 'party line', but are a deliberate attempt towards a talking position with Hanoi and the NLF.

People from other delegations might begin to talk in the same way to a familiar and trusted Friend. But there was no magic formula to deal with the problem. It was a matter of patient and laborious effort. He recalled the work of the India Conciliation Group, lasting for more than ten years – 'constantly confronting our British officials, who thought us profoundly misguided; but their doors were never shut against us. They always listened, and we had decent human relations with them.'[61]

Years earlier, as we have seen, Alexander formed the opinion that if the Kashmir conflict had been left to the Kashmiris, a settlement would have been reached quite quickly. Duncan Wood thought much the same about Vietnam. In the course of a tour of Vietnamese delegations in various capital cities, he found a flexible attitude in just one, Algiers. And the representative he spoke to was not, as was usual, from North Vietnam, but from the south, one of the dreaded Vietcong, the NLF, who had been directly engaged in the worst of the military action.[62]

The war dragged on with a violence which came to a climax in the massive bombing of North Vietnam at Christmas 1972. By that time Henry Kissinger was the US representative and he noted that although Le Duc Tho, who led the North Vietnam delegation, kept his distance in public, 'inside the negotiating room he moved at tremendous speed and with as much human warmth as he was capable of generating towards a representative of the capitalist system'. Another participant saw the same meeting rather differently, but with an admission that the parties had already gone beyond the stage of defending fixed positions with inflexibility. 'It was a very sombre meeting. No jollity, no joking as usually went on.'[63] Clearly there could have been a role for invisible intermediaries who might at least have had the effect of sparing Vietnam that last appalling paroxysm of military violence.

WORKING FOR THE PEACEABLE KINGDOM

A writer in the *Washington Post*, commenting on the award of the Padma Bushan medal to Horace Alexander, remarked that 'nothing had made as much sense for him as the teaching from his Quaker parents and Gandhi that the peaceable kingdom is eminently possible'.[64] Eminently possible, no doubt, but not easily possible. No one who looks at Alexander's encounters with the conflicts of the twentieth century can fail to be struck by the stubborn patience and resilience that he needed to bring to his work. The resilience was part of his temperament, nurtured by the optimistic atmosphere of pre-1914 Cambridge. The patience was something he had to cultivate. It was in part the patience of the experienced bird-watcher, but also that of someone who had convinced himself, rather against the grain, that 'anger does not help'.[65]

As we have seen, his native irritability was most evident in his dealings with fellow Quakers who did not share his vision of Quakerism in south Asia. Clearly, too, it was most apparent when his health was poor.[66] But in this he simply fell short of what he wanted to be, inexhaustibly ready to wait, to attend to the positive, the good outcome that he envisioned. There were two passages of poetry which meant a great deal to him. One was the stanza that closes Shelley's *Prometheus Unbound*, where the poet resolves

> To love and bear; to hope till hope creates
> From its own wreck the thing it contemplates.[67]

The other is from the epilogue to Browning's *Asolando*:

> One who never turned his back but marched breast forward,
> Never doubted clouds would break,
> Never dreamed though right were worsted wrong would triumph,
> Held we fall to rise, are baffled to fight better,
> Sleep to wake.

He applied these lines to that indomitable peace campaigner Marian Parmoor,[68] but they turn up elsewhere in his correspondence, and he evidently felt that they expressed something of himself, certainly something required of the dedicated peacemaker.

It would be difficult to exaggerate the importance of his friendship with Gandhi in sustaining him under the most discouraging circumstances. Gandhi himself was constantly conceding that his devotion to non-violence was imperfect, but that the principle of non-violence was unassailable. Nothing could divert him from this conviction. At the same time he was a man of such charm and resilience that he exercised a quite remarkable ability to attract almost anyone who came to know him personally. Those whose acquaintance with him was more than casual could not help being deeply influenced by him. As Dorothy Hogg observed, writing in 1965,

> one had to be with him in his prayer meetings, listen to his private conversations and discussions, take part in his anti-untouchability campaigns, travel with him, laugh with him, argue with him, watch him in his personal contacts with all and sundry, accompany him on his moving pilgrimages for Hindu–Muslim unity to be able to understand him and appreciate his true significance to India and the world.

In this respect, she felt, Alexander was admirably qualified to interpret Gandhi to those who had not known him, and she wanted him to go to the Pope to do just that, so that an effective papal intervention might be made in the war between India and Pakistan.[69] In 1944, as we have seen, she had been a stern critic of Alexander's shortcomings, so her confidence now in his ability to bring off this diplomatic coup is surprising, but that in itself reflects the enduring impact of Gandhi's personality on those who had known him. His faith could move mountains, and could empower others to do the same. She was, alas, disappointed. Alexander made no attempt to lobby the Pope.

Even so, Alexander's commitment to the creation of a peaceful and therefore sustainable world order should not be doubted. He was also acutely conscious of the complex pressures that made that objective almost impossibly difficult. That consciousness can often draw people towards acceptance of the established way of coping with international conflict, and rejection of what seem to be the naïve oversimplifications of the average peace activist. Gerald Bailey was a striking example of this. Alexander, on the other hand, managed to retain the vision of the activist without losing sight of the fact that politics is the art of the possible. We have seen that it was in a letter to Bailey that Alexander explained why he had 'a foot in both camps'. And it was central to his philosophy that people of goodwill needed to work together, no matter what their differences of opinion or interest might be. It was characteristic of him that he should have transformed Bailey's complaint that peace campaigning had sabotaged the Vietnam negotiations into an encouragement to get them going more effectively. As he wrote to Christopher Taylor years before, referring to opportunities for work in India after 1945, the reputation of the Quakers there enabled them 'to work with all parties and groups, and help to bring together into common enterprises people who are often sundered by political and communal antagonisms.'[70]

The lessons that Alexander learned from his experience are not easily presented in a compelling form. A formula such as 'Always attend to the positive aspects of a conflict situation' sounds pallid, inadequate. The picture one has of Alexander patiently if sadly listening to a bellicose rant, and brightening up, instantly on the alert, as soon as a note of flexibility surfaces, lacks the appeal of dynamic action. It has to be said, too, that some of those who encountered him found him devious: what, one wonders, did Gerald Bailey make of the Alexandrian metamorphosis of his indignant letter about the Vietnam negotiations? Richard Symonds recalls that the India Office found him 'slippery', in contrast to Agatha Harrison, who was seen as straightforward if misguided.

Perhaps one has to go back to the charismatic figure of Gandhi himself to make a proper assessment of Alexander's approach to the daunting problems of a world that seems hopelessly locked into cycles of violence. Alexander was quite unlike Gandhi, and was in many respects a typical western Quaker, invariably in western dress, and finding it quite natural, to the very end of his life, to speak of '*Mr* Gandhi'. He always tried to interpret Gandhi in terms with which western readers would feel at ease. It was Gandhi in translation – a very faithful translation, but most translations lack the brilliancy of the original. Of course, Alexander brought to his appreciation of Gandhi a rich Quaker tradition and his own carefully developed understanding of international relations. There was a genuine encounter of very different cultures. What they had in common was the willingness, if one may employ the Quaker phrase, to answer that of God in everyone. R. G. Casey, Governor of Bengal between 1944 and 1946, recalled that in his experience Gandhi never made 'any harsh or critical comment on other individuals, even on those who had said hard things about him'.[71] This was not, alas, a compliment that Alexander would have altogether deserved, but on occasion he did keep Gandhi up to the mark. In the summer of 1946 he was discussing the situation in Bengal with Gandhi, and mentioned how helpful Shaheed Suhrawardy had been to the FAU at the time of the Bengal famine.

> 'Do you realise he is a bad man?' asked Gandhi. I replied: 'Yes, I dare say; but I am not quite sure what you mean by that. We are mostly partly bad and partly good, aren't we?' 'Dr Jekyll and Mr Hyde,' he commented. 'I read that book by Robert Louis Stevenson in South Africa many years ago. There is much truth in it.'[72]

Alexander goes on to describe how Gandhi's relationship with Suhrawardy developed during his mission to East Bengal, coming to a climax in the cooperation between the two to maintain peace in Calcutta in August 1947. This is perhaps the most striking moment in the story told in *Gandhi through Western Eyes*, where Gandhi's influence on him is explored with scrupulous care and with an infectious warmth of affection. It is in part a straightforward and crisply presented account of Gandhi's career, which could be recommended to anyone wanting to understand how his thinking developed and what motivated him. But the book's distinction resides in its record of Alexander's personal response to him, or his use of anecdotes which his personal knowledge enabled him to appreciate. Thus he cites with relish Lord Templewood's account of the memorable encounter between Gandhi and King George, when the King reproached him for attacking his empire.

> I held my breath [Templewood wrote] in fear of an argument between the two. Gandhi's *savoir faire* saved the situation with a grave and deferential reply. 'I must not be drawn into a political argument in Your Majesty's Palace after receiving your Majesty's hospitality.' They then took leave of each other as friendly guest and host. A very honest King and a great diplomat, I thought to myself, and what exquisite worldly manners the unworldly possess.[73]

Alexander evidently savours every word of this testimony to Gandhi's adroitness, and it is such stories that prepare the reader for his analysis of the 'Quit India' movement of 1942, or the cooperation with Suhrawardy that made possible the 'miracle of Calcutta' in 1947. The 'Quit India' narrative, in particular is a model of fairness, bringing out the motivation of all those involved, and the difficulty each party had in understanding the other. An 'epilogue' considers how far Gandhi's rejection of 'the law of the jungle', his concern to substitute love for hate, truth for untruth, tolerance for intolerance, was realistically possible in the wider world. That world, says Alexander in conclusion, must choose between life and death: 'The old way will take us surely to death. The Gandhian way, the courageous way, seeking moral means to achieve the great end of 'One World', may bring life to mankind.'[74]

His book, inevitably, reached only a limited readership. But Alexander took a modest part in the most successful attempt in the late twentieth century to make Gandhi's significance understood by a mass audience: Richard Attenborough's film, *Gandhi*, released in 1982 at a rather dangerous moment in the Cold War between the USSR and the West. The film had a long period of gestation. The project had been conceived by Motilal Kothari, a civil servant in India's High Commission in London, as early as 1960, but it was only in 1962 that he approached Richard Attenborough to see if he was willing to take it on. He was, and realising the importance of getting the cooperation of the Government of India, he persuaded Lord Mountbatten to speak to Nehru about it, and he proved to be happy to give his blessing. Alexander first encountered the project when he and Rebecca were visiting India in the autumn of 1963. A first script was being prepared by the novelist Clifford Hanley, and Alexander had consulted the Cabinet Secretary, Sucha Singh Khera, about who needed to see it. Obviously Nehru was one, and Alexander spoke to him at a lunch party. Yes, he would like to see it, but it was mainly business for the Ministry of Information, where his daughter, Indira, was Minister. Pyarelal, the official biographer of Gandhi, of course wanted to see the script: he was cautious, but favourably impressed by Richard Attenborough.

Alexander received the Hanley script after his return to England, and sent a detailed comment to Kothari. On the whole he was pleased with its faithfulness to history, but did have some reservations. He was unhappy that the section dealing with Gandhi in South Africa had no African characters in it. He felt that Hanley was wrong to show Gandhi as angry: in stressful situations he could be stern, but not angry. The 'small talk' was wrong – 'He just did not talk like that. He had a very characteristic way of talking to his intimates, and it may be difficult to recapture; but it grates as it is now.' An important omission was Gandhi's village work, and his concern to improve the lot of the 'Harijans' – the untouchables. He suggested having a scene where Gandhi insisted on Harijans and caste Hindus sitting together – otherwise he would address them from among the Harijans. As for the last section, that was distinctly unsatisfactory. The script presented him as grieving over the casualties of communal riots. He did not stand grieving, but stimulated people to *do* things. Alexander was naturally disappointed that the script did not include 'the miracle of Calcutta', and he resented the portrayal of Gandhi as almost helpless and paralysed in the final episode. On the contrary he retained a 'tremendous vitality . . . right to the last moment', an unconquerable faith in truth and non-violence.[75]

For whatever reason, Hanley's script was rejected, and Alexander was kept informed of who else was being approached. Hallam Tennyson tried to secure Terence Rattigan; John Osborne, we learn, was evasive. Eventually Robert Bolt, the author of a fine play about Sir Thomas More, *A Man for All Seasons*, agreed to submit a script. Alexander read this too, and was again dissatisfied with the end. On 15 August 1947 he was *not* mourning in his ashram, as Bolt presented him, but actively ensuring peace in Calcutta. But his main objection was to the inadequacy of the subsidiary characters. He would like to have seen rugged characters disagreeing with the Mahatma, people such as Sardar Patel, Sarojini Naidu, Rajagopalachari.[76] This was his complaint, too, about the script by John Briley that formed the basis of the film that eventually emerged. By this time Alexander was in Pennsylvania, so he was not consulted. If he had been, one surmises that he would have taken particular exception to the way

Alexander's favourite Viceroy, Lord Irwin, was presented – as a stereotypical British official. But the film as a whole gave him unbounded satisfaction. The performance of Gandhi himself by Ben Kingsley was almost magically authentic. This was Gandhi as Alexander remembered him. He saw it four times, and was deeply moved by the response of the audiences, lingering silently in the auditorium as the credits rolled at the end, as though they could not bear to leave.

Alexander's faith in the practicability of building the peaceable kingdom was immensely strengthened by his association with Gandhi. The film made it possible for many others to have a glimpse of what Gandhi meant to those who knew him. As Alexander put it at the end of *Gandhi through Western Eyes*, 'Which of you, Gandhi asks every man and woman, is willing to dare the new way of life and hope with me?'

APPENDIX: FRITZ BERBER IN THE SECOND WORLD WAR

After their meeting in Geneva in November 1939, Alexander and Berber did not see each other again until they met in Delhi in April 1951. Berber has left an account of what happened to him during the war years in his autobiography, *Zwischen Macht und Gewissen*, 'between power and conscience' (1986). As we shall see, this provides a far from complete picture of his situation, but it can at least serve as a starting point for considering the issues involved. The book tells a story of increasing isolation and estrangement from his patron and protector Ribbentrop, beginning with his all-too-academic pamphlet on the attack by a British destroyer on a German ship, the *Altmark*. This took place in Norwegian territorial waters while Norway was still neutral, and Berber had no difficulty in showing how legally questionable the British action was. Unfortunately for him he presented the case in a moderate and objective way, and Ribbentrop, in an angry phone call, reminded him that Germany was engaged in a life-and-death struggle, in which scholarship in an ivory tower had no place. Thereafter Berber reckons that he further jeopardised his position by various memoranda expressing unwelcome views. In one, relating to the treatment of Britain after a successful German invasion, he emphasised the imprudence of introducing Gestapo methods there, as it would only alienate the population. In another he argued that the aerial bombardment of British cities was counterproductive if the strategic aim was to secure British cooperation. He left colleagues in no doubt about the adverse effects of the appalling treatment of the Jews. Bombing of civilians, as initially practised by the Germans, and later far more ruthlessly by the British and Americans, was clearly against international law.

His views were consistently ignored and his health deteriorated. Eventually he had to have an operation on his gall bladder, and his absence from work was timely, as Martin Luther, a fanatically Nazi Under-Secretary in the Foreign Ministry, was on the point of having him arrested. Friendly officials had time to intervene on his behalf, and in due course the flight of Rudolf Hess and the invasion of the Soviet Union served to distract attention from his offences. He continued editing his journal and, as far as possible, keeping out of harm's way. He received a warning, however, from an apparently sympathetic Gestapo officer that his position was still hazardous because Ribbentrop was known to have withdrawn his protection. It would be as well to seek a posting outside Germany. This became possible because one of his duties was to accompany Carl Burckhardt of the International Red Cross to camps holding Russian prisoners of war. Burckhardt was evidently impressed by Berber, and eventually, early in 1944, persuaded Ribbentrop to second him to Geneva. Ribbentrop was persuadable because the war was going badly for Germany, and he had formed hopes of concluding a separate peace with Britain. Because Berber was deemed to have good contacts with Britain, he could once again be regarded as useful.

In Geneva he concerned himself with an attempt, backed by the International Red Cross, to put limits on aerial bombardment by establishing well-defined areas which would be exempt from attack. This came to nothing. He did have the satisfaction, however, of taking part in the concerted effort to save some at least of Hungary's Jews, threatened by deportation to death camps after the German take-over of Hungary in 1944. Burckhardt sent him on a mission to urge Ribbentrop to withdraw the deportation order. Berber's narrative provides a dramatic account of Ribbentrop's receiving him angrily, accusing him of conspiring with British agents. Berber says that he responded with vigour, denying the accusation absolutely, and pointing out that Germany was clearly losing the war, that Ribbentrop would be prominent in any list of war criminals, and that he would be well advised to put a stop to what he must know was a wicked crime. Ribbentrop, Berber claims, was shaken by this outburst, and said that he would speak to Hitler. In due course the order was countermanded, and a quarter of a million Jews were thus saved from the gas chambers.

Berber's narrative is oversimplified and gives no indication of the full scope of the efforts made to frustrate the deportations, including the heroic role of Raoul Wallenberg and his Swedish colleagues, but his approach to Ribbentrop was clearly important, and sufficiently justified his long and unhappy career as an insider in the Nazi regime.[1] It must be said, however, that here as elsewhere the autobiography is an inadequate record of his wartime activities. There is, for one thing, no mention of his collaboration with Ulrich Noack over efforts to stop the war in the winter of 1939–40. And a completely different perspective on his standing in the Foreign Ministry emerges in a study by Robert Edwin Herzstein of wartime attempts to formulate a policy for Europe after a German victory.[2] In 1943 Ribbentrop set up a committee on the restructuring of Europe, which established three working groups. The first of these, assembling historical, geographical and statistical information, was chaired by Berber.[3] His approach to the new European order is illustrated by an article he published in his journal in which he considered ways and means of resolving future conflicts of interest.[4] The individuality of the different nations would have to be respected, and overbearing hegemony avoided. Berber himself mentions this article in his autobiography, and the fact that the *Frankfurter Zeitung* published long extracts from it. The authorities, however, issued a ban on such citations, and copies of that issue of the newspaper were confiscated.[5]

This incident throws some light on the ambiguity of his position. He had the status of an official who could be entrusted with the work of a government working group, but that did not mean that his work was acceptable to the Nazi establishment. Because of his official status opponents of the regime regarded him with suspicion. Thus, Ulrich von Hassell – later executed after the attempted assassination of Hitler in July 1944 – was invited to contribute an article on the political situation in Europe to Berber's journal. He agreed to do so, but only on condition that he was not expected to produce Nazi propaganda. 'Berber', von Hassell added, 'who gives the impression of being very clever but somewhat mysterious, agreed to my conditions.'[6] The 'mysteriousness' was a necessary camouflage for any attempt to find a place for dissent from the regime's orthodoxy, and he was not mysterious enough to escape the attention of Nazi zealots. At best his influence was limited, and if he ventured to express opinions too liberal he was in trouble. His personality evidently did not help. One of his Foreign Ministry superiors, Franz Alfred Six, dismissed him as a man who 'had little energy, ate too well, slept too much, and did not have a systematic mind'. Herzstein himself sees Berber as a 'pedantic, cranky professor'.[7] Woodbrooke colleagues fifteen years earlier might well have conceded that they could just about recognise this unkind caricature.

Berber seems to have had a guilty conscience about his role in this committee, and it is not mentioned in his autobiography. He is less than candid, too, about the extent to which he had accepted the views of the regime. Elizabeth Fox Howard was the first Quaker who was able to make contact with Berber after the war, and she met him in Baden-Baden on 21 and 22 May 1948. She sent an account of the meeting to Alexander and others who had known him before the war. It has to be said that she had never shared Alexander's and Corder Catchpool's appreciation of Berber's role, and had not been sympathetic to their concern to put before the Allied authorities evidence of his good faith.[8] She was evidently all too ready to be shocked by the extent to which he was willing to explain Hitler's actions as at least reasonable. The occupation of Bohemia/Moravia in March 1939 was justified by the fact that it could have been used as the pivot of an attack on Germany. The attack on the USSR was essentially pre-emptive: it sought to prevent an inevitable Russian attack at a later date. He insisted, too, that it was a mistake to suppose that Hitler aimed at world conquest. He wanted Germany to be the dominant power in Europe, and saw a permanent role for the British Empire and for the United States in their spheres of influence. This was all perhaps explanation rather than apology, and he insisted that as early as 1940 he had told Ribbentrop that he wanted to resign, ostensibly because of ill-health, but actually because he felt unable to support Nazi policy.[9]

It is certain that Berber was genuinely outraged by the Nazi treatment of the Jews, and also that he did what he could to promote free and open discussion in an environment intractably hostile to any such liberty. He had seen keeping open communications with his friends in Britain as a means of fostering such freedom. It is important to recognise, though, that this did not mean he shared their opinions. In particular, and in profound opposition to Alexander, he regarded the League of Nations as a radical mistake, a romantic idyll, a utopian vision that distracted attention from the opportunities for genuine cooperation between powerful nations.[10] Alexander was nevertheless right to see in Berber someone who represented a Germany with whom peace would have been possible, the more so because he managed to survive, however precariously, as part of the state apparatus. There were, of course, Germans who were much more at odds with the regime than he was. Whether their existence might have led to an earlier end to the war is far from clear, but the Churchillian doctrine of 'absolute silence' meant that it was impossible to find out.

NOTES

Preface

1. Chakravarty 1991: 178.
2. Tinker 1976: 238.

1 The making of an internationalist

1. Fox 1952: 399.
2. Alexander 1920: 15.
3. Ibid.: 136.
4. *The Friend of China*, vol.2, July 1877: 194.
5. Gavit 1925: 98. The role of the Royal Commission is assessed in Joyce A. Mandancy's introduction to a reprint of its report, see.*Royal Commission* 2003.
6. Alexander 1920: 136.
7. Ibid.,: 210.
8. Alexander 1983: 11–12. The arrival of the first chiffchaff was always a notable event for James Crosfield. In a manuscript collection of his poems there is one devoted to 'The Return of the Chiff Chaff, March 14 1893':

   From the leafless treetops high
   Sounds thy cheery well-known strain,
   Telling summer now is nigh,
   Soon will come long days again.

9. Bootham diary, 30 August 1900.
10. HGA to C. G. Syers-Gibson, 3 October 1980, LSF Temp. MSS 971/1/5/12.
11. Pollard 1926: 188.

12. HGA to Ranjit Chetsingh LSF Temp. MSS 972/2/1/2, undated, but replying to letter from him of 28 October 1944.
13. Alexander 1929b: 95.
14. MS in possession of Roger and Hilda Sturge, 1 October 1917.
15. Bootham diary, 4 February 1905.
16. *The Observer*, n.d., vol. 27 p. 227.
17. *The Friend*, 6 March 1925.
18. Morley 1889, ch. 10: 208, 206.
19. *The Observer*, n.d., vol. 27, p. 232.
20. Polland 1926: 152.
21. *Friends Quarterly Examiner*, vol. 48 1914 pp. 127–8.
22. See the autobiographical notes included in Woodbrooke MSS.
23. See Ashford 1985.
24. 'Log-books' were kept from very early days at Woodbrooke. They include essays and poems from the current students, photographs, and a facetious diary of the term's events.
25. Edith Longstreth (née Wood) to HGA, undated but evidently after 1950, LSF Temp. MSS. 971/1/6/8.
26. Alexander 1920: 151.
27. HGA to Browning, 25 April 1913, Oscar Browning MSS, KCMA.
28. Oscar Browning's role in Cambridge undergraduate society is vividly depicted in Anstruther 1983.
29. HGA to Browning, 9 January 1909, Oscar Browning MSS, KCMA.
30. Ibid., 6 November 1908.
31. HGA to Olive Graham, 4 October 1917, LSF Temp. MSS 971/1/7/1–7.
32. *The Friend*, 5 June 1964, p. 684. Review of Christopher Hassll's *Rupert Brooke* and Arthur Marwick's *Clifford Allen: The Open Conspirator.*
33. Keynes 1972: 435–6. Keynes wrote this memoir in September 1938, and it was first published in 1949.
34. HGA to Browning, 16 November 1909, Oscar Browning MSS, KCMA.
35. Ibid., 7 December 1909.
36. 14 February and 18 August 1910., ibid. See also letters of 28 June and 6 July.
37. 14th December 1909, ibid. The idea of a martyr nation was favoured by Neave Brayshaw. See Brayshaw 1905, where he cites a sermon by the Rev. Dr Mackennal, envisaging England's becoming 'a sacrificial nation' by disbanding her armies and calling her fleets from the sea, concerned only to serve the well-being of the world.
38. HGA to Browning, 24 July 1911, Oscar Browning MSS, KCMA.
39. 2 August 1911, ibid.
40. 24 June 1911, ibid.
41. HGA to Olive Graham, 25 October 1917, LSF Temp. MSS971/1/7/2.
42. It was established on the initiative of J. M. Keynes and J. T. Sheppard. See Skidelsky 1983: 114.
43. HGA to Browning, 4 and 30 November 1911, Oscar Browning MSS, KCMA.
44. 17 June 1912, ibid.
45. *Cambridge Review*, 2 and 9 May 1912.
46. HGA to Browning, 5 May 1912, Oscar Browning MSS, KCMA.
47. 11 February 1912, ibid.
48. Martin-Harvey 1933: 405.
49. *Punch*, vol. 142 24 January 1912 pp. 68–9. There is a full account of the production in Styan 1982: p. 80–5. Styan emphasises Reinhardt's method of '"Sprengung des Bühnenrahmens", extending the action past the footlights, "bursting out of the frame"'.

50. I speak from personal experience.
51. At a Young Friends' conference at Swanwick in Derbyshire, in August 1911, John William Graham was not well received when he ventured to speak about 'some difficulties of the peace problem'. Force, he said was needed when dealing with savages, lunatics, children and strikers, and 'when wife and children were threatened, all peace principles would go to the wall'. But speaker after speaker dissented from this, and 'expressed their belief in the need for an ideal, greater and higher than their practice' (*The Friend*, 15 September 1911, p. 606).
52. HGA to Olive Graham, 25 October 1917, LSF Temp. MSS 971/1/7/2.
53. HGA to Browning, 5 May 1912, Oscar Browning MSS, KCMA.
54. *Granta*, 7 May 1910.
55. Autobiographical notes included in woodbrooke MSS.
56. Ibid.
57. Ibid.
58. Keynes 1972: 325 and 340. Dickinson was writing an appreciation of C. P. Sanger and Frank Ramsey in *The Nation and Athenaeum*, 22 February 1930.
59. Autobiographical notes included in woodbrooke MSS.
60. The list of those associated with the congress includes many subsequently famous names, e.g. T. G. Masaryk, M. K. Gandhi, Alfred Zimmern, Olive Schreiner, Friedrich Meinecke, Lucien Lévy-Bruhl, Emile Durkheim, Georg Simmel, Fridtjof Nansen, Jane Addams. Some, such as Maurice Maeterlinck and H. G. Wells, were already well known.
61. Dryhurst 1911: 9–10.
62. Browne 1910: xii, xix.
63. E. G. Browne to E. D. Ross, December 1908; see Ross 1943: 62.
64. This could be the military attaché to the British embassy in Teheran mentioned in Browne 1990: 309–10. This letter is dated 9 October 1912; earlier letters were sent on 22 May and 29 September.
65. LSF Temp. MSS 971/1/1/1.
66. See, for example, Mangone 1954: 88.
67. Angell 1909: 62–3.
68. Alexander 1920: 185.
69. Graham 1912, ch. 8: 193–203.
70. Fayle 1934: 67.
71. *The Friend*, 21 August 1914, p. 613, reprinted from the previous week's issue of *The Nation*.
72. Dickinson 1973: 189.
73. W.B. Yeats, 'Nineteen Hundred and Nineteen', lines 29–32.
74. HGA to Browning, 1 February 1913, Oscar Browning MSS, KCMA.
75. Keynes 1972: 448–9.
76. Keynes 1949. This is almost certainly the edition that Alexander saw, but which he recalls with some indistinctness.
77. HGA, 'Peace', LSF Temp. MSS 971/1/1/1.
78. Schoolfellow of Rupert Brooke, and an artist whose work, according to Roger Fry, revealed a personality peculiarly spontaneous, unconstrained, unaffected (Fry 1924: v).
79. Nicholas Bagenal to HGA, 19 September 1917, Woodbrooke MS Box 1.
80. HGA, A Friend's Friend', LSF Temp. MSS 971/1/1/1.
81. *The Friend*, n.s., 18 September 1914, vol. 54, pp. 688–9.
82. John Rickman to HGA, 1 November 1914, LSF Temp. MSS 971/2/1/6.
83. Forster 1973: 136.
84. Carnegie 1933, vol. 2.

85. Egerton 1978.
86. Baker and Baker, 1927: 204.
87. *The Friend*, 26 February 1915, reporting a meeting on 15 February. While the reference to the Old Testament is doubtless of the most generalised kind, Angell may have recalled Deuteronomy 20.10, which explains the need for Cities of Refuge in order 'that innocent blood be not shed in the land'.
88. 28 May 1915, p. 419, ibid.
89. Sibinga MS 10.
90. Baker and Baker 1927: 228.
91. Lansbury 1928: 213.
92. *The Friend*, 16 June 1916, pp. 459–0.
93. Autobiographical notes included in woodbrooke MSS.

2 *The humanising of an intellectual*

1. MS in possession of Roger and Hilda Sturge, 1 October 1917.
2. Olive to HGA, 23 October 1917. Horace's letters to Olive are in LSF Temp. MSS 971/1/7/1–7, Olive's are in LSF ACC 11039, but have not as yet (2009) been catalogued.
3. Gairdner, 1909: 216, and see in particular chapter 5. A second edition, published in 1920 with the title *The Rebuke of Islam*, omits the more censorious passages, and concluded that there was much in Islam in the past that had been brilliant, and that much was still admirable today. But humanity's future cannot lie with Islam: 'At the end of the avenue, whether theologically, ethically, or socially, there is a blank wall' (pp.169–70).
4. Olive Graham to HGA, 16 October 1917.
5. Olive Graham to HGA, 11 October 1917.
6. Olive Graham to HGA,24 November 1917.
7. HGA to Olive Graham, 21 August 1917, LSF Temp MSS 971/1/7/1–7.
8. The missionary was Basil Backhouse.
9. HGA to Olive Graham, 30 September and 4 October 1917, LSF Temp. MSS 971/1/7/1–7.
10. The poem is in the Woodbrooke log-book for the spring term of 1924.
11. Information from Gwen Marriage's daughter, Greta Webb.
12. *The Friend*, 7 December 1917, p. 912.
13. *Friends' Fellowship Papers* 8, 1916, pp. 207–13.
14. Hirst 1920, Commission 2: 27.
15. 'An Essay on Human Association', p.2. in Sibinga MSS.
16. Ibid., 86–8.
17. Ibid., 90–1.
18. Ibid., 92–3.
19. Woolf 1923: 345–6.
20. Hobhouse 1920: 111–4.
21. Ibid.: 104.
22. Cole 1920b: 9.
23. Cole 1920a: 212.
24. G. L. Dickinson to HGA, 25 June 1920, LSF Temp. MSS 971/1/2/3.
25. 'An Essay on Human Association', p. 53, in Sibinga MSS.
26. There are references to Alexander in all the issues of *Portcullis* published in 1917. The remarkable extract from Thucydides may be found on pp. 16–17 of the February issue. Only the Captain of the First XV could have afforded to be so heretical.

27. C. F. Pierce was appointed headmaster in 1915. He had an undistinguished degree in theology from Oxford, and before going to Cranbrook had been Chaplain and assistant master at Giggleswick School.
28. Kendall 1913: 196. The book was published under the pseudonym of 'Fourth Form'.
29. HGA to Olive Graham, 29 March 1918, LSF Temp. MSS 971/1/7/1–7.
30. He might well have been. According to Guy Kendall, while many boys were allowed to smoke at home, 'to do so at school might entail expulsion' (Kendall 1913: 202.
31. Alexander 1920: 190.
32. Ibid. 202–3.
33. JGA to HGA, 12 January 1918.
34. Olive Graham to HGA, 13 September 1917, LSF ACC 11039.
35. Presumably he changed his mind in mid-sentence: did he think of writing 'or anyone else in my family', and then realise that some relatives would come even if the wedding were in Allonby? Having lost his father and his favourite brother so recently, he would none the less feel acutely bereft.
36. HGA to Olive Graham, 10 March and 24 July 1918, LSF Temp. MSS 971/1/7/1–7.
37. Olive Graham to HGA, 'Saturday', i.e. 27 July 1918, LSF ACC 11039.
38. LSF Temp. MSS 577/19 for the extensive correspondence on this matter, and *The Friend*, 9 March 1923.
39. When in London at this time, Alexander stayed either with John Rickman, recently returned from a revolutionised Russia, or at the 1917 Club in Gerrard Street, described by J. A. Hobson as 'a free meeting place for "advanced" men and women concerned with political and economic reforms, or with new literary or artistic movements.' Members included E. M. Forster, Ramsay MacDonald, Oswald Mosley, Henry W. Nevinson, Bertrand Russell and Olive Schreiner. It did not survive, Hobson suggests, because rents were too high and membership fees too low, and often unpaid (Hobson 1938: 125).
40. HGA to Olive Graham, 19 September 1919, LSF Temp. MSS 971/1/7/1–7.
41. Ibid. The Browns provided him with a copy of *The Young Visiters* to divert him on the journey to Birmingham: an indication of the household's cheerful character.
42. *The Friend*, 17 October 1919, pp. 638–9.
43. Olive Graham to HGA, 5 June 1919, LSF ACC 11039.
44. HGA to Olive Graham, 9 July 1919, and see 4 April 1919, LSF Temp. MSS 971/1/7/1–7.
45. HGA to Olive, 3 October 1919, LSF Temp. MSS 971/1/7/1–7. They soon moved to 78 Gibbons Road.
46. HGA to Olive, 1 October 1919, ibid.
47. Froude 1894a: 362, 379.
48. Froude 1894b, vol. 1: 98. Froude presumably has in mind here a letter Erasmus wrote to Louis Marlianus on 25 March 1520: 'We must bear almost anything rather than throw the world into confusion. There are seasons when we must even conceal the truth. The actual facts of things are not to be blurted out at all times and places, and in all companies' (Froude 1894a: 238). Alexander may have remembered this in his later diplomatic missions.
49. HGA to Olive Graham, 27 September 1919, LSF Temp. MSS 971/1/7/1–7.
50. Ibid., 10 October 1919.
51. Ibid., 18 October 1919.
52. Rickman to HGA, 11 January 1920, LSF Temp. MSS 971/2/1/6. John W. Graham made a similar assessment. He warned Olive that she must take great care not to be

too affected by Woodbrooke's 'excitiing atmosphere, particularly the atmosphere of religion'. It wasn't natural to have 'anything more than occasional outbursts of acute consciousness with regard to divine things. The ordinary religious life should be quietly natural and the more unconscious the better' (J. W. Graham to Olive Graham, 11 July 1919).

53. HGA to Olive Graham, 24 December 1919, LSF Temp. MSS 971/1/7/1–7.
54. Ibid.
55. HGA to Olive Graham, 31 December 1919, LSF Temp. MSS 971/1/7/1–7. See *The Friend*, 19 December 1919.

3 The discovery of Gandhi

1. Dickinson 1926: 492.
2. Dickinson 1920: 104.
3. See Porter, 1995: 58–78. Porter describes the Aberystwyth chair as 'a brilliant academic innovation', so perhaps some credit should go to Merttens and Woodbrooke too.
4. Zimmern 1918: 112.
5. See Zimmern 1922.
6. No one can argue that the Hitlerite campaign to annul Versailles was unexpected. In a debate in the National Constituent Assembly of German Austria, 7 June 1919, Otto Bauer pointed out the intrinsic instability of the new Czechoslovakian state, where six and a half million Czechs would rule three and a half million Germans – as well as large numbers of Hungarians, Ukrainians and Poles. How, he asked, could this new polyglot state, when it was 'ultimately destroyed by the desire of the nations for liberty, fall without setting the whole continent once more ablaze?' See a report filed in Philip Noel-Baker's papers in Churchill College Cambridge, 4.438.
7. HGA to Duncan Wood, 22 November 1974, Woodbrooke MSS, 4.438.
8. Alexander 1924: 15.
9. Ibid.: 205.
10. *The Friend*, 2 November 1923, p. 866.
11. Alexander 1924: 183–4.
12. Ibid.: 185.
13. Ibid.: 187–8.
14. Ibid.: 203.
15. Zimmern 1918.
16. Personal communication, 30 March 2004.
17. Berber and Schubert may have found their way to Woodbrooke through contact with Alexander's fellow Quaker John S. Stephens, who in the early 1920s was English lektor in Frankfurt University.
18. *The Friend*, 25 July 1930, p. 688.
19. Letters to H. G. Wood, 6 November 922, Woodbrooke MSS.
20. The provision of a strictly limited quantity of cake at tea-time remains an enduring characteristic of Woodbrooke life.
21. Log-book for autumn 1923, Woodbrocke MSS.
22. Each Woodbrooke student was assigned to a member of staff who was responsible for his or her general welfare, and was known as their 'shepherd'.
23. Log-book for spring 1924, Woodbroooke MSS. That same term one of the evening entertainments had been a 'shadowgraph' representation of the *Cautionary Tales*. 'The realism of the operation on the youth who ate bits of string was so ghastly, and the sight of yard after yard of string being drawn from his middle was so

sickening that it is believed several Woodbrookers gave up their tea and cocoa between meals for at least a week.'

24. W. Schubert to HGA, 27 March 1923, LSF Temp. MSS 971/2/1/1.
25. His standing may have been improved by the publication of an article of his in the April 1925 issue of the Union of Democratic Control's monthly *Foreign Affairs*, 'The Way of Austria', pp. 235–6.
26. W. Schubert to HGA, 4 November 1926 and 21 and February 1927, LSF Temp. MSS 971/2/1/1. Schubert's article on South Tyrol appeared in the 'World Outlook' section of *The Friend*, 4 December 1925, p. 1061.
27. LSF Temp. MSS 21 September 1926, 971/2/1/1.
28. 15 December 1925, ibid.
29. 28 January 1926, ibid.
30. 9 February 1927, ibid.
31. Schubert 1926. Schubert's unfavourable assessment is made in a letter dated 4 November 1926.
32. W, Schubert to HGA, 21 January 1925, LSF Temp. MSS 971/2/1/1.
33. Unpublished manuscript in Woodbrooke MSS.
34. Berber 1924: 24–37.
35. Philip Schwabe, 'The Good Samaritans', Woodbrooke log-book, autumn 1926.
36. D. Malcolm, 'Our Fellows', spring 1927 log-book, Woodbrooke MSS.
37. Autumn 1926 log-book, diary entry for 11 December, Woodbrooke MSS.
38. Sibinga MS 6. *The Undying Fire* is the title of a novel by H. G. Wells, published in 1919. It is a Wellsian version of the Book of Job, and shows how a schoolmaster's faith in his educational ideals survives discouragement after discouragement. Olive was particularly impressed by the title: 'It gave me a new conception of the indomitable spirit of man, and I have treasured the phrase through many a deep place.' Letter in possession of Sarah Graham, 28 October 1926.
39. Emile Coué, 1857–1926.
40. Brooks 1922: 116.
41. Olive Graham to HGA, 10 September 1924, LSF ACC 11039.
42. Quoted from an unpublished manuscript, 'Silence: An Indian Adventure', which Alexander wrote over several years in the early 1930s. See Sibibga MS 1, p. 7.
43. Alexander 1924a: 7. See LSF Temp. MSS 971/1/3/3/1 for a copy of this scarce pamphlet.
44. Sibinga MS 1, pp. 8–9.
45. Reports to India Sub-Committee of the Anti-Opium Board, LSF Temp. MSS 971/3/3, and *The Friend*, 11 April and 14 November 1924.
46. Alexander 1930: 8.
47. *The Friend*, 16 October 1925, p. 926.
48. *Times of Assam*, 12 September 1925.
49. Nehru was in Switzerland at the time, accompanying his wife while she was receiving medical treatment there. He evidently made a flying visit to Derbyshire to help Sinha, with whom he will have been acquainted in Allahabad. See India Office Library MSS, L/P&J/12/303. Nehru's younger sister, Krishna Hutheesing, relates how at this period her brother travelled widely in western Europe, so that his intervention on Sinha's behalf was natural enough. See Hutheesing 1944: 36.
50. A late autobiographical note says that Edward Cadbury was involved in the award of the Travelling Fellowship. One aspect of the tour which is obscure is what arrangements were made for the care of Olive during this prolonged absence from Birmingham. Her youngest sister, Agnes, may well have come to stay with her, as she did during Alexander's later mission in 1930.
51. Purcell and Hallsworth 1928: 42. The two men were anxious to promote trade

union organisation to lift the workers 'out of the morass of filthy and ghastly conditions' which they had witnessed.

52. Alexander 1929b: 24. Journal letter 3, HGA to Olive Graham, 6–7 October 1927, LSF Temp. MSS 971/2/1/7.
53. Ibid.; cf. Alexander 1929b: 21–3.
54. Shaw 1889: 82. Shaw originally delivered this lecture to the Economic Section of the British Association in 1888.
55. Alexander 1929b: 22.
56. Ibid.: 33–4.
57. Ibid.: 25–7.
58. HGA to Olive, journal letter 4, LSF Temp. MSS 971/2/1/7.
59. Sibinga MS 6.
60. Alexander 1929b: 63.
61. HGA to Olive, journal letter 5, LSF Temp. MSS 971/2/1/7.
62. Alexander 1929b: 78.
63. A. A. Purcell (1872–1935) and J. Hallsworth (1884–1974). Hallsworth was at this time Secretary-General of the National Union of Distributive and Allied Workers. Alexander makes a not uncomplimentary assessment of Purcell in journal letter 6 (HGA to Olive Temp. MSS 971/2/1/7). But did not venture to print it. He describes him as 'a great character – a real vulgar, shrewd Englishman, such as Chesterton might applaud, and a neo-Marxist. . . . He is a very shrewd observer, with a remarkable grasp of economic realities in many of the countries of the world, derived from personal observation.' He did not attach much importance to nationalism or to 'cultural ideals'. Alexander remarks that the Indians who met him took his 'vulgar humour' in their stride, and 'found him the most astonishing human being they had ever met'. After Purcell had returned to Britain he became active in the Commonwealth of India League, assisting Krishna Menon particularly in his contacts with the trade union movement. See Chakravarty, 1997: 117, 241–50.
64. Alexander 1929b: 99.
65. Ibid.: 102.
66. Alexander 1930: 36.
67. Information from Edward Milligan, 10 August 1998.
68. *The Friend*, 30 March and 15 June 1928, pp. 255, 540–1.
69. Alexander 1929b: 109.
70. Ibid.: 114.
71. Ibid.: 141.
72. HGA to Olive, journal letter 8, LSF Temp. MSS 971/2/1/7. Dutch familiarity with Woodbrooke is unsurprising. As former Woodbrookers were the nucleus of a considerable 'sect', based on the Woodbrooke outpost in Barchem. While some wished to remain in touch with Woodbrooke itself and with the Christian tradition, others were embarked on a quest 'for a new culture and a new religion' (*Woodbrooke Journal*, no. 2, December 1921: 29).
73. HGA to Olive, journal letter 5, LSF Temp. MSS 971/2/1/7. Cf. Alexander 1929b: 51.
74. Alexander 1929b: 177. Alexander does not mention Keynes or Lowes Dickinson, but the information is supplied from Gopal 1989: 79.
75. Alexander 1929b: 181–4.
76. Ibid.: 193.
77. Ibid.: 201.
78. Ibid.: 213–29.
79. *Woodbrooke Journal*, no. 15, June 1928: 19.
80. Purcell and Hallsworth 1928: 43.

81. Sibinga MS 1, p. 11. C. *Friends and Young India*, a pamphlet he wrote for the Friends' Service Council in 1929, especially p. 4: 'We may well look with awe and wonder at the rebirth of such a great people.' It is remarkable, he continues, that two of the people who rise pre-eminent out of the ferment, Gandhi and Tagore, have an affinity with Friends.

4 *Quaker interventions*

1. 'Responsible Government for India', pp. 4, 6., Sibinga MS 5.
2. Chakravarty 1997: 114.
3. Ibid.: 118, 151 n.161.
4. *The Spectator*, 18 and 25 January 1930.
5. Sibinga MS 1, p. 14.
6. Tagore 1930: 162.
7. *The Friend*, 23 May 1930. Cf. Tagore 1930: 169ff.
8. *The Spectator*, 'Thoughts on Mr Gandhi's Arrest', 10 May 1930; 10th May, *New Statesman* 'India after Gandhi', 1930.
9. Sibinga MS 1, pp.21–2.
10. *The Friend*, 30 May 1930, pp. 490–2. Cf. Tagore 1930: 163–4.
11. I am indebted to Edward Milligan for this anecdote, which he had from Elizabeth Painter (1891–1964) who had been present.
12. See *The Friend* for 30 May and 6 June 1930.
13. Andrews actually expected to leave Marseilles for Bombay on 13 June. But he seems to have asked Alexander to go instead at a meeting in Friends' House on Thursday 19 June. See, C. F. Andrew's to HGA, 2 and 21 June, LSF Temp. MSS 971/2/2/2.
14. Sibinga MS 1, pp.18–19.
15. Ibid., p.19.
16. Ibid., pp.20–1.
17. *The Times,* 8 June 1982. He was born in 1881.
18. Hugh Richardson to HGA, 2 June 1930, Woodbrooke Library.
19. Sibinga MS 1, pp. 23–4.
20. HGA to Olive, 23 July 1930, LSF Temp. MSS 577/119.
21. Sibinga MS 1, p. 28.
22. Ibid., p.27.
23. One is 'Silence: An Indian Adventure', a retrospective account already quoted; the other is an untitled series of chapters evidently written soon after leaving India, Sibinga MS. 1.
24. HGA to Olive, 18 August 1930. LSF Temp. MSS 577/119.
25. Sibinga MS 1, p. 30.
26. HGA to Olive, 19 August 1930, LSF Temp. MSS 577/119.
27. Ibid.
28. HGA to Olive, 29 August 1930, ibid.
29. Sibinga MS 1, pp. 31–2.
30. HGA to Olive, 4 September and 7 September 1930, LSF Temp. MSS 577/119.
31. Sibinga MS 1, pp. 38–9.
32. Letters to the Viceroy, 17 September 1930, Irwin Viceregal Correspondence, L/P&J/Irwin 653, India Office Library.
33. HGA to Olive, 4–6 September 1930, LSF Temp. MSS 577/119.
34. 7 September 1930, ibid.
35. 15–16 September 1930, ibid.
36. Letters from the Viceroy, 15 September 1930, Irwin Viceregal Correspondence,

L/P&J/Irwin Euro C152/25 487c, India Office Library. Cf. Irwin to HGA, LSF Temp. MSS 577/119, 18 September 1930, and Sibinga MS 1, p. 41.

37. Sibinga MS.1, pp. 34–5.
38. HGA to Olive, Sibinga MS 1, pp. 42–6. 1 October. 1930, LSF Temp. MSS 577/119.
39. Sibinga MS. 1, pp. 40–1.
40. Ibid., pp. 54–5.
41. Ibid.
42. Ibid., pp. 50–1.
43. Letters from Irwin, 8th October.1930, Irwin Viceregal Correspondence, L/P&J/ Irwin Euro C152/25 534a, India Office Library.
44. Roberts 1991: 42–3.
45. *The Friend*, 28 November 1930, p. 1076.
46. Ibid.
47. This was still the view held by experienced and influential commentators like Sir Reginald Craddock. His book *The Dilemma in India* 1929 betrays its unease in the ferocity of its judgements, but he will have been seen at the time as an authority difficult to challenge. And Roland Priestman, one of the Quaker missionaries in mid-India, affirmed that 'the Congress Party appears to be much stronger than it really is' – suggesting that it was supported by perhaps 10 per cent of the population. He encouraged Friends to 'follow the liberal and soundest thought of the best leaders, who are out for swaraj, with safeguards to the best interests of India' *The Friend*, 14 November 1930, p. 1041. Gandhi was *not* among the 'best leaders'.
48. *Indian Round Table Conference* 1931: 27.
49. Alexander 1984: 66–7.
50. The 24-page handwritten MS is entitled 'India's New Place in the World'.
51. The boycott had particularly damaged textile exports, where some categories had declined up to 45 per cent. See the figures quoted in Gopal 1957: 97. The impact of the boycott was emphasised by Sapru's colleague M. R. Jayakar in his first speech to the conference. See *Indian Round Table Conference* 1931: 45.
52. *The Times*, 19 January 1931.
53. V.L. Pandit to HGA, 24 March 1931, LSF Temp. MSS 971/2/2/2.
54. *Young India*, 16 April 1931. See Gandhi 1979–94, vol. 46: 3–8.
55. Chakravarty 1997, vol. 2: 96.
56. Ibid.: 120.
57. Ibid.: 130–1.
58. HGA to James Hunt, 23 January 1976, LSF Temp. MSS 577/69.
59. *The Friend,* 9 October and 23 October 1931.
60. From an account of 88 Knightsbridge read to the Woodbrooke 'Log Night', December 1931 Sibinga MS 2.
61. Alexander 1984: 76–7.
62. HGA, 'India and the National Congress', Sibinga MS. 2.
63. Agatha Harrison gives details in a letter to Gandhi, 5 May 1938. See Birla: 1977, vol 3: 164.
64. G. Lowes Dickinson to HGA, 5 November 1931, LSF Temp. MSS 971/2/1/2, and 11 March 1929, LSF Temp. MSS 971/1/2/3. Cf. *Young India*, 19 November 1931, included in Gandhi 1979–94, vol. 48: 261–4.
65. Scott 1971: 216.
66. The late Professor Paul Edwards, of Edinburgh University, was the then five-year-old child. He told me that he distinctly remembered thinking that, though no doubt as great a man as his father said, Gandhi didn't dress very well.
67. From Rolland's journal, September 1930, in Rolland 1969: 454.

68. Chakravarty 1991, vol. 2: 60–2, 173, 364, 368.
69. Ibid.: 62, 196, 259.
70. Ibid.: 96.
71. HGA to Sir Samuel Hoare, 20 January 1932, LSF Temp. MSS 577/100.
72. Gandhi 1979–94, vol. 48: 426–7.
73. Sir Samuel Hoare to Ramsay MacDonald, 8 and 13 April 1932, India Office Library MSS L/PO/6/65 ff.225–8.

5 The 1930s

1. Smuts, 1931: 13–15.
2. Fritz Berber to HGA, 28 February, 6 and 13 April, 19 May 1933, LSF Temp. MSS 971/1/2/5. The first words of the Sermon on the Mount are 'Blessed are the poor in spirit, for theirs is the kingdom of heaven' (Matthew 5.3).
3. HGA, report of journey through eastern Germany, August 1933, p. 3, LSF Temp MSS 577/97.
4. Ibid., p.1.
5. Ibid., p.4.
6. Ibid., p.6.
7. Ibid., pp. 12–13.
8. Evans 1929: 257–8.
9. Ibid.: 7, 9; T. P. Conwil Evans to HGA, 14 September 1933, LSF Temp. MSS 577/97; *Prometheus Unbound* IV, 570ff.
10. There is a note of contributions to pay the cost of Berber's January visit in LSF Temp. MSS 577/98.
11. Wordsworth, *The Prelude* (1805) IX, 19. The poet is embarking on his engagement with the French Revolution.
12. Text of talk by Berber on the political situation in Germany, 18 July 1933, pp. 8–9, LSF Temp. MSS 577/97.
13. Berber to HGA, 14 December 1933, LSF Temp. MSS 577/97.
14. Arnold-Forster to HGA, 13 January 1934, ibid. 577/98. Berber's examination of the doctrine of collective security in *Sicherheit und Gerechtigkeit* shows that he understood the doctrine of collective security very well, and rejected it.
15. Steed to HGA, 9 January 1934, ibid.
16. Berber to HGA, 14 March 1934, ibid.
17. Buxton to HGA, 9 March 1934, ibid.
18. In his correspondence before publication, Berber refers to this book as *Grundlagen Deutscher Völkerrechtspolitik*, basic principles of the German approach to international law, which sounds more acceptable to Nazi ears, and was perhaps the working title for the original project. The more provocative title was apparently inserted at the last moment. See Berber to HGA, 24 June 1934, LSF Temp. MSS 577/98.
19. Berber 1934: 54.
20. Berber to HGA, 4 May 1934, LSF Temp. MSS 577/98.
21. Arnold-Forster to HGA, 24 February 1934, ibid.
22. Toynbee 1967: 277–78, 286.
23. Berber 1986: 77–8.
24. Ibid.: 87.
25. Ibid.: 92–3.
26. Quotation untraced.
27. LSF Temp. MSS 577/91; 971/1/3/2.
28. Carl Heath to William Temple, 4 July 1932, LSF Temp. MSS 41/1.

29. Wyllie 1934: 190–1, 215–16. For good measure, Lieutenant-Colonel Wyllie thought that Hindus, as a matter of urgency, should be educated in elementary morality.
30. Agatha Harrison to Carl Heath, 13 February 1933, LSF Temp. MSS 577/7.
31. Birla 1977, vol.2: 80, 2 July 1935.
32. Agatha Harrison to Carl Heath, 16 October 1936, LSF Temp. MSS 577/7.
33. Agatha Harrison to HGA, 6 October 1933, LSF Temp. MSS 577/101.
34. See *The Friend*, 20 December 1935, p. 1202; 17 January 1936, p. 62.
35. Agatha Harrison to Carl Hoath, 2 April 1936, LSF Temp. MSS 577/7.
36. Letters from Atma S. Kamlani to HGA, 10 May and 19 June 1932, ibid. 577/101. Kamlani says that Reynolds' article on the Round Table Conference is 'written in an aggressive tone or it may be just vigorous.'
37. This was the suggestion made in a report to the Intelligence Bureau, 28 August 1930, India Office Papers L/P&J/12/314. Presumably Alexander had been observed listening politely to a patriotic song.
38. Low 1977: 174ff.
39. Address to the ICG by Nehru, LSF Temp. MSS 42/1/1935–6.
40. *The Friend*, 29 May 1936, p. 508.
41. India Office Papers L/P&J/12/314, 21 October 1936.
42. Birla 1977, vol. 2: 56–7, 20 June 1935.
43. 5 November 1936, RAB F4/173, Trinity College Cambridge.
44. 10 and 11 December 1936, RAB F3/1 8(1), 10 (3), Trinity College Cambridge.
45. R. T. Peel to Mr Crombie, 3 December 1936, India Office Papers L/P&J/12/314. Alexander's claims about government violence in Bengal in 1930–1 'is a monstrous distortion of the facts. So is the reference to the shooting at Hijli which, you will remember, the Court of Enquiry found was entirely justified.' Butler annotated this last claim, 'Unfortunately *no*'.
46. RAB F3/1 14, Trinity College Cambridge.
47. Alfred Jacob, the Friend in charge of the FSC programme in Spain, wrote that 'Our effort is simply to do the works of peace in the midst of war, affirming the rights of human personality which war denies. It is all that lovers of peace can do at a time like this. We have begun with children, because no one regards children as reds or anti-reds.' Alfred Jacob to Judith Corcoran of the British Youth Peace Assembly, 8 December 1936, Friends House MSS, FSC/R/SP/1/1.
48. 27 April 1937, RAB F3/1 15, Trinity College Cambridge.
49. *The Times*, 7 and 8 May 1937.
50. HGA to Butler, 9 May 1937, Butler to HGA, 11 May 1937, RAB F3/1 18, 19, Trinity College Cambridge.
51. 30th May 1937, RAB F1/82 (1), (4), Trinity College Cambridge. See the account of Gokhale in Alexander, 1961: 134–7. As was remarked at the end of the previous chapter, Alexander was much preoccupied at this time with plans for a society modelled on the Servants of India, and he may well have mentioned this to Butler.
52. Published by Gollancz for the New Fabian Research Bureau, Pamphlet 39.
53. R. A. Butler to HGA, 14 June 1938, LSF Temp. MSS 577/12.
54. *Hansard Parliamentary Debates, Lords*, vol. 83, cols. 1001–1011.
55. See LSF Temp. MSS 971/1/4/10. For a retrospective view, see ibid. 971/1/4/5.
56. Log-book for spring 1932. See Murray-Brown 1972: 155–6. Kenyatta's residence was paid for by Charles Roden Buxton.

6 *The Second World War*

1. *The Friend*, 4 June 1937, pp. 539–40. The story of the rich young man is told in Matthew 19.16–29, Mark 10.17–30, and Luke 18.18–30.

2. There is a copy of the petition with supporting names in the Lloyd George papers in the library of the House of Lords.
3. May/June 1937, quoted by Hughes 1964: 144. Catchpool is himself quoting words that he had written in 1933, and felt still to be valid.
4. Hughes 1964: 133–9, 154–5.
5. Report to Foreign Office by HGA on the situation in Germany, 30 November 1938, Foreign Office papers 371 21665, C15026.
6. Undated report by Muriel Lester to friends in Britain, LSF Temp. MSS 577/96.
7. Report to Foreign Office by HGA of a conversation with Fritz Berber, Foreign Office papers 371 22973, 10 June 1939.
8. Tennant 1957: 223.
9. HGA to Butler, 22 August 1939, Foreign Office papers 371 22976. The Nazi–Soviet Pact was signed the following day.
10. HGA to Butler, 3 September 1939, ibid. 371 23028. The letter evidently repeats the substance of the telephone call.
11. Ibid. 371 24407. The letter is dated 5 September 1939, but has been filed under 3 April 1940.
12. *Documents Concerning* . . . 1939: 152.
13. Noack 1952: 10.
14. Ibid.: 11–13.
15. Berggrav 1960.
16. See for example Deutsch 1968.
17. *Hansard's Parliamentary Debates, Commons*, vol. 351, col. 1922, 3 October 1939.
18. Ibid., cols 1870–4, 3 October 1939.
19. See the Lloyd George papers in the library of the House of Lords, G/50–60. In a letter to Sir Herbert Dunnico, of the eminently respectable International Peace Society, Lloyd George remarked that he had been 'overwhelmed with letters and messages from people of all parties, and from every part of the British Isles, supporting the line I took' (G/50/1, responding to Dunnico's letter of 4 October). The sheer quantity of this material is extraordinary, and very probably unique.
20. HGA to Chamberlain, 8 October 1939, LSF Temp. MSS 577/94. Writing on the 8 October, Chamberlain remarked that in the previous week he had received 1,860 letters urging him to 'stop the war'. Another 590 had urged him *not* to do so (1946: 424). Chamberlain could count his letters; Lloyd George would have had to take on extra staff to count *his*.
21. Meeting report, LSF Temp. MSS 577/95.
22. Ibid., 9th November 1939.
23. Noack 1952: 22–3.
24. The debate was on the peace appeal of the King of Belgium and the Queen of the Netherlands, an integral part of the Scandinavian peace strategy. Bell put forward the Berggrav proposals, but they were dismissed by peers like Lord Balfour of Burleigh, who said that any talk of negotiation would put an end to any change of heart in Germany: 'It will infallibly be interpreted as a sign of weakness' *Hansard's Parliamentary Debates, Lords*, vol. 115, cols. 251–6, 13 December 1939. Berggrav was in the gallery for the debate, and recalled this sentence when he interviewed Hermann Goering some five weeks later on 21 January. Goering told Berggrav that any German concessions would be seized upon by her enemies, who would simply assume that they were now free to exploit their advantage. Berggrav retorted that the British had exactly the same fear. Such mutual anxiety should not be allowed to take the world into total war. Berggrav 1960: 135–6].
25. HGA to Butler, 12 November 1939, LSF Temp. MSS 577/94.

26. 5 January 1940, RAB E3/6 220–5, Trinity College Cambridge. Butler was vehemently opposed to the so-called Narvik plan, comparing it with another Churchillian project in the First World War, the expedition to the Dardanelles. See Memoranda, Butler to Lord Halifax, 11 January 1940, RAB G11 12–13.
27. 2nd January 1940, Foreign Office papers 371 24405.
28. 10 January 1940, Foreign Office papers 371 24364. The broadcast is published in Temple 1940: 83–90.
29. Paul Sturge to R. A. Butler, RAB E3/6 211–19, Trinity College Cambridge.
30. *News Review*, 21 December 1939, vol. 8, no. 25, p. 1.
31. 16 and 18 March 1940, RAB E3/6 239, 243, Trinity College Cambridge.
32. Minutes of the Peace Committee Emergency Group, 7 February 1940, LSF Temp. MSS 577/95.
33. HGA to Butler, 29 February 1940, RAB E3/6 232–7, Trinity College Cambridge.
34. WM (40) 16th Conclusion, Minute 8, The Vatican, Public Record Office, Cab. 65.11.
35. Piotrowski 1961: 227–9.
36. The NPC letter, dated 5 March 1940, is filed in Foreign Office papers, 371 24406. FO officials' views may be seen in the same file. Robert Vansittart was particularly scornful of the way the Americans were behaving like ostriches in order, he suggested, to secure the re-election of Roosevelt as President later in the year.
37. Foreign Office papers 371 24407. Officials were commenting on Roosevelt's concern that the allies should make clear that they had no plans to dismember Germany.
38. Emergency Group of Friends Peace Committee minutes, 17 April 1940, LSF Temp. MSS 577/95.
39. Cotteridge Preparative Meeting minutes, 7 April 1940. A special Monthly Meeting on 19 March had encouraged meetings to hold such discussions.
40. HGA to Butler, 21 May 1940 and Butler to HGA, 22 May, LSF Temp. MSS 577/93.
41. HGA to Halifax, 30 December 1940, ibid.
42. George 1964: 128. The author is citing an account by Labour's Assistant National Agent in 1958.
43. Noel-Baker to HGA, 17 January 1941 and HGA to Noel-Baker, 19 January, LSF Temp. MSS 577/15.
44. See Louis 1992.
45. HGA to Agatha Harrison, 25 May 1940, LSF Temp. MSS 577/82a.
46. Carl Heath to HGA, 20 June 1940, ibid. 577/12, cf. RAB E3/6 246, Trinity College Cambridge.
47. HGA to R. A. Butler, RAB E3/6 257–8, Trinity College Cambridge.
48. These developments are detailed in Tendulkar 1952: 368–9.
49. The resolution is printed in Gandhi 1958–82, vol. 73: 1–3.
50. HGA to R. A. Butler, 1 October 1940, RAB E3/6 260, Trinity College Cambridge.
51. HGA to L. S. Amery, 3 October 1940, LSF Temp. MSS 577/12.
52. Amery to HGA, 14 October 1940, ibid.
53. Heath to Gandhi, 25 October 1940, ibid. 577/104; Heath to Amery, 25 October and Harrison to Heath, 31 October 1940; Heath to Alexander, 18 November 1940, ibid., 577/12.
54. HGA to Butler, 1 October and 1 November 1940, Butler to HGA? 2 November, RAB E3/6 260–6, Trinity College Cambridge.
55. HGA to Butler, 26 December 1940 and Butler to HGA ?28 December, ibid. 267–8.

56. William Pitt, Earl of Chatham, supported the aspirations of the American colonists to self-government, in opposition to the attempt at suppression by the government of Lord North.
57. HGA to Butler, 14 January 1941, LSF Temp. MSS 577/12.
58. HGA to Harrison, 21 February 1941, ibid. His various proposals may be found in the same folder, to Amery 8 and 18 October 1940, and to Sir George Schuster, 21, 28 February and 9 May 1941. See also HGA to Noel-Baker 28 January 1941, 577/15.
59. Carl Heath to Agatha Harrison, 25 February 1942, ibid., 47/1.
60. HGA to William Paton, 4 July 1941 and HGA to Agatha Harrison, 27th June, ibid., 577/12.
61. HGA to Amery, 25 July 1941, ibid. 577/106.
62. Wilfrid E. Littleboy to Churchill, 30 August 1941, based on Minute 25 of London Yearly Meeting, LSF Temp. MSS 971/1/2/11.
63. HGA to Amery, 14 November 1941, ibid., 577/11.
64. HGA to Amery, 4 December 1941 and HGA to ?, 17 December, ibid.
65. HGA to Stewart, 6 January 1942, ibid.
66. Alexander 1984: 112.
67. Agatha Harrison to Gandhi, 11 March 1942, LSF Temp. MSS 577/107.
68. HGA to Harrison, 2 May 1942, ibid.
69. Carl Heath to Agatha Harrison, 28 February 1942, LSF Temp. MSS 883/2/11. Cf. I. Harrison 1956 110–11.
70. Minute by Anthony Eden, 6 October 1941, Foreign Office papers 371/26543.
71. Ibid.
72. Butler to HGA, 20th October 1941, LSF Temp. MSS 577/14.
73. January 1941, Foreign Office papers 371 26542.
74. *The Friend*, 13 March 1942, pp. 85–6.
75. Norman Cartwright spoke to me in these terms when I interviewed him in 1995.
76. 8 September 1940, Cotteridge PM minutes.
77. *Woodbrooke International Journal*, June 1942, no. 43 pp. 2–5.

7 To India with the Friends' Ambulance Unit

1. From 1934 to 1940 Harold Loukes was on the staff of St Stephen's College, Delhi. He and his wife Mary then started a school in Darjeeling. After the end of the war they returned to Britain, and for many years he was Reader in Education in Oxford University.
2. Agatha Harrison to HGA, 27 January 1942, LSF Temp. MSS 577/113.
3. M. Desai's address to the Yearly Meeting of Friends, *Harijan*, 15 March 1942.
4. FAU Joint India Committee minutes for 27 July 1942 meeting (seen in AFSC archive).
5. Leo Amery to Lord Linlithgow, 10 August 1942, in Mansergh and Lumby 1971, vol. 2: 651.
6. Report by Richard Symonds to FAU about a meeting with Paul Patrick, 29 April 1942, LSF FSC/IN/9.
7. From Alexander's first journal letter to friends and colleagues in the UK, 6 June 1942, LSF Temp. MSS 577/82a.
8. HGA to Stewart Meacham, 26 March 1971, ibid., 577/67.
9. FAU Joint Indian Committee minutes, for 27 July 1942 (seen in AFSC archive).
10. Information from Richard Symonds.
11. *Harijan*, 5 July 1942, p. 214.
12. Mansergh and Lumby 1971: 385–7. 14 July 1942. This undertaking was reaffirmed

in the All-India Congress Committee resolution of 8 August, which precipitated the arrest of the Congress leaders: after independence India would cooperate with the Allies 'in the common task of resisting aggression'. (ibid.: 621–4).

13. Slade 1960: 230–3.
14. 1977, vol. 4: 310, June 1942.
15. Symonds 1988: 10. The senior official was Paul Patrick.
16. Davies 1947: 299.
17. Ibid.: 300.
18. Symonds 1988.
19. The introduction was provided by H. S. Suhrawardy's uncle, Sir Hassan Suhrawardy, one of Leo Amery's advisers in London.
20. There is a note about Suhrawardy among papers written by Alexander in 1979–80. He mentions the problem of the recruitment of Muslims in a letter to Agatha Harrison, 1 October 1942, LSF Temp. MSS 577/82a.
21. Symonds 1988: 16.
22. Letter to Brandon Cadbury, 18 January 1943 (AFSC archive).
23. Information from Richard Symonds, and from Clement Alexandre in a letter to the author dated 29 November 1993.
24. Wickenden 1989: 181ff., esp. 189–90.
25. HGA to Penderel Moon, 17 March 1944, LSF Temp. MSS 577/11. 'Expressed' is true, but Wickenden conjectures, with some plausibility, that Gandhi will have considered Allied defeat as a possibility.
26. HGA to Agatha Harrison, 6 August 1942, ibid. 577/82a.
27. Alexander 1984: 114.
28. C. Rajagopalachari to Gandhi, 18 July 1942.
29. 23 July 1942, quoted in Mansergh and Lumby 1971: 455n.
30. From a transcript of a private discussion at the Royal Institute of International Affairs, 9 March 1944, pp. 3–4, LSF Temp. MSS 577/11.
31. Ibid. Alexander formulated this position clearly in a cable sent to Harrison immediately after his conversations with Nehru, and she wrote to Cripps urging him to persuade the Viceroy to meet Gandhi, particularly since Congress was not going to make difficulties about the presence of foreign troops. A drastic overhaul of a complacent government was the precondition for effective participation in the war effort (20 and 24 July 1942, ibid., 577 82b).
32. Alexander 1984: 205.
33. Ibid.: 206–7.
34. See Hutchins 1973: 154. (An earlier version of this book was published in Delhi, 1971, with the title *Spontaneous Revolution*.)
35. 28th July 1942, quoted in Mansergh and Lumby 1977: A88.
36. Agatha Harrison to HGA, 17 July 1942 and Agatha Harrison to Gandhi, 29 July 1942, LSF Temp. MSS 42/2.
37. Mansergh and Lumby 1971: 486.
38. Ibid.: 651–2.
39. Ibid.: 667. H. J. Clauson of the India Office reassured the FAU's Tom Tanner that 'the Viceroy was inclined to be crotchety at times, and that the hot weather was probably affecting him adversely' (21 August 1942, LSF FSC/IN/9).
40. Mansergh and Lumby 1971: 873n.
41. 1 September 1942, ibid.: 874.
42. The then Governor of Bengal, Sir John Herbert, may have been helpful too. Alexander described him as 'an old Irwin man' who believed in 'the personal touch'. Herbert had been ADC to Irwin in the early years of his Viceroyalty, and of course he had personal knowledge of the practical work of the FAU in Calcutta.

43. Mansergh and Lumby 1971, vol. 3: 120, October 1942.
44. HGA to Agatha Harrison, 1 October 1942, LSF Temp. MSS 577/82a.
45. Published in 1944 as *Conflict and Co-operation in Modern History*.
46. Richard Symonds to HGA, 31 March 1944, LSF Temp. MSS 577/17. The toast was proposed months after Alexander's departure from India, but presumably reflects Blair's attitude earlier. The original meeting between Blair and the party leaders was probably in March 1943. See HGA to Christopher Taylor, 4 June 1945, AFSC archive.
47. HGA to ?, 2 September 1942, LSF FSC/IN/19.
48. Stephens 1966: 80ff.
49. Symonds 1988: 11.
50. Symonds to Tegla Davies, 26 September 1943, LSF Temp. MSS 577/17. Sujata Mookerjee had by this time married her FAU colleague Glan Davies.
51. From a report entitled 'Three Months after the Cyclone', ibid. 577/113.
52. HGA to Christopher Taylor, 4 June 1945, ibid.
53. Linlithgow to Gandhi, 5 February 1943 and Gandhi to Linlithgow, 7 February 1943, in Mansergh and Lumby 1971, vol. 3: 590, 616.
54. HGA to Sir Gilbert Laithwaite, 10 February 1943 and Laithwaite to HGA, 14 February 1943, ibid.: 714.
55. HGA to Sir Roger Lumby, ibid.: 734–5.
56. T. Linlithgow to Winston Churchil and L. S. Amery, ibid.: 737, 746.
57. Alexander 1944: 68–9.
58. Romans 12.21. Alexander says that he read the first few verses, and the last few, of this chapter. (LSF Temp. MSS 577/16).
59. The romanised spelling of the names of places visited by Alexander has been retained as it was in 1943. Kutsing is now Qujing, Pichieh is Bijie, Chengtu is Chengdu, Chungking is Chongqing. Luhsien has a new name, Luzhou, indicating a change in status.
60. Information from J. Gray Peile, who was based in Chengtu, and was in charge of vehicle maintenance. He recalls 'the interest and excitement surrounding the special Council meeting' attended by the two visitors (letter to the author, 19 September 2000).
61. Antony Reynolds, another member of the China Convoy, thinks that the converted Ford trucks used by the Convoy, fitted with Hercules diesel engines, used rapeseed oil as fuel (letter to the author, 20 January 2001). The trucks and their fuel are described in Morris 1948: 58–63. See also Smith 1998: 184–94.
62. From an article by Alexander entitled 'On the China Road', LSF Temp. MSS 577/16.
63. Ellen Ling to HGA, 6 October 1962, LSF Temp. MSS 971/1/6/8. Antony Reynolds suggests that Ellen Ling was a Methodist missionary, who will have been returning to her station in Chaotong (Zhaotong), some distance west of Weining. 'We sometimes had supplies to deliver to the hospital there.'
64. Technically associated with the China Inland Mission. For a brief account of its origins see Broomhall 1915: 364. Duncan Wood comments that the China Convoy established a close relationship with the Friedenshort sisters. Being Germans, they were classified by the Chinese authorities as enemy aliens, and forbidden to travel beyond the confines of Pichieh. This cut them off from a leper colony that was in their care. The Convoy lent them Laurie Baker to take charge of the colony and keep in touch with the sisters – one of the few instances of Anglo-German cooperation at that time. 'It was with a twinkle in her eye that one of the sisters said to a departing Convoy party which had enjoyed their hospitality, "Of course, we mustn't forget that we are enemies".'

65. Jones remarks that this was the longest time he had ever spent on that route. This was due in part to Alexander's bird-watching demands, but also to the 'diminished windshield', a day in Piechieh to repair a spring, and 'two days of rain which made for slow going through much mud'. He adds: 'As I look back on it, I would happily do it again. Alas, that was over half a century ago.'
66. Greenwood, 1978: 148, 154.
67. HGA report on the famine, 17 September 1943, LSF Temp. MSS 577/113. Additional information from Pamela Bankart.
68. Symonds to HGA, 13 March 1944, ibid., 577/17.
69. Duncan Wood records that Rich returned to Philadelphia having achieved the purpose of his mission. He could report that the seventy American conscientious objectors then being recruited would be warmly welcomed by members of the China Convoy. He had sampled a part of the work they might undertake and the conditions in which they would be working. He had also received the approval and support of missionary and diplomatic circles in Chungking and had even had an offer of some financial support from the Chinese Government. AFSC was thus encouraged to proceed with the recruitment of that large reinforcement, which may have caused some alarm in FAU headquarters since it would double the size of the Convoy and perhaps signal an American take-over. But AFSC had reckoned without Congress, where conscientious objectors were regarded as unpatriotic dissidents to be kept well out of public view in the USA, and certainly not to be on show elsewhere. A Bill was rushed through Congress banning foreign service for all US conscientious objectors and the vanguard party had to be recalled home from Capetown. So the China Convoy's American element, during the war years, consisted of the few US citizens who had somehow slipped through the net to become the very good companions of a largely British unit.
70. There is a list of the people Alexander saw in LSF Temp. MSS 971/2/1/5.

8 Campaigning in Britain and the USA

1. HGA to L. S. Amery, 16 September 1943 and Amery to HGA, 19 September 1943, LSF Temp. MSS 577/106.
2. Agatha Harrison to HGA, ibid. 971/2/2/2.
3. HGA to Agatha Harrison, ibid. 577/82b.
4. HGA to the Graham family, 5 January 1944, Sibinga MS 3.
5. David Owen to HGA, 28 January 1944, LSF Temp. MSS 971/2/2/2. See Nimocks 1970 and Symonds 1986: 63–6.
6. Dorothy Hogg to Edith Richards, 28 October 1943, LSF Temp. MSS 577/82b.
7. Ibid.
8. HGA to Agatha Harrison, 27 September 1943, ibid.
9. Dorothy Hogg to Agatha Harrison, 26 October 1943, ibid.
10. Dorothy Hogg to Agatha Harrison, 13 November 1943, ibid.
11. Ibid.
12. Agatha Harrison to HGA and Dorothy Hogg, 15 November 1943, ibid.
13. Dorothy Hogg to Agatha Harrison, 15 November 1943, ibid.
14. *Visva-Bharati Quarterly*, new ser., vol. 10, no.1, May–July 1944: 44. Kripalani later wrote to Alexander conceding that he had misunderstood Alexander's purpose in writing the book, and regretting that he had caused him pain 30 March 1945, (LSF Temp. MSS 971/2/1/3).
15. Transcript of discussion on 9 March 1944; Penderel Moon to HGA, 14 March 1944, LSF Temp. MSS 577/11.
16. HGA to S. P. Mookherjee, 2 August 1944, ibid. 577/114.

17. Glan Davies to HGA, 31 October 1943, ibid. 577/17.
18. Gandhi 1979, vol. 77: 1979 275. Gandhi to M. R. Jayakar, 20 May 1944, published in *The Bombay Chronicle*, 1 June, after a 'garbled and unauthorized version' had appeared in another newspaper. Also HGA to C. Rajagopalachari, 8 June 1944, LSF Temp. MSS 577/114.
19. 'Copy of airgraph letter from H. G. Alexander to Mr Gandhi', 22 June 1944, Sibinga MS 4.
20. Gandhi to HGA, 12 July 1944, quoted in Alexander 1984: 208. The date given in the book is incorrect.
21. Anna Barlow was personally on friendly terms with Alexander, and when he needed to stay in London at this time it was with her that he stayed. But on India she was uncompromising, and in Alexander's absence she could be formidable on the subject. In a letter of 3 March 1945, Agatha Harrison complained to Alexander that she had had 'a horrid time with Anna Barlow at the Peace Committee. With neither Carl [Heath] nor you present – it was most difficult. Quite honestly I thought she was outrageous' (LSF Temp. MSS 577/82c).
22. Dorothy Hogg to Agatha Harrison, 25 August 1944, ibid.
23. HGA to Agatha Harrison, 2 September 1944, ibid. 577/84.
24. The Bengal Civil Protection Committee. See Chapter 14, above.
25. HGA to Gandhi, 2 September 1944, Sibinga MS 4.
26. Gandhi 1979, vol. 78: 155. 'Agatha', of course, is Agatha Harrison, 'Muriel', Muriel Lester.
27. L. S. Amery to Arthur Eddington, 19 October 1944, LSF Temp. MSS 577/114.
28. HGA to R. A. Butler, 9 January 1945, ibid. 577/82c.
29. 11 September 1944, ibid. 577/82c. This appears to be the letter referred to by Suhash Chakravarty as an illustration of Harrison's anxiety about the prospect of India's severance from the Empire (Chakravarty 1991: 194). If so, it is an odd misreading of her impatience with those who were blind to the end of empires. Dr Chakravarty dates the letter 19 September 1944. but Dr H. D. Sharma of the Nehru Memorial Library informed me that this must be a misprint for 11 September.
30. HGA to Symonds, 17 March, and 24 April 1944, ibid., 577/17; Pamela Bankart to HGA, 1 April 1944, ibid. 577/17. The chipmunks were charming but rather helpless characters in *Bambi* (1942).
31. Papers of the India Relief Committee, organised by Krishna Menon and Clement Davies, a Liberal MP, ibid. 577/114.
32. Symonds to HGA, 9 March 1944, ibid., 971/2/2/1.
33. HGA to Symonds, 28 February 1944, ibid., 577/17; Symonds to HGA, 11 November 1943, ibid. 577/17.
34. *Woodbrooke International Journal*, no. 46, December 1943, p. 1. Certainly his cavalier attitude to drink is in contrast to that implied in a lecture he gave in February 1942, when he reluctantly admitted that 'many of the early Quakers were brewers'. The genial Edith Adams, who lived in a cottage in the Woodbrooke grounds, and took part in Woodbrooke social occasions, mocked his reluctance in a poem preserved in the log-book for the spring term, 1942.

    I'm sure those early Quakers were conscientious makers
    And ale of *their* concoction would breed a *pious mind*,
    And godly soberiety, run through the *whole* society –
    Yet everybody cheerful – after having dined.

    Many a solemn Quaker would be rejuvenated.

Just think of Horace Alexander – so *lean* and *lank* and *long*.
Did *ever* drinking cocoa make him break into a song
Or give him rosy countenance, or a *nice big enbonpoint*?

35. Clarence Pickett to HGA, 16 November and Anna Brinton to HGA. 15 December 1943, Sibinga MS 3.
36. HGA to Amery, 17 March 1944, ibid.; HGA to Symonds, 31 March 1944, LSF Temp. MSS 577/17. In a letter dated 13 March, Symonds mentioned a report in the Indian press about a meeting in Birmingham addressed by Amery. 'Mr Amery went on to speak of the work of the FAU . . . (a voice) Don't you go taking credit for them . . . (Mr Amery) It's not a question of taking credit . . . Mr Amery's words could not be heard owing to heckling.'
37. R. R. Williams to HGA, 8 May 1944, Sibinga MS 3.
38. HGA to Tegla Davies, 6 April 1945, and Dorothy Hogg to Agatha Harrison, ? May 1945, LSF Temp. MSS 577/82c.
39. A circular letter to Friends he had met in North America, November 1945, Sibinga MS 3.
40. HGA to Tegla Davies, 6 April 1945, ibid.
41. Sibinga MS 3 has a copy of the Meeting for Sufferings statement, printed as a leaflet for general circulation. Heath's questions are in a letter to Hubert Peet, 7 April 1945, also in Sibinga MS 3.
42. 'Dumbarton Oaks or Chaos?' *Fellowship*, vol. 17, pp. 69–84, April 1945.
43. HGA to Paul Sturgt, 5 June 1945, Sibinga MS 3.
44. Ibid.
45. *The Friend*, 4 May 1945, pp. 277–9.
46. HGA to Ralph Barlow, 19 May 1945, Sibinga MS 3.
47. HGA to Richard Graham, 17 June 1945, ibid.
48. HGA to Paul Sturge, 5 June 1945, ibid.
49. Circular letter to Friends he had met in North America, ibid., November 1945.
50. Bertram Pickard to friends and family, 1999: 13. 14 May 1935, in Pickard.
51. Information from Cecilia Sibinga. The following December Alexnder wrote that his name had been entered for a passage to India since July. See HGA to P. J. Patrick, 7 December 1945, LSF Temp. MSS 577/90.

9 Indian independence and its aftermath

1. Dorothy Hogg to Agatha Harrison, September 1945, LSF Temp. MSS 577/82c.
2. HGA to Cripps, 14 November 1945, ibid., 577/90.
3. A summary of Major Short's memorandum and Cripps's covering letter to Pethick-Lawrence, is item 261 in Mansergh and Moon, 1976: 592–3, 3 December 1945. See also Short to Cripps, 9 January 1946, item 349, pp. 765–6.
4. Agatha Harrison to Lord Pethick-Lawrence, 3 February 1946, LSF Temp. MSS 45/2/2.
5. Agatha Harrison to R. A. Kaur, 21 February 1946, ibid.
6. Penderel Moon to HGA, 15 December 1945, ibid., 577/90.
7. HGA to Pethick-Lawrence, 1 December 1945, ibid.
8. P. J. Patrick to HGA, 4 December 1945, ibid.
9. HGA to Agatha Harrison, 19 November 1945, 577/82c. ibid.
10. Dorothy Hogg to Agatha Harrison, late November 1945, ibid.
11. P. J. Patrick to HGA, 29 October 1945; HGA to P. J. Patrick, 7 December 1945, ibid. 577/90.

12. Brian Groves to Harry Abrahamson, 20 December 1945, AFSC archives, India 1945.
13. *The Friend*, 1 March 1946, pp. 165–6.
14. AFSC archives, India 1946.
15. Report to AFSC, 3 September 1945, and letter 94 to AFSC, from Allen Longshore, 8 December 1945, ibid., India 1945.
16. Mansergh and Moon 1976, 1090–1. Short's dealings with the Sikhs are indicated in Mansergh and Lumby 1977: 821–2, 957–8n., and 968–9.
17. Mansergh and Lumby 1977: 3.
18. *The Friend*, 19 April 1946, pp. 303–4.
19. HGA to Eric Johnson, 23 May 1946, Sibinga MS 7.
20. Harrison 1956: 119, and Ghosh 1967: 94–5.
21. Harrison 1956: 119–20.
22. Ghosh 1967: 95.
23. Sudhir Ghosh's account of how he became involved with the Quakers and with Gandhi is told in the first part of *Gandhi's Emissary* (1967).
24. Wavell 1997: 311.
25. Agatha Harrison to her sisters, 8 May 1946, LSF Temp. MSS 883/2/10.
26. Agatha Harrison to her sisters, 29 March 1946, ibid.
27. Agatha Harrison and her sisters, 8 May 1946, ibid.
28. Gandhi called them 'the three persons of the trinity'. Alexander 1984: 133.
29. Ibid.
30. Agatha Harrison to her sisters, 26 May 1946, LSF Temp. MSS 883/2/10.
31. Narrative of the Cabinet Mission negotiations in Simla, Sibinga MS 8.
32. Wavell's Broadcast Message, 17 May 1946, in Mansergh and Lumby 1977: 611–13.
33. Memorandum from the Cabinet Mission and the Viceroy to Prime Minister Attlee, 3 June 1946, ibid.: 787–95.
34. Gandhi Editorial in *Harijan*, 10 June 1946, ibid.: 861.
35. Gandhi to Woodraw Wyatt, 10 June 1946, ibid.: 857.
36. Wavell 1973: 292–3.
37. Judges 8.4.
38. Possibly chapter 16 of the first book, 'Of Bearing with the Defects of Others': 'Endeavour to be patient in bearing with the defects and infirmities of others . . .; for that thyself also hast many failings which must be borne with by others.' *Of the Imitation of Christ*, World's Classics edition, 1903, pp. 21–2. This edition was readily available, and would have slipped easily into Alexander's pocket.
39. The notes were written as a letter to Carl Heath, dated 17 June 1946.
40. As quoted in Azad 1959: 155.
41. See, for example, Nanda 1993: 95.
42. Journal letter to family and friends, 20 July 1946, LSF Temp. MSS 971/2/1/3.
43. Alexander 1984: 136.
44. HGA to Agatha Harrison, 30 July 1946, LSF Temp. MSS 577/82c.
45. *The Friend*, 9 August 1946, p. 637.
46. Wavell 1973: 339.
47. Mansergh and Moon 1979: 298.
48. Report from the FSU to the Friends' Service Council, LSF FSC reports IN/39.
49. Ibid., 19 August 1946.
50. HGA to Agatha Harrison, 4 September 1946, LSF Temp. MSS 577/82c
51. HGA to Agatha Harrison, 22 August 1946, ibid.
52. HGA to Agatha Harrison, 25 August 1946, ibid.

53. Sir Fredrick Burrows to Wavell, 28 August 1946, Pethick-Lawrence to Wavell, 9 September 1946, and Burrows to Wavell, 10 September 1946, See in Mansergh and Moon 1979, vol. 8: 324–5, 474, 485–7.
54. HGA to Agatha Harrison, 20 August 1946, LSF Temp. MSS 577/83a.
55. HGA to Agatha Harrison, 27 August 1946, ibid.
56. journal letter for circulation to friends and colleagues, October 1946, Sibinga MS 9.
57. HGA to Agatha Harrison, 18 September 1946, ibid.
58. 29 November 1946, ibid.
59. 24 October 1946, ibid. The incident is also described in Alexander 1984: 140–1.
60. Sykes 1997: 296–7.
61. Alexander 1984: 141–3.
62. HGA to Agatha Harrison, 22 November 1946, LSF Temp. MSS 577/83a.
63. Andrew Roberts' essay on the Viceroyalty of Mountbatten is in *Eminent Churchillians*, 1994. The public relations disaster is considered on p. 121.
64. Quoted in Brecher, 1959: 340.
65. HGA to Agatha to Harrison, 5 May 1997, LSF Temp. MSS 577 83a.
66. *The Friend*, 2 May 1947, pp. 333–4.
67. *The Friend*, 14 December 1951, p. 1093.
68. Alexander 1984: 147–8.
69. Symonds 2001: 5.
70. Alexander 1984: 211.
71. HGA to Gandhi, 22 July 1947 and Gandhi to HGA, 26 July, LSF Temp. 577/5.
72. Alexander 1984: 157.
73. Letter from Joan Court, July 1947, AFSC Program in India, Color and Background Material no.10.
74. HGA to Agatha Harrison, 31 August 1947, LSF Temp. MSS 577/83a. According to Sujata Davies, the meeting was held in extreme secrecy, and she and her husband were not party to any of the discussion. The competing claims of emergency work in the Punjab and the established projects in Bengal were a continuing source of friction in the Unit, as is evident in a letter from Colin Bell of the AFSC to Mervin Palmer, 17 November 1947, LSF MSS FSC IN/40.
75. Symonds 2001: 33.
76. Agnew 2001: 37. From a letter dated 24 September 1947. Agnew was an aristocratic Scot of no fixed occupation, who sought at this point to find employment in the new dominions.
77. Symonds 2001: 35.
78. Roderick Ede told Alexander that he had no idea where the money could be raised to pay Symonds's fare, 'but if there is a real need, something may happen to make it possible'. 27 August 1947, LSF FSC IN/19(ii).
79. Symonds 2001: 38.
80. Cf. HGA to Paul Sturge, 26 September 1947, Agnew 2001: 41–2. LSF FSC/IN/19(ii).
81. Symonds 2001: 41.
82. Ibid.: 48–72.
83. Journal letter for circulation to friends and colleagues, December 1947, LSF FSC/IN/19ii.
84. The National Conference was allied to the Indian National Congress, and had been suppressed by the Maharaja.
85. HGA to Paul Sturge, 17 November 1947, LSF FSC/IN/19.
86. Journal letter for circulation to friends and colleagues, December 1947, ibid.
87. Symonds 2001: 73–86.

88. Ibid.: 87–93.
89. HGA to Agatha Harrison, 13 January 1948, LSF Temp. MSS 577 83a.
90. Alexander 1984: 173. See also Symonds 2001: 92–3.
91. Journal letter for circulation to friends and colleagues, LSF FSC/IN/19 ii.
92. Symonds 2001: 137.
93. HGA to Clarence Pickett, 5 July 1948, LSF FSC IN/17.
94. Paul Sturge to Agatha Harrison, 27 February 1948, LSF Temp. MSS 577/83a.
95. HGA to Hugh Doncaster, 29 July 1947, ibid. 577/109.
96. ibid. 577/108. This folder contains several letters from Ranjit Chetsingh, Hugh Doncaster and Carl Heath on the issues raised by Mallik's application.
97. This meant that it was no longer a public lecture, and could only be attended by members of the Society.
98. HGA to Donald Groom, 23 May 1949, ibid. 577/25, Marjorie Sykes to Agatha Harrison, 23 June 1949, ibid. 577/27.
99. Agatha Harrison to Paul Sturge, 7 May 1948, LSF 577/83a.
100. HGA to Philip Noel-Baker, 2 March 1948, LSF Temp. MSS 577/83a.
101. Symonds 2001: 95–6. Symonds emphasises Noel-Baker's enjoyment of New York's social life, from which he was 'brutally' expelled. For an assessment of Noel-Baker's role in the Kashmir discussions, see Garner 1978: 323–4.
102. Personal communication, 30 March 2004.
103. HGA to Paul Sturge, 29 April 1948, LSF FSC MSS IN/17.
104. Agatha Harrison to HGA, 11 June 1948, LSF Temp. MSS 577.83a. Harrison was passing on a report by Myrtle Wright, who was present at the lecture.
105. Mrs Pandit, Nehru's sister, was at this time Indian ambassador to the USA. See account of the UN Commission in Symonds 2001: 96–105.
106. Ibid.: 116.
107. HGA to Paul Sturge, 25 August 1948, LSF Temp. MSS 577/83a.
108. HGA report to the FSC, 25 August 1948, ibid. FSC IN/19.
109. Agatha Harrison to HGA, 20 October 1948, LSF Temp. MSS 577/83a.
110. Agatha Harrison to HGA, 8 July 1948 HGA to Agatha Harrison, 8 July 1948, ibid.
111. Privat 1949: 63.
112. HGA to Robert Davis, 10 August 1949, LSF Temp. MSS 577/25.
113. HGA to Roderick Ede and others, 11 May 1949, Ibid. FSC/IN/19/iii.
114. Ibid. FSC/IN/11.
115. *The Friend*, 26 May 1950, p. 376.
116. HGA to Lucy Brown, 25 January 1970, Woodbrooke MSS.
117. Bose 1951: 156–7.
118. Agatha Harrison was the only person ever, I believe, to dress for dinner at the Unit's headquarters in 1 Upper Wood Street.
119. Harrison's reports are dated 7, 11 and 14 March, and 6 April 1950, LSF IN/17. For the importunate widow, see Luke 18.5.
120. HGA to Dr S. P. Mookherjee 9 April 1950 and Dr. S. P. Mookherjee to HGA, 11 April 1950. LSF Temp. MSS 971/2/1/5.
121. Dr S. P. Mookherjee to HGA, 6 May 1950, ibid.
122. HGA to Agatha Harrison, 2 September 1950, ibid. By this time I had left India.
123. Nehru to C. Rajagopalachari, 10 March 1950, in Nehru 1992: 97–8.
124. HGA to A. Chakravarty, 9 August 1949, LSF Temp. MSS 577/20.
125. Alexander 1951: 119–20.
126. HGA's journal letter for circulation to friends and colleagues, December 1950, LSF FSC IN/17.

127. HGA to V. P. Menon, 12 December 1950, LSF Temp. MSS 577/29.
128. J. Daulatram to HGA, 1 May 1951, ibid.
129. HGA to J. Daulatram, 5 May 1951, ibid.
130. J Daulatram to HGA, 7 May 1951, ibid.
131. For the sources of this narrative, see correspondence between HGA and Agatha Harrison, 3 and 12 April 1951, LSF Temp. MSS 577/83b.
132. Berber's wartime role is considered in Appendix A.
133. HGA to Agatha Harrison, 3 January 1951, LSF Temp. MSS 577/83b.
134. There are letters about Berber's appointment in LSF Temp. MSS 577/20.
135. HGA to Agatha Harrison, 6 May 1951, LSF Temp. MSS 577/83b.
136. HGA to Agatha Harrison, 11 June, ibid.
137. *Woodbrooke International Journal*, no. 62, December 1951, p. 6.
138. *The Friend*, 15 August 1952, p. 712.
139. *The Friend*, 3 October 1952, p. 875.
140. HGA to Agatha Harrison, 12 March 1953, LSF Temp. MSS 577/83c.
141. HGA, 'India Looks Ahead', LSF Temp. MSS 577/112.
142. Duncan Wood to HGA, 16 September 1948, Woodbrooke MSS Box 1.
143. The Bakers visited England in the winter of 1950–51, and Laurie Baker wrote an account of their work in *The Friend*, 16 February 1951, pp. 121–3: 'A Home-Hospital in the Himalaya'.
144. Ibid. There is a vivid account of the Bakers' work in Pithorigarh at this time by Bernard Llewellyn in *The Friendly Way*, no. 30, December 1954, reproduced more accessibly in Llewellyn 1955. See also Bhatia 1991.
145. Journal letter to friends and colleagues, 21 July 1953, LSF Temp. MSS 577/112.

10 India and the quest for a sustainable world order

1. Philip Noel-Baker to HGA, 15 April 1954 and HGA to Philip Noel-Baker, 4 May 1954, LSF Temp. MSS 577/90.
2. Alexander, 'The Foreign Policy of India', *The Friend*, 2 July 1954, pp. 623–5.
3. See Kahin 1956: 64–72.
4. Alexander, 'The British Press and India', *The Friend*, 16 December 1955, pp. 1231–2; letter from John Connell, *The Friend*, 30 December, pp. 1286–7. Bernard Canter's letter to Alexander, 2 January 1956, may be found in LSF Temp. MSS 577/33.
5. Hallam Tonnyson, 'India: Arena of "Peaceful Competition', *The Friend*, 30 December 1955, pp. 1285–6.
6. MS in private possession of Cecilia Sibinga.
7. Ian Stephens to HGA, 21 September 1954, LSF Temp. MSS 577/30.
8. Ibid. 577/43 contains documentation of this uncertainties that proceeded the couple's decision to marry.
9. Journal letter 28 February 1960, ibid. 577/47.
10. Journal letter to friends and colleagues, ibid. 577/56.
11. V. L. Pandit to HGA, 22 June 1964, ibid. 577?58.
12. *The Friend*, 10 September 1965, pp. 1074–5.
13. R. Chetsingh, 'Letter from India', *The Friend*, 8 October 1965.
14. HGA to V. L. Pandit, 4 November 1965, LSF Temp. MSS 577/60.
15. V. L. Pandit to HGA, 20 May 1967; HGA to Colin Bell, 3 June 1967, ibid.
16. *The Friend*, 21 January 1972, pp. 69–70.
17. HGA to T.N. Kaul, 21 July 1975, LSF Temp. MSS 577/78.
18. HGA to ? , 27 January 1976, ibid. 577/79.
19. Indira Gandhi to HGA, 23 December 1975, ibid.
20. HGA to Indira Gandhi, February 1976, ibid.

21. HGA to M. Daszi, 10 April 1977, ibid. 577/81.
22. HGA to J. P. Narayan, 2 April 1976, ibid. 577/79.
23. HGA to N. Desai, 22 November 1977, ibid. 577/81.
24. Ibid. 577/19. The letter was not published.
25. *The Friend*, 20 July 1984, p. 920.
26. HGA to Ilay Cooper, 4 August 1984 (in possession of recipient).
27. *The Friend*, 29 December 1961, p. 1702.
28. HGA to R. A. Butler, 16 August 1955; Butler to HGA, 30 August 1955, LSF Temp. MSS 577/34.
29. HGA to Marjorie Sykes, 7 April 1956, LSF Temp. MSS 577/34; Stella Alexander to J. P. Narayan, 15 January 1962, LSF Temp. MSS 577/33.
30. *The Friend*, 2 February 1956, p. 142.
31. Ibid., 7 December 1956, p. 1096.
32. HGA to G. Ramachandran, 21 August 1976, LSF Temp. MSS 577/79.
33. He provided a similar assessment in 'Some Thoughts on Indo-Pakistan Relations', *The Friends' Quarterly,* vol. 12 (1958), pp. 112–21.
34. HGA to John Linton, 15 December 1962, LSF Temp. MSS 577/52.
35. Journal letter 4 to friends and colleagues, 21 February 1958, ibid. 577/44.
36. Indira Gandhi to HGA, 24 May 1965, ibid. 577/60. According to Richard Symonds, who was a member of the first UN Kashmir Commission in 1948–9, the USA and the UK blocked all discussion of such a solution because of fears of Communist influence.
37. HGA to John Linton, 1 February 1963, ibid. 577/51.
38. Julian Harrison, *The Friend*, 28 December 1956, p. 1196; Horace Alexander, ibid., 4th January 1957, pp. 14–16; Philip Noel-Baker to HGA, 15 January 1957, LSF Temp. MSS 577/36; S. M. Haq, *The Friend*, 18 January 1957, pp. 65–6; HGA, ibid., 25 January 1957, pp. 88–90.
39. Report by HGA to Friends' Peace Committee, *The Friend*, 5 February 1982, pp. 150–1.
40. Stella Alexander to HGA, 18 April 1960, LSF Temp. MSS 577/29.
41. Ibid., 18 June 1960.
42. Stella Alexander to HGA, 21 June 1960, ibid.
43. Stella Alexander to HGA, 23 August 1960, ibid.
44. M. Scott to Friends Peace Committee, 25 August 1963, ibid. 577/56.
45. HGA to George Patterson, 17 September 1963, ibid.
46. See Hazarika 1994: pp. 359–61.
47. There is a detailed account of Scott's work on behalf of the Nagas in Scott 1980: 151–68. See also Dart 1993: 77–86.
48. Michael Scott to David Astor, 4 September 1968, LSF Temp. MSS 577/62.
49. *The Friend*, 2 January 1976, p. 19.
50. Ibid., 17 August 1962, p. 1016.
51. See LSF Temp. MSS 577/49.
52. *Everyman I* and *Everyman II* were small craft that, like *The Golden Rule*, had undertaken protest voyages in the Pacific.
53. *Guardian*, 14 September 1962; Anna Barlow to HGA, 21 September 1962 and Leslie Cross to HGA, n.d., LSF Temp. MSS 577/55.
54. HGA to G. Bailey, 12 June 1961, LSF Temp. MSS 577/56. See Luke 19.40.
55. The Editor of *The Friend* published extracts from Dr McKennal's sermon, as reproduced in Brayshaw 1905, as an editorial, 14 July 1961, p. 946. McKennal's text is hardly encouraging: 'And they shall fall by the edge of the sword, and shall be led away captive into all nations.' Luke 21.24.
56. *The Friend*, 7 July 1961, p. 923.

57. Ibid., 10 and 24th July 1970, pp. 814–5, 871–2.
58. HGA to Duncan Wood [and Kenneth Lee of Friends Peace Committee], 18 December 1970, LSF Temp. MSS 577/67.
59. HGA to Gilbert White, 21 December 1970, ibid.
60. Duncan Wood to HGA, 28 January, and 5 February 1971, ibid.
61. HGA to Duncan Wood and others, 10 March 1971, ibid.
62. Personal communication, March 2004.
63. From an internet transcript of *Vietnam: A Television History. Peace Is at Hand (1968–1973)*, broadcast in the US in 1983 by the Public Broadcasting Service, The transcript can be found at 'The American Experience Vietnam Online'.
64. McCarthy 1984: A21.
65. HGA to Jayaprakash Narayan, 29 March 1977, LSF Temp. MSS 577/81. This was immediately after the end of the 'Emergency', when he said he had tried *not* to be angry with Indira Gandhi, but had found it an effort.
66. It should be said that in my own dealings with him I never had the least intimation of the irritability that is so apparent in some of his letters.
67. It was through Alexander that Fritz Berber became acquainted with these lines, and he found them profoundly sustaining. See Berber 1986: 90.
68. *The Friend*, 1 August 1952, p. 666.
69. Dorothy Hogg to HGA, 12 September 1965, LSF Temp. MSS 577/60.
70. HGA to C. Taylor, 4 June 1945, ibid. 577/113.
71. Radhakrishnan1968: 24.
72. Alexander 1984: 139.
73. Lord Templewood, quoted ibid.: 82.
74. Ibid.: 187.
75. HGA to Motilal Kothari, 11 January 1964, LSF Temp. MSS 577/59.
76. HGA to Motilal Kothari, ibid., 17 May 1968.

Appendix

1. Berber's part in the Red Cross operation is considered in Favez 1988: 346, an account which emphasises uncertainties about his precise role.
2. Herzstein 1982.
3. Ibid.: 232. According to Paul Seabury, the Europe Committee was created on 5 April 1943 (Seabary 1954).
4. Berber 1942: 189ff. See Herzstein 1982: 231.
5. Berber 1986: 113.
6. Hassell 1948: 178. Entry for 18 May 1941.
7. Herzstein 1982: 231.
8. Corder Catchpool to HGA, 4 November 1945, Berber MSS in Woodbrooke Library, HGA MSS. Catchpool had seen references in the British press to Berber as 'a dangerous Nazi agent'.
9. LSF Temp. MSS 577/20. The typescript is unsigned, but is almost certainly Elizabeth Fox Howard's. She was in Germany just at this time: see *The Friend*, 14 May 1948, p. 399.
10. See Berber 1939, a lecture delivered in the Friedrich-Wilhelm University, 24 November 1938. This was exactly a week after the depressed interview with Alexander described in Chapter 6 in this volume, and the difference in tone is remarkable. His rejection of the League of Nations was, of course, of long standing, and is expounded at length in Berber 1934.

BIBLIOGRAPHY

Agnew, Sir Fulque (2001) *Witness to the Partition, India and Pakistan 1947–48*, Edinburgh: Centre for South Asian Studies.

Alexander, H. G. (1914) *Peace! Peace!*, Letchworth, Herts: Garden City Press.

— (1920) *Joseph Gundry Alexander*, London: Swarthmore Press.

— (1924a) *India and Opium*, Birmingham: privately printed [poss not by HGA]

— (1924b) *The Revival of Europe. Can the League of Nations Help?* London: Allen and Unwin.

— (1926) *The League of Nations and the Operation of Minority Treaties*, London: Friends Book Centre.

— (1929a) *Friends and Young India*, London: Society of Friends, Friends Service Council.

— (1929b) *Indian Ferment*, London: Williams and Norgate.

— (1930) *Narcotics in India and South Asia*, London: Williams and Norgate.

— (1933) *Indian Prisoners: A Case for Enquiry and an Opportunity for Progress*, London: Society of Friends.

— (1937) *Political Prisoners in India*, n.p.

— (1938) *Congress Rule in India*, London: Gollancz.

— (1944a) *Conflict and Co-operation in Modern History*, Calcutta: Calcutta University.

— (1944b) *India since Cripps*, Harmondsworth: Penguin.

— (1951) *New Citizens of India*, Bombay: Oxford University Press.
— (1952) *Kashmir: A Statement of Facts*, London: Friends Peace Committee.
— (1961) *Consider India*, London and Bombay: Asia Publishing House (first published 1954).
— (1984) *Gandhi through Western Eyes*, Philadelphia, PA: New Society Publishers (first published 1969).
— (1974) *Seventy Years of Birdwatching*, Berkhamsted: Poyser.
Andrews, C. F. (1935) *The Indian Earthquake*, London: Allen and Unwin.
Angell, Norman (1909) *Europe's Optical Illusion*, London: Simpkin, Marshall.
Anstruther, Ian (1983) *Oscar Browning*, London: John Murray.
Ashford, O. M. (1985) *Prophet – or Professor? The Life and Work of Lewis Fry Richardson*, Bristol: Hilger.
Azad, Maulana Abul Kalam (1959) *India Wins Freedom*, Bombay: Orient Longmans.
Baker, E. B. and Baker, Philip J. Noel (1927) *J. Allen Baker. A Memoir*, London: Swarthmore Press.
Berber, Friedrich (1924) 'Von der Gerechtigkeit', *Zwischen den Bunden. Drei Vortrage aus den Jugendring Munchen*, Munich: Christian Kaiser Verlag.
— (1934) *Sicherheit und Gerechtigkeit*, Berlin: C. Heymann.
— (1936) *Locarno*, Berlin: Junker.
— (1939) *Prinzipien der britisschen Aussenpolitik*, Berlin: Hochschule für Politik.
— (1942) 'Die neuordnung Europas und die Aufgabe der aussenpolitischen Wissenschaft', *Monatsschrift für aussenpolitischen Politik*, vol. 9, Berlin: Hochschule für Politik.
— (1986) *Zwischen Macht und Gewissen*, Munich: C. H. Beck'sche.
Berggrav, Eivind (1960) *Forgjeves for Fred*, Oslo: Forlaget Land og Kirke.
Bhatia, Gautam (1991) *Laurie Baker, Life, Work and Writings*, New Delhi: Penguin.
Birla, G. D. (1977) *Bapu: A Unique Association*, Bombay: Bharata Vidya Bhavan.
Bose, Hiralal (ed.) (1951) *The Task of Peace-making. Reports of the World Pacifist Meeting*, Calcutta: Visva-Bharati.
Brayshaw, Neave (1905) *Bible Notes on the Prophetic Period of Jewish History*, vol. 2, London: Summer School Continuation Committee.
Brecher, Michael (1959) *Nehru, a Political Biography*, London: Oxford University Press.
Brooks, Harry (1922) *The Pactice of Autosuggestion*, London: Allen and Unwin.
Broomhall, M. (1915) *The Jubilee Story of the China Inland Mission*, London: Religious Tract Society.

Browne, Edward Granville (1910) *The Persian Revolution of 1905–1909*, Cambridge: Cambridge University Press.

Carnegie, Andrew (1933) *Miscellaneous Writings*, vol. 2, New York: Doubleday, Doran.

Carr, E. H. (1939) *The Twenty Years' Crisis*, London: Macmillan.

Chakravarty, Suhash (1991) *The Raj Syndrome*, New Delhi: Penguin (first published 1989).

— (1997) *V. K. Krishna Menon and the India League*, vol. 1, New Delhi: Har-Anand.

Cole, G. D. H. (1920) *Guild Socialism Re-stated*, London: Leonard Parsons.

— (1920) *Social Theory*, London: Methuen.

Craddock, Reginald (1929) *The Dilemma in India*, London: Constable.

Dart, Martha (1993) *Marjorie Sykes, Quaker Gandhian*, York: Sessions.

Davies, A. Tegla (1947) *Friends' Ambulance Unit. The Story of the FAU in the Second World War*, London: Allen and Unwin.

Deutsch, Harold C. (1968) *The Conspiracy against Hitler in the Twilight War*. Minneapolis: University of Minnesota Press.

Dickinson, G. Lowes (1926) *The International Anarchy 1904–1913*, London: Allen and Unwin.

— (1973) *Autobiography*, London: Duckworth.

Documents Concerning German–Polish relations and the Outbreak of Hostilities between Britain and Germany on September 3, 1939 (1939).

Dryhurst, N. F. (ed.) (1911) *Nationalities and Subject Races: Report of Conference Held in Caxton Hall, Westminster, June 28–30, 1910*, London: P. S. King and Son.

Egerton, George W. (1978) *Great Britain and the Creation of the League of Nations*, Chapel Hill: University of North Carolina Press.

Evans, T. P. Conwil (1932) *Foreign Policy from a Back Bench, 1904–1918*, London: Oxford University Press.

— (1929) *The League Council in Action*, London: Oxford University Press.

— with N. Noel-Buxton (1922) *Oppressed Peoples and the League of Nations*, London: J. M. Dent.

Favez, Jean-Claude (1988) *Une mission impossible? Le CIRC, les déportations, et les camps de concentration Nazis*, Lausanne: Payot.

Fayle, C. E. (1934) *Harold Wright. A Memoir*, London: Allen and Unwin.

Feiling, Keith (1946) *Life of Neville Chamberlain*, London: Macmillan.

Forster, E. M. (1973) *Goldsworthy Lowes Dickinson*, London: Edward Arnold (first published 1934).

Fox, George (1952) *Journal of George Fox*, ed. J. Nickalls, Cambridge: Cambridge University Press.

Froude, J. A. (1894a) *Life and Letters of Erasmus*, London: Longman, Green.

— (1894b) *Short Studies on Great Subjects*, vol. 1, London: Longman Green.

Fry, Roger (1924) *Living Painters: Duncan Grant*, London: Hogarth Press.

Gairdner, H. T. (1909) *The Reproach of Islam*, Edinburgh: Foreign Mission Committee of the Church of Scotland.

— (1920) *The Rebuke of Islam*, Edinburgh: Foreign Mission Committee of the Church of Scotland.

Gandhi, M. K. (1958–82) *Collected Works of Mahatma Gandhi*, Ahmedabad: Navajivan Press.

Garner, Joe (1978) *The Commonwealth Office 1925–68*, London: Heinemann.

Gavit, J. P. (1925) *Opium*, London: Routledge.

George, T. J. S. (1964) *Krishna Menon. A Biography*, London: Jonathan Cape.

Ghosh, Sudhir (1967) *Gandhi's Emissary*, London: Cresset Press.

Gopal, S. (1989) *Radhakrishnan. A Biography*, London: Unwin Hyman.

— (1957) *The Viceroyalty of Lord Irwin*, Oxford, Clarendon Press.

Graham, John William (1912) *Evolution and Empire*, London: Headley Brothers.

Greenwood, Ormerod (1978) *Quaker Encounters*, vol. 3, York: Sessions.

Harrison, Irene (1956) *Agatha Harrison: An Impression by Her Sister*, London: Allen and Unwin.

Hassell, Ulrich von (1948) *The von Hassell Diaries*, ed. Hugh Gibson, London: Hamish Hamilton.

Hazarika, Sanjoy (1994) *Strangers of the Mist*, New Delhi: Penguin.

Herzstein, R. E. (1982) *When Nazi Dreams Come True*, London: Abacus.

Hirst, Margaret E. (ed.) (1920) *All Friends' Conference. Reports of Commissions*, London: Society of Friends.

Hobhouse, L. T. (1920) *The Metaphysical Theory of the State*, London: Allen and Unwin.

Hobson, J. A. (1938) *Confessions of an Economic Heretic*, London: Allen and Unwin.

Hogg, Dorothy (1981) *Memories for Tomorrow*, London: Regency Press.

Holmes, Edmond (1911) *What Is and What Might Be. A Study of Education in General and Elementary Education in Particular*, London: Constable.

Hughes, W. R. (1964) *Indomitable Friend*, London: Allen and Unwin.

Hutchins, Francis G. (1973) *India's Revolution. Gandhi and the Quit India Movement*, Cambridge, MA: Harvard University Press.

Hutheesing, K. (1944) *With No Regrets: An Autobiography*, Bombay: Padme Publications.

Indian Round Table Conference, 12th November 1930–9th January 1931 (1931).

Johnson, Bruce D. (1975) 'Righteousness before Revenue. The Forgotten Moral Crusade against the Indo-Chinese Opium Trade', *Journal of Drug Issues*, vol. 5.
Kahin, G. M. (1956) *The Asian-African Conference*, Ithaca, NY: Cornell University Press.
Kendall, Guy (1913) *The New Schoolmaster*, London: Smith, Elder.
Keynes, J. M. (1919) *The Economic Consequences of the Peace*, London: Macmillan.
— (1972) *Collected Writings*, vol. 10, London: Macmillan.
— (1949) *Two Memoirs*, ed. David Garnett, London: Rupert Hart Davis.
Lansbury, George (1928) *My Life*, London: Constable.
Llewellyn, Bernard (1955) *From the Back Streets of Bengal*, London: Allen and Unwin.
Louis, W. Roger (1992) *In the Name of God, Go! Leo Amery and the British Empire in the Age of Churchill*, New York: W. W. Norton.
Low, D. A. (1977) *Congress and the Raj*, London: Heinemann.
McCarthy, Colman (1984) 'A Pause from Violence', *Washington Post*, 9 June: A21.
MacMunn, Norman (1914) *The Path to Freedom in School*, London: G. Bell and Son.
Martin-Harvey, John (1933) *Autobiography*, London: Sampson Low.
Mangone, Gerard J. (1954) *A Short History of International Organization*, New York: McGraw Hill.
Mansergh, N. and Lumby, E. W. R. (eds) (1971) *The Transfer of Power*, vols 2 and 3, London: HMSO.
Mansergh, N. and Lumby, E. W. R. (eds) (1977) *The Transfer of Power*, vol. 7, London: HMSO.
Mansergh, N. and Moon, P. (eds) (1976) *The Transfer of Power*, vol. 6, London: HMSO.
Mansergh, N. and Moon, P. (eds) (1979) *The Transfer of Power*, vol. 8, London: HMSO.
Morley, John (1889) *Walpole*, London: Macmillan.
Morris, David (1948) *China Changed my Mind*, London: Cassell.
Murray-Brown, Jeremy (1972) *Kenyatta*, London: Allen and Unwin.
Nanda, B. R. (1993) *Gandhi and His Critics*, Delhi: Oxford University Press.
Nationalities and Subject Races: Report of a Conference Held in Caxton Hall, Westminster. June 28–30 1910 (1910).
Nehru, Jawaharlal (1992) *Selected Works*, Second Series, vol. 14, part 1, New Delhi: Orient Longmans.
Nehru, Jawaharlal (1936) *India and the World*, London: Allen and Unwin.
Nimocks, Walter (1970) *Milner's Young Men: The 'Kindergarten' in Edwardian Imperial Affairs*, London: Hodder and Stoughton.

Noack, Ulrich (1939) *Das politische Ethos in der europäische Diplomatie*, Hamburg: Hoffmann & Campe.

— (1952) *Norwegen zwischen Friedenssvermittlung und Fremdherrschaft*, Krefeld: Verlag Aufbau der Mitte.

Pickard, Bertram (1999) *Bertram Pickard of Geneva. His Journal Letters from USA in 1935 and 1937*, ed. Alison Bush, York Sessions.

Piotrowski, S. (1961) *Hans Frank*, Warsaw: Panstwowe Wydawnictwo Naukowe.

Porter, Brian (1995) 'David Davies and the Enforcement of Peace', *Thinkers of the Twenty Years Crisis*, ed. David Long and Peter Wilson, Oxford: Oxford University Press.

Privat, Edmond (1949) *The Clash of Loyalties*, London: Allen and Unwin.

Pollard, Francis E. (ed.) (1926) *Bootham School, 1823–1923*, London: J. M. Dent.

Purcell, A. A. and Hallsworth, J. (1928) *Report on Labour Conditions in India*, London: TUC General Council.

Radhakrishnan, S. (1968) *Mahatma Gandhi. 100 Years*, New Delhi: Gandhi Peace Foundation.

Rauschning, Herman (1938) *Germany's Revolution of Destruction*, London: Heinemann.

— (1942) *Makers of Destruction*, London: Eyre and Spottiswoode.

Roberts, Andrew (1994) *Eminent Churchillians*, London: Weidenfeld and Nicolson.

— (1992) *'Holy Fox', a Life of Lord Halifax*, London: Weidenfeld and Nicolson.

Rolland, Romain (1969) *Gandhi et Romain Rolland*, Paris: Cahiers Romain Rolland, 19.

Ross, Edward Denison (1943) *Both Ends of the Candle*, London: Faber.

The Royal Commission on Opium 1893–1895: First Report of the Royal Commission on Opium with Minutes of Evidence and Appendices (2003) intro. Joyce A. Mandancy, London: Ganesha Publishing.

Schubert, W. (1926) *The League of Nations and the Operation of Minority Treaties*, London: Friends Book Centre.

Scott, Drusilla (1971) *A. D. Lindsay: A Biography*, Oxford: Blackwell.

Scott, Michael (1980) *Search for Peace and Justice*, London: Rex Collings.

Seabury, Paul (1954) *The Wilhelmstrasse*, Berkeley and Los Angeles: University of California Press.

Shaw, George Bernard (1989) *Fabian Essays*, London: Fabian Society.

Slade, M. (1960) *The Spirit's Pilgrimage*, London: Longman.

Smith, Lyn (1998) *Pacifists in Action*, York: Sessions.

Smuts, Jan Christian (1931) *The Disarmed Peace*, Sheffield: J. W. Northend.

Stephens, Ian (1966) *Monsoon Morning*, London: Benn.

Styan, J. L. (1982) *Max Reinhardt*, Cambridge: Cambridge University Press.
Sykes, Marjorie (1997) *An Indian Tapestry*, York: Sessions.
Symonds, Richard (2001) *In the Margins of Independence*, Karachi: Oxford University Press.
— (1986) *Oxford and Empire*, London: Macmillan.
— (1988) 'Recollections of Horace Alexander and Gandhi', *Indo-British Review*, vol. 14.
Tagore, Rabindranath (1930) *The Religion of Man*, London: Allen and Unwin.
Temple, William (1940) *Thoughts in Wartime*, London: Macmillan.
Tendulkar, D. G. (1952) *Mahatma*, vol. 5, Bombay: Publications Division of the Ministry of Broadcasting and Information.
Tennant, W. D. (1957) *True Account*, London: Max Parrish.
Tinker, Hugh (1976) 'The India Conciliation Group, 1931–1950: Dilemmas of the Mediator', *Journal of Commonwealth and Comparative Politics*, vol. 14, issue 3.
Toynbee, Arnold (1967) *Acquaintances*, London: Oxford University Press.
Wavell, A. P. (1973) *The Viceroy's Journal*, ed. Penderel Moon, London: Oxford University Press.
Wells, H. G. (1919) *The Undying Fire*, London: Cassell.
Wickenden, T. (1989) *Report on the Disturbances of 1942–3*, ed. P. N. Chopra, New Delhi.
Woolf, Leonard (1923) *International Government*, London: Allen and Unwin (first published 1916).
Wyllie, J. A. (1934) *India at the Parting of the Ways*, London: L. Williams.
Yates, Ann, and Chester, Lewis (2006) *The Troublemaker: Michael Scott and His Lonely Struggle against Injustice*, London: Aurum.
Zimmern, Alfred (1918) 'Some Principles and Problems of the Settlement', *The Round Table*, vol. 9, no. 33.
— (1922) *Europe in Convalescence*, London Mills and Boon.

Periodicals consulted

Cambridge Review
Foreign Affairs (published by the Union of Democratic Control)
The Friend
The Friend of China
Friends' Fellowship Papers
Friends' Quarterly
Friends' Quarterly Examiner
Granta (Cambridge)
Harijan (Poona)
India Bulletin

The Nation and Athenaeum
The New Statesman
The Portcullis (Warwick)
Punch
The Round Table
The Spectator
The Times
Visva-Bharati Quarterly (Shantiniketan)
Woodbrooke International Journal (Birmingham)

INDEX

Note: Biographical sub-entries are in chronological order.